CASS SERIES ON SOVIET MILITARY THEORY AND PRACTICE

THE MILITARY STRATEGY OF THE SOVIET UNION:
A HISTORY

CASS SERIES ON SOVIET MILITARY THEORY AND PRACTICE

Series Editor – David M. Glantz
Ft. Leavenworth, Kansas

This series examines in detail the evolution of Soviet military science and the
way the Soviets have translated theoretical concepts for the conduct of war
into concrete military practice. Separate volumes focus on how the Soviets
have applied and refined theory in combat and on how they have structured
their forces to suit the requirement of changing times.

The Military Strategy of the Soviet Union
A HISTORY

DAVID M. GLANTZ

FRANK CASS

First published in 1992 in Great Britain by
FRANK CASS & CO. LTD.
Gainsborough House, Gainsborough Road,
London E11 1RS, England

and in the United States of America by
FRANK CASS
c/o International Specialized Book Services, Inc.
5602 N.E. Hassalo Street
Portland, Oregon 97213

Copyright © 1992 David M. Glantz

British Library Cataloguing in Publication Data

Glantz, David M.
  Military Strategy of the Soviet Union:
  History. – (Cass Series on Soviet
  Military Theory & Practice; Vol.5)
  I. Title   II. Series
  355.033547

ISBN 0 7146 3435 2

Library of Congress Cataloging-in-Publication Data
Glantz, David M.
    The military strategy of the Soviet Union : a history / David M.
  Glantz.
      p.   cm. — (Cass series on Soviet military theory and practice
  ; 5)
    Includes bibliographical references and index.
    ISBN 0-7146-3435-2
    1. Soviet Union—Military policy. 2. Soviet Union—History,
  Military—1917–   I. Title. II. Series: Glantz, David M. Cass
  series on Soviet military theory and practice ; 5.
  UA770.G55   1992
  355′.0335′47—dc20   91-43411
                                                              CIP

Typeset by Regent Typesetting, London
Printed in Great Britain by BPCC Wheatons Ltd, Exeter

CONTENTS

FIGURES

CHAPTER 1

INTRODUCTION

Since the formation of the Soviet state, the concept of military strategy (*voennaia strategiia*) has occupied a dominant position in the intellectual framework the Soviets use to explain the nature and content of war. In their view military strategy is the highest realm of military art (*voennoe iskusstvo*) "encompassing the theory and practice of preparing a country and its armed forces for war and of planning for and conducting war and strategic operations". Within the context of national and military policy, military strategy investigates the laws, mechanisms, and strategic nature of war and methods used to conduct it, and works out theoretical bases for planning, preparing for, and conducting war and strategic operations.[1]

In a practical sense, military strategy:

- determines the strategic missions of the armed forces and the manpower and resources necessary to accomplish these missions;
- formulates and implements measures to prepare the armed forces, theaters of military operations, national economy, and civilian population for war;
- plans war and strategic operations;
- organizes the deployment of the armed forces and their guidance during the conduct of strategic-scale operations; and
- studies the capabilities of probable enemies to wage war and conduct strategic operations.

The Western concept of national strategy approximates what the Soviets refer to as policy (*politika*), which they have, until now, defined as a class-derived, party-oriented, and historically predetermined concept related to the organic evolution of class and, hence, state relations. The Soviets recognize the unique realm of military policy (*voennaia politika*) as "the relations and activities of classes, governments, parties, and other social-political institutions, directly connected with the creation of military organizations and the use of means of armed force for the achievement of political ends".[2] Military policy "by its essence and content represents a distinct limited component of the general policy of classes and govern-

1

ments".[3] Military policy receives concrete expression in military doctrine and military strategy. The Soviets claim their military policy and the derivative fields of military doctrine and military strategy reflect the unique policy of the Communist Party of the Soviet Union, although this may change in the future.

While policy determines the goals and means of statecraft, military policy governs the use of the nation's armed forces within the context of general state policy. In its turn:

> military strategy is closely interlinked with policy, emanating from it and serving it . . . . This interdependence is produced by the nature of war as a continuation of the policy of classes and states by forceful means. The chief role of policy with respect to military strategy lies in the fact that policy elaborates the objectives of war, defines the methods to be used to conduct it, assigns military strategy its tasks, and creates the conditions required for their accomplishment, mobilizing the materials and human resources necessary to meet the needs of war."[4]

Thus, military strategy reflects the political aims and policies of the state as well as its economic and socio-political character. Conversely, military strategy in peacetime and wartime "exerts an inverse influence on policy".[5] As such, strategy also reflects military doctrine, whose tenets guide strategy in the fulfillment of practical tasks and are grounded upon the data of military science. Military strategy provides a framework for operational art and tactics, the other components of military art, and exploits the capabilities of operational art and tactics to convert operational and tactical successes into strategic success – the achievement of strategic aims.

Strategic force posture is the peacetime manifestation of military strategy and facilitates transition of the Soviet Armed Forces from peace to war. Force posture embraces active forces and forces which can be mobilized in time of crisis or war, and it provides the fundamental basis for deployment (*razvertyvanie*) of the armed forces prior to and during war. In essence, armed forces deployment encompasses the creation of armed forces groupings to conduct war and operations.[6] The Soviets consider the most basic and important level of armed forces deployment to be strategic – that is deployments in accordance with strategic plans.

Strategic deployment (*strategicheskie razvertyvanie*) consists of a series of interrelated issues, the most important of which are the following:

- transition of the armed forces from a peacetime to a wartime footing;

2

- concentration of forces on selective strategic axes (directions – *napravlenie*);
- operational deployment of forces to required wartime locations;
- deployment of "the rear" (rear services).[7]

Strategic deployment has "traditionally" been expressed in peacetime by Soviet force generation (mobilization) systems and in wartime by the creation of strategic echelons. Force generation involves the distinct and varied processes either for manning the force during transition from peace through crisis to war (mobilization) and, conversely, for shrinking the force in transition from war or crisis to peace (demobilization). Strategic echelonment permits phased generation and application of military forces in combat on a geographical basis. Strategic echelonment embraces all Soviet armed forces designated to perform strategic missions and achieve strategic objectives. It normally consists of two echelons and a reserve, each assigned a specific function.[8]

The first strategic echelon includes formations of all types of forces charged with conducting initial operations during the initial period of war. The initial period of war (*nachal'nyi period voiny*), by Soviet definition, is "the time, in the course of which, warring states conduct combat operations with armed forces groupings deployed before the beginning of war, to achieve immediate strategic aims at the start of war or to create favorable conditions for the introduction into the war of main forces and to conduct subsequent operations".[9]

Throughout the initial period of war, states conduct strategic deployment of their armed forces, mobilize their economies for war, and negotiate with potential allies as well as the enemy to improve their international position. The Soviets identified and defined the term during the 1920s, and it has been a focal point of Soviet military strategy since. It has, in fact, become a major subtopic in Soviet study of future war. Throughout the subsequent years, the duration of the initial period of war has varied from several weeks to several months.

The second strategic echelon consists of formations located or forming within the depth of the state as well as other newly-formed units created throughout the state over time. The strategic reserves include existing or mobilizable additional forces and materiel available to the High Command. The strategic second echelon and reserve serve the function of strengthening (*narashchivanie*) the state's armed force, permitting it to make the transition from initial to subsequent strategic operations.

Soviet military strategy, strategic force posture, and the related concepts of armed forces deployment, strategic deployment, force generation, and strategic echelonment all directly reflect the threat as defined by

3

Soviet political authorities. As such, these strategic issues have evolved and will continue to evolve in accordance with existing or predicted political, economic, social, and military realities of the time.

CHAPTER 2

THE CIVIL WAR AND MILITARY INTERVENTION (1917–1921)

MILITARY POLICY

In the chaotic, uncertain days following the Bolshevik Revolution of November 1917, the Red Army was born, and with it Marxist–Leninist military policy and doctrine. Policy and doctrine matured during the Civil War years, when internal struggle and foreign intervention threatened the fledgeling Bolshevik regime's existence. The Bolshevik Party maintained close control over political power and, understanding the political realities, also seized a commanding position in the formulation of official military policy. V. I. Lenin was the chief interpreter of Marxism, and the new Marxist–Leninist theory encompassed all aspects of man's existence, especially the relationship between statecraft and military power.

Lenin's voluminous theoretical work regarding war found partial expression in the concepts he formulated in *Imperialism, the Highest Stage of Capitalism (1916)*.[1] In it he described the economic and political essence of imperialism, the highest and final stage of capitalism. This stage, unforeseen by Karl Marx, explained why workers joyfully marched to war in 1914 in support of their capitalist masters. Bought off by the minimal social reforms of capitalist governments, workers now required longer to reach the point of full alienation. Thus, inevitable revolution would be delayed. Lenin, in describing the imperialist stage of history, broadened his definition of exploitation to include within it the exploitation of underdeveloped countries by capitalist powers. The inevitable world revolution would now include both workers and the peoples of colonial nations joined together in revolution against their capitalist oppressors. From this time forward, Soviet policy and military strategy sought to encourage revolution and ferment in lesser-developed lands.

MILITARY DOCTRINE

Lenin gave shape to Soviet military doctrine and, hence, military strategy. The Soviets have since credited him with having developed the most important Marxist views on war, the army, and military science, and with "developing the entire doctrine concerning the defense of socialism".[2] While confirming that war was a continuation of politics by other armed means, Lenin developed further the ideas of Marx and Engels that war and politics were inexorably related by underscoring the class nature of politics and its socio-economic roots. He recognized war as "a continuation of the policies of given interested powers – and various classes within them – at the present time" as a concentrated expression of economics. Lenin classified the types of war found in the imperialist stage of historical development (national-liberation, revolutionary, civil, imperialistic, in defense of socialism) and pointed out the role of economics and the morale-political factor in war, stating that "war will now be conducted by the people" and "the connection between the military organization of the nation and its entire economic and cultural structure was never as close as at the present."[3] Lenin's system for classifying types of war has endured into the 1980s. According to V. D. Sokolovsky's 1960 comprehensive study of Soviet military strategy:

> Lenin defined the nature of wars in the era of imperialism, showed the historical conditions and causes of their springing up, exposed the tendencies in the development of military matters and made a profound scientific analysis of the state of military matters in Russia early in the 20th Century.
>
> In developing and defining concretely the concepts of the Marxist theory of armed conflict, Lenin developed the doctrine of just and unjust wars and of the change of an imperialistic war into a civil war, into a war of the workers against the exploiters, thus arming the working class and its vanguard, the Communist party, with a clear program of action in the struggle for the liberation of the working people from capitalist slavery.[4]

During the Civil War, Lenin worked out and implemented the principles of military construction for a socialist state, which included:

- rule of the armed forces by the Communist Party;
- a class approach to construction of the armed forces;
- the unity of the army and the people;
- the truth of proletarian internationalism;
- centralized command and control and single command (*edinonachalie*);
- cadre organization;
- creation of soldierly discipline;
- constant readiness to repel aggression.[5]

Lenin's work created the basis of Soviet military science and, even-

6

tually, the military art of the armies of other socialist governments. According to Sokolovsky:

> The great works of V. I. Lenin devoted to the political struggle of the working class, armed uprising, and proletarian revolution, developed the most important concepts of Soviet military science and Soviet military strategy ... Thus, to Lenin belongs the great credit in the development of the Marxist military theory. The military theoretical views of Lenin are the foundation of the military theory of the Soviet government.[6]

In these works Lenin:

> formulated the views on the factors and the decisive course and outcome of struggle ... In his works he emphasized the most important principles for conducting armed combat: determining the main danger and the direction of the main attack; concentration of forces and weapons in the decisive place at the decisive moment; securing by all methods and means of struggle their use in accordance with existing conditions; the decisive role of the offensive; the objective evaluation of opposing forces; initiative and surprise; firmness and decisiveness; securing success; maneuver of forces; and pursuit of the enemy to his full destruction.[7]

The legacy of Lenin, also encompassing the exploits of his discredited and long-forgotten comrades (for example, Trotsky) and personifying the exploits of the new Red Army, became the foundation of future Soviet military doctrine. Only today is that legacy being re-examined and those forgotten comrades rediscovered.

MILITARY STRATEGY

As an armed conflict, the Russian Civil War and military intervention contrasted sharply with the nature of the First World War at all levels of war. Since the Civil War was a war for the political survival of the Bolsheviks against a hostile world, Soviet strategy incorporated the major recommendations of Lenin. Lenin's harsh program for "War Communism" resulted in the militarization of the entire nation (strategic rear) and the full mobilization of the limited economic power of the nation for war.

Soviet military strategy developed as an outgrowth of Bolshevik policy in tandem with emerging doctrine and the developing armed forces of the Soviet state. Marxist–Leninist teaching on war and armies provided the theoretical bases of Soviet military strategy, and Soviet military science as a whole. Military strategy encompassed the most important concepts of

7

the political strategy of the new Communist (Bolshevik) Party and the experience of the armed conflict of the working class. Thus:

> "The political question," wrote Lenin, "now closely approaches the military question ... The problem of politics is also the military problem: the organization of the headquarters, concentration of material forces, the provision of the soldier with everything necessary ..." This is the fundamental reason why the most important concepts of political strategy of the Communist Party – those dealing with the significance of the proper choice of the direction of the main blow, of creating superiority of forces and means in the direction of this blow, of the changes in form and methods of conflict depending on the situation, of the dependence of the organizational forms of the troops on the methods of warfare, of the significance of strategic reserves, and of the strategic leadership of the struggle – are the foundations of Soviet military strategy.[8]

In accordance with Lenin's belief in the absolute need for understanding the fundamental laws of any war, Soviet military strategy also exploited the experience of past wars, especially the wars of the imperialist era, as well as the most important theoretical strategic concepts of bourgeois military science. At the same time, Soviet military science and military strategy developed on a wholly new basis. Despite the fact that Soviet military strategy basically employed the same means and methods for the conduct of war as those used by the old regime, it had a number of peculiar characteristics when used as the strategy of a socialist state in the very first years of its existence.

Among the most important characteristics of Soviet military strategy during the Civil War were its self-proclaimed clarity of purpose and decisiveness as dictated by the class nature of the war and the nature of its political aims. Soviet ideologists have since claimed that:

> Both war, as a whole, and military strategy bear the imprint of class interests, the politics of which are reflected in a given war; the intensity of the political contradictions of the opposing sides exerts a direct influence on the decisiveness of the strategic aims of the war.
>
> The political aim of the Civil War on the part of the working classes of the Soviet Republic, the total destruction of the interventionists and White Guardists, required a very active and decisive strategy. Only by bold decisive actions could victory be achieved, and thus conditions for the peaceful building of socialism be created.[9]

The Civil War and military intervention grew organically as a natural outgrowth of revolution and the political forces which the revolution unleashed. While various political factions contended with one another militarily in search of power, the Bolshevik regime's decision to withdraw Russia from the World War prompted intervention by both the Central and Western powers. In addition, after the World War had ended, Eastern European successor states, in particular Poland, intervened militarily to capitalize on Russia's internal strife and to redress long-standing territorial grievances against the Russian state.

Given this turbulent and unstable situation, military operations between various factions developed in virtually every region and from every direction. As the natural focal point of this military action, the new Bolshevik government had to contend with threats from every quarter. It did, however, have the inherent advantage of operating from interior lines against threats from whatever direction they developed.

During the initial stages of the Civil War from November 1917 to March 1918, the Bolshevik government consolidated its power against various factions and by March 1918 established its authority over all former Russian territory except the Caucasus and regions held by the Germans and Austrians, with whom Russia was still at war.

In March 1918, after months of fruitless negotiations punctuated by a sharp and rapid German advance into the Baltic region, the Bolshevik government signed the Treaty of Brest–Litovsk, which ended Russian participation in the World War and recognized a German-supported puppet government in the Ukraine. While the Brest–Litovsk treaty provided respite from the World War, it also prompted Allied intervention, first in the Caucasus and later in other regions, and strengthened military opposition from White forces. By the summer of 1918, Civil War was a reality, spurred on by intervention in Russia by the forces of a host of Western nations.[10]

Strategic operations during the Civil War encompassed three major theaters (Eastern, Southern, and Western), with several strategic directions (axes) within each theater (see Figures 1–3). Chronologically, military campaigns occurred seasonally across the span of three years within each theater, with lesser operations punctuating the intervals between campaigns.

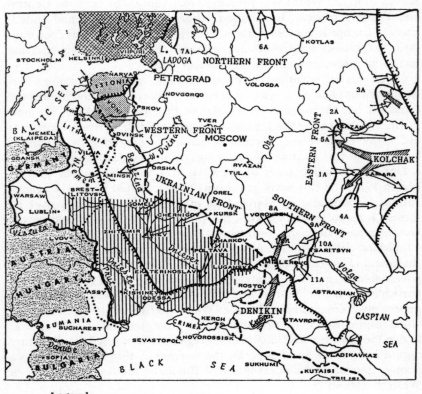

Legend
- - - - - Limit of German advance, March 1918
- Ukrainian separatists
- August 1918
- March 1919

1. Civil War and Intervention: March 1918–March 1919

Year	Southern Theater	Western Theater	Eastern Theater
1918	Denikin in the Kuban (Jan–Aug)		Czech Revolt (May–Nov) White Offensive (July–Aug) Red Offensive (Sept–Nov) Kolchak Revolt (coup) (Nov) Kolchak Advance (Dec)
1919	Bolsheviks secure Kiev and Ukraine	Iudenich Advance (May–June) (Sept–Oct)	Kolchak Advance (Feb–Apr)
	Denikin Offensive (May–Oct) Bolshevik Counteroffensive (Oct–Dec)	Bolshevik Counteroffensive (Oct–Nov)	Bolshevik Counteroffensive (Apr–Nov)
1920	Denikin defeat (Jan–Apr)	Polish Offensive (Apr–May)	
	Wrangel Offensive (June–Oct) Bolshevik Counteroffensive (Oct–Nov)	Bolshevik Offensive (May–Aug) Polish Counteroffensive (Aug–Oct) (peace)	

During the summer of 1918, the Bolsheviks faced threats from the south and east. After the defeat of General L. G. Kornilov's anti-Bolshevik force between January and April in the Kuban, General A. I. Denikin assumed command of White forces. By August his forces occupied Ekaterinodar and Novorossiisk, together with the bulk of the Kuban. As yet, however, he was unable to mount a more credible threat to Bolshevik power in southern Russia.[11]

A far more serious crisis erupted in the east, where, spurred on by a revolt by Czech troops (being transported from the Eastern to the Western Fronts by way of the Trans-Siberian railroad and Vladivostok), White forces advanced westward and, by 2 August 1918, seized Kazan.

11

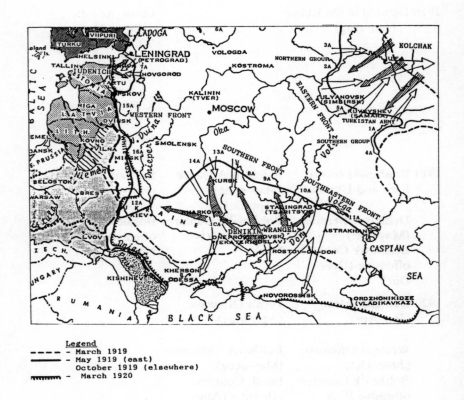

Legend
- - - - – March 1919
———— – May 1919 (east)
            October 1919 (elsewhere)
〰〰〰 – March 1920

2. Civil War and Intervention: March 1919–March 1920

Bolshevik forces concentrated by rail on the Eastern Front, counterattacked, and by early November recaptured Kazan, Samara, and Izhevsk. In the wake of the White defeat, Admiral A. V. Kolchak led a coup, formed a new White government, and organized a new White offensive, which by late December recaptured Perm. Yet another Bolshevik counteroffensive stopped Kolchak's forces by the end of the year, halting further fighting in the east until spring.

In 1919 the Bolsheviks faced their most perilous threat in the form of an extensive but poorly coordinated White offensive from the west, south, and east. Initially, in January the Bolshevik Ukrainian Front began the year auspiciously by crushing the Ukrainian separatist movement and securing Kiev (5 February). Meanwhile, the Southern Front crushed General P. N. Krasnov's pro-White Cossack forces in the Don region. The remnants of Krasnov's force joined Denikin's army in the Kuban. These Soviet successes were soon negated when in February Admiral Kolchak's forces commenced a new offensive, which became a harbinger of even more trying times for the Bolshevik government. Kolchak's attacking forces again seized Izhevsk and also threatened Kazan. Key Bolshevik grain regions were now in jeopardy as well as lines of communications with Turkestan. To counter this new threat, Bolshevik Commissar of War L. D. Trotsky reorganized Red forces, significantly reinforced the Eastern Front, and conducted a counteroffensive in late April. Ultimately, the counteroffensive broke the back of Kolchak's forces and forced a precipitous retreat, which ended on 14 November with Bolshevik seizure of Kolchak's headquarters at Omsk. The triumphant Soviet march eastward continued until late February 1920, when the Red Army took Irkutsk, where they temporarily halted to avoid provoking the Japanese (who occupied eastern Siberia).

While Trotsky was shifting his forces eastward and attacking Kolchak, in May White forces struck from Estonia toward Petrograd and northward from the Kuban. General N. N. Iudenich's White forces, backed by the British and Estonians, struck toward Pskov and Petrograd. In a halting, multi-stage offensive, by 15 October Iudenich penetrated Petrograd's southern suburbs. The subsequent failure of Iudenich to sever Petrograd's railline connections to Moscow permitted the Red Army to reinforce the city and, in late October, counterattack. Denied further active British support, Iudenich's forces collapsed and withdrew to Estonia, where they were interned.

Loosely cooperating with Iudenich, in May 1919 Denikin's Volunteer Army struck northward out of the Kuban, seized Rostov, and united with Ukrainian forces and General F. P. Wrangel's Caucasus Army, then operating south of Tsaritsyn. By June Denikin's combined force of three

13

armies (Volunteer, Caucasus, and newly-formed Don) cooperated with Ukrainian forces to seize territory extending from Khar'kov to Tsaritsyn. After a short pause, in July Denikin's armies began a concerted offensive toward Moscow.[12] The Red Army High Command hastily shifted 60,000 men from the east to meet the threat. An early Soviet counterattack in

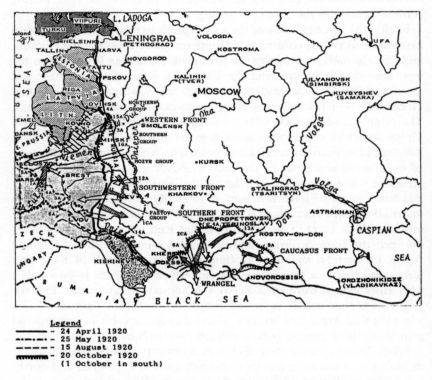

Legend
───────── – 24 April 1920
━·━·━·━ – 25 May 1920
────── – 15 August 1920
▮▮▮▮▮▮ – 20 October 1920
(1 October in south)

3. Civil War and Intervention: April–December 1920

July failed, and in September, after seizing Kiev, Denikin's armies drove north through Kursk and Voronezh toward Moscow. Finally, in mid-October near Orel, a heavy Soviet counteroffensive struck Denikin's overextended force. After weeks of heavy fighting, Denikin's armies collapsed. This victorious White advance now turned into a hasty retreat, and by January 1920 the Red Army had retaken Rostov. In March Denikin's armies abandoned the Kuban and withdrew to the Crimean Peninsula where Baron Wrangel took command of its remnants.

No sooner had the Red Army snuffed out the threat from the east and isolated the southern threat to the Crimean Peninsula than a new challenge emerged in the west, a challenge in the form of a hostile, expansionist Poland.[13] Already in the spring of 1919, while the Bolsheviks were preoccupied with the threat to Petrograd, Polish forces occupied eastern Galacia, Vilnius in Lithuania, and Baranovichi in Belorussia. By August Polish forces had seized Minsk but postponed a further advance to avoid facilitating a victory by Denikin and Kolchak and promoting the growth of Great Russian nationalism, which was likely to follow and benefit the Bolsheviks. In April 1920, however, after signing an agreement with the Ukrainian separatist government, Poland invaded the Soviet Union, and by 6 May seized Zhitimir, Korosten, and Kiev. Despite Polish hopes, the Ukrainians failed to support them, and, as they had feared, a wave of Russian nationalism buoyed the spirits and strength of the Red Army. In May M. N. Tukhachevsky's Soviet Western Front struck back at Polish forces between Polotsk and Minsk, but the counteroffensive failed. An even larger-scale counteroffensive in June by the Soviet Southwestern Front, spearheaded by S. M. Budenny's lst Cavalry Army, pierced Polish lines and reconquered Kiev. In early July the combined Soviet Western and Southwestern Fronts attacked, drove Polish forces from Belorussia and the Ukraine and by late July reached the Vistula River around Warsaw. Soviet command, control, and coordination problems during the climactic battle for Warsaw spelled doom for the offensive. A timely Polish counterstroke against the Soviet rear east of Warsaw (the "miracle on the Vistula") forced a subsequent Soviet withdrawal from Poland, which was hastened by news that White forces were again emerging from their southern bastions.

The last major White challenge to Bolshevik power began in June when Baron Wrangel's forces attacked from Crimea and seized the northern Tavria region to the north as well as the Kuban region. After containing Wrangel's forces in the Tavria (September), the Bolsheviks reestablished their Southern Front (under M. V. Frunze), reinforced it with troops from the Southwestern Front, and made the destruction of Wrangel a top strategic priority. In a subsequent two-month campaign, Frunze's forces drove Wrangel from the northern Tavria, penetrated heavy defenses covering the approaches into the Crimean Peninsula at Perekop, and overran the peninsula, forcing Wrangel to depart from Sevastopol on Western transports.[14]

By late November the major campaigns of the Civil War were over. Allied interventionist forces slowly left Russia throughout the Civil War. In October 1919 Allied troops in northern Russia evacuated Arkhangel'sk, in April 1919 the French and British left southern Russia, and by October 1922 the last to leave, the Japanese, departed from Vladivostok.

15

The Civil War continued in the Caucasus region and central Asia for up to two additional years before peace reigned in the war-ravaged nation.

The Civil War reflected the intensity of the political and ideological struggle. Bolshevik military strategy sought to achieve decisive aims, "since there was no talk whatsoever of coming to terms with the class enemy".[15] The armed forces sought to achieve strategic aims as quickly as possible, since victory in war became a prerequisite for the consolidation of Bolshevik political power. Operational-strategic planning by *fronts* avoided the achievement of limited objectives, but rather sought the total destruction of the enemy along each specific strategic direction (axis) and occupation of the enemy's territory. "Noting the importance and the need for a close survey of the military-political situation and the relationship of forces, Lenin wrote: 'We need not be tied down to any one strategic maneuver. Everything depends on the relationship of forces ...' "[16] Having accomplished the goal of destroying the White forces of Denikin, Kolchak, and Iudenich, by 1920 the Bolshevik High Command sought to achieve similar objectives against Poland during the Russo-Polish War. This tendency to treat war as a totality of military, economic, political, and social measures differentiated Bolshevik strategy from that of its opponents and left a lasting imprint on the minds of subsequent Soviet military strategists.

The perilous military situation facing the Bolsheviks, which often generated sheer desperation on the part of the Bolshevik High Command also conditioned military strategy:

> The Soviet Republic was in a fiery ring of fronts. The enemy, having superior forces and equipment, pressed against it from all sides and advanced toward the vital centers of the country. At the same time, limited manpower and material capabilities did not allow the Red Army to conduct simultaneously and with equal intensity broad offensive operations with decisive aims on several fronts.
>
> Therefore, the isolation of a decisive front from a multitude of the then-existing fronts was one of the most important problems of military strategy.[17]

Consequently, under the firm, and often ruthless, control of Lenin and the Party Central Committee, the relatively small Soviet armed force was massed and switched from one decisive strategic direction to another to meet the most critical threats.

An important feature of Soviet military strategy was its flexibility and its ability to select types of strategic operations appropriate to the situation and to employ them in various combinations. "We must never in any way tie our hands in a single strategic maneuver," said Lenin, illustrating his pragmatism when faced by reality.[18]

The most striking feature of ensuing Civil War military operations was the vastness of the regions involved. Vast space placed a high premium on rapid movement and careful concentration of forces. Soviet reliance on railroads to afford the Red Army strategic mobility gave rise to what the Soviets called *eshelonaia voina* (echelon – or railroad-war). Given the nature of the threat and geographical realities, the role and significance of individual *fronts* (equivalent to Western army groups) were ever-changing in accordance with the military-political situation.

Consequently, in the summer and the first half of the fall of 1918, of the then-existing Eastern, Southern Caspian–Caucasian, and Northern Fronts, and the Western Defense Area, the Eastern Front was recognized as the most important front. By the end of 1918, the Southern Front became the most prominent, by the spring of 1919 the Eastern Front was again the most important, and by the middle of the summer of 1919 the Southern Front again had become the most critical. This situation persisted to the end of the war. The Red Army, depending on the military and political situation, directed its main efforts against the enemy, first along one strategic direction, and then another, concentrating the bulk of its troops successively along each direction. Ensuing combat operations were aimed not only at destroying enemy manpower, but also, and simultaneously, at securing sources of raw materials, bread, and fuel, without which the country could not exist. Thus, during the Civil War, together with the destruction of the armed forces of the Whites and interventionists, the most important aim of strategic operations was also to find solutions to critical economic problems.

After defining and successfully solving the main strategic problem, that of recognizing the main enemy thrust and selecting the direction of the main blow, the next important characteristic of Soviet military strategy was the decisive concentration of forces and weapons along the selected direction of the main thrust. "To have an overwhelming advantage of forces at the decisive moment at the decisive point – that is the 'law' of military successes ...," wrote Lenin.[19] Given the overall paucity of forces and weapons characteristic of the Civil War, the solution of this problem involved great difficulties and was accomplished only by successful successive concentrations of forces in the decisive sectors at the expense of seriously weakening forces in other sectors.

Circumstances forced organs of strategic leadership to master the art of shifting and concentrating forces between key strategic directions, encompassing virtually all theaters of military operations. In a 10 August directive to the Main Military Soviet (*Vysshii voennyi Sovet*), Lenin wrote, "I consider it essential in every way possible to strengthen the Eastern Front ... All combat capable units must go."[20] *Front* commanders also had to mass their forces to the greatest possible extent to establish required superiority over the enemy on key directions. Often this shifting of forces caused temporary discomfiture or defeat in secondary sectors:

> This created conditions for the fulfillment of the main strategic aim presented by politics. In the history of the Civil War, there are known cases when, in the interest of strengthening the main front or deciding the main strategic problem, other fronts were weakened to such an extent that our troops were forced to retreat or even suffer temporary defeat ... This was the case, for example, with the Eastern Front by the end of 1918 and early 1919, when the concentration of the main forces on the Southern Front caused an excessive weakening of the Eastern Front.[21]

The principle of concentrating forces and weapons along priority directions was widely applied in all frontal sectors. The Soviet High Command strictly observed this principle of Soviet military strategy in the execution of most major offensive operations. For example, in the direction of the main thrust of the Southern Group of Frunze's Eastern Front, the Soviets concentrated 49,000 infantry and cavalry with 152 artillery pieces in a 200–220 kilometer sector, while only 22,500 infantry and cavalry with 70 artillery pieces were concentrated in the remaining 700 kilometer sector. During the July 1920 offensive, M. N. Tukhachevsky's Western Front concentrated three armies and one cavalry corps totalling 60,000 men in a 120 kilometer sector in the direction of the main thrust, while only one army and a small operational group concentrated in the auxiliary sector of some 300 kilometers.[22] In some Civil War operations, however, the principle of concentrating forces on the direction of the main thrust was not always observed and this often led to failure of the operation. This was the case, for example, during the August 1919 Southern Front offensive and the May 1920 offensive by the Western Front.

Soviet military strategy during the Civil War also embraced a wide variety of types and forms of armed conflict. Following Lenin's dictum that the methods of armed struggle against the enemy must be altered in accordance with changing conditions, Soviet military leaders exhibited exceptional flexibility in their selection of methods of warfare to fit existing circumstances. Military operations thus consisted of a mixture of offensives, counteroffensives or counterattacks, defensives, and even retreats, supported by widespread partisan activities. This required on the part of military strategy a high degree of flexibility in assigning priorities to threats and shifting military resources to meet these threats.

Military operations during the Civil War and military intervention substantially differed from operations during the World War and were characterized by their greater geographical scale, widespread resort to maneuver, and greater decisiveness. Red Army Civil War operations were continuous and extended to great depth; they were also of long duration (some of them lasted for several months) as shown by the following:

DIMENSIONS OF IMPORTANT RED ARMY STRATEGIC OPERATIONS DURING THE CIVIL WAR[23]

Operation	Forces Strength/ Divisions	Width of Offensive (km)	Depth of Offensive (km)	Duration of Operation (days)	Average rate of Advance (km/day)
Counterattack of Southern Group of Eastern Front:					
– on the entire front	73,500/ 8	up to 1600	up to 400	March 28, 1919–June 19, 1919 (53 days)	7–8
– in the direction of main thrust	49,000/ approx. 6	200– 220			
Offensive of Southern Front against Denikin:					
– on the entire front	95,000/ 20/5*	1400	150– 900	Oct. 10, 1919–Jan. 10 1920 (92 days)	8–10
– in the active sector	70,000/ 13/5	600			
Offensive of Western Front against the Poles:					
– on the entire front	89,000/ 20/2	500	700– 750	July 4, 1920–Aug. 15, 1920 (43 days)	16–18
– in the direction of main thrust	60,000 13/2	140			

*The first figure gives the number of infantry divisions, the second the number of cavalry divisions.

The scope and scale of Civil War military operations varied sharply. In theaters of military operations, Soviet *fronts* (first employed in June 1918) usually deployed in 700 to 1,800 kilometer-wide sectors and concentrated their offensive operations in sectors of from 400 to 1,000 kilometers against objectives which extended to depths of from 600 to 3,000 kilometers. Ensuing operations involved a tempo of advance of between 6 and 20 kilometers per day.[24]

STRATEGIC OFFENSE

The most important and decisive type of strategic operation was the strategic offensive. Red Army offensive operations sought to achieve the total defeat of the enemy, and these often ranged to great depths without significant operational pauses. Major offensive operations, as a rule, consisted of a series of successive operations by the forces of one or two *fronts*, unified by a single plan into an overall strategic effort along a given strategic direction. Each individual operation formed a link in the chain leading to accomplishment of the final aim of the entire operation. Usually offensive operations were against enemy groupings whose defeat would decisively alter the military-political situation. The relatively small forces, poor communications, and inadequate logistics limited the Bolsheviks' ability to sustain these strategic offensives and forced commanders to rely primarily on the use of successive operations, punctuated by short operational pauses.

On the broad, open and spacious battlefields of the Civil War, maneuver warfare predominated. Hence, the enemy, after his initial defeat, could then withdraw his troops and reorganize a defense or even a counteroffensive. Only by virtue of repeated blows, and by almost continuous and successive operations could the total destruction of the enemy be achieved. This combination of almost uninterrupted offensive operations and relentless pursuit was a characteristic feature of Red Army offensive operations during the Civil War. While it often produced decisive victories, on occasion Red Army overextension led to equally spectacular defeat (Poland 1920).

Offensive operations by the Eastern and Southern Fronts against the Kolchak's and Denikin's armies included a number of successive operations unified within a single plan to achieve a single decisive aim. During the period of the Eastern Front offensive from the Volga to the Urals (April–July 1919), the Buguruslan, Belebeia, Ufa, Zlatoust and Cheliabinsk operations were undertaken for a total penetration of up to 900–1,000 kilometers. Then from August to November, the same *front* conducted the Tobol'sk, Petropavlovsk and Omsk operations. From 20

November 1919 to 8 March 1920, the Eastern Front pursued Kolchak's armies from Omsk to Irkutsk, to a depth of 2,500–2,800 kilometers.[25] The strategic offensive operations of Southern Front's armies aimed at the destruction of Denikin's forces also consisted of a number of successive operations unified by a common aim: the Orel–Kromy, Voronezh–Kastornoe, Khar'kov, Donbas, and Rostov operations.

In most cases, the Red Army conducted major strategic offensive operations along a broad front, but, as a rule, delivered its main blows in narrow sectors, comprising only 23–28 per cent of the total front length. Strategic offensive operations were usually conducted by the forces of a single *front*, operating along a given strategic direction and consisting of from two to six armies each consisting of two to five divisions.[26] In some operations (against Denikin in the fall of 1919 and against the Poles in 1920), two *fronts* combined to conduct these offensives.

The achievement of decisive aims in offensive operations required that the governing military strategy be extraordinarily flexible in the creation of force groupings and in the employment of available forces and weapons. Therefore, during the Civil War, up to 75 per cent of the entire strength of the Red Army was subjected to strategic transfer from one front to another. Consequently, some divisions regrouped from one *front* to another as many as five times. Often offensives began in the form of a counteroffensive launched by Red forces after a period of defensive combat. The Soviets employed the counteroffensive to destroy attacking enemy shock groups and to regain the strategic initiative, usually by regrouping their forces and *launching* counteroffensives from a defensive posture, often against the enemy's flank.

Economic and political conditions exerted great influence on the nature and aims of Civil War strategic operations. In planning major offensive operations, for example, Soviet strategy took into account not only purely military considerations, but also the necessity for solving general political and economic problems. In a number of cases the solution of these problems was the chief aim of an operation. Thus, the report of the Supreme Commander on the strategic state of the Republic presented to V. I. Lenin on 7 October 1918 noted that "in developing our efforts primarily toward the south, we will obtain more rapidly the necessities of life, without which the center of the country could not exist".[27]

STRATEGIC DEFENSE

In the circumstances of maneuver warfare and limited quantities of forces and weapons, successful defense was of critical importance. While the Red Army conducted offensive operations on the front where enemy main forces and weapons were concentrated, it carried out defensive operations on fronts of secondary importance. Along some directions Red Army forces decided or were forced to retreat. Thus, during Eastern Front offensive operations against Kolchak's army, Southern Front forces were forced to abandon the Donbas and withdraw to the central region of the country. All the while, the Western Front conducted strenuous defensive operations covering the approaches to Petrograd. In the fall of 1919, when combat with Denikin's armies on the Southern Front entered its decisive phase, Eastern Front forces, under the pressure of a superior enemy, retreated to the Tobol River, while Western Front forces again resumed stubborn defense in the direction of Petrograd. Often defensive and offensive actions were combined within the same *front* when an unfavorable correlation of forces existed. For example, during operations along the Eastern Front in the spring of 1919, while Soviet forces launched counterattacks on the central frontal sector, other forces on both flanks engaged in stubborn defensive battles.

The Soviets resorted to the strategic defensive only when forced to because of limited forces and marked enemy superiority. In 1918 these defensive operations bought time for the Soviets to conduct mobilization, but by 1919 the Soviets used defensive operations deliberately to economize on forces necessary to conduct successful offensive operations in other sectors. Red Army defensive operations were clearly active in nature and were accompanied by decisive counterattacks against the flanks and rear of the enemy. Defense was intended to exhaust and bleed the enemy white, to eliminate his ability to maneuver, and to prepare conditions for a counterattack. An example of such operations was the defense of Tsaritsyn in the summer and fall of 1918, and also of Petrograd in the summer and fall of 1919.

STRATEGIC COOPERATION AND MANEUVER

Soviet military strategy during the Civil War left a valuable legacy of military experience in the organization of cooperation (*vzaimodeistvie*) between *fronts* and subordinate forces. For example, the Southern and Northern Groups of the Eastern Front closely cooperated in the defeat of Kolchak's army. During the struggle with Denikin, close cooperation was organized between the Southern and the Southeastern (Caucasian)

Fronts. There were, however, instances when cooperation between *fronts* was weak or altogether absent. The disruption of cooperation between the Western and Southwestern Fronts in 1920 was one of the major reasons for the Polish "miracle on the Vistula" and the subsequent unsuccessful outcome of the Warsaw operation. This lesson had a major impact on subsequent Soviet military strategists (for example the Soviet decision to halt their offensive along the Oder River in February 1945).

Red Army operations during the Civil War exhibited widely different forms of operational and strategic maneuver. Extensive use was made of such forms of maneuver as wide and close envelopment of the enemy by rapid flanking attacks, combined with deep penetration by the cavalry into the enemy rear. The Red Army employed extensive maneuver and flanking attacks to destroy the armies of Kolchak, Denikin and Wrangel. The Southwestern Front's counteroffensive against the Poles relied upon a double envelopment together with the simultaneous penetration by a cavalry army into the enemy rear, which led to the encirclement of a large Polish force in the Kiev region. Together with flanking attacks and deep penetrations, the Red Army employed such operational and strategic maneuvers as the deep cleaving attack, first used in the fall of 1919 in the defeat of Denikin's armies.

Soviet military strategy also succeeded in solving the problem of penetrating the enemy front throughout its entire depth within specific Civil War conditions. This problem was solved by massed use of cavalry organized into cavalry armies. These armies supported by artillery, armor, infantry, and aviation delivered strong attacks into the enemy rear and engaged the enemy's operational reserves.

Thus, during the Civil War, in accordance with the situation, the Red Army employed various forms of operational and strategic maneuver, while the interventionists and White forces relied primarily on frontal attacks across a wide sector. This linear type of offensive operation was the most characteristic feature of most interventionist and White Guard operations. A clear exception was the imaginative White employment of cavalry. General Mamontov's raid into the Red forces' rear during Denikin's advance to Orel so impressed the Bolsheviks that they modeled their subsequent cavalry operations after the experiences of Mamontov.

STRATEGIC RESERVES

Strategic reserves played an immensely decisive role in such a war of maneuver. Despite their importance, a characteristic feature of the Civil War was the extremely limited quantity of necessary strategic reserves at the disposal of the Soviet High Command. Although the Red Army enjoyed the advantage of internal operational lines, successful conduct of war by the Bolsheviks required they generate a large number of strategic (operational) reserves. Until 1920, however, *fronts* operating along principal strategic directions were reinforced primarily by transfer of troops from other less active *fronts*; even this feat was accomplished with great difficulty.

A report of the Supreme Commander to V. I. Lenin in March 1919, (for example, during Kolchak's offensive) illustrates the difficulties associated with the lack of numerous reserves, which Soviet military strategy had to overcome:

> The troops at the fronts have been fighting in their positions without any relief for almost a year. As a consequence of the vast extension of the combat sectors (frequently one division per 200 versts*) and the direct onslaught of the enemy, no army reserves or even front line reserves could be detached. Military units constantly on the front lines cannot be organized, reinforced, or correctly formed into a combat unit. In order to accomplish the strategic transfer of units from one front to another it is often necessary to take them directly from the battle lines, imposing the burden of defense on the neighboring units and often weakening the front seriously.[28]

To create reserves, in late 1918 the Red Army Supreme Command planned to form 11 infantry divisions within the interior military districts. If it had formed these divisions, by early spring of 1919 the Red Army Supreme Command would have possessed a reserve of 150,000–200,000 infantry. However, the worsening military situation on the Southern and Eastern Fronts made these measures impossible. Of the 11 divisions, seven were sent to the front before they had even completed their training. As a result, when Kolchak's 1919 offensive began, the Supreme Command had only approximately 60,000 infantry in reserve, and these reserves were not fully prepared since units and formations lacked artillery pieces and machine guns.[29] Because of insufficient reserves, the regrouping of forces within the Eastern Front was of even greater significance for the successful accomplishment of strategic tasks. The Soviet High Command throughout the entire Civil War resorted extensively to regrouping forces from secondary sectors to the direction of the main threat, thereby creating significant superiority in forces and weapons in most critical sectors.

The Central Committee of the Party, headed by Lenin, devoted considerable attention to the training and utilization of reserves.

---

* A Russian unit of length, equal to 1.0668 km or 3,500 feet.

Measures undertaken by the Party Central Committee constituted an extensive program for the creation not only of manpower, but also of materiel reserves. In the second half of 1919, the High Command formed reserve armies, which subsequently played an important role in the training of reserves. From July 1919 to December 1920, the reserve army of the Republic at Kazan alone supplied 34 per cent of the replacements to all the *fronts*, and up to 40 per cent to the most active *fronts*.[30] To create reserves for active armies, the High Command created special administrations (UPRAFORMS) at frontline headquarters to deal with manning and with the formation and training of the troops. These administrations formed their own reserve units. This centralized system for training manpower reserves made it possible, within a very short time, to reform units and formations at the front and also aided in the timely creation and employment of shock groups for specific operations.

Party, Komsomol, and trade-union mobilization, both in the Soviet Union and in liberated territories, also played an important part in the reinforcement of *fronts*. For example, by the time the armies of the Eastern Front had crossed the Ural Mountains in 1919, their personnel had been almost completely replaced by mobilized Ural workers. The Eastern Front's 5th Army had 24,000 soldiers on the Tobol River in August 1919. By October 1919, despite the losses sustained, it had increased to 37,000 by local mobilization.[31] Such a growth in force strength was characteristic of all the armies of the Eastern Front during their offensive and during the pursuit of Kolchak's army. The same was true of the Southern Front armies during operations which destroyed Denikin's forces.

PARTISAN WAR

A characteristic feature of Soviet military strategy during the Civil War was the skillful coordination of the military activities of the Red Army with the partisan movement in the rear of the interventionists and White Guardists. Partisan operations, a military manifestation of mobilizing the people and the rear for war, developed extensively on both sides and became an effective means of disrupting the enemy's strategic rear area. The Soviets credit this phenomenon to the ferocity of combat and the reign of terror which ensued:

> The unpopular terrorist regime of the military dictatorship, set up by the White Guardists with the active cooperation of the imperialists of Britain, France, and the United States on territory temporarily seized by them, caused profound universal indignation

25

among the working masses. Despite the severe terror, repressions, and persecutions, the workers and the peasants under the leadership of underground Bolshevik party organizations rose up to a decisive fight with the interventionists and White Guardists.[32]

Terror, in fact, generated a partisan movement on both contending sides, but Bolshevik ruthlessness in maintaining rear area security largely negated White partisan efforts.

The partisan movement, developed vigorously in the rear of Kolchak's and Denikin's forces, played an important role in the destruction of their armies. By quick surprise attacks, partisans paralyzed the functioning of the White forces' rear, disorganized supply lines to the front, and disrupted control of troops. This partisan struggle to the enemy rear was large-scale. The Soviets claim there were as many as 80,000 partisans active in Siberia in September 1919. In the Amur Oblast' of the Far East, a 25,000-man partisan army operated.[33] Strong partisan forces also existed in the Eastern Transbaikal region, in the Maritime Province, and in the Amur region. By fall 1919, vast regions had been captured by the partisan movement to the rear of Denikin's forces, thus helping to precipitate the rapid collapse of his army.

When planning and conducting major Civil War offensive operations, the Soviet High Command closely coordinated its combat activities with partisan operations. During Southern Front operations along the Don River against Krasnov and Denikin in the fall of 1918, an important role was assigned to insurrectional movements to the rear of the White Guardists. In preparing the counterattack of Southern Front forces in October 1919, the Party Central Committee informed the Central Committee of the Ukrainian Communist Party (Bolsheviks) of the strong support given to the Red Army by the Ukrainian partisans.

The Ukrainian Zafrontburo*, in accordance with the Central Committee of the Party's instructions, supplied detailed directives to Ukrainian partisans demanding the immediate initiation of military operations against Denikin, the capture and retention of the most important control points and railroad lines, and the disruption of Denikin's lines of retreat. Partisans were also to prevent the enemy destroying railroad lines, bridges, and other major railroad communica-

*The Zafrontburo (rear area Bureau) of the Central Committee of the Communist Party (Bolsheviks) of the Ukraine was formed in July 1919 to guide the underground communist organizations of the Ukraine and, through them, the up-risings and partisan movements in the rear area of the enemy. The Zafrontburo was headed by S. V. Kosior, secretary of the Central Committee of the Communist Party (Bolsheviks) of the Ukraine. The Central Committee of the Russia Communist Party (Bolsheviks) on 8 September 1919, approved the creation of the Zafrontburo.

tions in the path of the advancing Red Army. Ukrainian partisans consequently increased their attacks on Denikin and, as the troops of the Red Army approached, entered into direct contact with advancing formations and assisted them. The strength of the partisan units and of the forces of the uprising commanded by the Revolutionary Military Council, according to G. A. Kolos, Commander-in-Chief, reached 50,000 in December 1919.[34]

Bolshevik military operations were also closely coordinated with partisan activity during the destruction of Kolchak's, Miller's, Iudenich's and Wrangel's armies. Soviet strategists accord great importance to the partisan movement, noting, "The selfless heroic struggle of the workers, under the leadership of the Communist Party in the rear areas of the interventionists and White Guardists, played an important part in the successful outcome of the Civil War."[35]

CONCLUSIONS

Soviet military strategy during the Civil War was inseparably linked with the policy of the Soviet state. Soviet military strategy, like its military policy:

> was permeated with a unity of purpose, supported by the firm and unified leadership by the Central Committee of the Party headed by V. I. Lenin ... The Party Central Committee was the fighting headquarters, the true organizer and inspiration of the Soviet people in their fight with the interventionists and White Guardists.[36]

The Party Central Committee examined most important questions dealing with the conduct of war, including the building and reinforcement of the armed forces, strategic war planning, the creation and distribution of reserves, and the appointment of commanders. Strategic planning of all the most important campaigns of the Civil War and all the measures connected with their execution were developed under the direct leadership of Lenin and were fully discussed in the plenums and sessions of the Party Central Committee. For example, questions connected with all aspects of the preparation and conduct of the major Eastern Front strategic operation aimed at the destruction of Kolchak's Army were examined by the plenums of the Central Committee of the Russian Communist Party (Bolsheviks) on 13 April and 4 May 1919, at the session of the Politburo on 24 April, and at the joint session of the Orgburo and Politburo on 29 April 1919.[37]

The operation aimed at the destruction of Denikin's Army was based on the decisions of the July and September plenums of the Central

27

Committee of the Russian Communist Party (Bolsheviks) and on Polit-buro decisions of 15 October and 6 and 14 November 1919. Party Central Committee plenums and sessions developed the general strategic plans for each operation and outlined the measures to increase the defense potential of the country, improve supply of the active armies, strengthen the leadership within the *front* and armies, strengthen political agencies and Party organizations, and improve political Party work among the troops and the population.

In his speech at the closed session of the VIII Congress of the Russian Communist Party (Bolsheviks) on 21 March 1919, Lenin remarked that "questions of military construction were discussed at literally every session of the Central Committee. There was never a single question of strategy which had not been evaluated by the Central Committee or a bureau of the Central Committee and put into execution."[38]

The struggle at the fronts was only one aspect of the activity of the Party Central Committee. Simultaneously, and in parallel with providing military leadership, the Party Central Committee built the political institutions of the new Soviet state. Therefore, in the Soviet view:

> the history of the Civil War is inseparable from the history of the entire country. The close cooperation of the army and the people is one of the strongest aspects of Soviet military strategy as compared with that of the interventionists and White Guardists. In leading the defense of the country, the Central Committee of the Party encompassed all the aspects of its life and activity and created favorable internal as well as external conditions for Soviet military strategy in the execution of its tasks assigned by policy. As a result of vast organizational and political activity, the Communist Party changed the country into a single military camp and mobilized for the Red Army a maximum of manpower and material resources.[39]

In short, "The peace-loving foreign policy of the Communist Party and the Soviet government, inexorably pursued from the first victorious days of the socialist revolution in our country to the present day, played a major part in the victory over the interventionists and White Guardists."[40] This dominant role played by the party and its central committee established a pattern in the development and implementation of Soviet military strategy, which would endure unbroken for over 70 years. In essence, Frunze's 1920s dictum concerning the wartime unity of front and rear was born during the heat of the Civil War.

CHAPTER 3

THE EMERGENCE OF SOVIET MILITARY STRATEGY (1921–1935)

GENERAL

The Soviet Union emerged from the Civil War united under Lenin's Bolshevik Party, but faced serious problems associated with reconstructing national institutions. The Communist Party had to consolidate its political power, build state governmental institutions, restore the economic viability of the new Soviet Union, and overcome the state's technological backwardness, which placed her at a marked disadvantage in comparison with more highly industrialized Western nations. Lenin's New Economic Policy (NEP) supplanted the harsh repressive wartime policy of "War Communism" with a new system incorporating vestiges of capitalist practices. Nevertheless, the state "seized the commanding heights of industry" as a step on the march toward full Socialism. The New Economic Policy was designed to restore Soviet economic strength by providing for economic growth and a modicum of social peace. Throughout the early and mid-1920s, it created an atmosphere conducive for the ruling Communist Party to address successfully all facets of national reconstruction, one of the most important of which was the question of what sort of military establishment should the Soviet Union possess.

By the late 1920s it was apparent to Soviet leaders that unless they undertook drastic measures to industrialize the Soviet economy, their ill-equipped military establishment would continue to lag significantly behind those of other major European nations. Red Army strength had fallen to 562,000 men, the cadre-territorial system of manning the military had not produced a proficient fighting force, and everywhere advanced weaponry was in short supply. It was clear to all political and military leaders that a massive and expensive modernization program was necessary to transform the army into a modern force. It was equally clear that to finance such a program and build a new industrial base would require massive extracting of fresh financial and manpower resources from the population at large. This could only be done by unleashing a new social revolution against the landed-peasant class, which would destroy older institutions and free peasant labor for work in the industrial sector. The ensuing programs of collectivization and industrialization accorded with Commissar of War Frunze's recommended militarization of the state, prompted from above and controlled by centralized state planning. In October 1928, as a vehicle for these revolutionary changes, Stalin announced his first Five Year Plan, which was based in part on an earlier military five-year plan and which launched what he termed a "New Socialist Offensive".

Stalin's "New Socialist Offensive" expanded upon his concept of "Socialism in One Country", which he had enunciated several years before to discredit Trotsky's competing concept of "Permanent Revolution".[1] The "New Socialist Offensive" incorporated the dual programs of collectivization and industrialization, which wrought revolutionary change and produced massive human deprivation across the Soviet Union. Forced collectivization of agriculture demolished the rural landowning class (*kulaks*) and drove millions of people from the countryside into cities, labor camps, or death. In so doing it also created a larger proletariat to man the revitalized Soviet industrial base. Stalin's Five Year Plan emphasized the growth of heavy industry, and technological expertise required to build that industry, then absent in the Soviet Union. The expertise was obtained from the West, which provided thousands of technical advisers.

The ensuing industrialization program was a success, although at the expense of huge human cost. Soviet industrial production soared, in particular production of heavy equipment and armaments, some developed domestically, but many adopted from foreign designs. The fruits of this industrial revolution helped fuel a vigorous renaissance in military thought and, more importantly, permitted translation of new military theories into combat practice. Promises made in the form of theories in the late 1920s became realities in the 1930s, as the military benefits of a social and industrial revolution slowly transformed the Soviet Union into a leading military power.

In the early 1920s, while the Soviet Union began to repair the ravages of civil war and consolidate its political power domestically, it also began a thorough program of military reform to construct a military establishment compatible with the new Soviet state. Accordingly:

> In the first half of the 1920s, the political and economic system and the entire way of life of the Soviet people underwent decisive changes. Naturally, in the course of this, major changes occurred in the military area as well. A mass demobilization of the Red Army

took place while the ways and means of military building consistent with the new military and political situation were being developed theoretically and tested through practical experience, and pre-requisites were being created for ensuring the reliable protection of the peaceful toil of the Soviet people.[2]

Soviet analysts have called initial military reforms which followed in 1924–25 "the main and concluding act of the first *perestroika* in the armed forces of the Soviet republic". The inferred analogy to subsequent periods of reform is not simply coincidental. In late 1920, after the end of the Russian Civil War, the Red Army and Navy, which were organized on a regular/cadre basis, numbered 5.5 million men. National exhaustion produced by three years of bitter warfare, massive internal political uncertainty, and a devastated economic system prohibited the Soviets maintaining so large a force. International political and military realities and the concomitant imperative of preserving and strengthening the defense capabilities of the Soviet state required that it possess peacetime forces structured to expand during periods of crisis to meet any foresee-able external threat. In addition, the peacetime armed forces, in conjunc-tion with large internal security forces, had to be large enough to cope with lingering problems of internal security posed by internal political dissension and opposition of various ethnic groups to Soviet rule.[3] First and foremost, however, it was the external international threat juxta-posed against Soviet appreciation of the nature of future war that gave shape to Soviet military strategy.

THE NATURE OF FUTURE WAR AND THE THREAT

The nature of future war and how the state should prepare for and conduct it preoccupied Soviet military theoreticians in the 1920s and has done so ever since. Although every state's military must, to a certain extent, ponder the subject of future war, it was the unique combination of ideology and the warlike circumstances surrounding the Soviet Union's birth that made future war for the Soviets a well-defined discipline and, in fact, almost an obsession.

Future war encompassed not only a military aspect, but also a political context, and being driven by Marxist–Leninist ideology, the political aspect was deeply rooted in Soviet understanding of basic economic and social relationships. Thus, by definition, precise threat analysis required an acute understanding of a continuum of questions related to future war, including:

(1) the social-economic and political systems of existing states;

31

    (2) the nature of contradictions between and within them;
    (3) the capability of these contradictions to produce various types of wars;
    (4) the distribution of political forces (classes, nationalities, nations) and possible direction of development before and during war;
    (5) the political war aims of each separate enemy or contesting group;
    (6) the degree of popular support in war;
    (7) the social consequences of war.[4]

In the last analysis, Lenin believed that the economic, social, and political contradictions inherent in capitalism were the basic cause of war. "Capitalism – it is the reason for modern war."[5] Consequently, Soviet theoreticians defined four types of war, each with its own distinct characteristics:

    (1) wars among imperialist states;
    (2) wars between imperialist states and countries and peoples conducting national liberation revolutions;
    (3) wars between imperialist countries and countries either already socialist or completing socialist revolutions;
    (4) inescapable and revolutionary civil wars of the proletariat against the bourgeoise.

The inherent lawless, exploitative, and counterrevolutionary nature of capitalist states, in Lenin's view, made war theoretically inescapable. The ensuing war would be a violent death struggle between capitalism and socialism "of a class nature", with both history and morality on the side of socialism. Inescapably, warfare would reflect the horror experienced by the participants of the World War.

In the 1920s the Soviet leaders felt that "an attack of imperialist states on the Soviet Union would occur as a military intervention of an imperialist coalition," which could assume a wide variety of forms, including direct attack; financial, economic, and political support of other states for aggression by one state; subversion; intimidation; economic blockade; etc.[6] Stripped of its ideological clothing, this judgment made military sense as well.

Based on these assumptions, by 1928 Soviet threat analysis by the Red Army (RKKA) staff subdivided foreign states into four distinct threat groups:[7]

Group I: States obviously hostile to the Soviet Union

Britain	Rumania	Estonia
France	Finland	Latvia

| Poland | Italy | Lithuania |

Group 2: States which could affiliate with an anti-Soviet front

Germany	Bulgaria	Belgium
Czechoslovakia	Yugoslavia	Japan
Hungary	Greece	United States

Group 3: States not interested in war with Soviet Union for geographical, economic, and political reasons

Sweden	Switzerland	Persia
Norway	Austria	Latin American Countries
Denmark	Albania	

Group 4: States friendly to the Soviet Union

Turkey	Arab Middle East Countries	Indonesia
Afghanistan	African Countries	British India
China (potential)		Mongolia

Depending on political conditions, Soviet theorists believed that three variants existed for an attack on the Soviet Union by an imperialist state or a coalition of states.

Variant 1: Attack by its western neighbors with material-technical support by Britain, France and their allies, with Germany remaining neutral. In this variant the main blow would be struck by Poland and Romania.

Variant 2: Attack by contiguous western states (Poland, Rumania) with partial support (in the form of intervention) by the armed forces of Britain, France, and other major imperialist states.

Variant 3: Attack on the western, southern, and eastern borders of the Soviet state by the armed forces of a powerful imperialist bloc, which could include Finland, Estonia, Latvia, Lithuania, Poland, Rumania, Britain (through Turkish, Persian, and Afghan territory), reactionary Chinese militarists, and Japan.[8]

Further analysis of these threat variants inexorably drew the Soviets to several stark conclusions regarding the threat, which included recognition that:

(1) An attack by imperialist powers, sooner or later, was inescapable.

(2) The main threat emanated from the west.

(3) Secondary threats also existed from other directions.[9]

These conclusions impelled the Soviets to improve rapidly the state's

33

defense capabilities and "to work out, based on existing material means and moral-political capabilities, the most optimal means and forms of armed struggle".[10] The armed forces had to be readied for eventual war, and military theories were required for war with the most probable enemies. The apparent preeminence of the threat in the west required definition of a Western Theater of Military Operations (TVD), calculation of the capacity of strategic and operational directions, and estimation of the proper size of military formations, the width of offensive and defensive sectors, the depth and number of required successive operations, the duration of war, and a host of other operational-strategic and operational-tactical indices.

MILITARY POLICY AND DOCTRINE

The ensuing debate over military reform and reconstruction, which reflected Soviet understanding of the nature of future war, threat perception, and subsurface political struggles of the 1920s, encompassed several internal issues as well. Of paramount concern was the issue of ideology, or specifically, what role should the armed forces play in a socialist state, which was committed to extending world revolution. A corollary of this ideological question related to army composition: Should the army be socially pure (a workers' army) or should it contain "experts", that is, remnants of the former bourgeois class? A third more practical question related to the size and nature of the army. What size was feasible in light of the need for labor to revitalize industry and agriculture, and should the army be a large, well-trained permanent cadre force or a small, less tactically proficient militia force? All of these questions had sharp ideological ramifications.

Debate over these issues began in 1919, and, although basic questions had been resolved by 1922, the debates continued through 1924 with severe political overtones. Even though the main protagonists in the debate were Commissar of War L. D. Trotsky and one of the most preeminent Civil War Commanders, M. V. Frunze, the debate actually reflected deep-seated political struggles, which were occurring during Lenin's later years and which intensified after his death in 1924. Ultimately, these debates were central to the struggle for power over who would inherit Lenin's mantle.

Trotsky advocated a small, permanent, professional army supported by a large militia, incorporating within it the expertise of ex-Tsarist officers and NCOs. He also argued against the existence of a unique Socialist military doctrine. On the other hand, Frunze, in a series of articles written from 1921 to 1924, articulated an opposing view. His article, "The Unified Military Doctrine of the Red Army", advanced the concept of the necessity for a new Marxian (Socialist) doctrine of war, which he defined as:

> that concept accepted in the army of a given state which established the nature of the creation of the armed forces of the country, the method of combat training of the troops and their leadership on the basis of the views held by those ruling the state regarding the nature of the problems facing them and the methods of solving them, such methods arising from the class character of the state and determined by the level of productive forces of the country.[11]

Frunze concluded that:

> the character of the military doctrine of a given state is determined by the political line of the social class that stands at the head of it ... one of the fundamental theoretical tasks of those concerned with military affairs is the study of the peculiar nature of the building of the Red Army and its combat methods.[12]

Frunze's concept of Unified Military Doctrine resolved itself into four general statements. The first two were ideological in character and the latter two had far-reaching implications for the future development and tone of Soviet military doctrine. Theoretically Frunze asserted:

- there is a proletarian method of war, and
- the method of war must reflect the society and the means of production.

Practically he asserted:

- certain fundamentals, notably maneuver, offensive and *aktivnost'* (dynamism or activity) are essential in military operations;
- the Soviet military is a vehicle for spreading the revolution in the interests of the world proletariat.

A second article by Frunze, entitled "The Front and Rear in Future Warfare", demonstrated the necessity of mobilizing the full power of the state in future military conflicts. Frunze predicted that future war would be a "long and cruel conflict", which would draw upon the full economic and political forces of the belligerents. The immense importance of the rear, together with the impossibility of maintaining a large standing army in peacetime, created an:

> urgent, burning and immediate task: to strengthen the general work

of preparing the country for defense ... the adoption, while still at peace, of a firm course in the militarization of the work of all civil apparatus ... There must be established the same kind of definite plan for converting the national economy in time of war as we have worked out for the army.[13]

Frunze's general view prevailed, and Trotsky, undermined by the political machinations of Stalin and the death of Lenin, began to fade from the political scene. The concept of a Unified Military Doctrine has since remained a cardinal tenet of Soviet military doctrine, as have Frunze's concepts of the offensive and maneuver. In addition, the regular/cadre system, Frunze's officer training system, and his principles of one-man command (*edinonachal'stvo*) persist today. Above all, Frunze provided an ideological justification for the subsequent position of the armed forces in Soviet society.

The details and spirit of Frunze's Unified Military Doctrine endured into the 1930s and actually provided the theoretical justification for Stalin's attempts to mobilize the resources of the nation through collectivization and industrialization and to harness those resources for military development.

MILITARY STRATEGY

Evolving Soviet military strategic concepts of the 1920s closely reflected Soviet assessments of the nature of future war, their appreciation of potential threats, and the newly articulated Soviet doctrinal stance. Thus:

> The basic questions occupying the center of attention of Soviet military strategy were: working out the overall and concrete demands and recommendations for preparing the country and armed forces to repel imperialistic aggression, arising from views on the nature of future war, and the contents and nature of the initial period of war; analysis of the laws of armed struggle and the means and form of strategic-scale armed actions; determining the means of creating and employing all types of strategic reserves; and selection of optimal forms (systems) of strategic command and control and others.[14]

This methodology for tailoring strategy to political and military realities has remained fully operative ever since.

The focal point of Soviet study of the nature of future war and the centerpiece of their subsequently articulated military strategy was their understanding of the nature and content of what they termed the initial period of war. This the Soviets carefully defined as "the interval of time from the beginning of combat action to the entry into war of the contending sides' main forces".[15] Quite clearly, a state's military performance during the initial period of war would have substantial impact on the overall course and outcome of war.

The complex and critical problem of the initial period of war contained a series of lesser issues which required resolution, including:

(1) establishment of the essence and contents of the initial period;
(2) determination of the possible mechanisms for aggressors to unleash future war against the Soviet Union, and the contents and nature of enemy military actions at the beginning of war;
(3) selection of corresponding forms of initial strategic deployment and engineer preparation of theaters of military operations (TVDs);
(4) determination of the content and nature of first (initial) operations to repel aggression;
(5) resolution of questions of the functions of the rear from the commencement of military actions, including mobilization and deployment of the armed forces;
(6) calculation of the possible duration of the initial period.[16]

In essence, the initial period of war took the form of a struggle to seize the initiative, a fact which established the subject as the focal point for all aspects of subsequent Soviet strategic planning.

Soviet theorists judged that four immutable variants defined how enemies could initiate war:

Variant 1: Enemy states commence timely mobilization and concentration of forces before the beginning of war and finish relatively simultaneously, with neither side achieving any advantage. In this variant no state achieves surprise.

Variant 2: Each of the participants in war, while striving to forestall its enemy, begins timely mobilization and concentration of his main forces before the beginning of war and finishes it during initial military operations. In this circumstance one side achieves small advantage by attaining tactical surprise.

Variant 3: One of the enemy states begins the war by partially preempting the other from deploying its main forces. As a consequence, it is able to seize the operational-tactical initiative and begin operations with main force formations at a time when the second (state) continues mobilization and concentration of its main forces, while employing defensive actions

37

by limited forces of its covering army (covering forces). Thus, one side is able to achieve operational surprise.

Variant 4: One of the enemies carries out an attack with its fully deployed armed forces at a time when the other state, fearful of "provoking" war by beginning its mobilization and concentration of forces, still has not completed deployment of its main forces and is forced to do so during the course of unfolding war. As a result, the former state is able to secure strategic surprise and, consequently, the strategic initiative.[17]

During the 1920s Soviet military theorists assumed that mobilization and deployment patterns prevalent in 1914 would persist in the future. Thus, the most likely variants for the initiation of war appeared to be variants 1 and 2, where total or substantive preliminary mobilization on both sides would have to occur before war commenced. During the 1920s and during the following decade, the same theorists believed that there were distinct military requirements which had to be satisfied in order to attain or, conversely, deny the enemy the ability to attain the strategic initiative. These included:

(1) creation of a strong peacetime army, which would serve as a nucleus for main wartime forces;

(2) extensive advanced preparation of an infrastructure, especially a rail and road system, which would permit the timely deployment of main forces;

(3) detailed working out of mobilization, concentration, and operational-strategic deployment plans;

(4) creation of correspondingly extensive command and control organs for these processes;

(5) formation and concentration in the border regions of special motor-mechanized and aviation formations, designated from the start of military actions to disrupt the mobilization and deployment of enemy main forces;

(6) engineer preparation of the TVD;

(7) preparation of an air defense system for all of the state's territory;

(8) organization of cover along the state borders for the uninterrupted conduct of mobilization, concentration, and deployment of forces;

(9) procedures for advanced, secret conduct of partial mobilization and concentration of forces.[18]

Soviet leaders worked assiduously to fulfill these requirements.

Having worked out the general nature, circumstances, and requirements of future war, Soviet theorists turned to the question of strategic and operational military arenas – the spatial dimension of armed struggle. They retained the twin nineteenth-century concepts of theaters of war (*teatr voiny*) (TV) and theaters of military operations (*teatr voennykh deistvii*) (TVD). The former encompassed the entire region consumed by warfare, and the latter the territory where one or two armies conducted operations, each with its own objectives. Several theaters of military operations formed a theater of war. Within each theater of military operations, the Soviets designated operational zones (directions), where major portions of an army operated independently.

By 1928 most Soviet military theorists, and in particular V. K. Triandafillov, recognized the pre-eminence of the Western Theater of War, which they subdivided into six distinct theaters of military operations, as follows:

Theaters of Military Operations (TVDs): 1928

Name	Width (km)	Threat Dimensions (divisions)
1st Finnish	1500	–
2nd Finnish		–
Baltic	380	8–10
1st Polish	800	43
2nd Polish		20
Rumanian	320	35[19]

The Polish and Rumanian TVDs were considered the main strategic directions (axes).[20] Therefore, the Soviets planned to create initially at least one *front*-size formation to operate on each. Depending on political-military conditions, during wartime the Soviets planned to deal consecutively with the two Finnish, the Baltic, the two Polish, and the Rumanian groups. While each successive phase of offensive operations was being conducted within a single TVD, the Soviets would defend in the others (in the fashion of the Civil War period).

The premier force designated to operate strategically and to achieve strategic aims was the *front*, which was expected to conduct strategic or main operations. This meant that a *front* engaged all of an enemy's forces – in essence, the enemy's strategic grouping (*strategicheskaia gruppirovka*), either in a two-state war (Polish–Soviet) or within the context of a larger coalition war. The quintessential *front* objective was to "defeat the entire (enemy) state and drive it from the war".[21] The *front* itself functioned according to command and control capabilities prevalent in the 1920s. Until 1930 the Soviets considered the *front* "as a strategic

39

organization, accomplishing overall planning of army operations along a given strategic direction and managing the allocation of forces between armies".[22] Because the *front* lacked the full materiel means to influence the course of operations throughout its entire duration, rather than conducting a cohesive, distinct single *front* operation, each *front* conducted a combination of army operations designed *in toto* to achieve overall strategic goals. The *front* operation, as a single organic concept in its own right, would not become possible, and, hence, a major subject of study, until 1940.[23]

While Frunze and his successors worked out their reforms, concrete aspects of Soviet military art developed out of assessments of Civil War experiences and the growing necessity to harness technological changes to the development of new offensive concepts. Soviet military theoretical debates of the 1920s were marked by their freshness, candor and diversity, a fact often lost on posterity because of subsequent political developments, particularly the emergence of the Stalin dictatorship. This diversity particularly characterized the strategic debate, at the center of which was the issue of the role and essence of military strategy in contemporary and future war. Further, the debate focused on the relative role of offense and defense in the light of the experiences of the First World War and the Civil War. A number of key theoretical works gave definition to the ensuing discussion.

In 1923 B. M. Shaposhnikov, then First Deputy Chief of Staff of the Red Army, wrote a study entitled *Outline of Modern Strategy* (Abris sovrimennoi strategii) in which he critiqued the well-known military lectures of A. M. Zaionchkovsky, ex-Tsarist officer and Professor at the RKKA Military Academy. Zaionchkovsky's lectures tended to stress strategy over state policy and argued that "an offensive strategy is a natural type of military art as it corresponds to the nature of war".[24] Shaposhnikov, in his *Abris*, emphasized the essential relationship between military policy and strategy and stressed the primacy of the former, in particular when preparing for war. He distinguished between "the strategy of the state" and "the strategy of the command" during preparation for war and underscored the supremacy of the former. Hence, war planning had to be comprehensive and the work of both political and military authorities. He wrote, "The essence of the war plan consists precisely of drawing up the views on the conduct of war, as a whole, and a portion of which composes the indispensable work of the High Command."[25]

Shaposhnikov rejected Zaionchkovsky's faith in the offense, pointing out "policy should unconditionally influence the nature of a war, making it either offensive or defensive". He pointed out both the positive and negative aspects of the offensive and rejected "absolutizing" the offensive, stating, "In a war, the offensive and defensive are intertwined, and it is impossible to recommend only an offensive and may even be harmful."[26] Agreeing with A. A. Svechin, another former Tsarist officer and leading strategic theorist at the RKKA Military Academy, that "a defensive is a very strong form of waging war", B. M. Shaposhnikov advised Zaonchkovsky "to gain a good feeling for this and, with the light touch of a Suvorov, not to label in our days the defensive as 'false' and eradicate the spirit of the defensive from the Red Army".[27]

Subsequently, Shaposhnikov critiqued a report by Svechin to the Commissariat of Defense entitled, *Future War* (Budushchaia voina). The ensuing debate, which focused on such questions as the nature of future war, coalition warfare, and tasks involved in the initial period of war, provided a virtual catalogue of fundamental strategic issues debated in the 1920s.

Svechin warned against underestimating the value of the strategic defense, particularly in a coalition war. He wrote, "The disdain for the defensive noted in the Red Army is based upon a miscomprehension of the dialectical link between them: the one [state] which is unable to defend itself will also be unable to advance."[28] While Shaposhnikov agreed in general, he warned that "revolutionary armies in the course of history have always advanced better than defending themselves". Therefore, "It is essential to consider the essence of the Red Army and not deprive it of its spirit."[29]

In his major 1926 work *Strategy* (Strategiia), Svechin argued for the utility of a strategy of "attrition":

> Studying the totality of political, economic, and military-technical capabilities of the sides, A. A. Svechin concluded that today, when powerful states and their coalitions clash, wars inevitably take on a protracted nature in which the forms of struggle, above all armed struggle, can be quite diverse. The term "strategy of attrition," he wrote, "in no way reflects fundamentally the destruction of enemy personnel as the goal of the operation, but sees this as only part of the tasks of the armed front, but not the entire task; we have to think not only about the projecting of efforts, but also their dosage". Equally decisive military and political goals can be pursued with a "strategy of attrition" as with a "strategy of destruction".[30]

This accorded with Svechin's view that future war would be protracted in nature and would require step-by-step mobilization of tremendous national resources. In such warfare one could not count on rapid success and the implementation of a strategy of destruction, for which many Soviet theorists actively argued. Those who argued for a strategy of destruction believed it possible for the Soviet Union to win a war over its main capitalist adversaries by conducting a series of brilliant offensive operations in a short period. Svechin rejected this contention. Shaposhnikov also took issue with Svechin on this matter, accusing him of adhering to "a strategy of attrition, a strategy with limited goals and a strategy of major paths to the goals".[31]

Shaposhnikov and Svechin also disagreed regarding the nature of coalition war and the degree of offensiveness required to achieve victory. While they agreed that only the offensive would ultimately produce victory, Svechin clearly saw a role for defensive operations, writing, "The task of Red strategy in the initial period of a war consists in picking out the weakest point in the system of the configuration of enemy fronts, to achieve a dependable and major success and quickly regain the freedom of maneuver of the main forces."[32] This required initial defensive measures against the enemy main force, and, after they had been bled white, the conduct of a counteroffensive which would produce victory. Shaposhnikov, on the other hand, argued that "a war must begin with the defeat of the strongest and most dangerous enemy, and it must not be diverted by successes over a weak one leaving the stronger to hang over one's neck".[33] Shaposhnikov did, however, recognize that political issues warranted attention, stating:

> It must not be forgotten that for the resolution of a war, it is important to have not only military successes, but also obtain a political success, that is, win a victory over a politically important enemy ... Otherwise, only after an extended period accompanied even by military successes, will we be forced to return to the same fight against the main enemy against which we initially were only on the defensive.[34]

On these and other issues, Svechin and Shaposhnikov set the tone of the vigorous 1920s strategic debates, in which a multitude of other theorists participated. Contemporary Soviet strategists underscore the constructive work of the 1920s:

> In summing up what has been stated, let us emphasize that the 1920s until the mid-1930s were flourishing in the elaboration of the Soviet theory of military strategy. The objective needs of elaborating a military theory on a new methodological Marxist-Leninist basis, the necessity of analyzing the very rich combat experience of World War I and the Civil War, and the demands of ensuring the defense

capability of the world's first worker and peasant state – all of this was an impetus for the awakening of military thought. The catalyst of creative activity was also the atmosphere of debate and a critical approach to any, even the most authoritative opinions. The accomplishments of the theory of strategy of those times were a vivid reflection of the progressive nature of Soviet military science and its very rich potential.

All the finest that was elaborated by Soviet military thought in those years was employed with honor by Soviet military science as the starting point in terms of those new conditions which arose during the difficult years of the Great Patriotic War. Undoubtedly a large portion of the Soviet military leaders who headed the Armed Forces during the years of fiery testing was raised in the finest traditions of the military theoretical school of the 1920s and the mid-1930s. As the very rich experience of the operations and engagements indicates, during the war years there was a succession of advanced strategic views of that period.[35]

The same observers, however, underscore the sad implications when those constructive debates abruptly ended in the mid-1930s.

The conscious underestimation of the objective trends in military affairs, the violent instilling of strategic views and the elimination of broad strata of military theorists and practical workers from the elaboration of a theory of strategy – all of this naturally became established in the growing system at the end of the 1930s of command-administrative leadership over military science and could not but help cause the most negative consequences in the first encounter with combat reality. "The orientation of military theoretical thought on which our command was educated over the years, out of inertia, continued to influence the military mind, although it had long been in contradiction with the real facts of strategic reality ..." concluded G. Isserson. "For this reason, the situation in which the Great Patriotic War commenced in June 1941 was unexpected for the entire subjective strategic and military theoretical orientation of our higher command and this gave rise to definite confusion and an inability to understand events and to subordinate them to one's will and to seize the initiative."[36]

As an outgrowth of these debates and the political conditions in which they occurred, Soviet military strategists concluded, on the basis of experiences of the First World War and the Civil War, that future war would begin with extensive maneuver operations, it would occur over vast regions, and it would consume huge economic and human resources. S. S. Kamenev, Red Army commander from 1919 to 1924, wrote:

> In spite of all victorious fights before the battle, the fate of the campaign will be decided in the very last battle – interim defeats will be individual episodes ... In the warfare of modern large armies, defeat of the enemy results from the sum of continuous and planned victories on all fronts, successfully completed one after another and interconnected in time.[37]

Kamenev rejected the possibility of employing a grand strategic stroke like the Schlieffen Plan to win quick victory in war. Instead, he argued, "the uninterrupted conduct of operations is the main condition for victory". Tukhachevsky, drawing upon his experiences along the Vistula in 1920, concluded that "the impossibility, on a modern wide front, of destroying the enemy army by one blow forces the achievement of that end by a series of successive operations".[38] V. K. Triandafillov, in his 1929 work, *The Character of Operations of Modern Armies*, echoed and further developed Tukhachevsky's view of future war and concluded that only successive operations over a month to a depth of 150–200 kilometers could produce strategic victory. Triandafillov introduced the idea of using tanks supported by air forces to effect penetration of the tactical enemy defense and extend the offensive into the operational depth to achieve strategic aims.[39]

By 1929 the theory (but not yet the practice) of successive operations was fully developed. The *front*, with its component armies, as a strategic entity, accomplished missions assigned by the High Command. It united all forces in a theater of military operations and attacked with its armies along several operational directions (axes) to achieve overall strategic aims. The theoretical width of a *front*'s offensive sector was 300–400 kilometers, and its supposed depth of operations was 200 kilometers.[40] This view of strategic operations persisted into the 1930s and forced Soviet military theorists to seek an answer to the question of how to implement Triandafillov's views regarding mobile operations and escape the specter of attrition warfare. The evolution of a new level of war seemed to provide the tentative theoretical answer – the level of operational art.

Soviet rejection of the strategic concept of a single battle of annihilation and acceptance of the necessity for conducting successive military operations to destroy an enemy force focused the attention of military theorists on the realm between the traditional concepts of strategy and tactics – the realm that would become operational art. Slowly, new terminology and concepts evolved defining the limits of the operational

44

level of war. A May 1924 work entitled *Higher Commands–Official Guidance for Commanders and Field Commands of the Army and Fleet*, written in part by Frunze, focused on the subject of operations, stating:

> the aim of each operation and battle is the destruction of enemy forces and equipment by combat. The aim can be achieved only by skillful and decisive action, based on simple but artful maneuver, conducted violently and persistently.[41]

The subsequent work of Kamenev, Tukhachevsky and Triandafillov provided more detailed explanations of Frunze's general comments regarding the emerging operational level of war.

Svechin, in his 1926 work *Strategy*, articulated a new framework for all levels of war to meet the obvious needs of the time. Svechin described strategy as "the art of combining preparations for war and the grouping of operations to achieve aims put forth in war for the armed forces ... Strategy decides questions concerning both the use of the armed forces and all resources of the state for the achievement of final military aims". Based on this definition, Svechin considered the concept of successive operations and formulated a definition for operational art, which has since endured. Demonstrating the inter-relationship of all three levels of military art, Svechin wrote "tactics makes the steps from which operational leaps are assembled; strategy points out the path".[42]

The 1920s tendency to conceive of successive operations as the focal point for study of the operational level of war resulted from the technological backwardness within the Soviet state in general, and the poorly equipped state of the Red Army in particular. Industrial underdevelopment and the lack of a mature armaments industry dictated that the Soviets rely on infantry, artillery, and horse cavalry to conduct military operations. An optimistic view of successive operations postulated that a *front* could attack in a 300–400-kilometer sector to a depth of 200 kilometers, while an army, the basic operational large unit, designated to operate as part of a *front* or along a separate operational direction, could attack in a sector 50–80 kilometers wide to a depth of 25–30 kilometers. An army could also conduct a series of consecutive operations as part of a *front* offensive. Each operation would last 5–6 days, and would entail an advance of only 5–6 kilometers a day. By 1929 the Soviets were planning to increase that rate of advance to 25–30 kilometers a day by following Triandafillov's recommendation to introduce tanks and mechanized vehicles into the force structure.[43]

The 1929 *Field Regulation* (Ustav) developed the embryonic theory of successive offensive operations a step further by injecting into it the concept of future mechanization and motorization.[44] The *Ustav* enunciated the aim of conducting deep battle (*glubokii boi*) to achieve success in penetrating the tactical depth of enemy defenses by the simultaneous use of infantry support tanks and long-range action tanks cooperating with infantry, artillery, and aviation. In time, the theory of deep battle would develop into the broader concept of deep operations, which, in the 1930s, would become the hallmark and fundamental basis of Soviet military strategic concepts.

WAR PLANNING

Soviet war planning during the 1920s reflected contradictions between economic and political realities as well as Soviet theorists' strategic concerns. Philosophically, most of these theorists were imbued with an offensive spirit, and most military writings echoed that tendency. At the same time, some theorists like A. A. Svechin swam counter to the tide and incorporated defensive considerations in their theoretical writings.[45]

Of necessity, Soviet war planning took a realistic view of their offensive and defensive capabilities. Virtually all theorists and war planners identified the principal threat to the Soviet Union as a combination of eastern European successor states, possibly backed up by western European powers. The Soviets considered Poland and Rumania the principal threats, although prudence dictated that the Baltic states (Estonia, Latvia and Lithuania) and Finland should also be considered as potentially hostile. Triandafillov's 1929 study, *The Character of Operations of Modern Armies*, thoroughly assessed the combat potential of those nations, as did a host of other theorists.[46] Soviet war planning reflected the apparent realities of the military balance in eastern Europe. When those plans are juxtaposed against Triandafillov's analysis of the threat, one must conclude that Soviet strategic posture in the 1920s was indeed clearly defensive.

Several versions of Soviet war plans have recently surfaced, which emanated from formerly classified intelligence assessments of various nations during the late 1920s. All accord closely with published Soviet material on the period and Soviet strategic rationales dominant at that time. The most comprehensive version was an assessment made by the Latvian General Staff in 1927.[47] It postulated war between the Soviet Union, on the one hand, and Finland, Estonia, Latvia, Poland and Rumania on the other. While the assessment judged Poland and Rumania to be the most likely principal Soviet opponents and assumed the Baltic states would declare neutrality, the Latvians believed that the Soviets would disregard Baltic neutrality and automatically wage war against the Baltic states as well.

The Latvians noted that Soviet war plans were drafted by "ex-Imperial Army Staff officers", since "Red commanders, whose commissioned service dates from the Revolution and, subsequently, included the various crops of graduates of the General Staff School, have little to do with mobilization plans as a whole".[48]

This war plan presumed initial operations by two Soviet *fronts* against Poland and Rumania accompanied by defensive operations by a Soviet army along the long northern flank (see Figure 4). The Soviet Western Front, consisting of two armies (2nd and 3rd) and an operational group, deployed from Velikie Luki in the north to the Pripiat Marshes in the south, was to advance on the Dunaburg–Vilno–Warsaw railroad axis to capture Warsaw. The Southwestern Front, made up of three armies (4th, 5th, 6th), deployed from the Pripiat Marshes in the north to the Black Sea, would launch its main strategic attack with two armies toward Lemberg (L'vov) and Krakow, with an option of continuing an advance on Warsaw in conjunction with the Western Front's 3rd Army. First Independent Army in the north would remain on the defensive, guarding the Baltic frontier until major operations in the south had been completed. A reserve army of 15 divisions from the Moscow and the Volga Military Districts would function as GHQ strategic reserve. This war plan accorded with the threat portrayed in Triandafillov's work and closely corresponded to classified Soviet order of battle data maintained by the U.S. War Department General Staff in Washington.[49]

A second version of Soviet war planning came to the U.S. Army attaché in Riga from an "excellent source". Although the attaché questioned the veracity of the report because of its intricate details regarding mobilization, subsequent information on Soviet mobilization tends to verify the report's veracity.[50]

The war plan envisioned war only between the Soviet Union, Poland, and Rumania. The Soviet plan called for a Soviet attack on Rumania to seize Bessarabia, while Soviet forces facing Poland temporarily adopted a defensive stance. This plan accorded well with Soviet *ex post facto* statements that they intended dealing with their opponents consecutively. The plan involved Soviet employment of two cavalry groups as covering forces and two armies (1st, 2nd) and a separate army corps to conduct major operations against Rumania (see Figure 5). When the war began, the two cavalry groups (1st and 8th Cavalry Corps) were to conduct deep reconnaissance from the Iampol and Dubossary regions into Rumania before the main force advance.

Soviet main forces, consisting of 2nd Army, deployed north of Iampol and 1st Army, arrayed in the Tiraspol region, would subsequently advance into Bessarabia to secure Bratuglani, Kishinev, and Iassy. The

47

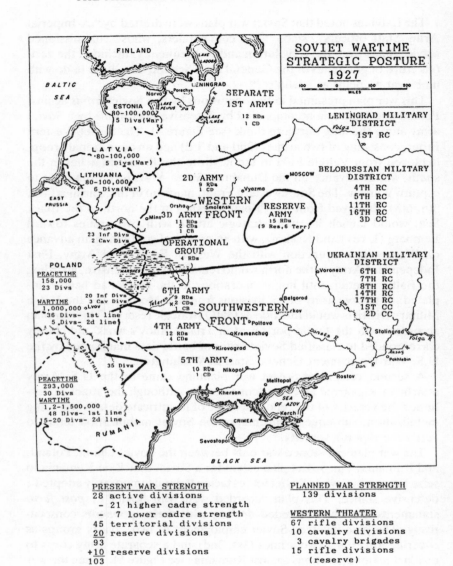

SOVIET WARTIME STRATEGIC POSTURE 1927

PRESENT WAR STRENGTH
28 active divisions
– 21 higher cadre strength
– 7 lower cadre strength
45 territorial divisions
20 reserve divisions
93
+10 reserve divisions
103

PLANNED WAR STRENGTH
139 divisions

WESTERN THEATER
67 rifle divisions
10 cavalry divisions
3 cavalry brigades
15 rifle divisions
(reserve)

4. Soviet wartime strategic posture: 1927

6th Separate Army Corps was to defend along lst Army's left flank to the Black Sea.

Both war plan variants accurately reflected Soviet strategic concerns, and the emergence of rudimentary *front* structures corresponded with 1920's realities. In effect, the plans involved operations by a combination of armies, whose actions were loosely coordinated by *front* headquarters.

FORCE GENERATION

To convert these strategic concepts and war plans from theory to reality, the Soviets required a scheme to transform the smaller peacetime Soviet force into one whose strength and posture were suited to conduct successful wartime operations against any prospective foes. This was a daunting task in light of the rapid demobilization, which drastically decreased the size of the Red Army after 1921. Over a period of four years, the Red Army shrank from a strength of 5.5 million to only 560,000, in a process which the Third Congress of Soviets of the USSR in May 1925 described as "irrefutable proof of such a peaceful policy".[51] Subsequent Soviet analysts have described the country's resulting military dilemma:

> With that strength the Red Army could ensure, although with a great deal of stress, the country's security under peacetime conditions. However, it was no longer in a condition to train the necessary number of strategic reserves, for of the existing cadre units (even with a minimal – 2 year – service) only 30 per cent of the contingent of the draftees could undergo army training. Ways of military training had to be found which would make it possible to provide military knowledge and skills to young inductees, without any major material outlays. As a whole, this difficult task was achieved in the course of the military reform.[52]

The ensuing military reform of 1924–25 focused on creating an army based on an active regular/cadre component, but with a mobilization capability founded on "territorial/militia" forces, which in peacetime trained conscripts and reservists and in wartime mobilized to expand the force several fold. While reducing the levels of peacetime military manpower sufficient to avoid straining the national economy, this system provided adequate reserves to fuel a mobilization system capable of producing a large enough wartime army to satisfy Soviet strategic needs. Succinctly stated:

> In accordance with the 1924–25 plan, the system for the organiza-

5. Soviet war plan against Rumania: 1927

tion of the country's defense, and all constituent elements, were subjected to a profound reorganization affecting the method of staffing the armed forces, the organizational-personnel structure of the troops, the procedure for fulfilling military service duties, the content and methods for combat and political training, the structure and principles governing the work of the management and procurement authorities, the organization of party-political work, and the ways and means of training command and political cadres. The main feature in this set of measures was the energetic completion of a conversion to a mixed system for the composition of the armed forces; by the end of 1925 46 out of 77 infantry divisions had already been converted into territorial-militia units. Infantry divisions deployed in the border military districts and most cavalry units and the naval and air forces and technical troops were kept as cadre forces.

The territorial formations were deployed in internal military districts, primarily in economically developed areas with adequate population density. As a rule, the boundaries of the districts where the divisions, regiments and battalions were staffed and deployed matched the lines of *guberniyas* (provinces), *uyezds* (districts), *rayons* (regions) and *volosts* (small rural districts). This made possible the close *rapprochement* and the merger of the armed forces with the masses of toiling people and the Soviets.[53]

Side by side with these formations, in both cadre and territorial formations, the Soviets experimented with the creation of a limited number of nationality-based military formations, predicated on the presumed reliability of those nationalities. This was, and to this day remains, a thorny question. While Soviet sources cite political and socioeconomic conditions as a prerequisite for permitting nationalities their own military formations, Western intelligence highlighted reliability problems by pointing out that, during Tsarist times, "Certain areas and peoples were entirely or partially exempt from conscription; for example, in the Caucasus, only the Cossacks were called to service, the Armenians, Georgians, and such, being exempt; the tribes of Turkestan and the Kirghiz were exempt; as were the Lapps in the tundra region of the north; conscription of manpower in Finland was started partially only late in the war."[54]

To provide manpower for all of these types of formations and to create a requisite manpower pool, in the autumn of 1925 the Soviet government passed a Law on Universal Military Service, which made all male citizens from the ages of 19 to 40 subject to military service. Each would undergo two years of pre-draft military training organized by local military commissariats, followed by five years of regular service. Thereafter, all personnel passed into the reserve.

The new Red Army then consisted of two basic elements: regular/cadre and territorial/militia (including national formations) manned as follows:

> All cadre formations and units were staffed on the basis of the extraterritorial principle; privates in the Red Army and Navy served in them, respectively, 2, 3, or 4 years (depending on the branch), after which for the balance of the active service they were granted long-term furlough and subsequently moved into the reserve. Administrative authorities, technical subunits, and supply agencies for the territorial troops drew their staffs from the cadres of army commanders, political workers and technical specialists. The bulk (as much as 90 per cent) of the renewable personnel of the territorial formations were military draftees living in that area. They were given combat and political training in their subunits and units for a period of 3 months during the first year of service and 1–2 months over the next 4 years; throughout that time, in between training periods, they lived at home and worked at their civilian jobs.[55]

Cadre forces in 1928 consisted of 28 rifle and 11 cavalry divisions, formed on a Union-wide basis. These divisions represented the core of the regular Red Army and, in turn, provided a nucleus for about 20 wartime rifle corps. Cadre forces were organized on the basis of two levels of peacetime fill. The first line cadre divisions numbered 6,300 permanent and 12,300 mobilization augmentees. The second line cadre divisions maintained a nucleus of 604 men, augmented by 11,750 during mobilization.[56]

Approximately 45 territorial divisions were stationed and manned on a regional basis, and, in wartime, they filled out rifle corps. The Soviets maintained territorial divisions at three manning levels. The first line territorial divisions numbered 2,400 cadre and 10,681 wartime augmentees. The second line divisions numbered from 604 to 622 permanent cadre and 11,734 to 11,750 augmentees. These divisions formed from cadre personnel of either cadre divisions or first line territorial divisions. A third type of territorial division, termed embryonic (*iacheiki*), consisted of 190 permanent cadre.[57] Upon mobilization, if sufficient reserves were present, this type of division would form from a first line territorial division. Thus, upon mobilization, the major portion of a first line territorial division could form two divisions (one first line and one second line) and, in some cases, a third (one third line).[58] Although this system also applied to cavalry forces, concern for the readiness of this important maneuver component of the armed forces prompted the Soviets to retain most cavalry divisions on cadre status. During mobilization all forces were to be filled out in time-phased fashion to form rifle corps (of mixed cadre and territorial composition) and, finally, rifle and shock armies.

As a concession to certain national groups within the Soviet Union, the Soviets also formed a small number of divisions and regiments consisting of specific nationalities. In October 1925 this amounted to one rifle division and three separate rifle regiments.

Between 1924 and 1935 these reforms produced the following composition for the Red Army:

Force Composition (in divisions)

	1924	1925	1928	1929	1930	1932	1933	1934	1935
Regular Cadre									
rifle	34	31	30	29	29	29	26	26	26
cavalry	8	10	11	12	10	12	9	9	16
Territorial militia									
rifle	15	46	39	37	41	42	47	47	58
cavalry	1	8*	8*	9*	3	4	5	5	–
Nationality	3								

1921 – experimentation with territorial brigade in Petrograd
1923 – 10 territorial militia divisions formed

*brigades[59]

In theory, this complex force manning and mobilization system provided for a smooth transition from peacetime to wartime footing. The mechanism offered a means for at least doubling, and possibly tripling, the size of the Red Army. Of course, training and equipping the force remained a serious problem, and the wartime efficiency of regular/cadre and territorial/militia forces remained suspect in the USSR and in Western assessments alike.

CONCLUSIONS

During the 1920s Soviet military strategy evolved in consonance with a variety of unique internal and external conditions. Internally, the Soviet Union faced severe political, economic, and social problems, including:

(1) political instability associated with a struggle for power and a debate over democracy, albeit within the party;

(2) economic crisis associated with Civil War dislocation of the economy and the adoption and subsequent rejection of the economic reforms of the New Economic Policy (NEP);

(3) Ethnic unrest, associated in the 1920s with Civil War and incorporation into the Soviet Union of nationalities, which, for a time during the Civil War, had regained their independence;

(4) military discontent associated with tension between "Red" officers and Tsarist "experts" and enlisted alienation connected with the collectivization and industrialization program of the late 1920s.

Externally, the Soviet Union confronted uncertainty concerning the emerging threat it faced, the need to plan for several variants, the uncertain impact of technology on military affairs, the apparent need to incorporate projected changes, and, of course, relationships with Germany in the midst of change.

Compounding these difficulties, the Soviet Union faced a Europe and world experiencing the drastic changes after the First World War and burdened with the Treaty of Versailles, which exacerbated international relations. Specifically, old alliances and blocs, which had kept a tense peace for over 40 years, crumbled by virtue of the World War with no apparent replacements; a truncated Germany emerged which lacked "historic" borders; independent successor states were born in eastern Europe, each of which was subject to internal political instablity, economic weakness, and ethnic tensions of their own; the global military and economic balance sharply shifted; and the world would soon experience a revolution in military weaponry, associated with further development of the airplane and the tank. Each of these realities would help shape Soviet strategy in the more harrowing period after 1935, ultimately with disastrous results.

CHAPTER 4

SOVIET MILITARY STRATEGY IN THE 1930s (1935–1941)

GENERAL

The 1930s was an ominous decade for the Soviet Union, Europe, and the world as a whole, particularly after 1935. Political, economic, and social changes had devastating consequences for a sizeable portion of the world. The most obvious product of the 1930s was a new world war, which, in addition to producing wholesale human carnage and misery, reshaped the global political structure.

Because of a variety of factors, the international concert which had fostered general European political stability in the 1920s mutated and failed in the 1930s. Soon after 1935, the utter collapse of that international concert in its struggle with resurgent totalitarianism led to unprecedented global disaster. In the beginning of the decade, the international concert consisted of the war-weary democratic Western European powers, the victors of the World War, backed up by a democratic, but increasingly detached United States, enforcing the Treaty of Versailles. The heart of the Versailles European structure was a still democratic, largely demobilized, but politically and economically troubled Weimar Germany, flanked on the east by independent but increasingly undemocratic and unstable eastern European successor states and even further east by the Soviet Union. Although the Western powers considered the Bolshevik Soviet Union a political pariah, its military weakness made it a relatively benign element of the European political and military balance.

New trends developing in the 1930s soon deprived the tenuous international system of its stability. An economic depression, which spread across Europe after 1929, exacerbated the debt and reparations problems of the 1920s, shook the foundations of political stability in Great Britain and France, drove the United States into further isolation, threatened German democracy with a virulent revisionist nationalism, further undermined the political viability of Eastern European states, and produced general European political and economic instability. Fascism, nazism, communism, and more traditional forms of totalitarianism fed on the

55

ensuing discontent and overturned the most basic assumption of the Versailles system by producing a revisionist and remilitarized German state. The reemergence of a German threat in turn produced alternating policies on the part of would-be opponents, designed on the one hand to assuage German demands (appeasement) and on the other to find new political combinations, which could contain the new Nazi Germany. Western ambivalence in the light of a disengaged United States endured even after it became clear that only war itself could thwart German aggression.

In the midst of this cauldron of seemingly unpredictable change, the Soviet Union itself underwent transformation from an agrarian, peasant-dominated Soviet state to a would-be industrial super-power armed with a significant mailed fist. It took a particularly virulent and ruthless brand of communist totalitarianism to accomplish this feat, and the international ramifications of these changes were no less significant than those produced by the transformation of Germany. Stalin's "New Socialist Offensive" of 1929 forceably collectivized Soviet agriculture, wiped out the Kulaks, set in motion large-scale industrialization governed by a system of five-year plans, and laid the basis for the revitalization of the Soviet military by exploiting the effects of a new technological revolution in weaponry (motor-mechanization, aviation, etc.).

During the early 1930s the Soviets followed the dual path of tacitly and verbally supporting revolution abroad, while pragmatically and simultaneously pursuing militarily useful secret contacts with Weimar Germany and arguing for general world disarmament. By the mid-1930s, intimidated by the rise of Nazi Germany, the Soviet government encouraged resistance to fascism through support of political "popular fronts", and alliances of all parties in opposition to fascism. By the late 1930s the progress of fascism was so pronounced that the Soviet Union offered to form outright political and military alliances with those threatened by Germany, although internal political oppression within the Soviet Union and the growth of her own military power prompted growing skepticism among those states she courted.

By 1939, after Munich and the Spanish Civil War had shown clearly the extent to which Western states would compromise with Germany, the Soviet Union, more for her own protection than out of conviction, sharply reversed her political course and signed the cynical Molotov–Ribbentrop Pact, which pledged mutual non-aggression between the Soviet Union and Germany and dismembered what was left of the major eastern European successor states. Finally in 1941, after Europe had been aflame for almost two years, the very thing Soviet policy was designed to deter occurred; Hitler invaded the Soviet Union.

It was within this complex and volatile context that Soviet military theorists formulated the state's strategy in the 1930s.

THE NATURE OF FUTURE WAR AND THE THREAT

The evolution of capitalism and European political currents in the 1930s, in the Soviet view, seemed to conform to Lenin's predictions that internal contradictions within capitalism and capitalist hostility to socialism would sharpen. With this evolution came a Soviet perception of an increased threat of war. An April 1936 Resolution of the Communist International commented, "Now war threatens every country, because in today's conditions of tensions of imperialistic contradictions, war, which fascist aggressors are unleashing, cannot be localized, it will develop into world war."[1]

Set amidst the context of these immense political changes, the nature of the threat to the Soviet Union altered significantly. Now the Soviets distinguished between four basic groups of states:

> Group 1: The Soviet Union – a proletarian state, which was the "greatest bulwark of peace";
>
> Group 2: Fascist aggressors (Germany, Italy, Japan);
>
> Group 3: A series of countries, confronted by constant threat of fascist aggression and loss of their governmental and national independence (Belgium, Czechoslovakia, Austria, etc.);
>
> Group 4: Other capitalist states, which, fearing losses as a result of the new re-partition of the world, were interested in securing for themselves peaceful conditions of existence.[2]

The Soviet policy of collective security and support for popular fronts across Europe became a distinct component of Soviet military policy and an adjunct to its military strategy. Throughout this period, as collective security failed, Germany became the Soviets' most obvious opponent in any future war. In addition, as German political successes multiplied, so also did Germany's allies or satellites, further increasing the threat. By September 1939, as a consequence of war and the subsequent German-Soviet partition of eastern Europe, Germany occupied borders contiguous to the Soviet Union. This stark reality compounded the task of

57

Soviet strategic theorists as they sought an adequate defensive strategic posture.

The sharpened contradictions evident in world capitalism and unbridled hostility of fascist states toward the Soviet Union, combined with the increased economic and military potential of prospective enemy states, led the Soviet Union to the inevitable conclusion that future war would be vaster and more intense than any earlier war. Thus:

> The basic position of Soviet military theory in evaluating indicators of the scale of war led to the following (conclusion). It was considered that future war would have the nature of a world war. In a definite stage, it would take the form of an attack on the USSR by a coalition of imperialist countries. From that moment it would be a struggle not for life, but for death, right up to the full destruction of imperialist forces who had unleashed the world war.[3]

This threat, so defined, meant that the Soviet Union had to be prepared for a two-front war; in the west against Germany and her allies, and in the east against Japan. Since the Soviet leadership considered the western threat the most serious, it was here that they concentrated the bulk of their attention. Preparations went far beyond simply the military realm for, "Future war was viewed as an aggregate of various types of struggle: armed, diplomatic, economic, etc. Advanced preparations to conduct each type of struggle were considered an obligatory condition for achieving victory."[4]

Soviet theorists continued to reason that war would be prolonged and could not be won by one or several lightning blows. Frunze's dictum of the 1920s remained valid that, "In a collision of first-class enemies, decision cannot be reached by one blow. War will take on the nature of a long and brutal contest, subjecting to the ordeal all the economic and political foundations of the struggling sides."[5]

Thus, the resources of the entire state had to be mobilized to deal with imperialist aggression, which could materialize in one of two variants:

Variant 1: from a condition described as "a peacetime situation";
Variant 2: from a condition arising as a result of our rendering international military assistance (Soviet supported revolution in capitalist or colonial states).

The Soviets also recognized that war could occur "in a period of forced participation by the Soviet state in a local armed conflict, unleashed by the reactionary forces of neighboring capitalist governments".[6]

In the 1930s Soviet theorists believed that future war would involve

58

million-man armies, equipped with all the fruits of modern science and technology. V. A. Melikov, in his 1939 work, *Strategic Deployment*, vividly described the nature of future war, writing: "The gigantic scale of contemporary war, in which the most powerful armed coalitions with millions of forces and many thousands of military-technical means will take part, can be resolved victoriously only by the artful use of three categories of armed forces; operating on the land, in the air, and on the sea."[7] The Soviets believed that ground forces, equipped with artillery, tanks, and aircraft would play the most decisive role.

As the 1930s progressed, and the General Staff digested, first, their combat experiences in the Spanish Civil War and then their experiences and those of the Germans in the conflict with Poland, Soviet views on the harshness and grave consequences of war matured, and assumed an even more pessimistic tone:

> Soviet military theorists allowed that, in some theaters of operations, unfavorable conditions could arise for Soviet forces, which would require the use of such forms of maneuver as the withdrawal and retreat into the depths of the country. In these cases, it was presumed that partisan detachments would be created on abandoned territory to organize struggle in the enemy rear.[8]

Throughout 1940 and 1941 Soviet military journals ominously began addressing such topics as battle in encirclement, as if contemplating conditions which they themselves would have to contend with in future conflict.[9] Despite these starkly realistic assessments, Soviet commentators today point out serious deficiencies in Soviet assessments of the nature of future war in the 1930s:

> Unfortunately, the absolute assertions that, to defend the socialist fatherland, we will fight "with little blood" and "on someone else's territory" led to a series of negative consequences:
>
> - the appearance of the elements of boasting, bragging, over-assessing one's own forces, and underassessing the enemy;
> - repudiating the very idea of partisan struggle (supposedly, it was not required in the future) and liquidating partisan bases;
> - mistakes in the preparation of the TVD and strategic deployment of forces, and many others.[10]

Contemporary Soviet military theorists credit their 1930s predecessors with "correctly reflecting the objective conditions for conducting war" in their consideration of the nature of future war. They note, however, the serious consequences of certain negative influences, the most serious of which they identify as the tyrannical political influence of Stalin. Of equal seriousness was the fact that, "in theoretical and practical planning, the possible variants for actions of Soviet forces in conditions of a forced withdrawal on all strategic axes and the necessity for creating a dense strategic defensive front were not worked out".[11] In short, the Soviets considered few strategic variants. In a message suitable for all times, Colonel R. A. Savushkin has written, "Experience shows that working out of the important questions of future war must consider many variants."[12]

MILITARY POLICY AND DOCTRINE

Soviet military doctrine in the 1930s remained an arena of dynamic analysis and debate, paradoxically at a time when Stalin was ruthlessly centralizing his political power and conducting bloodless party purges before physically liquidating of all potential competition within party circles. Stalin, for as yet unexplained reasons, allowed the military establishment to preside over the rapid and extensive rearmament program and to develop, in relative freedom, a military art markedly advanced for its time. Only when that military art was nearing maturity and full reflection in the Soviet force structure did Stalin strike at the one remaining potential threat to his achievement of absolute power – the military – in a purge of far-reaching consequences for the Soviet military and the Soviet Union in general.

Soviet military doctrine of the 1930s built upon the assumptions of the 1920s, although it was increasingly affected by the industrial and technological revolution occurring within the Soviet Union and by looming threats from hostile powers abroad. Soviet doctrine maintained that the class character of war would result in implacable and decisive future military combat, and that war would ultimately pit the Soviet Union against a coalition of imperialist nations. Long and bitter war would require the consecutive defeat of the Soviet Union's major enemies, the generation and use of large strategic reserves, resort to many means and forms of armed combat, and the conduct of large-scale maneuverable combat operations. War would require the achievement of decisive aims, including the full destruction of the enemy on his own territory. Quite naturally, the Soviets considered the offensive as the most decisive and fruitful form of strategic operation, although the verbiage associated with their military doctrine remained defensive.

In the light of these new doctrinal tenets, by the mid-1930s the Soviets felt they required a larger and more capable military force to deal with the burgeoning threat. Subsequent movement away from the cadre/territorial system toward a larger and better-equipped army promised to improve the peacetime readiness of the Soviet armed forces and, by extension, its capabilities for meeting wartime contingencies.

MILITARY STRATEGY

Throughout the 1930s Soviet interest in the theme of the initial period of war intensified. Although the Soviets recognized that the same range of variants regarding how war might begin was as valid as in the 1920s, they increasingly believed that the second and third variants were most likely – that is, that enemy mobilization was likely to begin before war broke out in an attempt by the enemy to gain tactical or operational advantage. This was likely because, to an increasing extent, enemy covering armies (deployed in peacetime) were equipped with even larger motor-mechanized and aviation forces. In essence, covering armies could now also function as the lead elements of an "army of invasion". Consequently, the principal mission now was to disrupt enemy mobilization and to destroy his covering army. The degree and success of subsequent mobilization then depended in part on the degree of advantage the invasion army achieved.[13]

Later in the 1930s, the Soviets became more concerned about German writings on the utility of surprise as a tool for securing the strategic initiative in war. Soviet theorists noted that it could be beneficial to begin war when no one foresaw it as a possibility. Consequently, "He who wishes to be victorious must not lose one unnecessary minute." To an increasing extent, "Soviet military theoreticians, while working out the problem of the initial period of war, studied the possibility of a surprise attack on our country by imperialist aggressors."[14]

This shifting Soviet evaluation of the seriousness of the initial period of war and the increased potential for an enemy to achieve surprise prompted sharp changes in Soviet military strategy. Most important, the Soviets decided to improve peacetime force readiness for war through a variety of measures, including the transformation of the territorial/militia system of force generation to a regular/cadre system, implementation of an extensive motor-mechanization program in the force structure, and creation of a program of technical reequipment for the most critical elements of the armed forces.[15]

New Soviet concepts associated with the redefined initial period of war recognized the possibility of an initial period when participants would attempt to forestall the enemy in mobilization and deployment of main forces. During this initial period, more powerful covering armies, deployed in border regions, interspersed with fortified regions and supported by armored and mechanized forces and aviation, would repel the enemy attack and carry the struggle to enemy territory. Simultaneously, main forces would mobilize, concentrate and deploy, and exploit the successful operations of covering armies on enemy territory by beginning their operations in more favorable conditions than was previously the case. The Soviets judged that the initial period of war would now last from 15 to 20 days.[16]

All of these judgements were based on the assumption that both warring states would be able to begin operations with only part of their forces. Meanwhile, main forces would continue their mobilization, concentration, and strategic deployment, protected by covering armies. The covering armies would form the first strategic echelon, and the main forces (mobilized and mobilizing) would constitute both the second strategic echelon and strategic reserves. According to General M. V. Zakharov, who worked on the General Staff in the late 1930s, "The possibility of forestalling enemy concentration and initiation of military operations was not considered possible."[17] The German experience in Poland validated that judgment.

The events in Poland in September 1939 and in Western Europe in May and June 1940 forced the Soviets to reconsider the likelihood of the fourth variant occurring, that is, a surprise attack by a fully mobilized enemy main force, specifically German. More recent Soviet military theorists have criticized themselves and their forebears for not fully working out this variant. Marshal G. K. Zhukov, then Red Army Chief of Staff, noted in his memoirs:

> In revising the operational plans in spring 1941, little attention was given to the new methods of warfare at the initial stage of hostilities.
> The People's Commissar for Defence and the General Staff believed that war between countries as big as Germany and the Soviet Union would follow the old scheme: the main forces engage in battle after several days of frontier fighting. As regards concentration and deployment deadlines, it was assumed that conditions for the two countries were the same. In fact, however, the forces and conditions proved to be far from equal.[18]

Faced with the prospect of potential large-scale German mobilization, the Soviet Union intended to respond with commensurate measures, either during the initial period of war or during the so-called "special threatening military period" (war imminent – *osoboe ugrozhaemyi voennyi period*), which would occur just before the beginning of war.[19] The outbreak of the Second World War in Poland on 1 September 1939 impelled the Soviets to begin conducting what was, in essence, "secret mobilizational deployment of the armed forces", which, between 1939 and June 1941, increased the armed forces' strength from 1.8 million to more than 5 million men. This was accompanied during the last six months before 22 June 1941 by a "secret strategic deployment of forces".[20]

By definition, the "special threatening military period" involved all measures required to repel aggression, including:

- bringing all armed forces to full military preparedness;
- carrying out immediate nation-wide force mobilization;
- building troops up to wartime strength in accordance with the mobilization plan;
- concentrating and deploying all mobilized troops in the western border regions in accordance with the plans of the border military districts and the High Command.[21]

As Zhukov later noted, "During the last few prewar months, the leadership did not provide for carrying out all necessary measures which would have to be taken during the special threatening military period."[22] Savushkin recently added:

> However, the introduction of those measures was too late because of Stalin's fear "of provoking" the enemy into armed attack ... Experience demonstrated that one could not forego combat preparedness of forces for the satisfaction of the desire to escape "provoking" conflict, which, in fact, can speed up the beginning of war. The inactivity of Stalin led to tragedy.[23]

Set against the backdrop of Soviet discussions regarding the nature of the initial period of war, the same theorists reevaluated prospective combat arenas and how forces would deploy within them. To the existing concept of a main Western Theater of War, by the end of the 1930s the Soviets had added four others (Near Eastern, Middle Eastern, Far Eastern, and Baltic-Scandinavian) to accommodate the expanding global scope of future war. Soviet incorporation into the Soviet Union in 1939 and 1940 of Eastern Poland, the Baltic states, Bessarabia, Northern Bukovina, and, finally, Karelia, expanded and improved the size and configuration of the Western and Baltic-Scandinavian theaters of war. The Soviets then subdivided the Western Theater into five theaters of military operations corresponding to the Leningrad, Baltic, Special Western, Special Kiev, and Odessa military districts. When war occurred, each military district was to transform itself into a *front* headquarters.

Since the principal military threat emanated from the west, the heaviest concentration of Soviet forces was in that region. Sufficient forces were left in the Far East and other border regions for defensive purposes. The Soviets organized wartime *fronts* and back-up forces in the west and elsewhere into strategic echelons. The first strategic echelon, encompassing *fronts* in the border military districts, contained two operational echelons made up of covering armies, a third operational echelon of forces designated to launch counteroffensives, and military district reserves. The second strategic echelon, consisting of mobilized or mobilizable main forces and reserves from internal military districts, was designated to cooperate with and reinforce the first strategic echelon.

Within the highest priority Western Theater of War, Soviet plans were designed to "repel the combined blows of aggressors by already prepared defensive force groupings in the border districts and subsequently go over to the counteroffensive. The sequence of destruction of respective members of opposing imperialist coalitions depended on military-political conditions."[24]

Throughout most of the 1930s, prevailing views regarding the role and missions of the *front* persisted. Late in the decade, however, changing Soviet perceptions of the nature of future war began to alter Soviet judgements regarding what missions a *front* could achieve in war. With the decrease in the number of potential opposing states and the increased size of the German Army, the concept of using one *front* against one enemy state was no longer realistic. It would clearly take several *fronts* deployed in several TVDs to deal with the German threat. In 1940 Soviet Defense Minister S.K. Timoshenko conceived the strategic offensive as successive *front* operations, in one or another TVD by means "... of the simultaneous conduct in a theater of war of two and even three offensive operations of various *fronts* with the strategic intention as extensively as possible, to shake the entire defensive capability of the enemy".[25]

The nature of *front* operations also changed because of the introduction into the force structure of aviation, motor-mechanized, and air assault forces, which extended the projected range and accelerated the speed of operations. Consequently, according to Savushkin:

> The *front* offensive operation from the sum of related single type –
> operations of shock and conventional armies – changed into a
> qualitatively new form of armed struggle, in addition including in it
> operations of aviation armies, armies to develop the penetration (or
> motor-mechanized armies), (and) groups of air assault formations
> (or forces of special designation – *osobogo naznacheniia* – ON).[26]

As a result:

> The *front* changed into an operational–strategic organization, in-

cluding in its function both the planning of combat efforts, and the continuous command and control of them in the process of developing operations (establishing coordination between air forces and ground forces, controlling mobile formations, conducting combined operations).[27]

Simultaneously, the importance of army operations diminished. According to Timoshenko, writing in 1940, "Even the shock army with maximum combat composition has been losing its independence in the achievement of large-scale operational objectives and even more so in strategic objectives."[28] In essence, by 1940 both the army and the *front* functioned at the operational level, and most theorists realized that only multiple *fronts* operating in tandem could achieve strategic objectives. As Timoshenko noted, however, despite the fact that January 1941 strategic war games held in Moscow postulated a strategic operation by two *fronts*, "by the beginning of war we had not succeeded in working out a theory for such operations. They were mastered and conducted only in the years of the Great Patriotic War."[29] In fact, even the theoretical basis of a single *front* operation had been only partially worked out in practice by June 1941.

The concept of the strategic operation (especially offensive) blossomed in the 1930s, particularly between 1932 and 1937, but late in the decade the purges curtailed most imaginative military thought. The creative work of the mid-1930s was largely due to technological and industrial developments and the theoretical work of a host of innovative military theorists. The impact of new weaponry, first felt in the tactical realm, by the mid-thirties affected the operational and strategic levels as well. In essence, the promise of the 1929 *Field Regulation* to achieve deep battle was being realized.

The most important aspect of Soviet military art and science in the 1930s was the full development of the concept of deep battle and the emergence of the concept of deep operations. The deep operation, a form of combat action conducted by operational large units:

> consisted of simultaneous attacks on the enemy defense with all means of attack to the entire depth of the defense; a penetration of the tactical defense zone on selected directions and subsequent decisive development of tactical success into operational success by means of introducing into battle an echelon to develop success (tanks, motorized infantry, cavalry) and the landing of air assaults to achieve rapidly the desired aims.[30]

The theory of deep operations represented a qualitative jump in the development of operational art and a total escape from the impasse of the First World War positional warfare. It provided the basis for Soviet military strategy, although the Soviets never fully integrated these operational theories into their strategic concepts.

The theory of deep operations evolved out of the earlier theory of deep battle formulated at the end of the 1920s in theoretical works of Tukhachevsky, Triandafillov, A.I. Egorov and others, who concluded that the appearance of new weapons (long-range artillery, tanks, aircraft) and types of forces (tank, air assault, mechanized) would permit the creation of more maneuverable forms of combat and ease the problem of penetrating tactical defenses. Early experimentation with deep battle techniques occurred in the Volga, Kiev, and Belorussian Military Districts, and, as a result, in February 1933 the Red Army gave official sanction to deep battle in its *Provisional Instructions on the Organization of Deep Battle*.[31] New and more explicit instructions appeared in March 1935, and the *Field Regulation* (*Ustav*) of 1936 made deep battle, as well as the larger scope deep operations, an established tenet of Soviet military art. While deep battle focused on the tactical defense and combat by units within an army, deep operations focused on operational level combat involving *fronts* and armies alike.

The theoretical basis of deep operations, field tested in military exercises in the mid-1930s, was established by 1936 and described in the *Regulation* of that year as:

> simultaneous assault on enemy defenses by aviation and artillery to the depths of the defense, penetration of the tactical zone of the defense by attacking units with widespread use of tank forces, and violent development of tactical success into operational success with the aim of the complete encirclement and destruction of the enemy. The main role is performed by the infantry and the mutual support of all types of forces are organized in its interests.[32]

The heart of deep operations involved the use of an operational formation consisting of: an attack echelon; an echelon to develop success; reserves; aviation forces; and air assault forces, all designated to achieve tactical and operational success. Deep operations could be conducted by a single *front* or (according to views of the late 1930s) by several *fronts* supported by large aviation forces. By this time the Soviets considered a *front* to be an operational-strategic large unit (earlier it had been considered only a strategic large unit).

Fronts conducted the largest-scale deep operations by employing successive army operations to penetrate enemy defenses along converging directions in order to encircle and destroy enemy main forces.

Successful penetration of an enemy defense required considerable over-all superiority in forces and creation of high force densities in penetration sectors. Development of the offensive into the operational depths required use of mechanized and cavalry corps, *front* reserves, and air assault landings in the enemy rear. To conduct deep operations, a *front* had to consist of:

3–4 shock armies
1–2 standard armies
1–2 mechanized, tank, or cavalry corps
15–30 aviation divisions.[33]

Such a *front* could attack in a sector 250–300 kilometers wide against objectives at a depth of 150–250 kilometers and deliver the main attack in a sector of 60–80 kilometers. Force densities of one division per 2–2.5 kilometers, 40–100 guns per one kilometer of front, and 50–100 tanks per one kilometer of front resulted. A *front* operation was to last 15–20 days with an average tempo of advance of 10–15 kilometers a day for infantry and 40–50 kilometers a day for mobile forces.[34] Within the *front* the attack echelon consisted of strong shock and combined-arms armies, and the echelon to develop success was composed of mobile groups formed from tank, mechanized, and cavalry corps. Aviation groups and reserves supported operating *fronts*.

Armies, as operational large units, operated within a *front* or independently along a separate operational direction. Armies participating in deep operations on *front* main attack directions consisted of:

4–5 rifle corps
1–2 mechanized or cavalry corps
7–9 artillery regiments
7–8 air defense artillery battalions
2–3 aviation divisions (in support).[35]

The army attack echelon, consisting of rifle corps reinforced by tanks and artillery, advanced in a sector 50–80 kilometers wide with its main strength concentrated in a penetration sector 20–30 kilometers wide to penetrate the tactical enemy defenses to a depth of 25–30 kilometers. The echelon to develop the penetration, an army mobile group of several mechanized or cavalry corps, completed the penetration of the enemy's tactical defense or attacked after penetration of the enemy's second defense belt to develop tactical success into operational success to a depth of 70–100 kilometers.[36] In both *front* and army deep operations, the Soviets paid particular attention to the organization of air defense using fighter aviation and air defense artillery units. The Soviets exercised deep operational concepts in maneuvers in the Kiev, Belorussian, Moscow, and Odessa Military Districts in the mid-thirties.

They also worked on the concept of the *front* defensive operation, although principally in secondary sectors, as an adjunct to offensive operations in main TVDs. In recent years virtually all Soviet sources have criticized Stalin and the General Staff for ignoring the defensive realm. Sokolovsky's 1963 book on military strategy and the Soviet *Military Encyclopedia* typify this view, stating, "Questions of the organization and conduct of the (strategic) defense were not worked out fully in our prewar theory ... The theory of front defensive operations up to the beginning of the Great Patriotic War was not sufficiently worked out."[37] Savushkin now states that: "It is difficult to establish the extent to which it was insufficient and to which it was incomplete. However, if you approach that question from the political, strategic, and theoretical point of view, in fact, one must directly state that such assertions are insufficiently objective."[38] Savushkin bases his claim on the following specific facts:

(1) From a political and strategic point of view the USSR had no desire or plans to attack the enemy or preempt an enemy attack. All planning was based on repelling an attack and launching counteroffensives.

(2) From the theoretical point of view, it was impossible to work out offensive questions on every scale without similar work on the defense. That is a single theoretical process. "Only thorough comprehension of defensive questions permitted Soviet theory to develop fully deep offensive operations."[39]

(3) From the factual point of view, all large maneuvers were two-sided in the sense that they developed questions of both offensive and defensive operations. This applied equally to mobile groups, air assault forces, air forces, and reserves.

And, as Savushkin summed up:

Finally, our theory, and this is documented, contained instructions on the general principles of constructing defensive systems on a frontal scale (defensive sectors, etc.); on its operational formation, on the function and order of using elements of the operational formation, on cooperation, etc. All of this says that defensive questions on the scale of the *front* were worked out roughly to the same degree as offensive questions.[40]

Savushkin explains the persistence of incorrect assertions, stating, "The thesis concerning the weak development of defensive theory appeared long ago. It became necessary at that time to shift responsibility for the failures in the initial period of war from Stalin to the military theoreticians."[41]

While theorists in the late 1930s and in 1940–41 pondered the diminished role of the *front* and the nature of strategic offensive and defensive questions, they also addressed the question of strategic reserves, which loomed larger as the projected scale of future war increased and warning time decreased. By late 1939 Soviet theorists had concluded that strategic reserves should be formed by two means: by creating new formations and units, and by restoring and regrouping forces from existing *fronts*.[42] These reserves would be used whenever possible in concentrated fashion to reinforce success.

WAR PLANNING

The theoretical work of Soviet military theorists found practical expression in Soviet war planning, exercises, and actual partial mobilizations conducted during the period 1936–41. This was true of the larger military district exercises, which helped work out theoretical questions of offense and defense within the context of potential external threats. During the Kiev exercise of 1935, in addition to testing concepts for deep battle, the Soviets employed a mechanized corps and cavalry division to encircle and destroy a deeply penetrating enemy force and an enemy air assault in the Soviet rear area.[43] During fall of the following year a Belorussian Military District exercise tested similar concepts.

Routine war and crisis planning also served as a vehicle for validating theory and prompted further theoretical work and practical changes. The Czech crisis of September 1938 was such an occasion, when the Soviet Union attempted to cooperate with Great Britain and France to give political and military guarantees to Czechoslovakia against German aggression. In addition to undertaking diplomatic measures, the Soviets conducted a partial mobilization and deployment of their armed forces to demonstrate their political solidarity with Czechoslovakia, Great Britain, and France against German actions. The mobilization, between 21 and 24 September, involved forces from the Kiev and Belorussian Special Military Districts and several other internal districts (see Figures 6–7). Precise mobilization measures included the alerting and raising to full strength of fortified regions along the border and in the depths and the full mobilization of one tank corps; 30 rifle and ten cavalry divisions; seven tank and motorized rifle and 12 aviation brigades; seven fortified regions, and two corps, one division, two brigades, 16 regiments, and numerous separate air defense battalions. Subsequently, by the end of the month, additional mobilization measures were implemented in many other military districts. In all, 60 rifle and 16 cavalry divisions, three tank corps, 22 separate tank brigades, and 17 aviation brigades were mobilized, for a total of 330,000 men.[44]

Subsequent squabbles with her potential allies and the ensuing tragic circumstances and terms of the Munich settlement negated the impact of Soviet actions, but the exercise was instructive. First, the Soviets apparently did not create *front* or army commands. Instead, they formed operational groups, some of army size, others smaller. This attested to the relatively immature state of Soviet command and control organs. Second, the Czech mobilization exercise prompted further work within the General Staff to smooth out mobilization plans and procedures and create more effective command and control. This work, in part, produced a new set of strategic deployment plans in 1938.

In November 1938 the Main Military Council approved a strategic deployment plan developed by Chief of the Red Army General Staff, B. M. Shaposhnikov. This plan "considered the most probable enemies, their armed forces and possible operational plans, and the basic strategic deployment of the Red Army in the west and in the east".[45] Although the General Staff had no real documentary proof of hostile enemy plans, the postulated threat rang true.

The plan identified Germany and Italy, possibly supported by Japan, as the most likely and most dangerous enemies. Although it assumed Germany would ultimately wage war on the Soviet Union, it judged that Germany was not yet materially capable of launching such an attack. Nor were political conditions (internal and external) suitable for Germany to do so. The policy of Great Britain and France toward fascist aggression had vacillated but, at least, it had imposed some limits on the conduct of Rumania, Bulgaria, Turkey, Finland, and the other Baltic states. Iran and Afghanistan would be neutral. In the east Japan, operating from her Asian bridgehead of Manchuria, could cooperate with a fascist attack in the west.

Thus, the plan assumed that the Soviet Union would face a two-front war, in the west against Germany, Italy, Poland and possibly Rumania, Finland, and the Baltic states; and in the east against Japan. The combined threat amounted to 194–210 infantry, four motorized and 15 cavalry divisions, equipped with 13,077 guns, 7,980 tanks, and 5,775 aircraft.[46] Over half of these forces threatened the western Soviet Union. In the event of crisis, the Soviets believed the Germans and Poles would jointly occupy Lithuania.

Accordingly, as before, the Soviets identified the Western (European) Theater of War as the priority theater and planned its main force

Verteilung der Truppen im europäischen Rußland

Distribution of Troops in European Russia   Enclosure No. 1 to

6. German assessment of Soviet force dispositions: 1937

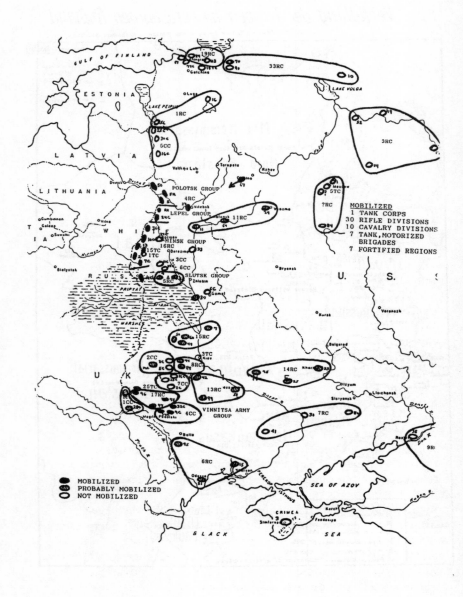

7. Soviet force posture during the Czech crisis: 21–24 September 1938

concentrations there. The location of the Pripiat Marshes, which divided the theater in two, posed a dilemma to Soviet strategic planners regarding where the main enemy thrust would occur – whether it would be north or south of the marshes.[47] Consequently, Shaposhnikov worked out two planning variants to meet either circumstance. Where the attack ultimately materialized would depend on specific German objectives and existing political and economic conditions. In either case, Finnish forces and those of the Baltic states could assist the Germans with an attack on Leningrad.

The Shaposhnikov plan contained two variants: the first, an enemy attack north of the Pripiat Marshes directed along the Minsk–Smolensk axis; and the second, an enemy thrust into the economically vital Ukraine. The first variant, considered most likely and decisive by Shaposhnikov and the General Staff, predicted the main German–Polish attack would occur in the north, while Polish forces would launch a secondary attack in the south (see Figure 8). The second variant postulated a main German–Polish drive into the Ukraine and a secondary combined allied attack in the north (see Figure 9). Preparation times for the attack varied between 20 and 30 days, depending on the variant. The Soviets presumed that Rumania would remain neutral in both cases. The Japanese threat of between 27 and 33 divisions also remained constant.[48]

Soviet strategic deployments in response to these threats sought to create force concentrations which could defeat the enemy in both the west and in the east, first by engaging the most dangerous threat, that in the west. While defending less critical theaters with covering forces, the Soviets intended to concentrate their forces in the west to meet either of the two enemy attacks. In the first variant, while forces on the southwestern and northwestern directions conducted active defense against the enemy, forces operating on the heavily weighted western direction would first defend and then launch a decisive counteroffensive toward Grodno and Warsaw.[49] The second variant provided for a main counteroffensive in the Ukraine and a smaller counteroffensive in the Minsk region. Soviet forces in the Far East would first defend the maritime provinces and then defeat Japanese forces in northern Manchuria and the coastal regions. To implement this plan, the Soviets had to maintain large well-equipped covering armies in peacetime, anchored on fortified regions. Only this type force could cope with the enemy first echelon invading armies and also cover the concentration of Soviet main forces designated to launch decisive counteroffensives.

Shaposhnikov's 1938 plan corresponded to those of 1914 regarding how it defined the initial period of war. In particular, it was predicated upon virtual full Soviet mobilization before hostilities commenced,

73

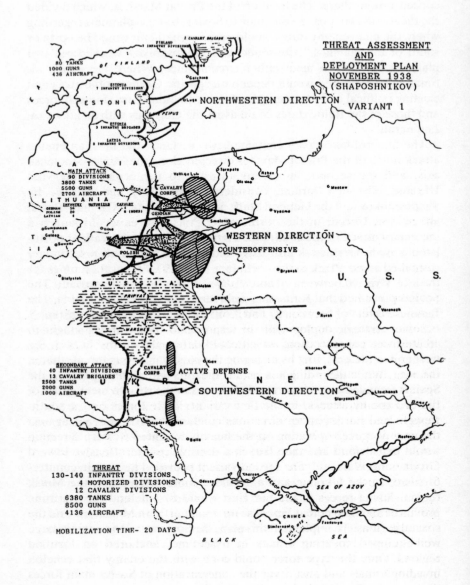

8. Soviet threat assessment and deployment plan: November 1938: Variant 1

although covering forces were considered adequate to cope with a degree of enemy advanced mobilization. While the plan did not designate use of a specific number of *fronts*, it did clearly foresee operations along three strategic directions, the most important of which was the Western.

The Polish crisis of summer 1939 and the ensuing war and partition of Poland impelled the General Staff to revisit the topic of strategic planning, this time on a limited offensive basis. Once the prospects for combined strategic action against Germany by the Soviet Union, Britain, and France had collapsed and the Soviets had signed their non-aggression pact with Germany, the Soviets partially mobilized and invaded eastern Poland. To conduct the operation, the Soviets formed two *front* commands (Belorussian and Ukrainian), each made up of armies and operational groups (see Figure 10). Although this command structure was far more elaborate than that formed during the Czech crisis a year before, the number of divisions mobilized was roughly the same. Because of a variety of severe command and control, logistical, and even morale problems, Soviet forces only muddled through the operation.[50] Their dismal military performances in Poland, and later in the Russo-Finnish War of 1939–40, proved embarrassing for the Soviet government and probably encouraged German aggressive plans against the Soviet Union.

As a result of the Polish partition, by September 1939 Germany occupied borders contiguous to the Soviet Union. Soon after, in October 1939 Soviet forces occupied the Baltic states, making that contiguous border even larger, but, in so doing, improving its strategic posture by insuring that attacks did not emanate from the "Baltic bridgehead" against Leningrad or Minsk (as had occurred in 1919). When the Polish buffer zone between Germany and the Soviet Union disappeared, although due in large part to Soviet actions, Soviet concern for security and defense deepened. One manifestation of this concern was the rapid Soviet expansion of her fortified positions along both the new and old Soviet borders (see Figure 11). In 1938 the Soviets had constructed 13 fortified regions (*ukreplennyi raion* – UR) along her old border manned by 25 machine gun battalions totalling 18,000 men. In late 1938 and early 1939, the Soviets added eight more fortified regions to the existing structure. During 1940 and 1941, while developing new strategic plans, which reflected the incorporation of Poland and the Baltic states into the Soviet Union, the Soviets constructed 20 new fortified regions along the new border, each consisting of two defensive belts to a depth of 15–20 kilometers.[51] The latter were only partially complete in June 1941. These belts of fortified regions were designed to form a base around which solid defenses could be constructed and to help protect and strengthen covering armies.

75

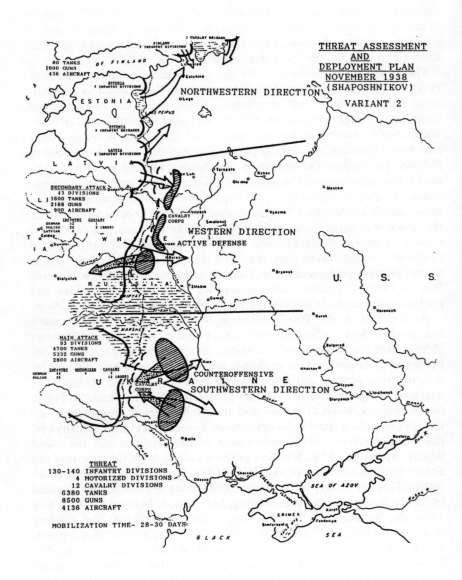

9. Soviet threat assessment and deployment plan: November 1938: Variant 2

10. Soviet force posture during the Polish crisis: 17–20 September 1939

The German conquests in western and northern Europe in the spring of 1940 lent an air of urgency to subsequent Soviet war planning. Clearly, the course of the European war required that the 1938 plan be updated. By July 1940 the General Staff had a new plan ready, prepared by Major General A. M. Vasilevsky, deputy chief of the General Staff's Operations Division, and approved by Shaposhnikov.[52] This plan, like its predecessor, postulated an attack by Germany, supported by Italy, Finland, Rumania, and possibly Hungary against the western Soviet Union and by Japan in the Far East. The Soviets assessed a total threat of 270 infantry divisions, 11,750 tanks, 22,000 guns, and 16,400 aircraft, the bulk of which would be directed against the most critical Western Theater (see figure 12). The July plan assessed that the main enemy attack would occur north of the San River along the Vilnius–Minsk and Brest–Baranovichi axes. In a second, less likely variant, German and Polish forces would concentrate in the Lublin region for an advance on Kiev. The plan concluded by stating "the chief, most politically favorable (course) for Germany and, consequently, the most probable is the first variant of her action – with deployment of the main force of the German Army north of the San River".[53]

Soviet strategic deployment in accordance with this plan required the formation of three *fronts* in the Western Theater; the Northwestern and Western covering the main strategic direction and the Southwestern covering the region south of the Pripiat Marshes. To deal with the Japanese threat in the Far East, the Soviets planned to form the Trans-Baikal and Far Eastern Fronts. Soviet critics have since noted several deficiencies in the plan, most important of which were the underassessment of the threat along the northwestern direction and the threat from Lublin toward Kiev.

After General K. A. Meretskov became Chief of the General Staff in August 1940, the General Staff reevaluated the July 1940 Shaposhnikov plan. The following month a new plan, which resembled Shaposhnikov's earlier plan, was approved by Minister of Defense Marshal S. K. Timoshenko and Meretskov and sent to Stalin for approval. The plan, depending on political conditions, provided for strategic deployments for both a northern and southern variant (north and south of Brest). A review of the plan by Stalin and the party and government leadership in early October 1940 resulted in greater emphasis being placed on the southern variant. During the course of the review, political leaders decided "that the Western theater of war was the main theater and that the main grouping here must be deployed on the Southwestern Direction".[54] As a result of the review, the decision was made to strengthen the Southwestern Front forces. Although the second variant for deployment of larger forces north

11. Soviet construction of fortified regions: 1938–1941

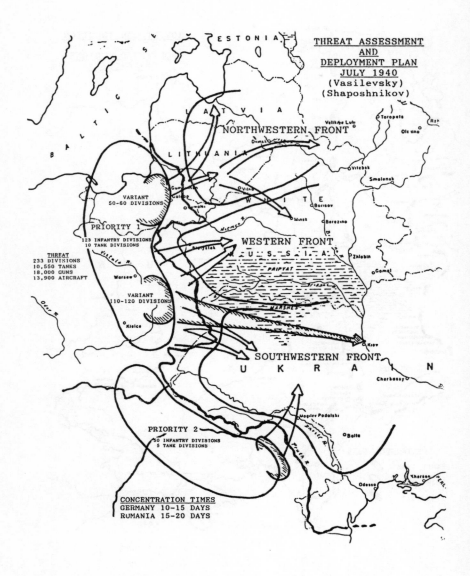

12. Soviet threat assessment and deployment plan: July 1940

of the Pripiat was not openly rejected, it did not, however, receive particular support. This new plan was then approved on 14 October (see Figure 13). As a consequence, "There occurred a full reorientation and reassessment of the basic strength of our forces from the Northwestern (as proposed by Shaposhnikov) to the Southwestern Direction."[55]

The October 1940 strategic deployment plan was again discussed and approved in the spring of 1941 after General G. K. Zhukov became Chief of the General Staff. The October changes and subsequent slight revisions before June 1941 resulted in reinforcement of the Southwestern Direction by 25 divisions.

To verify Soviet defense plans and judgments made regarding the nature of the initial period of war, in January 1941, after a high-level military-theoretical conference in Moscow had adjourned, the General Staff conducted an operational-strategic war game.[56] Minister of Defense Timoshenko and Chief of the General Staff Meretskov supervised, and 32 other senior commanders played significant roles in the game. The General Staff's operational directorate under Lieutenant General N. F. Vatutin and his assistant, Major General A. M. Vasilevsky, drew up the scenarios, which were based on actual threat estimates and war plans.

The war game scenario postulated an attack by Germany (Westerners) on the Soviet Union (Easterners) during which the Germans operated according to lessons learned in her wars of 1939 and 1940. The General Staff established the following goals for the games:

(1) to work out and master the basis of contemporary defensive and offensive operations;
(2) to provide to higher commanders practice in the organization and planning of *front* and army operations, in command and control of forces, and in organizing cooperation among main types of forces and the fleet;
(3) to work out questions of: defense of the state borders against an attack by a superior enemy; withdrawal to a prepared defensive line; conduct of particular operations to defeat the enemy in the border battles, overcoming the forward defensive positions, seizing fortified regions; penetrating enemy field defensive lines; organizing pursuit and river crossings by cavalry-mechanized armies, as well as overcoming mountain defiles;
(4) to study the Baltic and Southwestern Theaters of Military Operations.

According to Zakharov, then serving on the General Staff, "Conditions, created for the game, abounded in dramatic episodes for the eastern

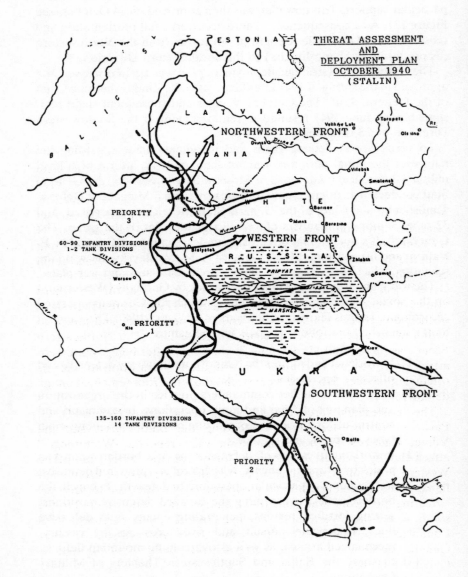

THREAT ASSESSMENT
AND
DEPLOYMENT PLAN
OCTOBER 1940
(STALIN)

13. Soviet threat assessment and deployment plan: October 1940

82

(Soviet) side; in many ways it resembled events which unfolded along our borders in June 1941 after the perfidious attack of German-Fascist forces on the Soviet Union."[57]

The Soviets played two games. In both games the "Westerners" deployed four *fronts*, extending from the Baltic to the Black Sea (Northeastern, Eastern, Southeastern, Southern), and the "Easterners" deployed three (Northwestern, Western, Southwestern). The principal differences in the two games were the conditions surrounding the attack and the location and nature of combat actions (see Figure 14).

In the first game (conducted from 2–6 January), the "Westerners" anticipated the "Easterners" in their deployment and on 15 July 1941 launched an attack with their Northeastern and Eastern Fronts. The main "Westerners" attack by the Southeastern and Southern Fronts (160 divisions) occurred south of Brest toward Vladimir–Volynskii and Tarnopol'. The northern attack (of 60 divisions), designed to distract "Eastern" attention from the real main attack area and the focal point of the game, was launched from East Prussia toward Riga and Dvinsk and from the Suwalki and Brest regions toward Baranovichi. It was to begin before full concentration of forces and was to reach the Riga–Dvinsk–Baranovichi line by 15 August. As the game unfolded the three northern armies of General G. K. Zhukov's Northeastern Front were halted short of their objectives by a 50-division enemy counterattack and forced to withdraw to a pre-planned prepared defense line. The Northeastern Front was then required to defend in place and, after being reinforced, attack on 10 August in conjunction with the Eastern Front to seize its original objectives. Up to 10 August, the Eastern Front remained on the defensive.

The "Easterners" forces defended with five armies of General D. G. Pavlov's Northwestern Front defending the Baltic coast and the Vilnius–Riga axis. The *front*'s main force was to repel the "Westerners'" attack and, by 1 August, expel enemy forces from the Soviet Union. The Western Front of 31 divisions supported the Northwestern Front's left flank, and a special operational group played the Southwestern Front.

During the second war game (8–11 January), the action shifted to the south, where the "Westerners" deployed in three *fronts* extending from Lublin to the Black Sea. For this game, commanders switched sides. General D. G. Pavlov's Southeastern Front struck first, followed by General F. I. Kuznetov's Southern Front in a joint drive toward Proskurov, designed to encircle and destroy the "Easterners'" L'vov–Ternopol' grouping and advance to the Shepetovka–Odessa line.[58] The Southern Front's 38 divisions were to penetrate enemy defenses and force the Dneistr River by 8 August. The Southeastern Front's 39 divisions,

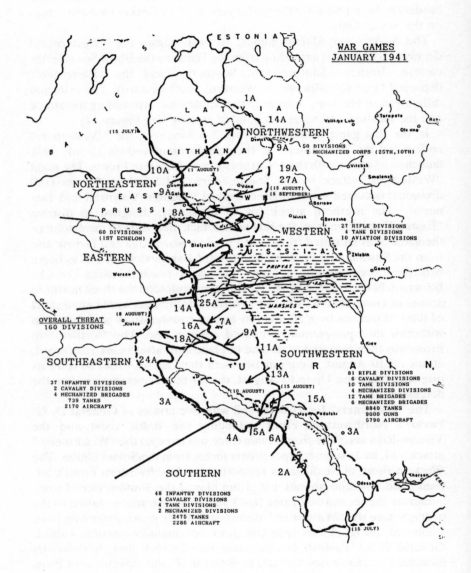

14. Soviet war games: January 1941

while seeking to encircle the enemy, were struck by an enemy counterattack, lost 20 divisions, and, by 8 August, had withdrawn to the Vistula River between Tarow and Demblin. The "Easterners'" Southwestern Front, commanded by General G. K. Zhukov and deployed from Brest to the Black Sea, consisted of 101 divisions. By 10 August (game time) the Southwestern Front had halted the drive from Rumania and defeated the drive from southern Poland.

The most interesting aspects of the war games were the reflections on strategic and operational questions during the subsequent critique. The most important question concerned the nature of initial operations as exemplified by the first game. Hitherto based on World War I experiences, the Soviets had presumed that initial operations would involve extensive meeting engagements. The example of the Russo-Finnish War, however, pointed out the problem of fortified boundaries and lines.[59] Despite the Germans in 1940 providing a clear example of how to circumvent fortifications, the first war game began with an operation to penetrate strongly fortified defenses.

The critique noted the following points: In chronological sequence, after the initial "Western" advance, the "Easterners" had to halt the enemy advance, finish regrouping their forces, conduct individual operations to liquidate the "Westerners", plan the entire *front* operation so that it followed individual operations without a pause, and deny the enemy time to recover after his initial defeat. Immediately thereafter the "Easterners" had to conduct a full-scale penetration operation.

The "Westerners", after initial operations and subsequent enemy counterattacks, had to stop the enemy offensive along the fortified border, defeat him, concentrate reserves, and regroup forces sufficiently to renew the offensive. To have prepared the counterattack in front of the fortified border could have led to defeat and subsequent failure to hold the fortified line. The solution, therefore, was to use firepower to inflict as many casualties as possible on the enemy forward of the fortified line and, consequently, avoid undue losses in that region. It would also have been pointless to abandon the Suwalki salient, since its possession facilitated subsequent encirclement of "Eastern" forces with an attack from the Suwalki area southeast and from the Brest area northwest.

The critique of "Eastern" operations noted that the counterattack by the *front*'s left wing 19th and 27th Armies and a mobile group had been proper, since it avoided an attack on prepared and fortified positions. Since it had been an enveloping maneuver and the frontage of attack had, quite naturally, lengthened, it would have required additional forces to be fully successful.

In summary, the critique concluded:

The operational-strategic horizons of many higher level commanders was far from perfection and required further painstaking and urgent work in sharpening the art of command and control and the leading of large units and deeper mastery of the nature of large-scale operations, and their organization, planning and subsequent implementation in practice.[60]

The second game was similarly critiqued. In both war games some game conditions clearly did not match reality and hence clouded the lessons derived. For example, the games:

- did not fully replicate an initial period of war;
- overestimated Soviet defensive capabilities;
- investigated subjects limited in scope;
- involved *fronts* which were too large and difficult to control;
- deployed *fronts* which covered too many operational axes;
- overemphasized the importance of the southwestern direction;
- failed to study adequately real conditions along the western border (for example, fortified regions and covering forces);
- accorded too little attention to the modern requirements of mobilization, deployment and concentration of forces in concert with real defense plans (for example, surprise)
- overassessed the strength of Soviet vis à vis German divisions and infantry vis à vis mechanized forces. Hence the correlation of forces was incorrect.[61]

In a more positive sense the game made use of mobile forces and provided considerable experience to higher commanders in commanding and controlling large-scale operations. For all that could be said of them, the January war games were an accurate representation of the state of Soviet strategic thinking on the eve of war.

Throughout the spring of 1941, tensions grew between Germany and the Soviet Union. The Germans intensified their intelligence collection against the Soviet Union and began mobilization for Barbarossa, prepared in December 1940, which called for a May 1941 invasion of the Soviet Union.[62] Ultimately, the Germans delayed Operation Barbarossa until 22 June to accommodate brief German operations in Yugoslavia, Greece, and Crete.

Soviet intelligence kept track of the German troop build-up in eastern Europe and received a significant amount of intelligence from diplomatic and military sources concerning the impending attack.[63] Soviet concern over increasing German offensive preparedness prompted Stalin and the General Staff to order preliminary mobilization measures on 13 May involving westward deployment of five armies. The record of this and other measures and excerpts from the extensive Soviet intelligence files have only recently been published.[64] Among the newly published material is an interesting proposal supposedly made in mid-May 1941 by Chief of the General Staff Zhukov to Stalin suggesting a Soviet preemptive strike against mobilizing German forces. Zhukov's proposal, probably only one of many made during 1941, and rejected, sits comfortably within the context of previous Soviet strategic planning and, in particular, the experiences of the January war games.

Entitled "Report on the Plan of Strategic Deployment of Armed Forces of the Soviet Union to the Chairman of the Council of People's Commissars on 15 May 1941" and co-signed by Timoshenko, Zhukov's report began with the words:

> 1 ... Considering that Germany, at this time, is mobilizing its forces and rear services, it has the capability of forestalling (pre-empting) our deployment and delivering a surprise blow. In order to avert such a situation, I consider it necessary on no account to give the initiative of action to the German command, to pre-empt the enemy deployment and to attack the German Army at that moment when it is in the process of deployment and has not yet succeeded in organizing the *front* and cooperation of its forces.[65]

The report then set out strategic objectives for the proposed operation designed to defeat and destroy the estimated 100 German divisions already assembling in eastern Poland. The first (initial) strategic objective was to destroy German forces assembled south of Brest and Demblin and, within 30 days, to advance to a line running from north of Ostrolenka, south along the Narew River, through Lowicz, Lodz, Kreuzberg, and Oppeln to Olomouc. Subsequently, Soviet forces were to attack north or northwest from the Katowice region to destroy German forces in the center and northwest wing of the front and seize the remainder of former Poland and East Prussia.

The immediate mission of Soviet forces during the first phase was to break up German forces east of the Vistula River and around Krakow, advance to the Narew and Vistula Rivers, and secure Katowice. Specific missions to carry out this task were:

(a) Strike the main blow by Southwestern Front forces toward Krakow and Katowice to cut Germany off from her southern allies.
(b) Deliver the secondary blow by the left wing of the Western Front toward Warsaw and Demblin to fix the Warsaw grouping

and secure Warsaw, and also to cooperate with the South-western Front in destroying the Lublin group.

(c) Conduct active defense against Finland, East Prussia, Hungary, and Rumania and be prepared to strike a blow against Rumania if favorable conditions arise.[66]

Zhukov calculated that the Soviet attacking force of 152 divisions would be faced by roughly 100 German divisions.

Zhukov's report suggests the following conclusions: first, as of 5 May 1941, Soviet intelligence estimated German strength opposite their borders in excess of 107 divisions.[67] This included: 23–24 divisions in East Prussia, 29 facing the Western Special MD, 31–34 opposite the Kiev MD, six located near Danzig and Poznan, four in the Carpathio–Ukraine, and 10–11 in Moldavia and Northern Dobrudja. Eighteen more divisions were then rumored to be en route. While Zhukov's estimate of German strength on 15 May was close to accurate, it certainly would not have been when the Soviets were able to mount their pre-emptive assault.

Second, Soviet deployments on 15 May were insufficient for the mounting of such an offensive. Between them, the Western and Southwestern Fronts counted about 102 divisions (see Figure 15). Strategic second echelon and reserve forces were just then beginning their deployment forward and would arrive in stages between early June and mid-July.[68] Thus, to establish requisite force strength for the offensive, Zhukov's plan could not have been implemented until mid-June (30 days) at the earliest, and by then German force strength would have also risen. For Zhukov to reach his desired correlation of forces, the attack would have had to occur after 60 days of preparation (in mid-July). That, of course, would have been too late to pre-empt the Germans and deny them surprise.

Third, in addition to correlation of force problems, the performance of Soviet forces in Poland and Finland, the sorry state of training and force readiness, the major equipment and logistical shortfalls in the Red Army, and the half-completed force reorganization would have made any offensive action by the Red Army simply folly. In the light of these realities, Stalin's decision to ignore Zhukov's proposal seems to have been prudent.

The plan itself bore close resemblence to the strategic deployment plan of October 1940 and the war games of January 1941 (see Figure 16). The southwestern direction received priority attention, and Zhukov hoped to replicate his performance in January, when, during the second war game, his Southwestern Front drove westward to the Vistula River. In this new proposal, however, his objectives were far more bold. Zhukov's plan is

15. The Zhukov proposal: 15 May 1941, availability of forces

16. The Zhukov proposal: 15 May 1941, concentration of forces (variant)

also of interest because it established limited objectives well short of the destruction of the German state. The Soviet decision to reveal the plan at this time adds to the current strategic debate a clear example of justifiable preventative war involving the conduct of a strategic offensive operation with definite limited aims.[69]

FORCE GENERATION

The changing, more threatening political atmosphere of Europe in the 1930s, as well as the demands of changing technology, altered Soviet strategic concepts and rendered the existing force generation system ineffective in meeting potential future threats. The territorial/cadre force served the Soviets well in the 1920s, but after 1935 it was apparent that the threat had outgrown the mobilization capability of the system. Wartime force expansion within existing mobilization plans was simply not large enough to meet new threats.

> It is important to note that by the mid-1930s the mixed territorial-cadre system of completing and organizing forces had already exhausted itself and become a brake on the path of their combat growth. There matured an actual necessity for a transformation to the unified cadre principle of formation. One of the main reasons was that the temporary manpower of territorial units and formations at short muster already were not in a condition to master the new complex technology and learn how to employ it in ever-changing conditions ... The transformation to a cadre system, to a considerable degree, was dictated by the growing demands for increased combat and mobilization preparedness, since the danger of a war with Fascist Germany grew.[70]

The transformation process began in 1937 and was completed by January 1939, by which time all troop formations and units had become cadre.

CADRE AND TERRITORIAL FORMATIONS AND UNITS OF THE RED ARMY

Formation and Unit	1 Jan 1937	1 Jan 1938	1 Jan 1939
Cadre rifle divisions	49	50	84
Mixed rifle divisions	4	2	0
Territorial divisions	35	34	0
Cadre mountain rifle divisions	9	10	14
Separate brigades	–	–	5
Territorial separate regiments	2	2	0
Total	97 divisions	96 divisions	98 divisions
	2 regiments	2 regiments	5 brigades[71]

91

During 1938 all nationality-based formations and schools were likewise abolished or replaced.

To provide an increased supply of manpower for these divisions and for future mobilization, on 1 September 1939 the Supreme Soviet accepted a new Law on Universal Military Service, which increased the term of military service of enlisted men and NCOs to three years and provided better training and more manpower. Similarily, the military district system was reformed to improve their efficiency in processing military manpower and the number of military districts grew to 16.[72]

The new force manning system and the reorganized administrative structure made possible expansion of the Red Army as it "crept up to war" between 1939 and June 1941. Between 1938 and 1941, the entire force structure grew from a total strength of 1.5 million men on 1 January 1938, through 4.2 million in December 1940, to 5 million in June 1941 (see Figure 17).[73]

By June 1941 the wartime establishment strength of rifle divisions was set at 14,483, and peacetime divisions were maintained at several levels of cadre strength. The strongest divisions (first line), deployed in border military districts, numbered 6,959 men; those in the interior (second line) had a strength of 5,220 men; and other reserve divisions (third line), with insignificant numbers of cadre in peacetime, would form during mobilization and wartime from existing divisions.[74]

FIGURE 17

EXPANSION OF THE RED ARMY: 1939–1941

Type Formation	1 June 1938	1 Sept 1939	Dec 1940	June 1941
armies	1	2	20	20
rifle corps	27	25	30	62
rifle divisions	71 regular 35 territorial	96	152	196
motorized rifle divisions	–	1	10 (approx)	31
cavalry corps	7	7	4	4
cavalry divisions	32	30	26	13
rifle brigades	–	5	5	3
tank divisions	4 (corps)	4 (corps)	18 (approx)	61
fortified regions (west)	13	21	21	41
(total)	?	?	?	120
airborne brigades	6	6	12	16
airborne corps	–	–	–	5
Red Army strength	1,513,000	1,520,000	4,207,000	5,000,000

Between April and June 1941, during the "special threatening military period", the Soviets accelerated "creeping up to war" by conducting a concealed strategic deployment of forces. This was, in essence, the first stage in a mobilization process which would continue into wartime and ultimately through early 1942 (see Figure 18). From 26 April 1941 the Trans-Baikal Military District and Far Eastern Front's military councils dispatched to the west one mechanized corps, two rifle corps, and two airborne brigades. On 10 May the Urals Military District received instructions to send two rifle divisions to the Baltic Military District, and five days later the Siberian Military District received similar orders to send single divisions to the Western and Kiev Special Military Districts.[75]

On 13 May the General Staff ordered 28 rifle divisions and the headquarters of four armies (16th, 19th, 21st, 22d) to move from interior military districts to districts along the border, and a fifth army (20th) to mobilize at Orel and assemble west of Moscow. "The troops were relocated secretly, under the guise of sending them to camp. Here the schedule for train traffic over the railroads was not altered."[76] Additional corps of these armies moved before 22 June and closed into deployment positions in early July, after hostilities had commenced. Ultimately, on 21 and 22 June, most of these forces were organized into a reserve group of armies (*front*) under Marshal S. M. Budenny.

From late May through early June the General Staff called up for service 800,000 reservists to fill out 100 divisions and numerous fortified regions. Finally, on 14 June formations within the border military districts secretly regrouped, most into positions between 20–80 kilometers from the border. This regrouping had been only partially completed on 22 June, when German forces struck. First echelon forces of covering armies, however, were forbidden to regroup. Instead, they required special orders to occupy wartime defensive positions.[77]

FIGURE 18

MOBILIZATION: MAY–JUNE 1941

Formation	Mobilization Location	Deployed Location
16th Army (12 divisions)	Trans-Baikal MD	Proskurov, Khmel'niki (Kiev Special MD by 22 June)
19th Army (10 divisions)	North Caucasus MD	Cherkassy, Belaia Tserkov (Kiev Special MD by 22 June)
25th Mechanized Corps (19th Army)	Orel MD (Khar'kov)	Mironovka (by 7 July)
20th Army (10 divisions)	Orel MD	Mogilev (61st RC), Smolensk (69th RC) Krichev (20th RC) Dorogobuzh (41st RC) (Moscow MD by 3–5 July)
7th Mechanized Corps (20th Army)	Orel MD	Orsha (Moscow MD by 5 July)
21st Army (14 divisions)	Volga MD	Chernigov (66th RC) Gomel (63rd RC)

		Ostera (45th RC) (all by 22 June)
		Bakhmacha (30th RC by 9 July)
		Gorodnia (33d RC by 10 July)
22rd Army (6 divisions)	Ural MD	Sebezh (62rd RC by 2 July)
		Vitebsk (51st RC by 2 July)

By 22 June, the strategic deployment had resulted in the following dispositions:

> The first echelon formations from the covering armies located close to the frontier were not to be moved. Their moving up directly to the frontier could be carried out only under a special order.
>
> By 22 June 1941, there were 56 rifle and cavalry divisions and 2 brigades in the first echelons of the covering armies in the Western border military districts. In the second echelons of the armies, there were 52 divisions located 50–100 km away from the frontier. There were 62 divisions in the reserve of the districts and these were spread out along a front of 4,500 km and to a depth from 100 to 400 km.[78]

An important aspect of the force generation process in the 1930s and on the eve of war was the question of generating a pool of individual reserves and strategic reserve formations.

> Soviet military theory considered that the exceptionally bitter nature of impending war, the use of automatic weapons and combat equipment possessing great destructive force, would lead to considerable manpower and materiel losses. "On average," pointed out the well-known Soviet theorist S. M. Belitsky, "the basic mass of personnel in an operating army must be changed (replaced) every 4–8 months of a long war." Military theorists felt that this required first, and foremost, timely and uninterrupted military training of called-up contingents.[79]

To accomplish this end, as noted, the government and military authorities shifted to the regular/cadre system of force generation, passed the 1939 Law on Universal Military Service, increased the age of reserve service to 50, created an extensive system of schools and training institutions, and instituted military training among the population by *Osoaviakhim*.[80] By June 1941 14 million men had received required training. These collective measures to establish a larger manpower base and a mechanism for converting manpower into actual military formations enabled the Soviet High Command before and during the initial period of war to field a massive number of new corps and armies (see Figure 19). In the last analysis, these strategic reserves made major contributions to the survival of the Red Army and the Soviet state in 1941.

STRATEGIC POSTURE ON THE EVE OF WAR: JUNE 1941

By 22 June 1941 the Soviets had implemented many of the military requirements of the "special threatening military period". Long-term preparedness programs were well under way, partial mobilization proceeded apace, forces were being converted to wartime establishments, and strategic and operational force concentration and deployment were progressing. These measures reached the forward military districts, but, because of Stalin's "concerns over provocations", similar provisions at the tactical and lower operational levels were severely restricted.[81]

Soviet forces were clearly postured to go to war in the near future, but only in a defensive stance. Actual Soviet force dispositions on the eve of the German attack amplify that judgment (see Figures 20 and 21). The Soviet first strategic echelon in the Western Theater of War consisted of forces in the border military districts, which formed four *fronts* and one army as follows:

Military District	Force
Baltic	Northwestern Front
Special Western	Western Front
Special Kiev	Southwestern Front
Leningrad	Leningrad Front
Odessa	9th Army

The High Command ordered these *fronts*, in the event of war, to prohibit enemy land and air intrusion, cover and protect the mobilization and deployment of the main force by conducting a stubborn defense along the borders, detect enemy mobilization and deployment, gain air superiority and disrupt enemy force concentration, protect Soviet mobilization and concentration of forces against enemy air attack, and block any actions by enemy air assault or reconnaissance-diversionary groups.[82] All of these missions were inherently defensive in nature.

To accomplish these missions, border military district (*front*) commanders formed three operational echelons. The first echelon of border

95

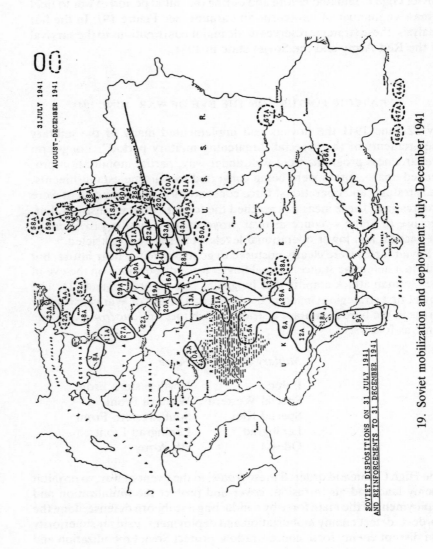

19. Soviet mobilization and deployment: July–December 1941

SOVIET MILITARY STRATEGY 1935–1941

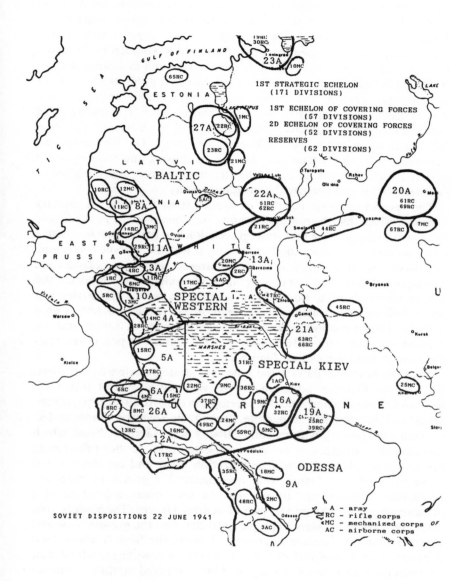

20. Soviet force dispositions, Western Theater, 22 June 1941

guards and rifle and fortification forces of covering armies, arrayed to a depth of 100 kilometers in the immediate border region, consisted of several tactical echelons backed up by the most combat-ready mechanized corps. To their rear, to a depth of 150 kilometers, formed a second operational echelon of army reserve rifle and mechanized corps positioned to add depth to the defense and launch counterattacks. A third operational echelon, consisting of reserve armies or corps and mechanized corps deployed before or shortly after the outbreak of hostilities along or forward of the Dnepr and Sozh River lines from Vitebsk in the north to west of Kiev in the south. The first defending echelon of covering armies had the task of slowing and wearing down enemy forces, the second of halting the enemy drive, and the third of counterattacking to destroy the invading enemy.

The second strategic echelon of armies from the internal military districts, which had begun mobilization and deployment in April and May, was to support the first strategic echelon and participate in decisive counterattacks to restore the border and, if feasible, pursue the enemy into his own territory. In the case of both strategic echelons, defenses and subsequent deployments were geographically weighted in support of the southwestern strategic direction in accordance with 1941 Soviet war plans. Subsequent strategic assessments in late June and July shifted priority of force commitment to the Western direction. Soviet strategic deployment plans and systems were flexible enough to permit the real-location of these forces (see Figure 22).

There were serious flaws in the June 1941 strategic defense plan. First, the surprise German offensive caught virtually all Soviet forces off balance and unprepared, and this preemption rendered a large part of the Soviet mobilization plan inoperable. Second, the Soviets seriously under-estimated the power, swiftness, and lethality of the German thrust, which subsequently advanced at twice the expected rate, further preempting Soviet plans. Third, German mobilization plans and capabilities and those of the Soviet Union were asymmetrical. German mobilization postulated "creeping-up" to war and the subsequent unleashing of a massive attack with the greater part of its armed forces. The Soviets, too, "crept up" to war but were unprepared to deal with the massive scale and surprise nature of German operations. Fourth, the Soviets misassessed the location of the main effort and were unable or unwilling to adjust their dispositions before major damage had been inflicted on their defensive forces. Fifth, Soviet force reorganization and regroupment programs were only half-completed, leaving a patchwork quilt of prepared and unprepared units to face the German onslaught. Systemic problems at every level included a logistic system which was utterly unprepared,

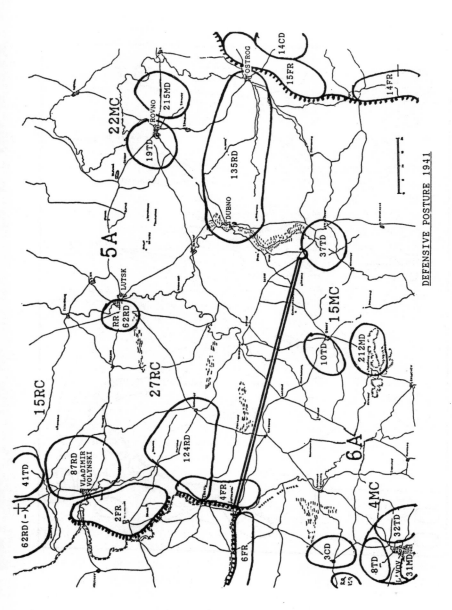

21. Soviet force deployment, Southwestern Front, 22 June 1941

DEFENSIVE POSTURE 1941

99

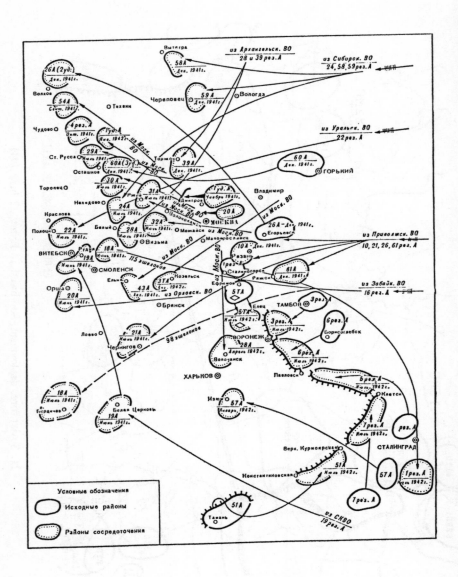

22. Soviet mobilization and deployment, April 1941–July 1942

organizationally or in terms of resources, to support large-scale offensive or defensive operations. Existing resources were badly deployed and unevenly distributed. And sixth, the purges of the military from 1937 to 1941 had left inexperienced commanders at every level of command. In short, Soviet defenses were not ready to cope with the threat. These hard lessons must be fully digested if, in the future, the Soviets formulate a new and similar defensive strategy. This strategic defense, to be viable, must avoid all of the major pitfalls of 1941.[83]

CONCLUSIONS

From the end of the Second World War until very recently, the Soviets have maintained that their military strategy in the 1930s and on the eve of Operation Barbarossa (June 1941) was essentially offensive. They attribute their dismal military performance during the initial period of war on the Eastern Front to wholesale neglect of the defense.[84] While this was partially true of operational thinking in the decade of the 1930s as a whole, it certainly was not true of Soviet military strategy during the years preceding Operation Barbarossa.

Soviet military strategy in the 1930s and up to June 1941 reacted to sharply altered international conditions in general and, specifically, to the emergence of potentially powerful military threats. In Savushkin's words, "Soviet military strategy correctly defined the political nature and scale of future war, the role and proportional weight of all types of armed forces, the character of armed struggle, and the types and means of strategic actions."[85]

During the 1930s the Soviets worked out the theoretical and, to some extent, the practical bases for the theories of *front* successive offensive operations and *front* deep offensive operations. Likewise, they developed concepts for echelonment at the strategic level and the maneuver use of mobile forces as a *front* "echelon to develop success" in offensive operations. Similar defensive concepts developed within the context of this theoretical work, particularly after 1939, when necessity dictated the likelihood of Soviet forces conducting a strategic defense. Despite this advanced theoretical work and some practical work as well, it was not until 1940 that *front* operations or operations by groups of *fronts*, in an offensive or a defensive sense, received adequate attention. When they did, severe technological deficiencies, in particular associated with communication, inhibited development of requisite command, control, and coordination techniques. This became abundantly clear in June 1941.

While recent Soviet critics stress the positive results of military

101

theoretical and practical work on both offensive and defensive issues in the 1930s, they now attribute many of the failures in the system to Stalin:

> However, not all that was planned on the matter of strengthening the defense and increasing its insurmountability was successfully brought to fruition . . . The development of Soviet military art would have led to more notable results if there had not been the tragedy of 1937–1938 resulting from the Stalin personality cult. It not only destroyed its creators but also fully negated the most important of its theories.[86]

Soviet military strategy on the eve of Operation Barbarossa was clearly defensive, despite the fact that Soviet military theorists throughout the 1930s had been thoroughly imbued with the "spirit of the offensive". The purge of the Soviet military from 1937 to the outbreak of European war stifled military thought and analysis, while the experiences of Soviet military specialists and units in the Spanish Civil War, the invasion of Poland, and the Russo-Finnish War cast serious doubt on the feasibility of conducting deep offensive operations in the manner envisioned by their 1930s regulations. Soviet faith in the utility of an offensive posture was further shaken by the course and outcome of the German-Polish War and the 1940 War in the west. Soviet theorists largely discounted German success in Poland and explained it as a product of Polish ineptitude; they could not, however, dismiss the precipitous fall of France in so cavalier a fashion. Soviet theorists were shocked to realize that Germany had successfully implemented the offensive theories of deep battle and deep operations, which the Soviets had developed and now, in part, discarded. These events also shook Soviet faith in their own offensive prowess.

Soviet military analyses published during 1940 and 1941 accurately assessed what the Germans had done and clearly articulated the implications of German success for the Soviet state in general and the Red Army in particular. These analyses conveyed the sobering message that a fate similar to that of France might befall the Soviet Union, and it provided a stimulus for subsequent Soviet defensive planning. Overnight, Soviet strategic plans began focusing on defensive measures, if only to permit the General Staff time to correct recent errors and restore a genuine deep operational capability to the Red Army.

Soviet strategic planning on the eve of Barbarossa reflected an understandable dichotomy between adherence to traditional offensive concepts (which was, in part, ideologically driven) and Soviet realization that only a well-founded defense could guarantee the near-term safety of the Soviet state. While the Soviets embarked on a program to increase the size of the Red Army and restructure and reequip it to make it a formidable offensive tool (ostensibly by summer 1942), Soviet planners formulated strategic defensive plans to protect the state during this transitional period.

The program to increase the strength of the Red Army proceeded apace. Drawing upon the experiences of the Soviet–Finnish War and the War in the west, the Soviets refined their views on contemporary war, reworked mobilization plans and operational-strategic war plans, accelerated force training, created central control organs, and prepared command cadre. While implementing this program, they began a force regrouping, which culminated in a major strategic deployment of forces from May into June 1941. Despite extreme turbulence in the High Command (which saw three chiefs of the General Staff between August 1940 and July 1941), a new strategic defensive plan emerged. Actual Soviet force deployments before Operation Barbarossa evidenced the nature of that strategic defense, which, in turn, provided context for combat in the initial stages of Barbarossa.

During the 1930s international conditions turned ugly and threatening for all actors on the international stage. Economic dislocation, growth of totalitarianism, and rampant social discord raised international tensions, increased the likelihood of future war, and altered the very nature of war. In the Soviet Union, it resulted in a major rearmament program and an intense focus on war plans and strategic defense. In the end, despite all Soviet exertions, the strategic defense essentially failed.

CHAPTER 5

SOVIET MILITARY STRATEGY IN THE SECOND WORLD WAR (1941–1945)

THE FIRST PERIOD OF WAR (22 JUNE 1941–18 NOVEMBER 1942)

General

The first period of war, by Soviet definition, encompassed the 17-month period from 22 June 1941, the day Operation Barbarossa began, to 19 November 1942, the day the Soviet Stalingrad counteroffensive began. Throughout this period the Germans maintained the strategic initiative, except from December 1941 to February 1942, when Soviet forces conducted the Moscow counteroffensive and temporarily forced the Germans to go on the defense. The first period of war was marked by the near destruction of the Soviet prewar army; severe alterations of the Soviet force structure to accommodate the demands of war; and serious testing of Soviet prewar operational concepts, which had proven difficult, if not impossible, to implement in wartime.

Marked weaknesses in the force structure and combat technique of the Red Army, so apparent in Soviet military operations in Poland and Finland in 1939 and 1940, were also strikingly evident during the initial period of war. The surprise German offensive accentuated these weaknesses, wrought havoc in the Red Army, and threatened its virtual destruction. Throughout the summer and fall of 1941, the Soviets sought, at huge cost, to slow and halt the expanding German offensive (see Figure 23). In late fall, assisted by deteriorating weather and overextension of German forces, the Red Army was able to halt the German onslaught and regain the initiative. In November and December, first on the flanks (Tikhvin and Rostov) and then in the center (Moscow), the Red Army launched counteroffensives that halted and threw back German forces (see figure 24). These hastily planned and crudely conducted counteroffensives surprised the Germans and thwarted achievement of ultimate German strategic aims.

In late winter 1941, as fighting waned and the front stabilized, both contending High Commands began planning operations in the spring.

104

23. The Summer–Fall Campaign, June–December 1941

The Germans postured their forces as if to continue their attack on Moscow. In actuality, however, they regrouped for a major strategic offensive across southern Russia. The Soviets were deceived by the ruse and prepared to conduct a strategic defense-in-depth in the Moscow region. To supplement that defense, the Soviet High Command planned offensives in the south, near Khar'kov and Kerch, to distract German attention and forces from the critical Moscow axis and perhaps to unhinge German defenses in the south as well. In May 1942 German forces, which had been secretly concentrated for the strategic drive in the south, utterly defeated the twin Soviet May offensives (see Figure 25).

After inflicting heavy losses on Soviet forces in the Khar'kov and Kerch operations, German Army Group South advanced on a broad front into the Donbas and toward the Don River. By mid-fall, after repelling a series of local Soviet counterattacks, German forces reached the Stalingrad and Caucasus regions. The Soviet High Command struggled to halt the German advance and simultaneously prepared for major counterstrokes of their own. Throughout the summer and fall of 1942, Soviet forces in the Leningrad and Moscow regions postured for or launched limited offensives to weaken the German southern thrust. By November 1942 the momentum of the German drive across southern Russia had ebbed, establishing favorable conditions for a Soviet offensive.

MILITARY POLICY AND STRATEGY

Soviet military policy during this critical first period of war sought to achieve the dual aims of forging an international alliance against Nazi Germany, while mobilizing the full power of the state to repel the German onslaught. The first priority was to deal with the direct military threat. Meanwhile, Stalin began pressing his Western Allies to open a second front on the continent of Europe.

The increasing scale and intensity of armed struggle on the Eastern Front, in comparison with that of previous wars, tested the traditional limits of military art. The complex demands of modern operations broadened the scope of military strategy, which, during the Great Patriotic War years, had to encompass an ever-widening circle of missions placed before it by the state's political leadership. Among military strategy's most demanding tasks were:

- working out plans for the mobilization of men and materiél, for the formation and strategic deployment of the armed forces and their use in war;

24. The Winter Campaign, December 1941–April 1942

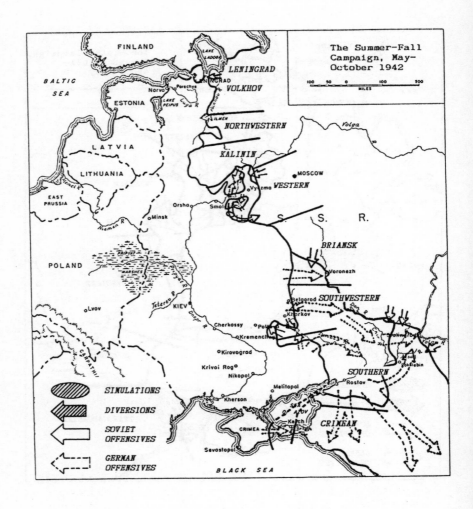

25. The Summer–Fall Campaign, May–October 1942

- working out plans for the conduct of military actions in campaigns and strategic operations;
- organizing and effecting the strategic leadership of the armed forces;
- creating strategic shock groupings;
- preparing and employing strategic reserves;
- organizing the country's air defenses;
- preparing theaters of military operations;
- determining, in accordance with existing conditions, the most effective means and forms of conducting armed struggle;
- organizing strategic cooperation between *fronts*, groups of *fronts*, and types of armed forces, and other all-around protection;
- effective use of the military-economic capabilities of the state for the achievement of victory over the enemy.

During the war years, the Soviets defined such important categories of military strategy as "periods of war", "military campaigns", "strategic operations", and other forms of strategic actions.[1]

Official Soviet statements concerning their military strategy in the first period of war emphasize the defensive nature of that strategy and the titanic struggle to regain the strategic initiative:

During the first period of the war, when the enemy held the strategic initiative, military strategy performed the tasks involved in setting up an active strategic defense, mainly employing the tactics of exhausting the enemy with determined resistance at existing created and natural positions, frustrating the enemy's plans with determined counterstrokes and conducting individual offensive operations (army and *front*). In the process the strategic defense in 1941 was established, as a rule, as a forced measure, during the course of active enemy offensive operations; in 1942 it was prepared in advance, and in 1943 it was deliberately conducted with the objective of exhausting the enemy and switching to a counteroffensive. Characteristic was an increase in the depth and number of defensive zones (*polosa oborony*). An important achievement of Soviet military strategy in the first and second periods of the war was the execution of a strategic counteroffensive near Moscow and its development into a general offensive by Soviet troops in the winter of 1941–42, and also in 1942–43 at Stalingrad.[2]

The growing scope and scale of warfare placed new demands on strategy in general and strategic leadership in particular.

War demanded the mobilization of all the strength and resources of the nation, their concentrated use in the interests of achieving victory in war, maximum centralized leadership of the state and concentration of all power in the hands of one all-powerful organ. Such an organ was the State Committee of Defense (GKO) under the chairmanship of General Secretary of the Party I.V. Stalin, which was organized on 30 June 1941 by decision of the Communist Party Central Committee, the Presidium of the USSR Supreme Soviet and the Council of Ministers of the USSR. The direction of all aspects of national life and the work of governmental and social organs was concentrated in it. Its directives became law in all matters.[3]

Based on the overall political war aims of the Soviet state, the State Defense Committee (GKO) established for the Supreme High Command (VKG) and, in general, for the armed forces, all military-political missions. In addition, the GKO determined necessary forces and equipment to fulfill these missions; established the strength of the armed forces, based on the requirements of armed conflict, economic resources needs, and existing manpower resources in the country; determined armed forces structure, equipment, and overall combat employment; and made decisions regarding changes in the organs of higher command and the appointment of command cadres for the central and *front* apparatus. Creation of the GKO and the concentration of extensive powers in its hands played a decisive role in the development of a more effective system of strategic leadership.

STRATEGIC DEFENSE

The foremost strategic problem confronting the Soviet High Command during this period was to orchestrate a successful strategic defense. Specifically, the Soviets had to halt the German general offensive, negate the advantages the Germans had derived from achieving initial surprise, counter the clear German superiority in operational and tactical skills, and establish defenses along an immense front while defending the key cities of Moscow, Leningrad and Kiev. As they struggled to halt the seemingly invincible German advance, the Soviets had to prepare and then conduct crucial counteroffensives. All this had to be done over tremendous distances and in the face of catastrophic losses in manpower, equipment, territory and in the nation's productive base.

The Red Army conducted its strategic defensive operations simultanously along several strategic directions, employing on each direction several *fronts* cooperating according to *Stavka* (High Command) plans. The practice of employing multiple *fronts* in a single strategic operation contradicted predominant prewar beliefs that single *fronts* would be able to conduct strategic defensive operations in their own right. This departure from prewar theory ultimately gave birth to new concepts involving the conduct of strategic operations by groups of *fronts*. In these strategic operations, the Soviet High Command sought to inflict maximum casualties on the enemy by weakening and bleeding his main offensive groups to slow his offensive while denying him possession of economically and politically vital regions and to create conditions suitable for counteroffensives. Strategic defensive operations raged along frontages of from 200 to 800 kilometers to depths of from 100 to 600 kilometers over a period of from 20 to 100 days.

Transition of the armed forces to the strategic defense took place under varying conditions. During the summer-fall campaign of 1941 the surprise German attack accorded German forces the strategic initiative throughout the entire initial period of war. The Soviets regained the strategic initiative temporarily between December 1941 and April 1942. Soviet operational disasters in the Crimea and around Khar'kov in May 1942 and the subsequent German strategic thrust across southern Russia mounted under a cloak of strategic deception again accorded the German High Command the strategic initiative throughout the 1942 summer and fall campaign.

During the initial period of war, the Soviet strategic defense was characterized by intense, fragmented fighting across a broad front. Within weeks of the German attack, operations had spread to encompass a front of 3,000 kilometers to depths of 400–600 kilometers. Over 350 Soviet divisions and thousands of tanks took part in the massive operation. Well organized, equipped, and trained German forces took advantage of the poorly organized and supplied Soviet formations, which also lacked sufficiently prepared engineer defenses. Soviet commands were unable to plan defensive operations in advance and simply reacted to the German thrusts. With their planning crippled, Soviet forces could only react until the attrition and exhaustion of German forces and the presence of newly mobilized Soviet forces could combine to halt the German offensive and restore stability to the front. The experiences of the initial strategic defense in 1941 and 1942 convinced the Soviets that defense with inadequate forces in an unprepared theater of operations led to catastrophic losses in territory, equipment, and manpower.

To halt the German offensive, ultimately the Soviets had to organize

111

and conduct between two and four distinct consecutive strategic defensive operations along each strategic direction, which developed as follows:

Leningrad (Northwestern) Direction –
   Defensive operations in Lithuania and Latvia – 22 June–9 July 1941
   Leningrad defensive operation – 10 July–30 September 1941

Moscow (Western) Direction –
   Defensive operations in Belorussia – 22 June–10 July 1941
   Smolensk operation – 10 July–10 September 1941
   Distant approaches to Moscow – 3 September–7 November 1941
   Close approaches to Moscow – 14 November–5 December 1941

Kiev (Southwestern) Direction –
   Defensive operations in the western Ukraine – 22 June–11 July 1941
   Defensive operations at the Korosten and Kiev Fortified Regions – 10 July–9 September 1941
   Uman defensive operation – 15 July–4 August 1941
   Kiev defensive operation – 10–29 September 1941

During 1942 strategic defensive operations developed in an entirely different fashion. The German High Command struck only along the southwestern direction, where Soviet forces engaged in both positional and maneuver defense, while forces along the remainder of the front defended or launched local offensives. Over the course of the long five-month summer campaign, Soviet forces conducted three consecutive defensive operations along the southwestern direction. These operations included Voronezh–Voroshilovgrad (28 June–24 July 1942), Stalingrad (17 July–18 November 1942), and North Caucasus (28 July–31 December 1942).

Among the features which increased the effectiveness of the strategic defense in 1942 were timely detection of enemy strategic aims and concentration of main forces on the axis of his advance; skillful construction of strategic defenses; timely reestablishment of a strategic defensive front; creation and more skillful employment of strategic reserves; and the successful organization of close coordination between large groups of forces operating on various strategic directions.

In 1941 Soviet failure to determine quickly German priority strategic aims led, in part, to the great depth of the German advance. Only after almost six months of combat were the Soviets able to halt the advance on

112

the outskirts of Moscow, at a time when German forces had already advanced between 850 and 1,200 kilometers. According to Soviet judgements:

> The ultimate aims of the strategic defense in that campaign were achieved to a considerable degree thanks to the fact that the *Stavka* VGK, in spite of huge errors in determining the main blow of the enemy on the eve of war, was able to determine correctly the Moscow direction as the main and decisive one, and during the course of the entire campaign devoted special attention to it.[4]

By skillfully shifting strategic reserves and concentrating them on the western direction, the *Stavka* was able to tilt the correlation of forces in the Soviets' favor and halt the enemy offensive.

Unlike the case in 1941, in 1942 the Soviet High Command was able to detect the axis of the main German thrust earlier during the initial defensive operation (Voronezh). Consequently, the *Stavka* could withdraw successfully most of its forces and, in the course of almost five months, halt the German thrust at a depth of from 650–1,000 kilometers.

From these massive 1941 and 1942 operations, the Soviets learned that the resilience of strategic defenses depended directly on the depth of the strategic grouping of forces and the extensiveness of engineer preparations in the theater of military operations. This was a particularly vexing problem for the Soviets in 1941, when their force densities were low, reserves were inadequate, and engineer fortifications weak and scattered. While the High Command formed and committed some reserves to combat during the early days and weeks, only during the strategic defensive operation at Moscow did the Soviets possess enough forces to establish a full two-echelon strategic defense. At Moscow the first echelon consisted of the Western and Briansk Fronts and the second, of the Reserve Front. Despite the two-echelon configuration, the depth of the defense still did not exceed 80 kilometers. In 1942 the depth of Soviet strategic defenses increased to 100 to 120 kilometers, and, as a consequence, the defenses were far more credible and resilient.

During the first period of war, the Soviets amassed considerable experience in conducting *front* and army defensive operations. *Fronts* defended along operational directions under *Stavka* control, and armies defended according to *front* plans. Shortages of men and material forced the Soviets to deploy the bulk of their forces in a single shallow operational echelon with only small reserves (in violation of prewar concepts). Concentrated German armor supported by aviation easily pierced these shallow, poorly prepared defenses. As Soviet mobilization progressed and weapons production improved, however, they were able to increase

113

weapons densities and create deeper defenses. By the fall of 1942 Soviet combined-arms armies formed their first army artillery groups, air defense groups, and artillery and antitank reserves. The combined-arms army's defensive depth increased to as much as 20 kilometers, its average operational density to 10 kilometers of front per rifle division, and the average weapons density to 15–25 guns per kilometer of front. By the end of 1942, army and *front* defensive depths averaged 15 and 30 kilometers respectively, with the first defensive belt best developed, consisting of battalion defensive regions. The fragmented nature of the defense, however, isolated subunits and hindered maneuver of forces along the front and in its depths.

Throughout the first period of war, the Soviets emphasized improvements in antitank defenses, which had been ineffective early in the war due to the paucity of weapons and the tendency of commanders to scatter them evenly across the front. Heavy caliber artillery and aviation had similarly been ineffective against enemy armor. Although antitank artillery remained scarce (less than five guns per kilometer), by mid-1942 the Soviets began creating antitank regions (strong points) echeloned in depth along likely tank axes of advance. Eventually Soviet attachment of antitank reserves from *front* and army commands to lower command echlons increased the density and mobility of antitank defenses. After the summer of 1941, artillery customarily engaged enemy armor units to supplement other antitank defenses (often in a direct fire role).

Engineer preparations of the theater of military operations, which were woefully weak in 1941, likewise improved in 1942. This was particularly important with regard to rear defensive lines, which operational and strategic reserves could occupy before and during each operation. In 1941 German offensive progress was slowest where such defensive lines and fortifications existed, such as along the southwestern direction, where the Rava–Russkaia, Peremysl', Novogorod–Volynskii, Korosten', and other fortified regions impeded forward progress. The significant impact of these regions on the course of operations led the *Stavka* early in the war to order construction of a series of new rear defensive lines (24 June – Luga defensive belt to cover approaches to Leningrad; 25 June–defensive line from Nevel' through Vitebsk and Mogilev to Kremenchug; 28 June – Viaz'ma defensive line; mid-July – Mozhaisk defensive line). This process continued as German forces penetrated existing defenses. On 12 October 1941 the *Stavka* ordered construction of extensive defenses around Moscow, and soon after the GKO ordered creation of yet another defensive line along the east bank of the Volga River anchored on the cities of Iaroslavl', Saratov, Stalingrad and Astrakhan. Similar measures were implemented along the southwestern direction covering Kiev,

Odessa, the Crimea, the Donbas, Stalingrad, and finally the Caucasus. These defenses were built by engineer-sapper units (later sapper armies) and by the local population.[5]

This extensive engineering work ultimately produced rear defensive lines to a depth of 200–400 kilometers in late 1941 and a depth of up to 600 kilometers in 1942. Despite this immense work, a wide range of problems continued to inhibit the effectiveness of deep strategic defenses. Lack of engineer expertise and requisite construction materials hindered timely erection of defensive lines, and the rapid enemy advance often pre-empted their occupation by Soviet forces. Compounding these problems, withdrawing forces had insufficient strength to occupy the deep defenses before the arrival of newly assembled strategic reserves.

> Thus, of 291 rifle divisions and 66 rifle brigades dispatched by the *Stavka* VGK in the summer of 1941 to operating armies, only 66 divisions (22.6 per cent) and 4 brigades (6 per cent) were used ahead of time for the occupation of rear defensive lines ... The complex problem of strategic defense, which the *Stavka* VGK devoted much attention to during the course of war, was a problem of preservation of the integrity of the strategic front.[6]

Once strategic defenses had been penetrated, the Soviet High Command faced a series of serious problems associated with their reestablishment. First, the combat capability of first strategic echelon forces had to be restored. Then new strategic defenses had to be erected and occupied by newly created and regrouped strategic reserves. This was done in 1941 and 1942, first by determining enemy strategic intentions, identifying the most critical strategic sectors and estimating the size of the potential strategic penetration, and then by correctly selecting and occupying new strategic defensive lines. The first such experience occurred in June and July 1941 along the northwestern and western directions. To forestall the German advance, the *Stavka* created a new defensive line extending from Pskov and Ostrov southward along the Western Dvina and Dnepr Rivers, at a depth of 200 kilometers. Between 27 June and 10 July 1941, the *Stavka* occupied this line with five combined-arms armies from the strategic reserve. Consequently, on the northwestern direction by 20 July, a contiguous defensive front had been restored, and German plans to seize Leningrad from the march were disrupted.

On the western direction, although German forces successfully pene-trated Dnepr River defenses, fresh Soviet reserves halted German forces during the Smolensk operation (10 July–10 September 1941), which eventually had a major impact on the timing and success of the sub-sequent German thrust on Moscow.

115

For the first time in World War II, German-fascist forces were forced to cease their offensive on the main direction and go over to the defense. An important result of the Smolensk operation was the winning of time for the strengthening of the restored strategic defensive front in the Moscow direction, for the preparation of the capital's defenses and for the subsequent defeat of the Hitlerites before Moscow.[7]

In the fall of 1941 the Soviet task of restoring the strategic defensive front was complicated by the Germans having penetrated Soviet defenses along both the southwestern and western directions, and *Stavka* reserves were inadequate to restore the entire front. Ultimately, stabilization of the front along the Mozhaisk defense line west of Moscow permitted the High Command to regroup and concentrate sufficient strategic reserves both to halt the Germans and to launch the 5 December 1941 counter-offensive. Along the southwestern direction, the Soviets were unable to erect such strong defenses. Only the gradual weakening of German forces through attrition and Soviet reestablishment of its Southwestern and Southern Fronts' strength permitted restoration and stabilization of the front in November. Even with the front stabilized, the Soviets still erected another web of rearward defense lines through Kostroma, Vladimir, Tambov and Stalingrad.

Stabilization of the front required, first and foremost, the reestablishment of first echelon strength by means of reinforcement or restoration of formations during the defensive operation. During fall 1941 this process involved full or partial restoration of 23 Western Front divisions and 27 Southwestern Front divisions. Regrouping of forces also played a critical role in restoring the stability and viability of strategic defenses. To strengthen the Mozhaisk line, the *Stavka* regrouped into the region 14 rifle divisions, 16 tank brigades, and over 40 artillery regiments, many transferred from the Northwestern and Southwestern Fronts.[8]

Among the many combat techniques the Soviets relied on to slow the German advance were successive delaying operations and counterattacks in the Southwestern Front sector and fighting in encirclement (although not by design) and from positional defenses along the Moscow direction. Throughout these operations constant counterattacks and counter-strokes sapped German strength and gained time for the assembly of reserves. Ultimately, in addition to reestablishing a strategic defense in the fall of 1941, the *Stavka* orchestrated a regrouping of strategic reserves sufficient to launch the first Soviet strategic counteroffensive of the war, the Moscow counteroffensive.

During the summer of 1942 the *Stavka* faced the task of restoring the strategic defense after a major German strategic thrust had shattered the Soviet defensive front along the southwestern direction. Complicating this task was the fact that the German thrust isolated Soviet strategic reserves north of the Middle Don River by cutting north-south rail lines and forced all Soviet strategic regrouping to move southward via the Volga River and central Asia. Initial *Stavka* attempts to reestablish first strategic echelon defenses in the vicinity of Veshensk, Millerovo, and Rostov failed, and German forces penetrated 150–400 kilometers toward Stalingrad along a front of 500 kilometers. Faced with these realities, the *Stavka* designated a new defense line along the Don River through Stalingrad and Astrakhan' to the Caucasus Mountains.

Unlike the situation in 1941, in 1942 the *Stavka* relied on ten newly formed reserve armies and other divisions transferred from the Far East to reestablish its strategic defenses. The *Stavka* also conducted offensive operations elsewhere along the front to tie down German forces and prevent their transfer south (Western and Kalinin Fronts' Rzhev–Sychevka Operation, Northwestern Front's Demiansk operation, and the Leningrad and Volkhov Fronts' Siniavinsk operation). Once the strategic defense had been reestablished, the Soviets again seized the strategic initiative in the Stalingrad sector.

Strategic reserves played a significant role in the strategic defense by establishing new defense lines, liquidating enemy penetrations, and providing forces necessary to launch counteroffensives. During this period the *Stavka* retained from two to ten reserve armies under its direct control. These reserve armies were instrumental in slowing and containing the German onslaught and launching the winter counteroffensive around Moscow in 1941–42, the abortive Khar'kov offensive in May 1942, and finally the Stalingrad offensive of November 1942 (see Appendix 1).

Stavka employment of strategic reserves during the summer–fall campaign of 1941 was of unprecedented scale. From 22 June to 1 December 1941, the *Stavka* committed to combat from its reserves 291 rifle divisions and 94 rifle brigades. The basic mass of the reserves (85 per cent) consisted of new formations prepared for combat in a short period. Hence, these were often undersize, and their combat capabilities were limited. The *Stavka* committed 150 divisions and 44 brigades to the critical western direction and 141 divisions and 50 brigades to the northwestern and southwestern directions. During the summer–fall campaign of 1942 strategic reserves consisting of 72 rifle divisions, 11 tank and mechanized corps, two cavalry corps, 38 tank brigades, 100 artillery regiments, and 10 aviation regiments reinforced Soviet forces operating on the Stalingrad direction. Of these reserves, 25 rifle divisions, three

117

tank corps, and three mechanized corps stiffened the principal shock forces which conducted the Stalingrad counteroffensive operation.[9]

Strategic reserves increased both the strength and the depth of strategic defenses and, ultimately, provided numerical superiority necessary for the Red Army to make the transition to the offensive. For example, between 1 October and 5 December 1941, Western Front strength increased as follows:

Western Front Composition

Type Force	1 October 1941	5 December 1941
rifle divisions	30	50
rifle brigades	1	16
aviation divisions	5	8
cavalry divisions	3	16
tank brigades	3	22
artillery regiments-RVGK	28	53
guards mortar battalions	1	30
separate antiaircraft battalions	11	16[10]

The *Stavka* increased defensive depths during the Smolensk operation by assignment of six strategic reserve armies (29th, 30th, 24th, 28th, 31st, 33rd) to the second echelon of the Western Front. These armies were assembled from NKVD units, regular forces, and people's militia forces of the Moscow Military District.[11] At Moscow a reserve *front* and forces of the Moscow defense zone backed up first echelon defending *fronts*. Throughout defensive operations on high priority directions, strategic reserves also participated in more than 40 local offensives or counterattacks to tie down and weaken enemy forces.

Soviet assessments accord great importance to the use of strategic reserves, in particular during the harrowing first two years of war.

Timely and skillful introduction into battle of *Stavka* VGK strategic reserves during the summer-fall campaign of 1941 and 1942 was one of the important factors in the achievement of the aims of strategic defense in the first period of war. In both campaigns strategic reserves not only permitted the exhaustion and bleeding white of ememy shock groups and the halting of their offensive, but also guaranteed the successful transition of Soviet forces to the counteroffensive and the development of a general offensive.[12]

Strategic cooperation (*vzaimodeistvie*) also facilitated successful erection of strategic defenses. Cooperation was organized:

by mission, by direction, and by variant of action: strategic (*Stavka* VGK and General Staff) – between groups of Soviet Armed Forces operating on various strategic directions; and operational-strategic within the realm of one strategic defensive operation (high command of strategic directions and representatives of the *Stavka* VGK) – between elements of the operational-strategic formation of forces and large formations of types of armed forces.[13]

The Soviet High Command had particular difficulty in organizing strategic cooperation in 1941 and 1942 because of the circumstances surrounding the German offensives, in particular the loss of strategic initiative. During the strategic defense, the *Stavka* specified measures to disrupt the implementation of German plans. First and foremost, it planned and conducted operations on secondary directions to tie down German forces and prevent reinforcement of main German efforts (the Leningrad, Tikhvin and Rostov operations in 1941 and Rzhev–Sychevka operation in 1942). On main axis the Soviets conducted counterattacks and local offensive operations to distract and weaken the enemy. During the Stalingrad defense, these local attacks forced the Germans to commit segments of their Sixth Army and Third Rumanian and Eighth Italian Armies to combat along the Don River, thus weakening German forces at Stalingrad proper. Whenever possible, Soviet commands shifted aviation forces from secondary sectors to weight the defense on critical strategic directions. In defensive operations near major population centers (Leningrad, Moscow), air defense forces (PVO) and systems were thoroughly integrated into the ground defense to the extent of even directly engaging ground forces. The same applied to naval forces operating along coastal regions.

The basic functions of strategic cooperation during conduct of a strategic defense were:

coordination of the strength of strategic groups of forces operating on important directions with the aim of disrupting enemy plans for penetrating into large political-industrial centers; the organization and realization of counterstroke and individual offensive operations to pin down groups on one direction and to prohibit transfer of part of the force to another direction; the covering of flanks and gaps in the strategic groupings defending on main directions, and determining the time and place of commitment of strategic reserves to restore the strategic defensive front; coordination of the strength of *fronts* and fleets when conducting an operation on coastal directions; and organization of joint operations of national PVO

119

forces with *fronts* during defense of large political and economic centers.[14]

Prewar Soviet military theory had postulated that single *fronts* could successfully conduct strategic operations. During Operation Barbarossa Soviet *fronts* in the border military districts attempted to do so, but for a variety of reasons had little success. Experience quickly indicated "that one *front* was not capable of halting an offensive by a large enemy shock group and that for the achievement of strategic missions it was necessary to concentrate the forces of several *fronts* under single command".[15] This gave birth to a new form of strategic defense – a defensive operation by a group of *fronts*. By August 1941 two to three *fronts* cooperated to conduct such a defense.

During the first period of war a strategic defensive operation of a group of *fronts* became defined as "an aggregate of interconnected defensive operations of *front* large formations, operations, and combat actions of large formations and formations of long-range aviation, PVO *strany* (national air defense) forces, and fleet forces conducted according to a single concept to achieve strategic aims".[16] The aims of strategic defensive operations were varied and depended on concrete conditions and missions performed by the actual forces engaged in each campaign. While the primary Soviet objective in summer 1941 was to disrupt German offensive plans and halt the offensive, in the fall the Soviets also sought to prevent German seizure of key large cities and to prepare for counteroffensives. In 1942 the High Command defensive aims were to defend Stalingrad and the Volga River defense lines and to gain time to assemble strategic reserves with which to conduct a counteroffensive. The scale of the defense grew accordingly, as follows:

	Moscow Defensive Operation	*Stalingrad Defensive Operation*
personnel	160,000	1,250,000
guns/mortars	2,200	7,600
tanks	400	990
aircraft	454	677[17]

During the first period of war, insufficient preparation time and severe manpower and equipment deficiences plagued Soviet planning and conduct of strategic defensive operations. German achievement of initial surprise and surprise in several subsequent operations only exacerbated these problems. The Soviet penchant for overestimating their own capabilities and underestimating enemy capabilities, especially regarding armored forces, resulted in huge Soviet losses in personnel, equipment and territory. Ensuing defensive operations were of a "forced nature, and the basic means for (their) conduct was a combination of positional and maneuver forms of defensive actions, the essence of which involved successive conduct of defensive engagements and battles along lines designated beforehand and echeloned in depth, with counterattacks and counterstrokes".[18] These operations were prolonged in nature, lasting from 50 to 125 days and extending in depth from 150 to 800 kilometers.

COMMAND AND CONTROL

Strict centralization of command and control at the highest level made successful Soviet strategic defense possible. Early Soviet attempts to create three separate groups of *fronts* to cover the three main strategic directions (northwestern, western, and southwestern) failed because of inept command and control during the disastrous operations in the summer of 1941. Even before the creation of separate "direction" high commands, on 23 June 1941 Stalin and the Communist Party Politburo had created the *Stavka* of the High Command (Stavka GK) under Commissar of Defense Marshal S. K. Timoshenko, to provide "uninterrupted and qualified command and control". On 10 July 1941, when high commands were established for strategic directions, Stalin became Chairman of the renamed Supreme Command (*Stavka* VK). By 8 August Stalin reorganized the *Stavka* into the Supreme High Command (*Stavka* VGK) with himself as Supreme High Commander.[19] "Full authority for strategic leadership of the Soviet Army, Navy, border and internal forces and partisan forces was concentrated in the *Stavka* VGK. It carried all responsibility to the party Central Committee and the GKO for the conduct of military operations and the combat readiness of forces."[20]

The *Stavka* consisted of the most powerful and capable political and military leaders in the nation, and throughout wartime its composition fluctuated only slightly. In addition to Stalin, it always included the Chief of the General Staff, who was, in succession, Marshal B. M. Shaposhnikov (29 June 1941), Colonel General A. M. Vasilevsky (11 May 1942), and Army General A. I. Antonov (17 February 1945). After 17 February 1945, the *Stavka* consisted of Stalin, G. K. Zhukov, A. M. Vasilevsky, A. I. Antonov, N. A. Bulganin, and N. G. Kuznetsov.[21]

The *Stavka* was responsible for addressing an extraordinarily wide range of military-strategic questions, including:

- assessing military-political and strategic conditions,
- determining strategic missions of the armed forces in accordance with military-political aims,
- making decisions on the preparation and conduct of military campaigns and strategic operations,

- creating strategic groupings of forces,
- organizing cooperation between strategic groupings and large operational forces of all types and partisans,
- coordinating Soviet armed forces with those of allied states,
- organizing strategic *razvedka* and *maskirovka*,
- preparing and employing strategic reserves,
- materiel-technical provisioning of forces in accordance with assigned missions,
- mastering and exploiting armed forces' combat experiences.[22]

The *Stavka*, either directly or through its representatives, familiarized commanders of directions and *fronts* with the aims of each operation, provided forces and weaponry, designated missions, and organized cooperation between *fronts* and other large units. It thus provided linkages between political and military leaders and, hence, clear political control over the conduct of the war.

The working organs of the *Stavka* were the General Staff, the administration of the People's Commissariat of Defense (*Narkomat oborony* – NKO) and the People's Commissariat of the Navy (*Narkomat Voenno–Morskogo Flota* – NVMF). All three were throughly reorganized in 1941. The most important of these organs was the General Staff. The 1941 reorganization of the General Staff was designed to "concentrate to a maximum degree the strength of that organ on the operational-strategic leadership of the armed forces and free it from organizational functions".[23] A GKO order of 23 July 1941 removed from the General Staff the functions of creating new units and formations, preparing reinforcements for operating armies, and other force generation questions, leaving it to focus on strategic and operational matters.

The General Staff, functioning as a staff of the Supreme High Command, "in the course of war fulfilled a great volume of work, being in full concept its creative laboratory".[24] Among its precise functions were:

- studying and analyzing conditions at the front and reporting on these conditions to the *Stavka*,
- on the basis of *Stavka* decisions, working out plans for the use of the armed forces,
- preparing and conducting military campaigns and strategic operations,
- organizing strategic cooperation among the armed forces branches and *fronts*,
- transmitting to forces decisions, orders, and directives of the *Stavka* and supervising their fulfillment,

- supervising military *razvedka*,
- controlling the formation of reserves and their use in accordance with *Stavka* decisions,
- monitoring the condition and combat readiness of forces.

In short, the General Staff was the "main organization for the practical realization of strategic concepts and plans of military operations".[25]

The General Staff created special groups of officers, known as the General Staff Officers Corps, which provided liaison between the General Staff and operating forces. These officers provided a constant General Staff presence in *front*, army, and even corps and division staffs. Representatives of the General Staff "systematically informed the General Staff about conditions in regions of force operations, fulfilled combat missions, directives, orders and instructions of the Supreme High Command and actively assisted commanders and staffs in organizing command and control of forces".[26]

The People's Commissariat of Defense (NKO) and its subordinate organs provided all-round support for the armed forces. One of the most important NKO organs, created in August 1941, was the Main Directorate for the Formation and Manning of the Soviet Armed Forces, which raised strategic reserves and provided reinforcements for operating armies. The Main Directorate of General Military Training (*Vsevobuch*) provided military training for civilians. To provide logistical support for the Armed Forces, in July 1941 the NKO formed the Main Directorate for the Rear, headed by the Chief of Rear Services of the Red Army, who was directly responsible to the Supreme High Command. Similar positions were created in all *fronts* and armies. In the Soviet view these organs fulfilled Frunze's dictum of close cooperation between *front* and rear in both a military and an economic sense.

To further rationalize the connection between national military authorities and operating armed forces, the Soviets created chiefs of branches and types of armed and specialized forces, such as artillery, aviation, armored, engineer, signal, and air defense. These chiefs and their staffs coordinated the raising, training, allocation, and use of these forces in combat. Analogous organs with similar functions also evolved within the navy. Ultimately, by May 1942 a like staff evolved to coordinate military operations conducted by the partisan movement, the Central Staff of the Partisan Movement (TsShPD).

Other centralized organs evolved to extend tight political presence and control into military units at all levels. The Main Political Directorate of the Red Army and Navy supervised activities of the political directorates of *fronts* and fleets and political departments of armies and flotillas. Their mission was to "realize party policies and secure the fulfillment of *Stavka* orders and directives".[27] This "commissar" system extended to the tactical level within military forces. By fall 1941 the Main Political Directorate had also created special cells to organize political work in partisan formations and among the population of German occupied territories.

Party involvement in the prosecution of the war effort was nearly total. The party Politburo approved *Stavka* strategic plans. Politburo members and candidate members, serving as members of the military council of *fronts*, systematically "assisted" *front* commanders and staffs in the planning and conduct of operations. The same system extended throughout the political structure of republics, *kraes* (territories), *oblasts* (districts), and cities and, in the form of the commissar system, throughout the military chain of command.[28]

Throughout the first period of war, the *Stavka* struggled to find a system suitable for strategic direction of its armed forces, in particular the proper relationship between *Stavka* and operating *fronts*. It became apparent very quickly after 22 June 1941 that the prewar concept of single *fronts* conducting strategic-scale operations in their own right was not feasible. *Fronts* had neither the experienced personnel, the communications, nor the forces to conduct effectively operations over so large an expanse and against so experienced an enemy. On 10 July 1941, as combat raged out of control along a front extending from the Barents Sea to the Black Sea, the *Stavka* created commands of strategic directions (*glavnykh komandovanii strategicheskikh napravlenii*) as intermediate headquarters between operating *fronts* and the *Stavka*. These commands were organized as follows:

Strategic Direction	Large Formations	Commanders
Northwestern	Northern, Northwestern Fronts, Northern and Baltic Fleets	Marshal K. E. Voroshilov
Western	Western Front Pinsk River Flotilla	Marshal S. K. Timoshenko
Southwestern	Southwestern, Southern Fronts, Black Sea Fleet, Danube River Flotilla	Marshal S. M. Budenny

On 21 April 1942, in response to deteriorating military conditions in the southern Soviet Union, the *Stavka* created the North Caucasus Direction under Marshal S. M. Budenny, consisting of the Crimean Front, Sevas-

topol' defensive region, North Caucasus Military District, Black Sea Fleet, and Azov Flotilla.

Strategic direction headquarters received the missions of "exercising operational-strategic supervision of *fronts* and fleets operating on main strategic directions, coordinating their strength, insuring control over the fulfillment of *Stavka* missions, and supervising the work of the rear".[29] Although strategic directions provided a modicum of unity of command, their lack of staff and other assets hindered their effectiveness. "As war experience demonstrated, in the concrete conditions of the summer of 1941, they did not play the role assigned to them, and could not sharply improve the supervision of fronts."[30] In short, they lacked well-defined responsibilities, functions, and powers, and, since they had at their disposal no reserves, they could not influence the outcome of operations. Consequently, the *Stavka* still had to intervene directly and often in the conduct of significant operations.

As the front stabilized and communications improved in late 1941 the need for directions lessened, and they were gradually abolished. The High Command of the Northwestern Direction was dissolved on 5 September 1941, the Western on 5 May 1942, the Southwestern on 23 June 1942, and the Northern Caucasus on 19 May 1942. By the summer of 1942 the *Stavka* had assumed direct responsibility for all *front* and fleet operations without use of intermediate headquarters, but often by use of *Stavka* representatives dispatched from Moscow to field headquarters to help plan and conduct operations by *fronts* or groups of *fronts*.

"The *Stavka* VGK, having direct contact with *fronts* and fleets, possessed the capability of continuously monitoring conditions in regions of their operations, reacting early to changing conditions and rendering an influence over the combat operations of forces."[31]

Basic strategic decision-making, in principle, was accomplished in a collegial manner, although during the first two years of war, Stalin often dominated decision-making. The *Stavka* itself was a collective organ. "Important decisions on strategic questions were made after careful preparations by the General Staff and discussions within the *Stavka* with participation by leading General Staff figures."[32] Armed force and branch commanders, commanders and military council members of *fronts* and other responsible leaders and specialists participated in formulating the concept of strategic operations.

Balancing this collegiality was the principle of single command (*edinonachalie*), which meant "in all cases final strategic decisions were made and affirmed by the High Command and that no one besides the *Stavka* VGK had the right to supervise the operational activities of the Armed Forces overall, separate campaigns, and strategic operations."[33]

125

Only the *Stavka* approved plans for conducting campaigns and operations, and allocated necessary manpower and materiel resources. All other decision-making powers at lower command levels were specifically delegated by the *Stavka*.

The *Stavka* issued its decisions to *front*, fleet, and flotilla commanders in the form of directives of the High Command. The directives usually designated

> the missions, time and place of conducted operations, the forces and means allocated for their accomplishment, the direction for concentrating the main strength, the order of cooperation with neighbors, long-range aviation and the fleet (on coastal directions), and also the period provided to the *front* for the *Stavka* to approve the plan of operation. When preparing an offensive operation, as a rule the directive designated the immediate and subsequent *front* missions, the width of the penetration sector, density of forces and means, operational formations, and the means of using mobile groups and second echelons.[34]

In formulating *Stavka* directives, the General Staff, branch commanders, and chiefs of service of the People's Commissariat of Defense provided personal assistance to *front* directorates. When it was necessary during the course of operations, the *Stavka* VGK assigned *fronts* additional missions, clarified existing missions, and issued directives for the preparation of subsequent operations.

A common practice during the first period of war, which continued to occur on a lesser scale in later periods, was personal direct involvement in operations by the High Command and *Stavka*. By telephone or by personal contact (in the field or in Moscow), the *Stavka* or *Stavka* representatives issued orders to *fronts* and sometimes armies, and, reciprocally, received reports from subordinate headquarters. If oral missions were given, they were later followed by written orders. Later in the war, the *Stavka* employed its representatives to provide closer liaison with operating forces, and often *front* commanders returned to Moscow for direct face-to-face consultations with the *Stavka*.

STRATEGIC OFFENSE

The Soviets considered, and still consider, the strategic offensive to have been the basic and most decisive type of strategic action. They defined it as "a system of offensive operations, related according to single *Stavka* concept, conducted ... to achieve military-political aims of the campaign."[35] Soviet strategic offensives, usually begun as counteroffensives, developed in sectors of from 50 to 550 kilometers and penetrated to depths of from 50 to 250 kilometers. All were overly ambitious, and, because of force and logistical inadequacies, fell far short of expectations. The Soviet High Command still had to learn the art of the possible (see Appendix 2).

Normally, during the first period of war, strategic offensives were launched in the form of strategic counteroffensives after the aims of a strategic defense had been achieved. Strategic counteroffensives were designed "to destroy the enemy offensive grouping, disrupt his offensive, secure strategically important regions or lines, and secure the strategic initiative".[36] They usually took the form of a large strategic offensive operation of groups of *fronts* with attached strategic reserves. Defending *fronts* and adjacent *fronts* often participated. Just as was the case with strategic defenses, the scale of strategic counteroffensives grew throughout the first period of war:

Scale of Strategic Counteroffensive (Offensive) Operations

Forces	Moscow	Stalingrad
Fronts	3	3
Combined Arms Armies	15	10
Tank Armies	0	1
Air Armies	0	4
Divisions–Friendly	110	83
–Enemy	74	50
Tank and Mechanized Corps	0	7
Personnel–Friendly	1,000	1,103
–Enemy	1,708	1,011
Guns and Mortars–Friendly	7,652	15,501
–Enemy	13,500	10,290
Tanks and SP Guns–Friendly	774	1,463
–Enemy	1,170	675
Combat Aircraft–Friendly	1,100	1,350
–Enemy	615	1,210[37]

At Moscow Soviet forces conducted their counteroffensive against attacking German forces, while at Stalingrad the Soviets struck after the Germans had gone over to the defense, but before they had erected strong defensive positions. In both cases Soviet forces had only marginal or local force superiority.

Soviet success in counteroffensives depended directly on a number of factors, including correct calculation of the correlation of forces and selection of main attack axis; skillful creation of favorable conditions for making the transition to the offensive; timely regrouping and concentration of all types of forces; proper determination of deployment positions; careful marshalling of reserves for commitment at the decisive moment; selection of the proper time for the counteroffensive; and the attainment of secrecy in preparing the counteroffensive and to achieve surprise during its conduct. Both the Moscow and Stalingrad counteroffensives accorded the Soviets the strategic initiative. They also represented the first step in the development of a general Soviet strategic offensive across major portions of the Eastern Front.

The Soviet High Command chose as the focal point of its counteroffensives those enemy groups whose destruction would lead to "a fundamental change in the military-political conditions in a theater of military operations, on a strategic direction, or on the entire strategic front".[38] During the first period of war, German seizure of the strategic initiative largely dictated to the *Stavka* where the counteroffensive would have to focus, specifically against German Army Group Center around Moscow in the winter campaign of 1941–42 and against German Army Group South (A, B, Don) in the Stalingrad and Caucasus regions during the winter campaign of 1942–43. Both strategic counteroffensives had decisive impacts on the outcome of the war.

The factor of surprise, and its corollary, deception, played a considerable role in Soviet offensive and counteroffensive planning, although its effects were less significant in the first period of war than later. Soviet offensive action at Tikhvin and Rostov in November 1941, surprises in their own right, also contributed to Soviet achievement of surprise at Moscow in the December 1941 counteroffensive, as did the Soviet decision to shift to the counteroffensive without any operational pause. The Soviets repeatedly attempted to conduct operational deception (*maskirovka*) in accordance with well-defined prewar views. While their attempts to do so were often unsuccessful, they did succeed in preparing and implementing effective deception plans for their limited offensives at Rostov (December 1941), Moscow–Toropets (January 1942), and Barvenkovo–Lozovaia (January 1942). An effective Soviet operational deception at Khar'kov (May 1942) fell victim to an even more successful German strategic deception plan.[39]

During the first period of war, when Soviet force superiorities were lacking or only marginal, strategic offensives consisted of consecutive offensive operations launched in separate sectors of the front. In the winter campaigns of 1941–42 and 1942–43, these offensives embraced less than 50 per cent of the front. In the case of 1941–42, the Moscow, Tikhvin, Demiansk, Barvenkovo, Rostov, and Kerch operations encompassed up to 2,000 kilometers of the total 4,000 kilometer front. The winter campaign the next year expanded to include 3,000 kilometers of the 6,000-kilometer front.

Offensive operations conducted during 1941 and 1942 provided the Soviets with combat experience necessary to effect improvements in their offensive operational techniques. In their largest scale offensive, the Moscow winter offensive of 1941–42, Soviet *fronts* advanced in sectors 300–400 kilometers wide and armies in sectors 20–80 kilometers wide, with objectives at depths of 120–250 kilometers for *fronts* and 30–35 kilometers for armies. These objectives were to be secured within a period of 6–8 days. The tendency on the part of Soviet commanders to disperse their attacking forces over too broad a front prompted *Stavka* corrective action. *Stavka* Directive No. 3 (dated 10 January 1942) required commanders at all levels to concentrate their forces and to create shock groups, which they could employ to achieve penetrations in relatively narrow and critical *front* sectors.[40] The directive established penetration sectors of 30 kilometers for *fronts* and 15 kilometers for armies. These measures permitted generation of higher artillery densities on main attack direction (from 7–12 guns/mortars per kilometer in summer–autumn 1941 to 45–65 guns/mortars in the summer of 1942).

The offensive operational formation of *fronts* throughout the entire first period of war was single echelon, at first with a two- or three-rifle division reserve, and later with a tank or cavalry corps in reserve. Armies also formed in single echelon throughout 1941. In 1942, however, an increase in army strength permitted army commanders to deploy their forces in two echelons with a combined-arms reserve; mobile forces (a mobile group); artillery groups; and antitank, tank, and engineer reserves. As a result, the depth of the army operational formation increased to 15–20 kilometers and, in some instances, 30–40 kilometers.[41]

The operational role of Soviet armor increased both offensively and defensively. The Soviets used the small tank brigades of 1941–42 in close coordination with cavalry and airborne forces to stiffen infantry defense, launch counterattacks and spearhead pursuits. These mobile forces, however, had limited sustaining power and were difficult to resupply and coordinate with infantry. In 1942 newly formed tank armies, tank corps, and mechanized corps provided better means for countering German armored thrusts and exploiting success while functioning as mobile groups of *fronts* and armies. The composition of these fledgling armored forces, however, was unbalanced because of a marked shortage of mechanized infantry and their strange mixture of hoofbound, footbound, and trackbound forces. Hence, they were difficult to coordinate with other types of forces, they were vulnerable when isolated from their supporting infantry, and Soviet commanders simply had not learned how to use them properly. A special order of the People's Commissariat of Defense (Order No. 325), issued on 16 October 1942, pondered mobile group failures (such as the débâcle at Khar'kov in May 1942), directed that tank and mechanized corps be used as single entities for powerful attacks or counterattacks, and prohibited the fragmented use of those valuable operational formations.[42]

Strategic reserves also played a significant role in strategic offensive operations in the form of reserve armies, divisions, regiments, and even *fronts* (Reserve *Front* at Moscow in 1941). During the two critical periods of strategic defense in 1941 and 1942, 85 per cent of reserve forces consisted of new formations in the strategic rear, while 15 per cent were units withdrawn from the front for reorganization and refitting.[43] This reflected the difficulty in withdrawing large formations from existing *fronts* when the enemy possessed the strategic initiative.

Strategic cooperation during strategic offensive operations during the first period of war was more difficult to achieve than in later periods, primarily because offensive operations were usually hastily planned. From its central position, the *Stavka* was able to coordinate operations on the flanks (at Tikhvin and Rostov) with the most critical Moscow counteroffensive. Further refinements of cooperation during offensives would mature in later periods of war.

As was the case with strategic defensive operations, by late 1941 the *Stavka* realized the utility of groups of *fronts* conducting strategic offensive operations. Beginning with the counteroffensive at Moscow "large military-political missions in campaigns were resolved by the forces of several *fronts* in cooperation with other types of armed forces".[44] At Moscow nine *fronts* operated offensively in a 2,000-kilometer sector. As yet, however, operations by groups of *fronts* remained crude. *Stavka* and *front* commands had much to learn regarding concentration, selection of principal offensive axes, support of ground forces, and the intricacies of large-scale envelopment operations. At Moscow, although the Soviets achieved some success, they failed to execute operations properly in virtually all of these respects.

CONCLUSIONS

Soviet military strategy in the first 17 months of war evidenced unevenness and uncertainty, which, in turn, reflected the complex nature of the initial period of war, the unpredictable subsequent course of combat, inexperience within the Soviet High Command, and the heightened role of personality (namely Stalin's) on the workings of the *Stavka*. The "Stalin" factor operated throughout to pervert the nature of prewar assessments and shape military strategy once war had commenced.

The catastrophic course of combat in June and July 1941, produced in part by erroneous prewar assessments, stripped the initiative from Soviet strategic planners. As a result, the newly emergent *Stavka* was limited to reactive planning based on the single imperative of restoring stability to the front. Virtually all strategic decisions throughout the summer and fall reflected that reality. Throughout the period, the single most redeeming factor was the single-minded effort by the *Stavka* to amass strategic reserves and apply them at the point of most acute danger. This process capitalized on the innate strength of the Soviet state – her large population – and exploited the most obvious German weaknesses – a limited supply of manpower and an inability to establish strategic priorities. By playing that strength against German weakness, the Soviets were able to maintain a reasonable correlation of forces and, ultimately, achieve their preeminent strategic aim of conducting a viable strategic defense and halting the German drive, albeit just short of its initial strategic objectives. Exploitation of this strength enabled the Soviets to survive several strategic defeats and compensated for a host of obvious Soviet weaknesses. All the while, Soviet military leaders amassed experience, realizing that failure educates those who survive.

Throughout this period Stalin was the dominant figure. Although he personally unified the Soviet strategic effort, his personal power and threatening demeanor intimidated the General Staff and high-level military leaders. Often operating on the basis of whim and prejudice, his subjective judgments frequently overcame objective reality. His single-minded insistence upon marshaling reserves and his ruthless, but often stingy, allocation of those reserves strengthened the Red Army strategically, but his meddling in strategic and operational decision-making often produced disaster. At Moscow the energy and determination of the counterattacking Red Army, in part, reflected his strength of will. Strategic blunders notwithstanding, the threadbare Red Army of December 1941 fought with a ferocity and desperation mirroring the determination and ruthlessness of its leader.

Again, in 1942 Stalin's misjudgements, which he forcibly imposed on the High Command, produced disaster after disaster until in November 1942 he replicated his positive performance of December 1941. According to one Soviet critic:

The defeat of the Red Army on the southern wing of the Soviet-

131

German front could not be explained by the peculiarity of conditions, since it served in some measure to justify our defeat in the summer of 1941. The chief reason for the failure of the summer's campaign of 1942 was the mistaken decision of the High Command "to affix" to the strategic defensive operation numerous individual offensive operations on all fronts. This resulted in a dispersal of strength and a premature expenditure of strategic reserves that certainly doomed the Stalin plan to failure.[45]

By fall 1942, however, there was increasing evidence that Stalin was heeding the counsel of his, by now, tested and more trusted key military advisors (such as Zhukov, Vasilevsky, Antonov, and Voronev).

Throughout the first period of war, Stalin retained tight control over his political and military subordinates. He undertook harsh disciplinary measures against those he suspected of being disloyal, and he often confused individuals' combat failures or ineptitude with disloyalty.[46] To insure political reliablity of commanders, Stalin retained the onerous commissar system in the chain of command, and he backed up his strategic concepts with arbitrary and often extreme orders (like the "not a step back (*ne shagu nazad*)" order of the Stalingrad period). Commissars validated all commanders' orders, and failure to carry out these orders provided grounds for arbitrary arrest or even execution.

THE SECOND PERIOD OF WAR (19 NOVEMBER 1942– 31 DECEMBER 1943)

General

In November 1942 the *Stavka*, using several reserve armies, one tank army, and the majority of its new tank and mechanized corps, launched a surprise counterattack against overextended German, Rumanian, Hungarian, and Italian forces in the Stalingrad region (see Figure 26). The success of the ensuing operation exceeded Soviet expectations. The Soviets smashed Rumanian Third and Fourth Armies and encircled German Sixth Army and a major portion of German Fourth Panzer Army at Stalingrad. This first successful Soviet encirclement operation wrested the strategic initiative from German hands. Thereafter, the *Stavka* attempted simultaneously to reduce German forces surrounded at Stalingrad, defeat German relief attempts, and expand the Soviet offensive to encompass the entire southern wing of the Eastern Front.

As had been the case during the winter campaign of 1941–42, Stalin was overoptimistic and tried to achieve too much too soon, with too little. Soviet forces reduced the Stalingrad "Cauldron", forced the upper and

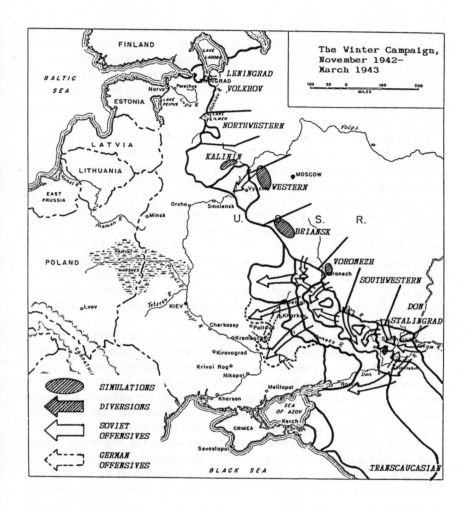

26. The Winter Campaign, November 1942–March 1943

middle reaches of the Don River, cleared the Caucasus region, and pressed westward through Khar'kov and into the Donets Basin (Donbas). Threadbare Soviet armies, led by weakened tank corps at the end of tenuous supply lines, advanced too far. A brilliant counterstroke by Field Marshal Erich von Manstein's Army Group South struck the overextended Soviet force and drove it back across the Northern Donets River, liberating Khar'kov and forming the inviting yet ominous Soviet salient around Kursk. It was on that salient that the Germans next focused their attention.

Hitler and the German High Command selected the relatively narrow Kursk sector for their next major offensive, an offensive finally launched in July 1943 in an attempt to crush Soviet operational and strategic reserves, restore equilibrium to the Eastern Front and, if possible, restore the strategic initiative to Germany (see Figure 27). For the first time in the war, at Kursk the Soviets eschewed conducting a precipitous strategic offensive and instead prepared an imposing strategic plan, unparalleled in its size and complexity, designed first to crush the advancing Germans and then to hurl them back in disorder. The strategic plan incorporated a uniquely premeditated defensive first phase to absorb the shock of the German offensive. Once the German offensive had stalled, the Soviets planned to launch massive offensives north and south of Kursk and then in other sectors as well.

The script played as the Soviets wrote it. The titanic German effort at Kursk failed at huge cost, and a wave of ensuing Soviet offensives rippled along the Eastern Front, ultimately driving German forces through Smolensk and Khar'kov back to the line of the Dnepr River. There, in a brilliantly conceived operation during the late fall, Soviet forces suddenly forded the Dnepr River north of Kiev, liberated the city, and created an extensive strategic bridgehead on the river's right bank.

The monumental struggles of mid-1943 marked the beginning of the end for the Germans. Never again could they launch a major offensive. Stripped of most of their allies and increasingly bereft of operational reserves, the Germans could only defend and delay, relying on scorched earth tactics, overtaxed Soviet logistics, and a tenuous defense to erode Soviet combat capability and impede the Soviet advance. The Germans hoped in vain that Soviet exhaustion and depleted manpower would produce stalemate or Soviet collapse in the east.

MILITARY POLICY AND STRATEGY

Soviet policy during the second period of war sought to capitalize on cascading German defeats by orchestrating a fundamental turning point

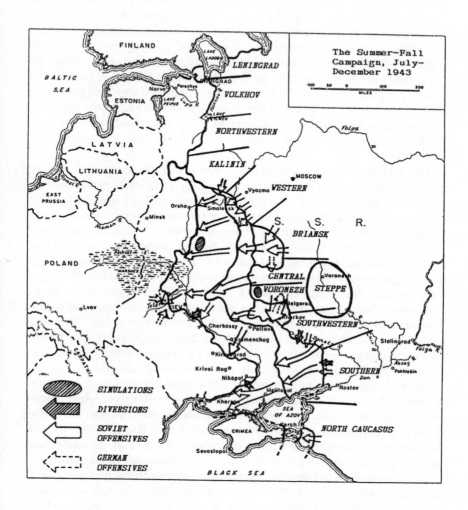

27. The Summer–Fall Campaign, July–December 1943

(*perelom*) in the war, through her own active military operations and increased cooperation with the Allies. While emphasizing the necessity for joint Soviet-Allied political and military action, principally by establishment of a strategic second front, the Soviets implemented a military strategy which would enable them to resolve the conflict, if necessary, on their own. Official Soviet pronouncements regarding its military strategy reflect that policy, stating: "During the second period of the war the Soviet Army seized the strategic initiative and secured it once and for all. All subsequent development of Soviet military strategy was related to the main type of strategic operations – the strategic offensive."[47]

The principal strategic aim of the Soviet armed forces in 1943 was to secure and maintain the initiative by using all types of strategic operations (defensive and offensive), by carefully employing field forces on critical strategic directions, by judiciously using strategic reserves, and by implementing ambitious strategic deception plans to achieve surprise. Multiple strategic offensives formed distinct campaigns, and, to an increasing extent, the Soviets planned for the entirety of the campaign. The winter and summer–fall campaigns commenced with Soviet strategic offensives at Stalingrad and Kursk, each of which began as counter-offensives. These counteroffensives were conducted by a group of *fronts* and directed by a *Stavka* representative. Each was larger in scale than any earlier counteroffensive, and involved simultaneous or successive blows delivered across a broad front. The winter offensive, conducted on the heels of the Stalingrad counteroffensive, involved four *fronts* and 18 combined-arms armies advancing in a 700 to 900 kilometer-wide sector to a depth of 120 to 400 kilometers. The summer offensive, which commenced at Kursk, involved ten fronts, 40 combined-arms and five tank armies, operating on a 2,000-kilometer front to a depth of 600 to 700 kilometers. Although the winter offensive fell short of its ambitious objectives, the summer offensive achieved virtually all of its aims.

The Soviets focused their strategic efforts during the winter campaign along the southern and southwestern strategic directions and these were far better coordinated than the Moscow operations a year earlier. The summer 1943 strategic offensive (and the summer–fall campaign) commenced in the Kursk region with initial defensive operations by a group of *fronts*. Sufficient time existed to prepare and fully man a deeply echeloned and fortified defense extending to a depth of more than 100 kilometers. Simultaneously, the Soviets massed deeply echeloned forces along the Moscow and Voronezh directions to deal with any altered German threat and to participate in the summer offensive as it developed. Soviet strategic planning included extensive deception, use of diversionary operations, and secret movement of reserves. After initial operations in the Kursk region, the Soviet strategic offensive grew to encompass the entire Eastern Front from the Moscow area southward to the Black Sea. The year 1943 also saw the rise of a strategically significant partisan movement, which disrupted the German rear area and tied down a considerable number of German.

STRATEGIC OFFENSE

The dominant form of strategic operation in the second period of war was the strategic offensive. From November 1942, with the exception of the period February–July 1943, Soviet forces possessed the strategic initiative and were almost constantly on the offensive. Throughout this period strategic offensive operation increased in scale, complexity, and decisiveness. As in 1941, strategic offensive operations normally took the form of counteroffensives, in particular those at Stalingrad and Kursk. The Kursk counteroffensive of July 1943, however, following a period of premeditated defense, gave the Soviets numerical superiority of 2.7:1 with a clearly offensive campaign plan. By August 1943 all pretext of defense disappeared, and a general Soviet offensive developed, which endured throughout the fall.

The scale of Soviet strategic counteroffensive/offensive operations grew significantly, as the statistics of the Stalingrad and Kursk operations indicate:

Scale of Strategic Counteroffensive/Offensive Operations

Forces	Stalingrad	Kursk
Fronts	3	5
Combined-Arms Armies	10	19
Tank Armies	1	5
Air Armies	4	5
Divisions – Friendly	83	134
Enemy	50	55
Separate Tank and Mechanized Corps	7	14
Personnel – Friendly	1,103,000	2,226,000
Enemy	1,011,000	900,000
Guns and Mortars – Friendly	15,501	33,000
Enemy	10,290	10,000

Tanks and SP Guns – Friendly	1,463	4,800
Enemy	675	1,800
Aircraft – Friendly	1,350	4,300
Enemy	1,210	2,100[48]

Soviet counteroffensives during the second period of war achieved greater success and were more complex than earlier efforts. At Stalingrad Soviet forces conducted their first successful large-scale encirclement of German, Rumanian, and Italian forces, in the process destroying the better part of four enemy armies (German Sixth, Rumanian Third and Fourth, and Italian Eighth). In the Belgorod–Khar'kov operation (Kursk), Soviet forces conducted a direct, deep, cutting offensive along a broad front to isolate and destroy German forces piecemeal. This offensive method ultimately forced the Germans to withdraw across the breadth of the Soviet Union to the Sozh and Dnepr River lines. Throughout this period the *Stavka* and *fronts* relied on tank armies, tank and mechanized corps, and combined-arms armies from the strategic reserve to attain strategic objectives. Strategic offensives encompassed a front of 1,000 kilometers and ranged to a depth of 250 kilometers. While the Stalingrad counteroffensive temporarily accorded the Soviets the strategic initiative, the Kursk counteroffensive forced the Germans to abandon offensive action throughout the remainder of the war. After August 1943 the Soviet armed forces conducted strategic offensives almost continuously to war's end.

Soviet strategic offensives in the summer and fall of 1943 sought to destroy German strategic groupings in the central and southern Soviet Union and clear the enemy from the RSFSR, eastern Belorussia, and the eastern Ukraine. While the Soviets achieved these aims, they were unable to destroy *in toto* any large German force grouping (army or army group).

Equipped with an almost completely revitalized force structure, manned by an increasingly experienced command cadre, and guided by new regulations which efficiently generalized war experiences, the Soviets used 1943 to experiment with strategic and operational concepts and techniques. Of particular importance was the problem of coordinating the more elaborate forces and evolving operational techniques for their use. The Soviets sought to create a capability for conducting large-scale offensive operations on a broad front in order to achieve multiple penetrations of German defenses. To do so, they relied on artful and increasingly concealed concentrations of forces and the use of shock groups. After successfully penetrating enemy tactical defenses, mobile groups of armies (tank and mechanized corps) and *fronts* (tank armies) developed the tactical successes into the operational depths. A characteristic of 1943 offensive operations was the decisive conduct of the penetration and the subsequent use of maneuver to increase the scale of the exploitation. Unlike the first period of war, when attack sectors were wide and penetration sectors imprecise, in the second period of war these sectors narrowed and became better defined. *Fronts* attacked in sectors 150–200 kilometers wide and armies in 20 to 35-kilometer-wide sectors. *Front* penetration sectors shrunk to 25–30 kilometers and army penetration sectors to 6–12 kilometers. Offensive operational densities in penetration sectors increased to 2.5–3 kilometers per rifle division and 150– 180 guns/mortars and 30–40 tanks per kilometer of front.[49]

Operational formations also matured. During the winter offensive of 1942–43, *fronts* deployed in a single echelon configuration backed up by a combined-arms reserve; however, the single echelon was stronger than before, sometimes even consisting of a tank army (of mixed composition). Responding to the growth of German defenses, by the summer of 1943, *fronts* formed in two echelons with the *front* mobile group (tank army) following the first echelon on the main attack axis. Combined-arms armies during the winter offensive organized in two echelons supported by an army mobile group (tank or mechanized corps). By the summer of 1943, combined-arms armies often formed in a single echelon of rifle corps with artillery and antiaircraft artillery groups, mobile obstacle detachments, and reserves to fulfill the immediate mission of the *front* at a depth of 60–90 kilometers. On the offense these armies used greater cover and deception and, after October 1942, routinely employed extensive operational reconnaissance before an offensive.

Mobile groups increased in importance and expanded the scope of offensive operations. Army and *front* commanders usually secretly regrouped their mobile groups and committed them on the first day of the offensive to complete or exploit the tactical penetration. The new tank armies experimented with uninterrupted operations deep in the operational depth of enemy defenses. These first experiences (not always fully successful) served as a basis for subsequent use of tank armies, singly or in combination. In sectors where mobile groups were not available, *front* and army commanders used second echelons to develop the attack, although at a slower pace.

Soviet use of artillery and air support in offensives markedly improved through development of the concepts of the artillery and air offensives. The centrally controlled artillery offensive provided better support of ground troops by subdividing army artillery groups into support groups for first echelon rifle corps. Supporting fires were designed to precede and accompany the attack through the tactical defense, and provide artillery coverage for the advance into the operational depths.[50] The aviation offensive provided similar phasing of air support throughout the offensive.

During offensive operations the Soviets regrouped forces to develop success, to switch the impetus of attack to secondary directions, and to defeat German counterattacks. Increasingly they were able to hide this regrouping from German intelligence. High attack and pursuit tempos were achieved by the use of task-organized forward detachments, which raced ahead of main forces (in particular, in advance of mobile groups) to secure key terrain features, river crossings and road junctions, and hold them for the main force. While tempos of advance increased and the scale of operations grew, corresponding growth of German defenses continued to limit the scale of Soviet offensive success, as did the systematic German destruction of the regions they abandoned.

The role of surprise increased in importance considerably during the second period of war. The necessity of penetrating heavier enemy defenses required the High Command to launch unexpected attacks to avoid undue casualties and prevent the enemy repelling the attack. Better Soviet understanding of German operational methods and more experienced commanders and forces permitted the Soviets to plan and conduct surprise offensives regarding the timing, location, and form of attack. This was facilitated by greater Soviet planning secrecy and more effective use of feints, demonstrations, and both active and passive deception (*maskirovka*).[51]

At Stalingrad the *Stavka* conducted a secret strategic regrouping of forces, concealed the bulk of its offensive preparations, and orchestrated diversionary operations on the Moscow direction to achieve strategic surprise along the Don and Volga Rivers. At Kursk it was even more difficult to achieve surprise because of heavier force concentrations on both sides and the relative transparency of both German and Soviet intent. The Soviets did achieve operational surprise largely due to the concealed scale of their defensive preparations and a degree of strategic surprise in the counteroffensive phase because of their large-scale secret regrouping of strategic reserves, diversionary operations in the south, and their decision to launch their counteroffensive so soon after the German Kursk offensive had failed. In the fall of 1943, the Soviets again successfully achieved strategic surprise through deception, particularly in the conduct of the Kiev operation, which provided Soviet forces with a strategic bridgehead across the Dnepr River.

Complexity of strategic operations also grew. Two principal methods evolved: a series of successive operations (by front or in depth) by groups of *fronts* operating on various strategic directions; and the launching of simultaneous operations on many or all strategic directions. The *Stavka* resorted to the first method in the winter campaign of 1942–43 until the offensive momentum ebbed along the Northern Donets River in February 1943. It used the same method in the summer–fall campaign (Kursk and post-Kursk), although the breadth of the offensive frontage and the frequency and strength of the offensives grew to embrace all operating *fronts* from north of Smolensk to the Black Sea.

Throughout the second period of war, strategic reserves continued to play a critical role. While during the first period most reserves had been formed anew in the rear, during the second period the correlation of forces and strategic initiative shifted in the Soviets' favor. This permitted the *Stavka* to withdraw and reequip large formations from operating forces. Thus 70 per cent of strategic reserves comprised formations withdrawn from operating *fronts* and 30 per cent were new formations. Most reserves maintained their former organizational structure, as well as a nucleus of trained and combat-experienced individuals (for example 3,000 per rifle division) and were, hence, more effective when again committed to combat.[52] This, in turn, reduced the preparation time for new strategic offensives.

The quantity of strategic reserves under *Stavka* control doubled in the second period of war in comparison with the first period, particularly regarding mobile ground and air formations. Most of these reserves were employed to conduct ever larger-scale offensive operations. For example, during the summer–fall campaign of 1943, the *Stavka* strengthened its forces on the southern wing of the Eastern Front by committing from *Stavka* reserves nine combined-arms armies, two tank armies, one cavalry and two tank corps, and three cavalry divisions. During the Kursk operation, the *Stavka* released the reserve Steppe Front to combat, and its armies participated first in the Kursk defense, and then provided shock group forces to spearhead the Belgorod–Khar'kov operation (5th Guards, 5th Guards Tank, 53rd Armies). Once the Belgorod–Khar'kov operation had commenced, the *Stavka* strengthened attacking *fronts* by releasing additional armies from its control (47th Army). Still other *Stavka* reserves secured the flanks of offensives and helped repulse enemy counterattacks (4th Guards Army). In general terms, all these uses of the strategic reserves contributed to the strength, sustainability, and depth of offensive operations.

The *Stavka* and *front* commands gained a tremendous amount of experience in command and control (cooperation) of massive multi-*front* forces on an expanding frontage and to great depths in the winter campaign of 1942–43. From 19 November 1942 to 24 January 1943, the *Stavka* committed eight *fronts* into offensive action. Beginning in the immediate environs of Stalingrad, by late January the offensive had

141

expanded to embrace the region from Kursk in the north to Novorossiisk in the south. The forward progress of the offensive waned only after Soviet forces themselves had become overextended, and fresh German reserves (II SS Panzer Corps) were available to participate in counterstrokes of their own.

Prior to and during the summer–fall campaign of 1943 Soviet long-range and frontal aviation for the first time conducted several large-scale air operations to disrupt German transport and communications and weaken German air power.[53] In the accompanying ground counteroffensive and offensives, the *Stavka* coordinated the operations of strategic groupings in both the center and on the left wing of the Eastern Front. Supplementing these complex efforts, Soviet partisans, under strategic guidance of the *Stavka*, also conducted special operations like "Railroad War" and "Concert" to disrupt German communication networks further and inhibit movement of reserves.[54] In August–September 1943 five *fronts* on the southwestern direction cooperated with long-range air and naval forces to clear German forces from the left bank of the Ukraine and the Donbas region to a depth of 600 kilometers. These and other massive operations coordinated by the *Stavka* produced significant strategic gains but, even more important, paved the way for even larger-scale strategic operations in the future.

Strategic offensive operations by groups of *fronts* matured during the second period of war. After the Battle of Kursk, they became the preeminent method of conducting strategic offensive operations, although until 1944 groups of *fronts* conducted relatively linear operations, while avoiding the more complex and difficult to coordinate envelopment and encirclement operations (with the exception of the earlier Stalingrad operation). The most characteristic form of strategic offensive operation in 1943 was the deep cutting blow (*glubokii rassekaiushchii udar*) designed to penetrate to the depth of the enemy's defensive formation. The Belgorod–Khar'kov operation (August 1943) was most representative of this technique and was one of the first such operations.[55] Forces from the adjoining flanks of two *fronts* (Voronezh and Steppe), supported by two tank armies, launched the main blow. Resulting overwhelming force superiorities (3:1 operationally and 8:1 tactically) produced rapid penetration of German defenses and exploitation to a depth of 120 kilometers within seven days. Characteristic of this period of war, however, this form of operation resulted in only limited enemy encirclements, and the advance of exploiting forces was finally checked by redeployed German operational reserves. A similar pattern characterized the Soviet Kiev offensive operation of November 1943.

In 1943 the Soviets also broke up large defending enemy groups by a series of powerful strikes by groups of *fronts* across a broad front and along several axes. Subsequently, Soviet forces developed the offensive into the depths along parallel or diverging directions. This produced fragmentation of enemy defenses, isolation of enemy units from one another, and often a general enemy withdrawal. (An exception was the January–February 1943 Donbas and Khar'kov operations where the Soviet offensive expanded to such an extent that attacking forces became dispersed and weak, thus becoming susceptible to counterattack and defeat in detail.) The first successful operation of this type took place at Orel in July and August 1943. Although these methods did confuse the German defenders, ultimately causing them to withdraw from the Orel salient, they produced no encirclements, developed slowly, and proved costly to the Soviets in terms of casualties.

The Soviets also conducted their general strategic offensive in the fall of 1943 along numerous axes across an exceedingly broad front. The ensuing unremitting pressure on German defenders caused them to collapse, and subsequently Soviet forces, spearheaded by tank armies, exploited along parallel lines to the Sozh and Dnepr River lines. While the advance was spectacular, Soviet forces in any single sector were insufficiently strong to seize a sizeable bridgehead across those two major rivers. Consequently, it would require a major strategic build-up and over a month to gain such a bridgehead on the right bank of the Ukraine.

Throughout the second period of war, the *Stavka* conducted large-scale strategic operations with ever increasing effectiveness. All indices associated with offensive success showed marked improvement. By the end of 1943 single offensive operations pushed to depths of 100–150 kilometers and operational pursuits of up to 300 kilometers. Most important, unlike the case in February 1943, when German counterattacks had forced Soviet forces back several hundred kilometers to the Northern Donets River, by year's end German counterattacks had only negligible effect on these territorial gains (Belgorod–Khar'kov, Kiev). Understandable Soviet numerical and force superiorities over the Germans also grew, permitting the *Stavka* to experiment with more complex operational methods and conditioning, to a degree, greater Soviet offensive success.

STRATEGIC DEFENSE

Unlike the first period of war, during the second period the *Stavka* employed strategic defense in the service of overall strategic offensive aims. With the maturation of defensive principles and techniques in 1943 (both Soviet and German), the nature of Soviet defenses changed.

Defensive frontages decreased as the depth of the defenses increased, thus improving defensive operational densities. By the summer of 1943, *fronts* defended sectors 250–300 kilometers wide and armies sectors of 40–70 kilometers. Defensive depths increased to 120–150 kilometers for a *front* and 30–40 kilometers for an army. Resultant operational densities in main defensive sectors amounted to 7–13 kilometers per rifle division, 30–80 guns/mortars and 7–27 tanks/self-propelled guns per kilometer of front. A defending *front* deployed in two echelons, often with a tank army in second echelon. The *front* reserve sometimes included tank and mechanized corps in addition to rifle forces. Combined-arms armies and tank armies defended in single echelon formation, supported by artillery and air defense artillery groups, antitank reserves, and mobile obstacle detachments. During the organization of a defense following an offensive operation, a *front* formed in single echelon with a tank army defending along the main direction.[56]

Antitank defenses matured considerably in the second period of war, a consequence of the increased number of army antitank regions and the presence of distinct *front* and army antitank reserves and mobile obstacle detachments. Antitank densities in main defense sectors grew to 20–25 guns per kilometer of front.[57] The general resilience of defenses also benefited from more extensive and sophisticated use of antiaircraft fire, engineer obstacles, and artillery fire, as well as from more flexible maneuvering on the part of defending units.

The most notable strategic defense in the period (and perhaps the war as a whole), the Kursk defense of summer 1943, was premeditated and rested within the clear context of an ambitious strategic offensive campaign plan. Soviet forces possessed overall force superiority in virtually every regard, but still the Germans had regained at least the operational initiative after their successful counterstrokes in the Donbas and at Khar'kov in February and March 1943. The *Stavka* decided to commence the new campaign (an inherently offensive one) by conducting a premeditated defense based on prepared defensive positions around Kursk. Knowing German propensities for attack, they wished to smash German forces in defensive fighting and then make the transition to an ever broader strategic counteroffensive. The *Stavka* planned the first two counteroffensive thrusts, one in detail at Orel and one in outline at Belgorod, before the defensive phase of the operation had begun.

Thus, the strategic defense of 1943 was fundamentally different from those of 1941 and 1942. Superior Soviet forces in possession of the strategic initiative occupied defenses of unprecedented strength designed to exploit the most prominent of German vulnerabilities – their almost irrational faith in their own invincibility. At Kursk the Soviet High

Command was able to anticipate the German offensive, "The plan of the Hitlerite command to develop a large-scale strategic offensive on the Kursk direction was detected up to three months before its commencement, which permitted Soviet forces to make all-round preparations to repel the powerful enemy attack."[58] Consequently, in the Kursk bulge, which comprised 13 per cent of the Eastern Front, the Soviet High Command concentrated in advance around one-third of its personnel and aircraft strength, half of its armor, and one-quarter of its artillery. The strategic defense successfully repulsed the German offensive in only 19 days.

Much of the Soviet success at Kursk was due to the nature of the defense itself. Strategic defenses were of unprecedented depth and well-organized in an engineer sense. The total strategic depth of 300 kilometers was more than twice as deep as the best prepared defense of 1942. Consequently, German offensive thrusts along the two principal attack axes penetrated to depths of only 12 and 35 kilometers respectively. The Kursk operation was the first instance when all defensive lines were fully developed and manned by forces in advance. First echelon defending *fronts* created five to six defensive belts, including two tactical belts with first echelon rifle corps, one army belt for second echelon rifle corps, and three *front* belts for *front* reserves and mobile forces. To the rear, the reserve Steppe Front formed additional defensive belts backed up by a "state defensive belt" along the left bank of the Don River. The tactical defensive zone alone was 15–20 kilometers deep. Heavy defensive positions on expected enemy main attack axes included three belts of up to 70 kilometers depth occupied by unprecedented densities of forces and equipment. The minefield densities of up to 2,000 mines per kilometer of front were two to three times higher than the best defenses in 1941 and 1942.[59]

The *Stavka* employed strategic reserves at Kursk to create large defensive concentrations and deeply echeloned defenses; to reinforce *fronts* during defensive operations; to create shock groups with which to conduct counteroffensives (such as 5th Guards Army and 5th Guards Tank Army transferred from the Steppe to the Voronezh Front); and to strengthen the counteroffensive blow (introduction of Steppe Front before the Belgorod–Khar'kov operation). Assembly of strategic reserves before the operation was of unprecedented scale. *Stavka* redeployed nine armies from the Northwestern and North Caucasus Fronts into the region between Moscow and Voroshilovgrad, seven of which German intelligence failed to detect.[60] In addition, it regrouped and refitted three tank armies under its control (3rd Guards, 4th, 5th Guards), one of which it used during the defensive phase (5th Guards)

145

and all of which spearheaded the offensive phases of the strategic operation, side by side with two other tank armies (1st, 2nd), which had initially taken part in the defense.

The Kursk operation was also a premier example of strategic defense conducted by a group of *fronts* with *Stavka* representatives closely coordinating operations on each strategic direction. Compared with the aims of similar operations in the first period of war, the objectives and accomplishments of the Kursk defense were far more ambitious and successful. This, in turn, was reflected by the strategic defensive indices of the operation compared with its largest scale predecessor:

Defensive Indices

Forces and Means	Stalingrad Defense	Kursk Defense
personnel	1,250,000	1,909,000
guns and mortars	7,600	26,499
tanks and SP guns	990	4,995
aircraft	677	2,172[61]

Since Soviet forces already possessed the strategic initiative and force superiority, in the second period of war the German High Command was forced to limit its offensive action to a smaller strategic sector. Soviet forces were able to concentrate their defenses in these regions and create denser, more resilient defenses than previously. While defensive operations by groups of *fronts* in the first period of war had occurred over a period of 50 to 125 days and to depths of 150–800 kilometers, during the second period defenses endured from 19 to 35 days at depths of 12–150 kilometers.[62] In essence, by July 1943 Soviet strategic defenses were virtually impenetrable.

COMMAND AND CONTROL

Command relationships between the *Stavka* and operating *fronts*, which were fully developed by late 1942, persisted throughout the second period of war. *Stavka* decisions were dispatched to *front* and fleet commands in the form of directives of the High Command. Directives specified the objectives, timing, and location of operations; forces and equipment to be employed; place of concentration and key operational directions; cooperation measures for adjacent *fronts* and fleets and supporting aviation; and time constraints on *front* planning. Directives also provided initial and subsequent *front* missions, the width of penetration sectors, force densities, operational formation, and the use of mobile groups and second echelons. The General Staff, armed forces branch chiefs, and chiefs of services of the Commissariat of Defense provided input for *Stavka* directives. During operations the *Stavka* issued additional missions to *fronts* as well as instructions regarding subsequent operations.

While during the first period of war *front* and even army commanders personally received *Stavka* instructions, in the second period *front* commanders seldom made personal visits to the *Stavka*. Instead they submitted written proposals, often on the initiative of the *Front* Military Council (the commander, chief of staff, and military commissar). The *Stavka* then studied and, if necessary, corrected *front* proposals before converting them into formal *Stavka* directives. Throughout this period *Stavka* representatives were assigned to assist planning and coordinate major operations by groups of *fronts*.

CONCLUSIONS

In earlier years no single unifying plan had provided a basis for a campaign, but this situation changed in the second period of the war. The Stalingrad operations took place in the context of broader strategic aims, and subsequent operations were envisioned in at least outline form. The rapid development of the offensive, however, blurred the intended strategic aim and ultimately produced confusion and limited operational defeat. During the latter stages of the operation, Stalin and, to some extent, other *Stavka* members and staff personnel, reverted to earlier bad habits. They stubbornly insisted on continuing operations despite unsettling intelligence reports. They chose to follow subjective judgment rather than objective fact, as they had in the winter of 1941–42. Similarly, they ignored the eroded strength of their forces and again fell victim to the mistake of seeking strategic ends that were disproportionate to the forces at hand. These lessons were not lost on the High Command. In the future, forces and means would be better matched against desired ends. This became a marked characteristic of the summer–fall campaign.

The summer–fall strategic campaign plan was more mature than that which had governed winter operations. The *Stavka* and General Staff planned in advance, and in some detail, for both the defensive and offensive phases of the Kursk operation. They also sketched out the principal objectives and lines of operations for the subsequent drive to the Dnepr.

After the Soviet victory at Stalingrad, Stalin initiated changes in the Red Army designed to harness the latent power of Russian nationalism in

147

the service of military victory. The changes also reflected Stalin's new confidence that he could maintain his dominant political position. A *Stavka* order converted the onerous position of military commissar into one of political deputy. Whereas the former commissar could veto a commander's military decision, the new political deputy lacked that authority. Simultaneously, the *Stavka* restored the rank of marshal and created for individual and unit battlefield prowess a series of new orders, honorifics, and decorations named after former heroes from Russian military history (Suvurov, Kutuzov, Alexander Nevsky, Bogdan Khmel'nitsky). In addition to drawing upon national sentiment, these changes seemed to offer hope for a reformed postwar Soviet Union. Collectively they formed a less tangible moral aspect of Soviet military strategy.

THE THIRD PERIOD OF WAR (1 JANUARY 1944–MAY 1945)

General

In 1944 the Soviets initiated the first of a series of successive strategic offensives collectively forming a series of campaigns, which continued virtually unabated until war's end. The January strategic offensives at the extremities of the Eastern Front against German forces around Leningrad and at Krivoi Rog and Nikopol', south of the Dnepr River, gave way in early spring to the multi-*front* Korsun'–Shevchenkovskii encirclement operation (see Figure 28). Unlike the practice in previous springs, the Soviets ignored the thaw (*rasputitsa*) and continued a series of successive *front* offensive operations, which liberated the right bank of the Ukraine and brought Soviet forces to the Rumanian borders by the end of April. While Soviet armies chopped away at the German northern flank, ultimately driving Finland from the war, a multi-*front* strategic offensive in June 1944, using successive encirclement operations within a brilliantly conceived strategic deception plan, crushed German Army Group Center in Belorussia and penetrated to the East Prussian borders (see Figure 29). A subsequent strategic blow in the Ukraine brought Soviet forces deep into Poland; they held bridgeheads across the Narev and Vistula rivers north and south of Warsaw. In August, reflecting Soviet political as well as military concerns, the Soviets launched a series of successive strategic offensives into and through the Balkans that drove Rumania from the war and propelled Soviet forces into Hungary and Yugoslavia while other Soviet *fronts* continued to grind up German forces in the Baltic region.

The Soviets began operations in 1945 with a series of simultaneous

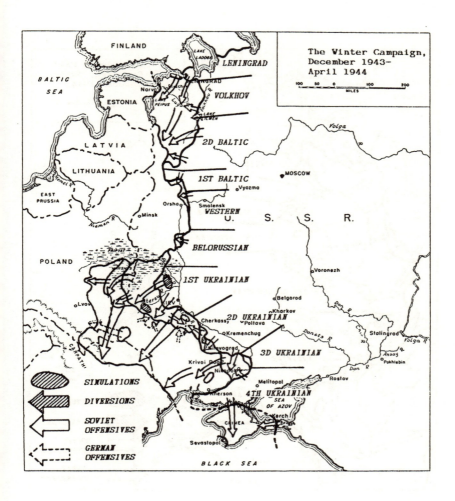

28. The Winter Campaign, December 1943–April 1944

29. The Summer–Fall Campaign, June–October 1944

SOVIET MILITARY STRATEGY 1941–1945

strategic offensive operations extending from the Baltic Sea to the Balkans (see Figure 30). The East Prussian and Vistula–Oder offensive operations propelled Soviet troops to the Baltic Sea and across the Oder River, only 60 kilometers from Berlin, while in the south Soviet forces parried a German counteroffensive at Budapest and then continued the advance into Austria. After conducting operations in February and March 1945 to clear German forces from the flanks of the Soviet main thrust, the Soviets began the titanic, almost ceremonial struggle to conquer Berlin and liquidate the Nazis in their own lair, thus ending the Great Patriotic War. However, combat for Soviet forces was not over. In August 1945, responding to requests for assistance from their allies, the Soviets organized and conducted their largest-scale strategic offensive of the war (in terms of space) which crushed Japanese forces in Manchuria and won for the Soviet Union a place in subsequent negotiations for peace and postwar reconstruction in the Far East.

MILITARY POLICY AND STRATEGY

Having irrevocably seized the strategic military initiative in 1943, in the third period of war, Soviet policy matured to reflect political as well as military realities. While the Soviets still sought the military destruction of Nazi Germany, they did so within the context of their view of the postwar world. Central to that view was their desire to establish political relationships which would insure the future security of the Soviet state in particular, and socialism in general. At a minimum, this involved the extension of Soviet influence into eastern Europe and northeastern and southern Asia to create a cordon sanitaire around her borders and to support any subsequent advance of socialism. This intent was underscored by Soviet policy statements at wartime conferences with her allies in 1944 and 1945 and by evolving military policy, doctrine, and strategy, as well as military operations themselves.

Officially, the Soviets say the following about their military strategy in the third period of war:

> In the third period of the war, under conditions of increasing combat strength of the armed forces and the build-up of large strategic reserves, the development of Soviet military strategy was manifested in the successive and continuous conduct of strategic offensive operations over the entire Soviet-German front. Fundamentally new forms of strategic operations by the armed forces were discovered and successfully employed. These were *front* group operations (*operatsiia gruppi frontov*) involving from 100 to 200

151

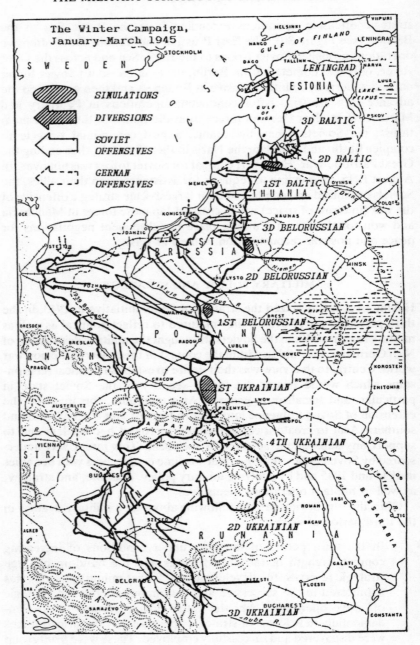

30. The Winter Campaign, January–March 1945

divisions, 20,000–40,000 guns and mortars, between 3,000 and 6,000 tanks and self-propelled artillery units and from 2,000 to 7,500 aircraft. Such operations were carried out on the most important strategic axes and were characterized by the decisiveness of the objectives, great spatial scope, the dynamic nature of the combat operations, and the achievement of important military-political and strategic results. Some of them were carried out on a front of 800–1,000 kilometers and extended to a depth of up to 500–600 kilometers. From 50 to 100 enemy divisions were destroyed in the process.

One of the most characteristic features of the strategic operations carried out was the encirclement and destruction of large groupings of enemy troops. Military strategy underwent considerable development with respect to the organization and conduct of large joint operations involving long-range aviation and naval forces.[63]

Soviet strategy in the third period of war grew in scope and ambition and took on a more subtle political flavor. With the strategic initiative firmly in Soviet hands, strategic operations became totally offensive, more grandiose, and incessant. While earlier operations occurred along separate strategic directions, by 1944 they took place along the entire strategic front, successively in 1944 and simultaneously in 1945. Each operation was conducted with a deception plan coordinated by the *Stavka*, a plan that encompassed the entire campaign. These plans successfully concealed both the location and scale of the strategic offensives and, to some extent, the timing of operations.

By war's end the *front* group operations described above had decisive objectives (usually the encirclement and destruction of large enemy groups), huge scope, high maneuverability, and significant military-political or economic results. They spanned frontages from 450 to 1,400 kilometers (4,400 kilometers in Manchuria) and thrust to a depth of 500–600 kilometers while destroying as many as 50–100 enemy divisions. Often the political and economic goal of the operation was as important as the military goal, and these goals affected the nature of military operations (for example, the operations against Finland, the drive into the Balkans, and the Manchurian offensive).

COMMAND AND CONTROL

Command and control of strategic operations reached full maturation during the third and final period of war and involved sophisticated cooperation between the political leadership (Stalin and NKO), the

153

Stavka, front commanders, and chief of types of forces. *Stavka* representatives played a key role in the planning and conduct of virtually every strategic operation up to 1945. K.E. Voroshilov, G.K. Zhukov, S.K. Timoshenko, A.M. Vasilevsky, B.M. Shaposhnikov, N.N. Voronov, A.I. Antonov, S.M. Shtemenko, L.E. Mekhlis, L.A. Govorov, K.K. Rokossovsky, and others served, sometimes repeatedly, as *Stavka* representatives. Zhukov gave high praise to their work, writing, "The presence of such a command and control link in the strategic command system was extremely necessary and unconditionally beneficial."[64] The institution of representative of the *Stavka* endured throughout 1944.

In 1945, however, because of requirements for ever tighter coordination of political and military objectives, the shorter frontages, the greater experience of *front* commanders and staffs, and perhaps a desire to diminish the prestige of certain key *Stavka* representatives in light of the impending end of hostilities, Stalin and the *Stavka* resorted to working directly through *front* commanders on key strategic directions (Berlin, for example). Still later, during preparations for the Manchurian strategic offensive, the *Stavka* created a joint high command (*glavnoe komandovanie*) for all Soviet forces operating in the Far East. This became the first fully-fledged theater of military operations headquarters, supported by a full staff.

STRATEGIC OFFENSE

The scope, scale and intensity of Soviet offensive operations grew during the third period of war. Planned and conducted under an impenetrable veil of secrecy and deception, strategic offensive operations dominated Soviet military actions as Soviet forces employed a wide range of offensive methods to achieve strategic success. No longer did they rely on counteroffensives, for the correlation of forces had shifted decisively in their favor, and, from August 1943 on, the Soviets maintained firm control of the strategic initiative.

The principal goal of all campaigns and separate operations was the destruction of German forces and the liberation, first, of Soviet territory, and then of territory and peoples in eastern, southeastern, and central Europe. As in late 1943, in early 1944 the priority strategic direction of Soviet offensive efforts was the southern wing of the Eastern Front, largely because of political, economic, and military factors. The main German force concentrations were located in the Ukraine, as was much of the economic heartland of the old Soviet state. A southern drive also threatened the interests of Germany's remaining allies (Rumania, Hungary), and Soviet success there promised to drive them from the war.

During the final campaigns of the war on the Eastern Front (summer–fall 1944 and 1945 in Europe), Soviet forces struck again along the western direction, which by then was the shortest route to Berlin and the heart of Germany. Auxiliary strategic operations along the flanks maintained pressure on the Germans and satisfied other political and economic objectives. This shifting of main attack axes had a beneficial effect on operations. "Such a means of conducting armed struggle permitted achievement of important results on the main attack direction, and then using that success for rapid widening of the front of the strategic offensive and developing it in depth forced the enemy to disperse his forces on many directions."[65]

Having determined the principal strategic offensive direction, the *Stavka* concentrated its forces on it to an increasingly effective extent. Strategic shock groups during 1944 and 1945 generally consisted of 50 per cent or more of the total force operating on the Eastern Front. During the summer–fall campaign of 1944, the *Stavka* concentrated 3,076,000 men (50 per cent of the total), 46,335 guns and mortars (53 per cent of the total), 4,190 tanks and SP guns (58 per cent of the total), and 5,000 aircraft (56 per cent of the total) in the direction of the main blow between Nevel' and Chernovtsy (about 37 per cent of the front). This granted the Soviets strategic force superiority over the enemy of 1.6:1 in personnel, 1.8:1 in guns and mortars, 1.1:1 in tanks and SP guns, and 2.7:1 in aircraft.[66] Such force concentration guaranteed rapid penetration of German tactical defenses and ever deeper exploitation of Soviet mobile forces into the operational depths (150 kilometers) and operational-strategic depths (up to 400 kilometers) over ever shorter periods of time.

Soviet strategy and operational art matured with the refinement of concepts and techniques developed in 1943 and the creation of new techniques during the last two years of war. *Front* operations, an integral part of strategic operations, ranged to depths of 150–300 kilometers and destroyed 16–18 enemy divisions. Armies within *fronts* attacked to depths of 100–150 kilometers and destroyed enemy operational forces (3–6 divisions).[67] During each *front* operation, armies conducted one or two successive operations.

The form of *front* operations also matured. During the first two periods of war, *front* offensives had been conducted by several armies attacking along separate directions. In the third period of war, because of increased manpower and weaponry, *fronts* conducted frontal attacks against the enemy center and one or both of the enemy flanks to encircle and destroy multiple enemy groups (Belorussia 1944). In instances where encirclement operations were impossible or infeasible, each *front*, supported by heavy artillery and aviation, delivered one or two frontal blows to a great

155

THE MILITARY STRATEGY OF THE SOVIET UNION

depth, cut up enemy forces, and destroyed them piecemeal (Vistula–Oder 1945). Armies customarily struck one blow against the enemy center or along the enemy flank and advanced into the depth of the defense to cooperate with other armies in encircling enemy forces. By the third period of the war, *fronts* could launch, in addition to a main attack, a strong secondary attack and one or two supporting attacks.

The increased strength of *fronts* and greater concentration of forces permitted creation of greater operational densities and increased superiority. Major operations achieved operational densities of 200–250 guns/mortars and 70–85 tanks/self-propelled guns per kilometer of frontage, and superiorities were attained amounting to 3–5:1 in manpower, 6–8:1 in tanks and artillery, and 3–5:1 in combat aircraft.[68]

Operational formations also increased in depth and complexity. The *front* operational formation included a strong first echelon; an optional second echelon of one or sometimes two combined armies; a mobile group of one, two or sometimes three tank armies, or in the absence of a tank army, one or two tank corps or one or two cavalry-mechanized groups; strong reserves of all types; and mobile obstacle detachments. The army operational formation was similar, with one or two tank or mechanized corps functioning as mobile groups and with army artillery and antiaircraft groups in support. The depth of the *front* operational formation reached 70–100 kilometers and that of the army 30 kilometers. Operational formations were flexible and tailored to the existing situation. Thus, in Manchuria two out of three *fronts* attacked in single echelon formation, as did the majority of armies. *Front* air armies (generally one) supported *front* and army operations.

Offensive operations began with penetration operations, which by 1944 were conducted using shock groups, heavy artillery concentrations, artillery and air offensives, and a greater number of infantry support tanks. By 1945 infantry support tanks were often attached in from company to regimental strength to individual rifle battalions. As a rule, the Soviets overcame the enemy's first defensive belt on the first day of operations and the second belt on the second or third day. By the third period of war, the penetration of the enemy's tactical defense was followed by an operational exploitation, the encirclement of the enemy, and the creation of an inner encircling line to choke those entrapped and an outer encircling line to hold off enemy relief attempts (Korsun'–Shevchenkovskii). By mid-1944 the outer encirclement line continued the offensive, while encircled enemy forces were being destroyed (Belorussia, Iassy-Kishinev).

Operational pursuit became important, for it determined the ultimate depth of the operation. While earlier in the war pursuit rates had amounted to 8–12 kilometers per day on distinct directions in close contact with the enemy, by the third period pursuit occurred on a wide front, both day and night, along separate directions, and at high tempos. Tank armies and tank corps led the pursuit along parallel routes separated by 60–80 kilometers or more from the main rifle forces. Strong tank-heavy task-organized forward detachments led the pursuit and also the advance of main rifle forces, and contributed to maintaining the high momentum of the advance.* By August 1945, in some instances forward detachments initiated offensive operations to preempt or disrupt enemy defenses before they solidified.[69] From 1944 onward, mobile forces engaged in deception during pursuit operations, often using forward detachments to portray false axes of advance. Aviation units supported all elements of the pursuing force. The numerous river crossings in pursuit operations were undertaken by forward detachments or by carefully planned and conducted river crossing operations.

In general, *front* offensive operations by 1944 evidenced considerable maneuver and demonstrated Soviet mastery of the problem of coordinating the use of all types of combat arms. Rapid and often secret regrouping and shifting of forces, and quick and effective cross attachment of units promoted more flexibility in Soviet operations and permitted successful conduct of successive army operations with little or no pause. All of these measures increased the tempo of the advance to 20–30 kilometers per day for rifle forces and 50–60 kilometers per day for tank forces, and permitted advances by *fronts* and armies to depths of 400–500 kilometers and 150–180 kilometers respectively. The duration of these operations averaged 15–20 days per *front* and 5–15 days for armies.

Tank and mechanized forces, which imparted much of the long-range offensive punch to the Red Army, reached their heyday in 1944–45.[70] When functioning as the mobile group of a *front*, tank armies on several occasions operated in first echelon, but more often operated in second echelon. The commitment of tank armies to action created operational armored densities of 30–100 tanks per kilometer of front on main attack directions. By the end of the war, separate tank corps operated to a depth of 180 kilometers and tank armies to a depth of 400 kilometers or more. Separate tank corps or mechanized corps, acting as army mobile groups, would complete the penetration of the tactical defense zone to a depth of

---

* Distinct from advanced guards, forward detachments led the advance with the mission of seizing key terrain features to facilitate the advance of main force units. Later, these detachments also disrupted enemy defenses before they jelled. Tank armies and tank corps used tank corps and tank brigades as forward detachments. Rifle corps used tank brigades, and rifle divisions used reinforced rifle battlaions, self-propelled artillery battalions, or tank brigades.

25–40 kilometers, after which tank armies as the *front*'s mobile group would develop success to the entire depth of the *front* offensive operation. By 1944–45 a weakening of German operational reserves permitted Soviet tank armies to repulse counterattacks more easily and thus gave the tank armies greater operational freedom. Tank armies conducted pursuit operations rapidly in corps column (pre-combat)* formation led by strong forward detachments deployed to preempt any enemy counteraction. Tank army night operations were particularly effective. Separate tank or mechanized corps covered the flanks of advancing tank armies, while forward detachments of advancing rifle forces (reinforced tank brigades, self-propelled artillery battalions, or truck-mounted rifle battalions with tanks) linked rifle forces with advancing tank and mechanized forces.

The Soviets achieved efficient command and control of mobile forces operating in extended formation deep in the enemy rear area by using operational groups (forward command points), first echelon staffs (command points), and second echelon command and control (rear command points) posts. To provide continuous command and control during deep offensives, operational groups and first echelon staffs displaced one another in turn. Throughout the war a persistent problem which inhibited the effectiveness of Soviet tank and mechanized units was the absence of an armored personnel carrier. Hence, the Soviets never had real armored infantry.

Aviation support of offensives became more sophisticated in the third period of war. Larger echeloned aircraft attack groups provided continuous close air and interdiction support and concentrated on the most important enemy objectives. Fighters and assault aircraft provided immediate troop support throughout the enemy tactical defense, while bombers and assault aircraft supported forces operating in the operational depths or blocked enemy withdrawal and forward movement of enemy reserves or supplies. Throughout the war, however, air support in the deep operational realm was spotty because of limited airfields, short aircraft combat radii, and limited fuel and ammunition (a result of German scorched earth policies).

During 1944 and 1945 successful Soviet conduct of strategic deception became a motive force in the routine achievement of surprise and strategic success.[71] In 1943 the Soviets had been able to conceal their operational intent on numerous occasions, but the Germans were able to discover where Soviet strategic priorities lay. Consequently, Soviet strategic offensives were more difficult and costly. In 1944, however, the

*Precombat formation is a march formation from which units can deploy rapidly and fight against an opponent attacking from any quarter.

158

Soviets were able to conceal their strategic priorities and capitalize on strategic patterns formed in 1943, as well as on German preconceptions and political notions (mostly Hitler's).

Thus, in the winter campaign of 1944, the German High Command, considering that Soviet forces would not further develop offensive operation so soon after the battle for the Dnepr and in *rasputitsa* conditions of spring, was not prepared to deal with the Soviet March and April thrust deep into the Ukraine. The surprise Soviet offensive conducted by the four Ukrainian *fronts* from January to April 1944 seriously damaged German Army Group South and drove 250–450 kilometers westward through the Ukraine.

As a result of the winter campaign of 1944, the Soviets conditioned the Germans to expect a subsequent year-long drive through the Ukraine into Poland and Rumania by constantly conducting operations in that direction. Then, in the spring, the Soviets implemented an elaborate strategic deception plan to conceal a strategic redeployment of forces and prepare a secret strategic strike against German forces in Belorussia. As at Kursk, the Soviets planned in advance for all stages of the summer campaign, and all of those stages were based on the premise that the initial strategic deception would accomplish its aims. The deception succeeded, and Soviet intelligence effectively kept track of the movement of German operational and tactical reserves.

Within a tight cloak of planning secrecy, the Soviets regrouped into new offensive positions five combined-arms armies; two tank and one air army; 1st Polish Army; five separate tank, two mechanized, and four cavalry corps; tens of separate brigades and regiments; and 11 aviation regiments. The secret strategic regrouping was supplemented by a major disinformation plan and diversionary planning by adjacent *fronts* (3rd Ukrainian and 3rd Baltic).[72]

The success of the June strategic offensive against Army Group Center exceeded Soviet expectations. As German reserves moved north to stabilize the situation, the 1st Ukrainian Front struck German Army Group Northern Ukraine in coordination with a 1st Belorussian Front attack toward Lublin. As both forces reached the Vistula River, Soviet forces struck in the Baltic and in Rumania, driving back German Army Group North and shattering Army Group South Ukraine. By late fall continued Soviet operations on both flanks had drawn German reserves from the center and created new German vulnerabilities in Poland and southern East Prussia, thus paving the way for future Soviet successes in the forthcoming winter offensive.

These successes were made possible by improved Soviet capabilities for shifting large strategic reserves secretly across the front and moving them into the forward area without the Germans' knowledge and by effective Soviet monitoring of German troops movements and defensive dispositions. The Soviets timed and concealed these regroupings so well that the Germans were unable to counter them, even if specific portions of the strategic deception plan failed.

Increasing Soviet force superiorities and Soviet commanders' greater experience permitted more complex forms of operations. In 1943 successive offensive operations along the front characterized offensive campaigns. While this form persisted into 1944, to an increasing extent the *Stavka* was able to organize and conduct simultaneous operations along critical strategic directions and, finally, along the entire front.

During the winter–spring campaign of 1944 the Soviets organized two consecutive waves of successive *front* operations. The first wave began in December toward Vinnitsa (the Zhitomir–Berdichev operation) and ultimately developed into the Korsun'–Shevchenkovskii operation of January–February 1944, during which the 1st and 2rd Ukrainian Fronts jointly encircled two German corps. The second wave began in early March, when, within three days, the 1st, 2rd, and 3rd Ukrainian Fronts commenced operations (the Proskurov–Chernovtsy, Uman', and Bereznegovatoe–Snigirevka operations), which ultimately reached the Rumanian borders and encircled, but failed to destroy, German First Panzer Army. Abruptly, during the second wave of operations, the Soviets shifted the axis of their main thrust from Vinnitsa westward toward Ternopol' and Chernovtsy.

The Soviet summer–fall campaign was of even grander scale, involving as it did consecutive strategic offensives against German Army Group Center in Belorussia, German Army Group North Ukraine in southern Poland, and German Army Group South Ukraine in Rumania. These consecutive strategic operations ultimately embraced virtually the entire 4,500 kilometer Eastern Front and penetrated in some sectors to a depth of 1,100 kilometers. In the south alone, between 20 August and late October 1944, the Soviet 2nd, 3rd, and 4th Ukrainian Fronts conducted the Iassy-Kishinev, Transylvanian, Debrecan, Belgrade, and Budapest operations, while at the same time occupying Bulgaria. All planning took place during the operations, denying the Germans benefit of any appreciable operational pause. The pace of the Soviet advance accelerated throughout these operations to achieve rates of up to 100 kilometers per day for mobile forces and 15 to 20 kilometers per day for rifle forces. The damage done to the Germans also mounted as the Soviets heavily damaged two entire German army groups (Center and South Ukraine).

In 1945, when the breadth of the Eastern Front had shrunken to 2,200 kilometers, the *Stavka* commenced strategic operations simultaneously across the entire front (the Vistula–Oder and East Prussian operations, 12–15 January 1945). Within a short period the entire German strategic defensive front had been fractured as remnants of German forces were bypassed, encircled, or simply rendered irrelevant on a series of strategic directions (Courland, Zemland). In this campaign, Soviet offensive impulses slowed or halted only when Soviet forces were exhausted or had outrun their supplies.

Strategic reserves played a reduced role in the third period of war when the problem of creating and reestablishing strategic reserves occurred in more favorable military-political conditions. While Soviet strength rose in both an economic and military sense, that of Germany fell sharply. Moreover, while the Soviets added significant allied strength to their military host (Poland, Rumania, Bulgaria, and Czechoslovakia), German allies were driven one by one from the war (Italy, Rumania and Hungary).[73] By 1945 the truncated front (less than half of 1943) also reduced the need for strategic reserves, although new political realities still prompted their creation.

As in the second period of war, the *Stavka* used most strategic reserves to create offensive shock groups, strengthen the offensive during its course, cover vulnerable flanks, and repel counterattacks. Special reserve armies were also created for specialized offensive missions (9th Guards Army). During preparations for the Belorussian operation (summer–fall campaign 1944) the *Stavka* allocated to *fronts* operating on the main direction four combined-arms armies, two tank armies, 52 rifle and cavalry divisions, six separate tank and mechanized corps, 33 aviation divisions, hundreds of separate brigades and regiments, and 210,000 personnel replacements.[74] Even greater reserves were allocated for the 1945 campaign. During the Belorussian operation, the *Stavka* reinforced the 1st Baltic Front with two armies, so that it could strike a supporting blow toward the Baltic coast. When the Soviet advance into the Ukraine during the winter campaign of 1944 left a major gap on 1st Ukrainian Front's right flank, the *Stavka* created the new 2nd Belorussian Front and allocated to it from strategic reserves one combined-arms army and one air army. This new *front* immediately began an offensive toward Kovel' in support of 1st Ukrainian Front. During operations in Hungary in March 1945 *Stavka* commitment of a reserve army (9th Guards) permitted the 2nd Ukrainian Front to commence the Vienna offensive operation, virtually at the same time that the 3rd Ukrainian Front was halting a German offensive in the adjacent Lake Balaton sector.

Strategic cooperation further improved during the third period of war and expanded to embrace closer cooperation with allies in liberated eastern Europe and other theaters. To achieve strategic aims in every campaign, it was necessary to attack and destroy the enemy on several directions. This required each separate operation to be coordinated according to aim, place, time, and method. In the 1944 campaigns special attention was devoted to selecting correctly the time for introducing into action strategic force groupings operating on different axes. Experience indicated that it was beneficial for each strategic grouping to begin its operations at a time when the opposing enemy force had been weakened and lacked sufficient reserves due to the influence of operations going on elsewhere and when Soviet forces had already been fully regrouped and reequipped. Thus:

> The shattering blows and decisive offensives of Soviet forces in Belorussia and the western Ukraine in June and July 1944 forced the Hitlerite command to transfer considerable forces there from the Baltic region and Rumania, thus weakening the operating forces of Army Groups North and South Ukraine. This permitted the Soviet High Command to develop operations along all decisive directions of the Soviet-German front.[75]

In the 1945 campaign, when all offensive operations began simultaneously across the strategic front, the organization of strategic cooperation became easier. The success of each of these groups prevented German maneuver, thus easing the task of achieving strategic aims in all sectors. The principal Soviet concern in these operations was to secure the flanks of each strategic grouping, as occurred during the latter stages of the Vistula-Oder operation when the *Stavka* halted operations in order to clear the Germans from their extended flanks by launching the Pomeranian and Silesian operations.[76]

During the last period of war the *Stavka* also had to organize cooperation between Soviet forces and the growing number of allied armies, raised, equipped, and deployed to fight within Soviet strategic formations. These included two Polish armies, two Rumanian armies, one Bulgarian army, a Czechoslovak corps, and several Hungarian divisions. These forces had been raised in the Soviet Union and were led by Soviet senior officers. Once the Soviet government had created "governments in exile" for each nation and had begun to liberate these national territories from German control, the allied forces grew in number, but still essentially remained under Soviet control, usually integrated into specific *fronts* and armies.[77] In some operations the *Stavka* assigned these forces highly visible military-political objectives. For example, the 1st Polish Army participated in the liberation of Warsaw and later in the Berlin operation, while the Czech corps assisted in the liberation of Slovak and Czech territory.

162

Strategic cooperation between Soviet forces and the Western allies also improved after the opening of the "second front" in June 1944. Co-operation took the form of more closely coordinated timing of major operations based on existing conditions. Operational cooperation was more concrete and involved the negotiation of "designated boundaries for the meeting of coalition forces, aviation zones of operation, and agreements on administrative questions". Soviet critiques of cooperation judge that "overall, the existing system of cooperation, despite the absence of a single (unifying) organ, was sufficiently flexible and played a positive role".[78] To effect this closer cooperation, in 1941 and early 1942 the Allies sent missions to Moscow to coordinate with the Soviet General Staff (the U.S. representative was General Deane). After June 1944 Major General I. A. Susloparov represented the Soviet General Staff in Eisenhower's European headquarters, and Major General Kislenko served with Allied forces in the Mediterranean theater.[79] Despite marginal cooperation between Soviet and Allied forces and extensive shipment of U.S. lend-lease material to the Soviet Union, the relationship was marred by great mutual suspicion of one another's motives, particularly during the last two years of war.

Strategic operations by groups of Soviet *fronts* fully matured in the third period of war. The most typical aim of these operations was the outright destruction of large strategic enemy groupings of between 20 and 60 divisions and the occupation of strategically important economic, political, and military regions. In 1944 this involved the destruction of entire enemy army groups and the forcing of German allies to leave the war (Finland, Rumania, Hungary, and Bulgaria). The scale of these operations was immense. Operations by groups of *fronts* occurred along decisive directions, had decisive objectives, were huge, and achieved important military-political results.

To a greater extent than before, operations by groups of *fronts* became more complex and often involved extensive encirclement operations, although in some instances the Soviets still resorted to "deep cutting" (*rassekaiushchaia*) operations or attacking enemy defenses on a broad front (splitting – *droblenie*). At times all three methods were used in a single strategic operation.

Most characteristic of groups of *fronts'* operations in 1944 and 1945 was the encirclement operation, conducted in two principal ways. In the Korsun'–Shevchenkovskii, Iassy-Kishinev, Prague, and, later, Manchurian operations, Soviet groups of *fronts* launched two almost simultaneous strikes along converging directions to encircle the enemy force. In the East Prussian operation, two *fronts* conducted one powerful enveloping attack to pin German forces against the sea and other natural

THE MILITARY STRATEGY OF THE SOVIET UNION

obstacles. In the Belorussian operation three Soviet *fronts* conducted two simultaneous and rapid encirclement operations of German multi-corps-size forces at Vitebsk and Bobruisk and then developed the operation without pause into a subsequent encirclement of 105,000 Germans at Minsk. The operational encirclements took only two to three days to complete, and the larger strategic encirclements only seven days. As a result, German Army Group Center lost well over half of its strength.[80]

The Belorussian operation demonstrated Soviet mastery of the long-standing problem of creating effective inner and outer encirclement lines during an encirclement operation. The inner encirclement effectively contained surrounded enemy forces, while the outer encirclement line not only prevented relief by German reserves, but also continued to develop the offensive, further sealing the fate of the encircled forces.

The larger and more effective Soviet tank and mechanized forces available in the third period of war made successful encirclement operations possible. These tank armies and mobile (tank, mechanized, and cavalry) corps, attacking and exploiting at a high tempo, extended the range and lethality of Soviet offensives. While the effective range of these forces had been roughly 120–150 kilometers during the second period of war, during 1944 they often reached depths of 250–300 kilometers, and during 1945 they operated as deep as 500–600 kilometers without extended pauses to regroup and reequip.[81]

The *Stavka* continued to conduct "deep cutting" operations where conditions dictated, for example in the Right Bank of the Ukraine Operation (March–April 1944) and the Vistula–Oder operation (January–February 1945). The latter was the most fully developed instance of this type of operation, which was characterized by decisive Soviet force superiorities (four- to eight-fold), created in part by massive use of deception, and extensive deep maneuver by *front*, army, and lower operational and tactical maneuver forces (mobile groups and forward detachments). Extensive maneuver by Soviet forces resulted in the encirclement of German forces in Warsaw, in the Silesian industrial region, and in numerous pockets throughout Poland, virtual "floating bubbles" of by-passed German forces left behind as Soviet main forces pushed on westward to the Oder River. The offensive developed rapidly along numerous axes with advances of up to 70 kilometers per day to an ultimate depth of over 500 kilometers achieved in less than three weeks.[82]

In the Belorussian operation Soviet groups of *fronts* employed, consecutively, several forms of offensive action. Initially, Soviet forces penetrated German defenses simultaneously in six separate sectors, thus splitting enemy forces. Subsequently, they exploited and encircled three major enemy groups at Vitebsk, Bobruisk, and Minsk. After destroying these concentrations, the group of three *fronts* continued the offensive westward along diverging directions to dismember further German Army Group Center.

As a postscript to European operations, in August 1945 the Soviets conducted their most geographically challenging and extensive strategic operation of the war. In response to Allied requests for Soviet assistance against Japan, the Soviets planned joint operations against Japanese forces in Manchuria and on the northern island possessions of the Kuriles and Sakhalin.[83]

Unique strategic circumstances conditioned the precise form and ultimate outcome of the Manchurian operation. First, the immense size of the theater of operations and its distance from European Russia required the Soviets to move almost 700,000 men and massive amounts of equipment and supplies over 9,000 kilometers along the limited umbilical of the Trans-Siberian railroad from the European theater to the Far East. To maintain strategic surprise, secrecy was important. Second, the Soviets were confronted with severe time constraints. Japanese reinforcement of Manchuria, American use of the atomic bomb, and possible ensuing Japanese collapse, made it imperative that the offensive achieve its goals in a matter of days, rather than weeks or months. Manchuria had to be secured within 30 days and the main entrances into central Manchuria within one week, as much for political as for military considerations.

From virtually every perspective, strategic deception and ensuing surprise made the difference between success and failure. Deception in the form of political finesse dulled Japanese apprehensions over possible Soviet war intentions and the Soviets created and orchestrated a deception plan without the context of ongoing combat. The Soviets did not rely on the "noise" of war to conceal their deception. Ultimately, they concealed their intention to attack, as well as the locations, scale, and form of the attack.

The Soviets conducted a three-front offensive to conquer Manchuria. The Trans-Baikal Front, attacked from eastern Mongolia, spearheaded by 6th Guards Tank Army, penetrated the forbidding terrain of western Manchuria, while the 1st Far Eastern Front struck westward from the Vladivostok area against heavier Japanese troop concentrations in eastern Manchuria. These two fronts linked up and entrapped all Japanese forces in the region, while the 2nd Far Eastern Front, in the north, pressured the Japanese along a wide front. Deception to conceal the deployment of the Trans-Baikal Front was particularly important. The Soviet attack achieved surprise and paralyzed Japanese defenders. By 15 August the Soviets had achieved most of their objectives in a strategic operation whose success has since made it a model of how the Soviets would like to operate in the initial period of any future war.

Soviet offensive operations in the third period of war remain the most massive in recent history and have provided much of the base of experience for postwar Soviet military theorists. The operations destroyed enemy forces as large as 90 divisions and penetrated to strategic depths of up to 600 kilometers (800 in Manchuria) within several weeks. Political effects were also significant. The Iassy-Kishinev operation drove Rumania and Bulgaria from the war. The Budapest operation did likewise for Hungary, while the Berlin and Manchurian operations completed the war against Germany and Japan.

The systematic growth of strategic offensive operations is measurable by a wide range of indices relating the size of forces, the dimensions of strategic operations, and the scale of destruction inflicted on the enemy. Most important is the impact of these operations on future war. In the view of one eminent Soviet military strategist:

> As a whole, the successful resolution of the problem of preparing and conducting strategic operations in the Great Patriotic War years was a considerable step in the development of Soviet military strategy. The experience of that resolution has not lost its importance for contemporary conditions, when the scale of military operations and the volume and contents of strategic missions has grown considerably. Experiences in struggling to seize and maintain the strategic initiative, in preparing and employing strategic reserves, in securing high tempos on the offensive and in operation of groups of forces in rapidly and sharply changing conditions, and in achieving surprise blows deserve special attention.[84]

STRATEGIC DEFENSE

As strategic offensive operations expanded to unprecedented scale during the third period of war, defensive operations shrank in scope and importance. Since Soviet forces were continuously on the strategic offensive, there was no requirement for strategic defense. *Front* defensive operations decreased in scope and frequency during the third period of war. *Fronts* and armies went on the defense at the end of major offensive operations to resupply and regroup, to repel enemy counterattacks, or to fortify a region just secured. Defenses continued to strengthen at all levels. *Fronts* defended sectors 250–350 kilometers wide and armies sectors 30–70 kilometers wide. Operational densities increased to one rifle division per 7–8 kilometers of frontage and 24–36 guns/mortars and 7 tanks/self-propelled guns per kilometer.[85] *Fronts* defended in two-echelon formation with a combined-arms or tank army in second echelon and several tank, rifle, and antitank formations in reserve, while armies deployed for defense in one or two echelons. Engineers prepared defenses to depths of 40–50 and 150–180 kilometers, respectively, for armies and *fronts*, thus permitting creation of three army defensive belts and one to three additional defensive belts for *fronts* (Lake Balaton 1945). Antitank, tank, artillery, and aviation support for defensive operations improved as well. Second echelon tank or combined-arms armies launched *front* counterattacks during defensive operations.

Within the larger context of the European war, from June 1941 until 1944, the necessity of defeating Hitler's Germany compelled the Soviets to maintain a strategic defensive posture *vis à vis* Japanese forces in the Far East. Throughout 1944 Soviet strategic posture in that region began to shift subtly. The number of Soviet Far Eastern divisions increased from 48 in January to 59.5 in December.[86] Soviet forces still remained arrayed defensively behind a curtain of fortified regions deployed along the border. Although the possibility of a Japanese attack lessened as Japanese fortunes fell, Japanese planning *vis à vis* the Soviet Far East remained offensive into 1944. Reflecting the realities of the Pacific War, Japanese planning shifted to a defensive orientation in mid-1944.

Between May and August 1945, after the Soviet government had agreed with the U.S. and other allies to enter the war against Japan, Soviet strategic posture in the Far East shifted from a defensive to an offensive one. Within a tight cloak of secrecy, the *Stavka* conducted a strategic regrouping, which raised the strength of their forces in the Far East from 59.5 to 87.5 divisions, thus transforming a clearly defensive posture into an offensive one.[87]

Elsewhere during the third period of war, the Soviets resorted to a large-scale operational defense in March 1945 when the Germans conducted their last major offensive in the Lake Balaton region of Hungary to retake Budapest and the Balaton oil fields and restore Germany's position in Hungary.[88] Even in this operation, Soviet defensive measures took place within the context of a planned strategic offensive toward Vienna.

CONCLUSIONS

Soviet military strategy in the last two years of war did more than simply defeat Nazi Germany and assist in the defeat of Japan. It also helped shape the political geography of postwar Europe and Asia. Through military action and diplomacy, the Soviets were able to extend their political influence well beyond their prewar borders. Where the Red Army conquered, political control ensued. The Soviets routinely created "national" armies, in advance, for each nation which they intended to liberate and formed embryonic political organs for "liberated" nations. Thus, militarily the liberation was a joint one. Meanwhile, in negotiations with her Western Allies at Teheran, Yalta and Potsdam, the Soviets insisted on political power-sharing between political authorities sponsored by them and those based in, and backed by, the West. In the final analysis, Soviet military strategy and the ensuing presence of military forces dictated political outcome. Hence, by 1948 all nations liberated by the Red Army were firmly embedded in the Soviet camp.

In Asia the same phenomena resulted. Manchuria became the supply base for the emergence of Communist China, and Soviet-occupied North Korea became a new Communist bastion. On the other hand, failure by the Soviets to gain Allied agreement for a Soviet role in the conquest of Japan guaranteed the future emergence of a non-Communist Japan (minus her northern islands, which to this day remain in the hands of their conquerers).

In the last year of war, internal aspects of Stalin's military strategy subtly reflected his appreciation of postwar realities. In 1945 he reduced his reliance on *Stavka* representatives to coordinate strategic operations and, instead, assigned his most prestigious representative (Zhukov) to command the most important operating front (1st Belorussian). This brought his most powerful *fronts*, and their prestigious commanders, under even closer personal control.

Soviet military strategy during the last year of war accorded priority to establishing Soviet military power in the Baltic and Balkans, where Soviet postwar interests lay and where wartime agreements with the Allies were least firm. It was no coincidence that the Soviets launched the Vienna operation from Hungary deep into Austria before they mounted the climactic Berlin operation. The Berlin operation itself was carefully timed to coincide with (and forestall) the Allied advance toward Berlin from the west. While the Berlin operation unfolded, the Soviets maintained powerful reserves to insure against any failure of the West to abide by wartime agreements.[89]

CHAPTER 6

POST-SECOND WORLD WAR SOVIET MILITARY STRATEGY

OVERVIEW

Since the end of the Second World War, Soviet military strategy has been conditioned by "experiences of the war and the new distribution of military-political forces in the world".[1] The Soviets claim their policy has been based on the "fact that the governments of the former allies in the anti-Hitlerite coalition (primarily the United States and Britain) had departed from the principles agreed upon for the postwar organization of the world"[2] During the ensuing Cold War, which the Soviets now imply began in 1949, Soviet military strategy recognized the dual realities of nuclear and conventional war. While their views regarding the domination of nuclear weapons have on several occasions shifted, until very recently they have steadfastly insisted that "the offensive was the main type of strategic operation, in either a nuclear or non-nuclear context".[3]

During the 1950s Soviet military strategy sought to defend the gains made by communism in the Second World War and immediate postwar years against what they perceived as a concerted Western effort, led by the United States, to "contain" the expansion of communism. Containment, in their view, typified Western political efforts to restore the global status quo by the restoration of the economic, political, and, ultimately, the military power of West Germany and Japan. Containment also entailed creation of anti-communist political-military alliances, such as NATO, CENTO, and SEATO, and the provision of direct military and political assistance in the form of the Truman Doctrine to states threatened by communism, such as Turkey and Greece. The economic corollary of these political programs was the Marshall Plan.

Militarily, the Soviets considered themselves threatened by, first, the United States' atomic monopoly (broken in 1949) and, second, by the emergence of United States dominated military alliances, the most menacing of which was NATO. The Soviet Union responded strategically by preserving a large, expandable peacetime military establishment, keeping large military forces in conquered regions of Eastern Europe,

169

and cloaking these forces within the political guise of an alliance (the Warsaw Pact), which could contend with NATO on a multilateral basis. The major thrust of Soviet military strategy was to possess a conventional military force whose offensive capabilities could check Western nuclear and conventional military power.

In the late 1950s, the growing Western thermonuclear threat caused the Soviets to modify their strategy. In 1960 Khrushchev enunciated a strategy, soon delineated in detail by Marshal V. D. Sokolovsky's book, *Military Strategy* (*Voennoe strategiia*), which was premised on Soviet creation of a thermonuclear capability equal to that of the West and a presumed reduced Soviet conventional capability, designed, in part, to respond to internal Soviet imperatives and facilitate expansion of the Soviet economy.[4] The central feature of this strategy was the assumption that future war would be inescapably global and nuclear.

Although Khrushchev fell from power in 1964, the "single option" concept of global nuclear war continued to dominate Soviet military strategy for several years thereafter. Lessons of the 1960s, including the Cuban missile crisis, and the reluctance of key personnel in military-theoretical circles to accept fully the implications of the "single option", led to a gradual shift in Soviet strategy, apparent by the end of the decade. In short, the shift involved a lessened emphasis on the nuclear component of strategy and a belief that conventional forces would still play a significant role in future war.

From the early 1970s to the mid 1980s, in response to the perceived U.S. and NATO threat, Soviet military theorists embraced the concept of the theater-strategic operation, which replaced the nuclear-dominant strategy of the 1960s and emphasized conventional aspects of future war.[5] With broadening prospects for large-scale combined-arms operations occurring in future war, with or without the use of nuclear weapons, the Soviets sought to develop concepts which could produce strategic victory within continental theaters of military operations. As a vehicle for understanding the potential for theater-strategic operations, the Soviets thoroughly analyzed their Great Patriotic War strategic and operational experiences, believing that basic principles and combat techniques of that period retained their relevance.

Soviet study of strategic operations in the Second World War produced a series of models, which seemed to provide a sound basis on which to formulate contemporary concepts for the conduct of the theater-strategic operation. Among the many criteria for selecting these models were characteristics of modern war which the Soviets considered most dominant and significant. These included the greater scale and scope of operations, the increased role of highly mobile operational and tactical

170

maneuver forces as the motive force for development of operations, the rapid maturation of operations to operational and strategic depths, increased complexity of political aims and military missions, and the necessity for sustaining operations, in terms of manpower, equipment, and logistics, to greater depths over ever-lengthening time periods. The four examples the Soviets focused on most were the Belorussian operation (June–August 1944), the Iassy-Kishinev operation (August 1944), the Vistula-Oder operation (January 1945), and the Manchurian operation (August 1945). The last two, in fact, became virtual models of the theater-strategic offensive for Soviet strategists in the early 1980s.[6]

During the mid-1980s a wide range of new factors coalesced to influence significantly Soviet military strategy. First, the Soviet military fundamentally reassessed the nature and requirements of future war, especially regarding the perceived technological revolution in new weaponry (in particular, high-precision weaponry), whose effects could not readily be predicted. Second, a wave of internal uncertainty swept through the ruling and intellectual circles within the Soviet Union regarding the political, economic and, finally, ideological bases of the Soviet state. Third, there occurred a growing disenchantment with the nature and effects of existing Soviet military policy and strategy, characterized by active Soviet intervention abroad and an intense and seemingly unlimited arms race, which placed immense burdens on the Soviet economy and seemed to offer little real gain in the Soviet Union's international stature.

THE FIRST POSTWAR PERIOD (1946–1960)

General

Although the Soviet Union emerged from the Second World War victorious, problems confronting the nation in general, and the military in particular, were immense. War had wrought extensive economic loss and social dislocation within the Soviet Union and had exacted a catastrophic toll in human lives. Massive wartime population transfers combined with extensive postwar adjustment of borders and juggling of peoples and a sizeable demobilization of armed forces personnel threatened further social instability. These factors juxtaposed against wartime popular hopes for postwar liberalization of the totalitarian Soviet state created great potential for political unrest as well. These largely domestic concerns of Stalin were coupled with his anxiety over the political nature of the postwar world. By war's end it was clear that a new combination of capitalistic competitor states had emerged – one dominated by the United

States. It was also clear that, while war had drained Soviet economic strength and peacetime reconstruction would continue to drain it, war had enhanced the United States' economic potential. American development and use of atomic weapons vividly underscored this point. The preeminent postwar Soviet international concern was the creation around the Soviet Union's borders of a *cordon sanitaire*, a buffer against future foreign military aggression and the threat of foreign ideas. The ideological imperative of spreading revolution (liberation) and the realities of the principle "to the victor belongs the spoils" justified this policy.

A third problem confronting Stalin was a military one, namely the United States' monopoly in atomic weaponry. Although Stalin publicly denigrated the importance of such weapons (or, for that matter, any single weapon) and continued to do so until his death, he evidenced his concern for such weapons by developing military and technological programs to counter and ultimately end the U.S. monopoly.

Given the realities of 1945 and the potential for political ferment, even before war's end, Stalin worked swiftly to ensure his continued firm control over the Soviet Union and its adjacent territories. He created and sponsored Communist governments in exile complete with military forces (Polish, Czech), and the Red Army entered Eastern Europe with those governments and armies in tow. Once returned to their native lands, these exile governments, with Red Army and NKVD assistance, engaged in a process of consolidating "socialist" governments. Within the Soviet Union, Stalin carefully eliminated potential challenges to his authority and crushed guerrilla bands operating in territories formerly occupied by Germany. Harsh treatment of Soviet ethnic minorities who had cooperated with Germans and of Soviet prisoners returned from German POW camps was indicative of Stalin's desire to insulate the Soviet Union against any alien ideas or political dissonance.

The death of Stalin in 1953 and growing Soviet realization that future war was likely to be nuclear had an enormous impact on Soviet military thought and the structure of Soviet military forces. Stalin's demise threw the Soviet leadership into a struggle for power reminiscent of that during Lenin's last days and the years immediately following his death. Once again there were two main groups who conducted their political struggle within the context of a doctrinal argument focused on the scale of armaments and heavy industry expenditures *vis-à-vis* production to satisfy consumer demand. G.N. Malenkov, who argued for greater production of consumer goods, wanted military expenditures to be concentrated on the development and production of nuclear weapons and delivery means to deter possible American attack, and favored a corresponding decrease in expenditures on massive ground forces. N. S. Khrushchev, perhaps to curry military support, advocated continued emphasis on conventional armaments, large ground forces and expanded heavy industry. Eventually Khrushchev won a political victory and, hence, the debate. Consequently, until 1960 Soviet ground forces continued to develop at current levels supplemented by steady improvements in nuclear forces. By 1960, however, Khrushchev had co-opted Malenkov's views and embraced accelerated reliance on nuclear forces at the expense of ground forces, a trend which would endure until well after Khrushchev was ousted from power in 1964.

Within the military establishment, Stalin's death permitted Soviet military theorists to strip off slowly the veneer of Stalinist principles which had insulated that theory from detailed critical examination and which had prevented more active and open discussion of operational and tactical questions. It also encouraged theorists to ponder more fully the likelihood and nature of future nuclear warfare. Soviet recognition of the increased importance of nuclear weapons and the enhanced potential impact of surprise attained by initial wartime use of these weapons triggered a basic revision of military theory and wholesale reorganization of the armed forces.

The following period, which lasted until 1960 and which is usually identified as the period of the Zhukov reforms, was characterized by intense Soviet reinvestigation of all areas of military science in the light of recent technological changes. This study resulted in a thorough reorganization of the armed forces, a redefinition of the role and capabilities of the various arms and services within a new concept of military operations, and accelerated development and fielding of new weaponry. Characterizing these intense debates were a flood of articles in the classified journal *Military thought* (*Voennaia mysl'*) and in the *Military-Historical journal* (*Voenno-istoricheskii zhurnal* – founded in 1959) on topics hitherto little discussed. Among the important themes discussed in early issues of *Military-Historical journal* was that of the nature of the initial period of war, a topic which assumed greater importance in a nuclear era. A second wave of changes began in the early 1960s, keynoted by Khrushchev's January 1960 speech, which announced Soviet recognition that a revolution had occurred in military affairs. The second wave represented a full maturation of theoretical concepts already developed during the first, or Zhukov, phase.

MILITARY POLICY AND DOCTRINE

In the military realm, Stalin firmly controlled all matters, just as he had in wartime. Characteristically, Stalin selected his chief military advisors carefully, making certain no "man on a white horse" would appear to challenge his authority. The leading Soviet wartime military figure, Marshal G. K. Zhukov, suffered for his fame by being posted as Odessa Military District Commander in 1946, in virtual exile. A similar fate befell other leading military figures. Stalin had himself portrayed as the architect of wartime victories and the premier military theoretician of the war. His theoretical prowess rested on five "permanently operating factors", which he articulated in 1918 and repeated throughout his life. These factors were:

    (1) the stability of the rear;
    (2) the morale of the army;
    (3) the quantity and quality of divisions;
    (4) the armaments of the army;
    (5) the organizational ability of command personnel.[7]

Most Soviet theoretical military articles of this period dutifully and understandably echoed those judgements. Stalin's permanent operating factors in war dominated Soviet military doctrine and were often used to explain away the importance in war of what Stalin labeled as transitory factors, such as surprise and other Western-derived "principles" Although viewed derisively by most Westerners, the overly broad and seemingly basic factors, in essence, summed up the Soviet wartime experience at the national level and provided rationale for avoiding panic over the United States' atomic monopoly.

    Western observers have characterized the Stalinist period as one devoid of constructive military debate in the strategic, operational, and tactical realms and as a period of marked retrenchment in military thought, since the Soviet Union seemed to refuse to recognize the impact of technological change (atomic weapons) on warfare. Soviet statements made during de-Stalinization after Stalin's death have reinforced this negative view. One critic stated:

> The cult of personality, appearing especially in postwar literature, has had a negative influence on the development of Soviet military science in this period. To please Stalin, the truths of the war were trampled upon. All military success was attributed to him and the role of military leaders became that of simple functionaries. At the time misfortunes of the war were explained as mistakes of his functionaries – *front* and army commanders. One could not talk about our major failures in the first months of war, much less analyze them ...[8]

The same critic cited Stalin's insistence on the validity of the permament operating factors at the expense of an adequate understanding of the dangers of surprise as a harmful influence on Soviet military science in the atomic age. Other critics considered Stalin's somewhat understandable refusal to analyze the initial period of war in June 1941 as equally harmful. Yet these judgements were prompted in part by contemporary political considerations, and after de-Stalinization was over, more recent Soviet writers (probably also for political reasons) have corrected these judgements, writing:

> Actually there was no lagging of Soviet military strategy and, furthermore, there was no military weakness of the USSR in that period. The fighting strength of our armed forces, their structure, equipment, and combat readiness, as well as military art, completely corresponded to the requirements of that time and ensured the Motherland's security.[9]

Thus the extreme denigration of Stalin's role in the formulation of military doctrine is probably as unjustified as the extreme adulation accorded to him during his lifetime for his military skill. The public and now declassified written record during the period 1946–53 does evidence extensive Soviet discussion of the major themes of military science (strategic operations, *front* and army operations, tactics, use of airborne forces, etc.) primarily on the basis of evaluating war experience. The actual record of Soviet political, economic, and military accomplishments, which had their genesis under Stalin's leadership, is impressive. Stalin tackled the problem of rebuilding a nearly destroyed nation, orchestrated socialist revolutions (coups) in eastern European nations, developed nuclear weapons and delivery means, and tried to extend revolution in Europe and Asia, all the while confronting the overwhelming strategic military superiority of the United States.

In the military realm, Stalin maintained, reorganized and reequipped a large and formidable ground force capable of deterring potential United States use of atomic weapons by holding central and western Europe hostage to Soviet ground power. Stalin demobilized Soviet ground forces from a 1945 strength of more than 6 million men and about 550 divisions to a force of under 3 million men organized into about 180 divisions.[10] His postwar military reorganization program increased the firepower and mobility of the ground forces by introducing new generations of weapons and vehicles into the force structure and by mechanizing a larger segment of these forces. Slowly throughout the 1950s, Soviet armed forces strength rose, reaching 3.6 million men in 1958.

While reforming the most visible elements of Soviet military power, Stalin diverted resources from national recovery programs into programs for developing nuclear weapons and delivery systems. His concentration in word and deed on improving ground force power distracted public attention from the critical atomic arena. Feverish activity in the atomic field, which also involved adroit intelligence work and the cooperation of dragooned German scientists, resulted in production of a Soviet atomic device by 1949, a thermonuclear bomb by 1953, and three new long-range bombers by 1955 (and, by extension, development of a *sputnik* by 1957).

The emergence of a new Soviet view of war, in general, and of offensive operations, in particular, was fundamental to the wholesale changes after Stalin's death in 1953. This new view held that general war would likely begin with or include a nuclear exchange (by strategic aircraft) and would involve use of nuclear weapons on the battlefield. In the late 1950s, however, while the Soviets recognized the importance of nuclear weapons, they tempered their assessment of the impact of those weapons on the battlefield. Thus, a leading military theorist noted that "under contemporary conditions the use of weapons of mass destruction in operations can achieve greater success only in combination with artillery fire and aviation strikes". Moreover, "the use of atomic weapons considerably lessens the requirements for artillery in the conduct of an offensive operation, but that new weapon cannot entirely abolish or replace artillery and aviation, which will play a large role in the course of an operation"[11] The same analyst warned that the appearance of new weapons always required careful reassessment of military theory and the development of powerful nuclear weapons made such study essential. Thus, while Khrushchev consolidated his power, Soviet military doctrine began taking cognizance of the nuclear age. The Zhukov force reorganization, which involved the replacement of the cumbersome mechanized divisions and relatively immobile rifle divisions by new motorized rifle divisions, reflected that evolving doctrine.

MILITARY STRATEGY

Soviet postwar military art, in general, and military strategy, in particular, fully reflected basic concepts expressed in the Red Army field regulations of 1944 amended by the experiences of 1945 operations, in particular the Vistula–Oder, Berlin, and Manchurian operations. Military art emphasized reliance on the offensive, characterized by widespread maneuver and judicious use of massed armor, artillery, and airpower to effect success on the battlefield. The offensive model was that of 1944–45, although infantry (rifle) forces were gradually motorized and mechanized, and the last cavalry formations soon faded from the scene.

These offensive concepts reflected older deep battle themes, so evident in the 1936 and 1944 field regulations, by stressing that:

> offensive combat consists in suppressing the enemy by mighty fire of all means and by a blow in his entire depth of defense, and is conducted by a decisive offensive of the entire combat formation.[12]

In the strategic realm, the Soviets emphasized study of the fundamental theme of conducting strategic operations and also devoted time to study the nature of the strategic defense and how to effect a transition from the defensive to an offensive. In view of the Zhukov force reorganization, combined-arms operations became an important focus of study. In this context the Soviets studied extensively the military art of foreign nations, particularly the United States. Unique postwar conditions, including rapid technological change and increased mechanization of forces, required intensive reflection on wartime strategic operations.

The Soviets assumed a future world war would be an armed clash between two powerful coalitions of states with differing political systems, each fielding armed forces of many millions of men, and each with fully mobilized "economic and morale capabilities".[13] War involved not only defeat of enemy forces within theaters of war, but also the undermining of a nation's economic potential, the occupation of important regions, and the dismemberment of the opposing coalition by forcing its members to surrender unconditionally. Since a number of intermediate military-political objectives had to be accomplished to achieve final war aims, it was necessary to conduct a series of successive strategic offensive operations. In these strategic operations, the ground forces bore the main burden of struggle assisted by other armed forces elements. The Soviets recognized the existance of several types of strategic operations, including the strategic offensive, the strategic defense, and the counteroffensive. They considered the strategic offensive, however, to be most important.

The Soviets defined the strategic offensive as the:

> main and decisive form of strategic operations by the armed forces and only as a result of it was it possible to defeat the strategic formation of the enemy armed forces in the theater, capture vitally important territory and finally smash enemy resistance and ensure victory.[14]

Offensive operations by groups of *fronts* as before:

> were considered the basic form of strategic actions. All questions of

177

their preparation and conduct within the theory of strategy were resolved on the basis of generalizing the rich experience of the Great Patriotic War. In addition, it was believed that the parameters of strategic offensive operations (operations by groups of *fronts*) in comparison with the past war increased somewhat in light of the growing armed strength, mobility, and fire-power of the ground forces.

Strategic defense, as before, was recognized as a temporary form of strategic action. Its form remained defensive operations by groups of *fronts* with the participation of formations and large formations of all types of armed forces.[15]

The Soviets reckoned that the scale of future strategic operations corresponded with the scale of 1944 and 1945 operations. Consequently, they believed that each strategic operation encompassed one or two strategic directions or a full theater of military operations to its entire depth. In larger theaters of war, full execution of strategic missions required two or more successive strategic operations. A strategic operation involved participation of a group of reinforced *fronts*, one or two air armies, airborne divisions, military transport aviation, air defense forces, and, in coastal regions, naval forces.[16]

The General Staff developed the concept for and planned the strategic operation and determined the composition and formation of forces, the direction of the main effort, the strategic missions of the group of *fronts*, and the approximate timing of the offensive. The width of the strategic offensive sector ranged from 400–600 kilometers (two *fronts*) to 800–1,200 kilometers (four *fronts*), and within this sector, forces concentrated in one or several *front* penetration sectors. Extensive artillery and air preparations preceded the offensive. *Front* commands controlled the artillery preparation, and the air force commander or one of the *front* commanders controlled the critical air offensive operation. The air operation, which was planned to last two to three days, involved one or two air armies, long-range aviation, and national air defense forces. Its objective was to achieve air supremacy by destroying enemy tactical air forces in the air or on their own airfields; by destroying airfields, ammunition and POL dumps; and by neutralizing enemy radar systems. The strategic offensive commenced simultaneously with the air operation and sought to encircle enemy forces or fragment the enemy strategic front by direct attack and destroy enemy forces piecemeal.[17]

Encirclement operations by groups of *fronts*, the most decisive form of offensive actions, involved two *front* operations conducted along converging directions (as in the Belorussian operation) or one or two *fronts* conducting enveloping attacks to force the enemy against a natural obstacle (sea, mountains) (as in the East Prussian operation). Swift development of the offensive into the depths and toward the flanks would result in the encirclement of enemy strategic groups. Mechanized armies launched deep sustained strikes and cooperated with airborne divisions dropped deep in the enemy rear to complete the envelopment.

Direct attacks by *fronts* deployed on a broad frontage were designed to achieve multiple penetrations (as in the Vistula–Oder and Manchurian operations) and paralyze the enemy's ability to maneuver forces laterally. This, however, required considerable concentration of manpower and weaponry in critical penetration sectors. Both forms of the offensive, the envelopment and the direct attack, were to begin with penetration operations conducted by *fronts* and armies. This Soviet view on the nature of strategic operations and internal security requirements within the Soviet bloc dictated armed forces' strength and the organization of military forces stationed in peacetime central and eastern Europe.

Within the context of strategic operations, the premier operational level organization was the *front*, designated to perform both operational and strategic missions. Front operations involved a "series of army operations executed either simultaneously or successively". By exploiting the operational capabilities of new weapons, *fronts* were to "split the operational structure of the enemy along the front and in the depths into isolated pockets and destroy them one by one ... to encircle and defeat resisting enemy forces in a given direction with the envelopment of the whole depth of his operational organization".[18] *Fronts*, operating in sectors of from 200–300 kilometers, deployed strong shock groups in one or several penetration sectors of up to 50 kilometers wide.

The *front*'s operational formation consisted of a first echelon of combined-arms armies, *front* mobile groups consisting of one or two mechanized armies, a second echelon, frontal aviation, airborne forces (one or two divisions), a *front* antiaircraft group, and a reserve. *Fronts* employed mechanized armies in first echelon when operating against hasty enemy defenses. *Front* operations had the immediate mission of penetrating enemy army group defenses on the first day of the operation with first echelon armies, then encircling and destroying first echelon enemy forces. Subsequently, the *front* developed the offensive by committing its mechanized armies through 8–12-kilometer sectors on the second day of the operation. The mechanized armies and follow-on second echelon forces then conducted the exploitation operation to destroy enemy operational and strategic reserves to a depth of 200 kilometers.[19] Thus, the *front*'s operational frontage and depth of mission increased dramatically in comparison with norms of the third period of the Great Patriotic War. The Soviets expected the duration of *front* (and army) operations to be shorter than those in the war years.

WAR PLANNING:

Forward Defense (The GOFG 1946 Plan)

Faint glimpses of Soviet postwar war planning offer a contradictory picture regarding the relative degree of offensiveness of Soviet military strategy. While theoretical writings underscored Soviet faith in the offensive, recently declassified Soviet materials argue that Soviet strategy was more subtle, at least prior to 1949, when the Soviets now claim the Cold War began.

In February 1989 the Soviets surfaced a "pre-Cold War" model for a future Soviet strategic defensive posture when they published in their *Military-historical journal* excerpts from a 1946 operations plan for the Group of Occupation Forces, Germany (GOFG) (see figure 31). The 1946 plan was probably indicative of General Staff concepts current in 1988 and early 1989. Although the operational plan had certain paragraphs deleted, those published portrayed a defense in sector followed by a counteroffensive to restore the international borders. Comparison of the plan's details with Western intelligence materials affirm its overall authenticity, but also raises some critical issues associated with deleted elements of the plan.

The introduction to the plan, entitled "Whence the Threat" described what it termed the Soviet "defensive" strategic posture in 1946, stating:

> At the end of 1946–beginning of 1947, the General Staff of the Armed Forces of the USSR presented the Higher Military Council with "A Plan for the Active Defense of the Territory of The Soviet Union." In accordance with this plan, the following tasks were put before the Armed Forces:
> – to assure the reliable repulsion of aggression and the integrity of the borders established by international agreements after the Second World War;
> – to be prepared to repel an enemy air attack, including one with the possible use of atomic weapons;
> – for the Navy to be prepared to repel air aggression from maritime directions [axes] and to provide support to Ground Forces operating in coastal regions.

To resolve these tasks it was envisioned that on the primary directions the Armed Forces should consist of the following:
a. a repulsion (blocking) army including troops of fortified regions;
b. troops of the reserve of the Supreme High Command;
c. secondary troops and new formations, above all for supplying these directions during military operations. It was planned to deploy the second and third components only in time of war to repel aggression.[20]

Blocking armies (*armiia otpora*), located in the groups of forces deployed in central Europe, had the mission of "shattering the enemy in the border defensive zone and preparing conditions for going over to the counter-offensive"[21] High Command reserve forces were to strike advancing enemy main forces in conjunction with blocking armies, defeat them, and participate in the counteroffensive. Secondary (mobilization) forces, maintained at cadre strength in peacetime, were to mobilize within seven days and concentrate in designated assembly areas between ten and 20 days after receipt of the mobilization order.[22]

Within this strategic context the GOFG plan concentrated Soviet defenses within a 50 to 150-kilometer belt inside the Soviet Occupation Zone of Germany. Regimental-size covering forces deployed in a 50-kilometer security zone (belt) along the border, backed up by two combined-arms armies, which occupied three subsequent defensive belts. Further to the rear, two mechanized armies concentrated in assembly areas from which they could launch coordinated counter-strokes. The GOFG plan indicated the numerical designations of all combat divisions and major supporting units participating in the defense.

The plan required Soviet forces to operate in classic World War II fashion (see Figure 32). The two combined-arms armies (3rd Shock and 8th Guards) defended in three defensive belts 50, 100, and 150 kilometers from the border. Each rifle division in the first defensive belt deployed one regiment forward, which, with police units, functioned as a covering force along all roads leading into the Soviet Zone of Occupation. Covering forces were to delay in sector as the enemy attack developed.

The main defensive belt ran through Wismar to Ludwigslust and then along the Elbe and Saal rivers to the Czech border. The "primary forces of rifle and mechanized divisions of 3rd Shock Army and 8th Guards Army". together with army and reinforcing units occupied this belt.[23] Each army formed in two echelons with its rifle divisions and mechanized regiments of mechanized divisions in first echelon and tank regiments of mechanized divisions and 11th Tank Division of 3rd Shock Army in

Фотокопия первой страницы обложки дела, в котором
находятся оперативные планы Группы советских оккупа-
ционных войск в Германии, разработанные в 1946 году.

31. Cover sheet, Soviet GOFG operational plan, 1946

second echelon. Forward armies had orders to "prevent enemy penetration of the main defense belt before the approach of counterattacking mechanized armies"[24] The second and third defense belts were reconnoitered but initially left unoccupied.

1st and 2nd Guards Mechanized Armies, located in the operational rear, received orders to "annihilate the advancing enemy".[25] After concentration in assembly areas, the two mechanized armies were to strike simultaneously along the Berlin–Magdeburg axis. They also received secondary missions of launching strikes toward Schwerin (2nd Guards Mech) and Leipzig (1st Guards Mech).

This then was the basic GOFG defensive scheme. One can judge how well this plan accorded with reality by comparing its contents with the U.S. intelligence picture of GOFG in 1946–47, particularly regarding the composition of the force and how it was disposed (see Figure 33). In both respects, interesting relationships emerge, which, on the one hand, tend to validate the plan and provide hints as to what paragraphs were deleted from it and, on the other hand, raise disturbing issues, which the original plan neglected to mention.[26]

The GOFG order of battle matched U.S. intelligence estimates with two notable exceptions. Most divisions shown as subordinate to 3rd Shock and 8th Guards Armies reflected period intelligence assessments. The 82nd Guards Rifle Division of 8th Guards Army, which is included in the plan, according to intelligence assessments returned to the Soviet Union from GOFG some time in 1947 or 1948. The divisions of the two mechanized armies also conformed to intelligence estimates, but with two notable exceptions: the 1st Tank Division of 2nd Guards Mechanized Army and the 19th Guards Mechanized Division of 1st Guards Mechanized Army did not appear in intelligence assessments. Their location, however, corresponded to the assessed locations of two cadre regiments of cadre divisions U.S. intelligence detected northwest and southwest of Berlin.[27]

According to U.S. intelligence estimates, Soviet force dispositions also matched those of the defensive plan. Four regiments from the 94th Guards and 207th Rifle Divisions of 3rd Shock Army and the 57th Guards and 39th Guards Rifle Divisions of 8th Guards Army were, indeed, positioned well forward of their parent units in a 50-kilometer security zone east of the international border. Rifle and mechanized divisions of the two armies were garrisoned along the line Wismar–Ludwigslust–Elbe River–Saal River; that is, where the GOFG's plan showed the forward edge of the first defensive belt to be located. The locations of all other divisions of GOFG in the plan conformed to U.S. intelligence estimates.[28]

The GOFG plan, however, differed in one important respect from

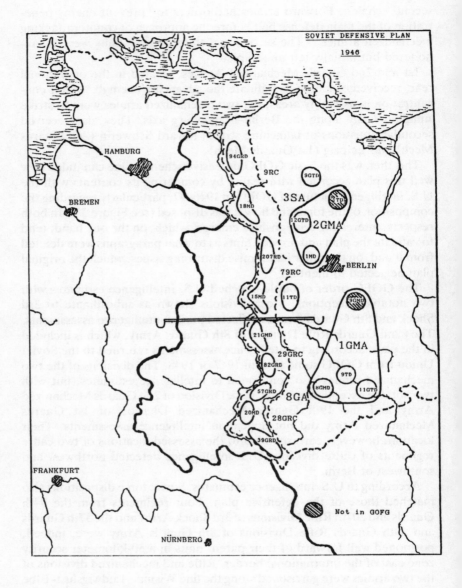

32. Soviet force dispositions, Soviet GOFG operation plan, 1946

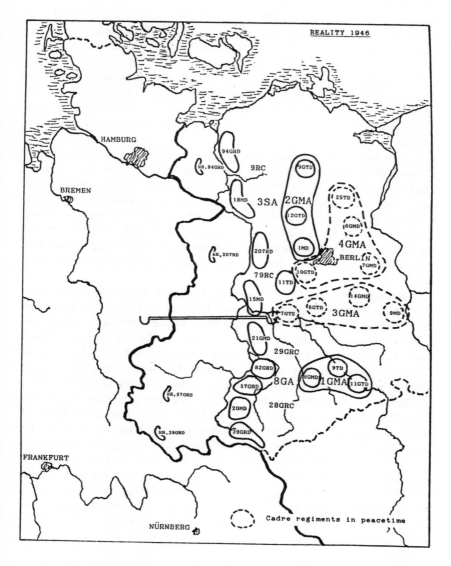

33. Soviet GOFG force dispositions, 1946 (according to U.S. intelligence assessments)

intelligence assessments, and this probably explained the appearance in the plan of the two divisions (1st Tank and 19th Guards Mechanized) not listed in U.S. intelligence reports. According to those intelligence estimates, from 1946 to 1948 the Soviets maintained eight divisions at cadre strength, above and beyond those full-strength divisions listed in both the GOFG plan and U.S. intelligence estimates. These divisions belonged to the former 3rd and 4th Guards Tank Armies, which had been a part of GOFG in 1945 and early 1946. These two armies, renamed mechanized, were demobilized during 1946, and their eight divisions reverted to cadre status.[29]

According to the same intelligence reports, after demobilization, each of these divisions was reduced to cadre regiment strength, that is, 25th Tank Division became the 25th Cadre Tank Regiment. In wartime each cadre regiment would be mobilized into a full division, and the eight divisions would operate under 3rd and 4th Guards Mechanized Army control. (The army headquarters remained in GOFG.) Although the published GOFG plan mentioned neither army, they were apparently among those "secondary" forces which could be mobilized within seven days.

In all likelihood, the GOFG plan, as published, demonstrated an even shorter mobilization option. The two mystery divisions, 1st Tank and 19th Guards Mechanized Divisions, were located precisely where two cadre regiments existed according to U.S. intelligence reports. These were designated the 25th Cadre Tank Regiment and the 14th Guards Cadre Mechanized Regiment. 1st Tank Division and 19th Guards Mechanized Division probably formed around a nucleus of these two regiments, reinforced with the six other full-strength cadre regiments from the other cadre divisions of 3rd and 4th Guards Mechanized Armies. Thus, in a short-warning circumstance (short of seven days), the four cadre regiments of 3rd and 4th Guards Mechanized Armies could rapidly form two new divisions for GOFG, which would then be assigned to 1st and 2nd Guards Mechanized Armies. In a longer warning scenario, and certainly within seven days, the full 3rd and 4th Guards Mechanized Armies would emerge in the GOFG Order of Battle, increasing GOFG strength from 16 to 24 divisions. During the Berlin Crisis, both 3rd and 4th Guards Mechanized Armies were rapidly brought up to full strength, where they remained until 1958, when the two armies again disappeared, and their divisions were reassigned to 18th and 20th Guards Armies.[30]

From 1949 until 1987, powerful groups of forces (potential wartime *fronts*) maintained in peacetime at full combat strength and based in the forward area (central and eastern Europe) represented the focal point of the Soviet strategic force posture. These forward forces provided Soviet strategic planners with the potential capability for conducting major strategic offensive operations with minimal additional initial force generation. Large-scale exercises within the Soviet Union and eastern Europe confirmed this planning focus. Despite these powerful forward forces, experience convinced Soviet military planners that even this force required significant wartime augmentation, which could only be provided by an extensive force generation system incorporating the best of tested, traditional features.

FORCE GENERATION

During the initial postwar years, after the demobilization of 1946–48, which reduced Soviet Army strength from over 6 million men and 550 divisions to fewer than 3 million men and about 180 divisions, Soviet military strategy required a force fully capable of executing wartime plans. This entailed creation of a force generation system which could increase the army at least three-fold in the event of war to 9 million men and 540 divisions.

	Manpower	*Divisions*
Peacetime	3m	180
Wartime		
M+5	3m	180
M+30	6m	360
M+120	9m	540[31]

As before June 1941, the Soviets maintained forces at several levels of readiness, with forces in the forward region at the highest level. They employed the following tested techniques to form new wartime divisions:

(1) maintaining formations at varous levels of peacetime fill;
(2) cadreing formations at the next lower unit level (cadre regiments for divisions);
(3) splitting peacetime higher-fill formations into two or more like wartime formations;
(4) employing cadre from higher-fill formations to form the nucleus of similar new formations.[32]

The Soviets elevated peacetime formations at varying levels of fill or status to a wartime status according to mobilization priorities, each with its own mobilizations time-table (M+5, M+30, M+120). Collectively, these mobilization schemes exhausted the supply of manpower under 35 years of age. Finally, mobilized forces were integrated into the active armed force in accordance with postwar concepts of strategic echelonment, which mirrored somewhat the echelonment structure of 1941 amended to reflect forward basing of forces.[33] This structure included a first strategic echelon of forces deployed in the forward groups of forces and perhaps augmented by high-readiness divisions within the western military districts, a second strategic echelon within the Soviet Union (probably the border military districts), and a strategic reserve drawn from the interior military districts and mobilization base. During the late 1950s, this strategic echelonment became a subject of controversy, as many argued it did not fully reflect the realities of nuclear warfare. Specifically, the two strategic echelons seemed to lack requisite strength and depth. Consequently, by 1960 the Soviets altered this traditional echelonment.

THE SECOND POSTWAR PERIOD (1961–1970): THE REVOLUTION IN
MILITARY AFFAIRS

General

During the late 1950s internal change within the Soviet Union accelerated and created conditions for continued de-Stalinization. The Soviet Union emerged as a fully qualified superpower capable of challenging the United States politically and technologically. These trends provided the basis for a fundamental shift in Soviet military policy, doctrine and strategy. Internally, by 1960 Khrushchev had emerged as first among equals on the political stage, although the principle of collective leadership remained intact. Consequently, Khrushchev was able to undertake internal economic initiatives within an overall program designed to insure future Soviet economic supremacy over the United States. This ambitious program involved the industrial sector as well as agricultural production (the virgin lands program).

Externally, Khrushchev prepared to exploit Soviet technological achievements (Sputnik's launch in 1957) to carve out for the Soviet Union a more active role in international affairs, one which would, in essence, challenge U.S. global supremacy. In January 1960 Khrushchev provided a framework for the Soviet Union's new strategic posture by declaring that a "revolution" had occurred in military affairs. That revolution accentuated the importance of nuclear war and, in so doing, dictated the

188

global preeminence of the two principal nuclear powers. Almost simultaneously, Khrushchev recognized and exploited the realities of a decaying world colonial structure. By announcing Soviet support for "wars of liberation", he promised blanket Soviet support to nationalities struggling to gain independence from Western colonial powers, and exploited nationalistic trends which had been growing since the end of the Second World War. In a larger sense, the Soviet Union attempted to facilitate the revolutionary process sketched out by Lenin to pit nations against one another on a class basis. These fundamental changes in Soviet foreign policy had an inevitable effect on Soviet military policy, doctrine, and strategy. One of the more viable effects was a more aggressive Soviet policy stance evidenced by the Berlin Wall and the Cuban Missile Crisis.

In 1964 Khrushchev was removed as Party First Secretary in a test of the durability of collective leadership. In part, at least, his removal was prompted by political and military dissatisfaction with increased global tensions, resulting from U.S. challenges to the more offensive Soviet policy (in Laos, Cuba, Berlin, and S.E. Asia). Despite Khrushchev's removal from power, the basic tenets of Soviet policy persisted for several years, propelled forward by a basic inertia. Beneath the surface, however, by the mid and late 1960s, there was a growing Soviet uneasiness over the possible consequences of a policy of confrontation, particularly confrontation in a nuclear arena with a superior nuclear power. The Soviet response was to seek to end U.S. nuclear supremacy by the achievement of nuclear parity and simultaneously to find solutions other than nuclear for the resolution of military problems.

MILITARY POLICY AND DOCTRINE

Khrushchev's 1960 speech signaled his full commitment to the idea that "a revolution in military affairs" had occurred.[34] That "revolution" recognized the preeminence of nuclear weapons in war, elevated the importance of strategy (signified by the establishment of strategic rocket forces and their emphasis) and diminished the importance of operational art (and, by extension, the ground forces). Among the myriad of works explaining the nature of the revolution in military affairs was V. D. Sokolovsky's 1962 book *Military Strategy* (*Voennaia strategiia*). His description of future war echoed Khrushchev's view that "both gigantic military coalitions will deploy massive armies in a future decisive world war; all modern, powerful and long-range means of combat, including multi-megaton nuclear-rocket weapons, will be used in it on a huge scale; and the most decisive methods of military operations will be used".[35] Sokolovsky maintained that strategic nuclear forces could themselves

189

decide the outcome of war without resort to extended ground operations, and even if ground operations occurred:

> mass nuclear-rocket strikes will be of decisive importance for the attainment of goals in a future world war. The infliction of these assaults will be the main, decisive method of waging war...armed conflicts in ground theaters of military operations will also take place differently. The defeat of the enemy's groupings of ground troops, the destruction of his rockets, aircraft and nuclear weapons ... will be achieved mainly by nuclear-rocket strikes.[36]

Ground forces were to exploit the effects of nuclear strikes, defeat enemy forces, and conquer and occupy territory. Within this nuclear context, ground forces played a distinctly secondary role to strategic rocket forces, and strategy became dominant over operational art:

> All this shows that the relationship between the role and importance of armed combat waged by forces in direct contact with the enemy in the zone of combat operations, employing simultaneously tactical, operational and strategic means of destruction on the one hand, and the role and importance of armed combat waged beyond the confines of this zone by strategic means alone on the other hand has shifted abruptly toward an increase in the role and importance of the latter.[37]

This belief in the predominance of nuclear weapons in warfare persisted for several years after Khrushchev's ouster from power. In 1966, A. A. Strokov noted in his classic work on the history of military art that the existence of nuclear rockets and the equipping of large units and formations with them had prompted a fundamental change in operational art and tactics. Specifically, the use of nuclear weapons could achieve strategic results "independently from the conduct of operations and battles".[38] In a general war situation, the Soviets viewed operational art as clearly subordinate to nuclear strategy, although it did retain its importance for local wars.

Strokov's comments illuminated another aspect of doctrinal change, which emerged in the 1960s and continued to develop in subsequent years. Responding to the changing world order, specifically the breakdown of old colonial empires and the emergence of a "third" world, in 1960 Khrushchev committed the Soviet Union to support "wars of national liberation". These wars, while contributing to instability in capitalist societies, promised fresh opportunities for the expansion of socialism, as developments in Vietnam and Cuba had indicated. In subsequent years Soviet support for this new type of warfare matured from simple verbal support, through even more extensive materiel assistance, to the direct employment of military advisers and proxies in specific regions of the world. In essence, this new Soviet policy represented the practical implementation of Lenin's description of revolution in the imperialist stage of development – revolution of a proletariat of underdeveloped nations against their capitalist masters. Thus, at the highest levels of military doctrine, significant changes occurred in the post-Stalin years, reflected by the evolving Soviet force structure and in new Soviet concepts for conducting war at the strategic, operational, and tactical levels.

After 1960 Khrushchev reduced the size of the armed forces to facilitate the requirements of the new Soviet doctrinal stance. From a strength of 3.6 million and 180 divisions in 1958, the force shrank to 2.5 million and 160 divisions in 1962 and to 2 million men organized in 138 divisions in 1968. This truncation program benefited the newly-created strategic rocket forces at the expense of the ground forces, which, for a time, lost their independent status.

The force generation (mobilization) system of the 1950s continued until the late 1960s and was based on the same 1939 Law of Universal Military Service.[39] A new universal military service law, adopted in 1967, decreased the term of service in some services (for example, from three years to two years in the ground forces), but adjusted age and time limitations for reserve obligations. This accorded with the reduced peacetime strength of the army, but maintained a significant mobilization capability.

MILITARY STRATEGY

While older operational concepts endured, coexisting with a growing nuclear arsenal, Soviet theorists worked feverishly to develop less ambiguous strategic, operational, and tactical concepts governing the use of the Soviet armed forces. By the time Sokolovsky had given full definition to the "revolution in military affairs", those concepts had finally received more complete definition. His work *Military Strategy* provided the context within which other authors could define the role of the armed forces in war – which by definition would be nuclear. Having accorded to strategic rocket forces the key role of deciding the ultimate outcome of war, Sokolovsky said that ground operations, if required, were to be conducted in close concert with nuclear strikes. With the use of nuclear strikes, "great possibilities are created for waging extensive mobile offensive operations with highly mobile mechanized troops."[40] War was likely to begin with a nuclear exchange. Ground operations would occur against this nuclear backdrop, and theater ground forces would have the mission of mopping up enemy theater forces after the devastating initial nuclear exchange. Ground operations would involve use of mobile tank and motorized rifle formations, supported by nuclear rocket forces, conducting deep operations at high speed, often on multiple axes, in order to exploit the effects of nuclear strikes, defeat enemy forces, and conquer and occupy territory.

Given the increased vulnerability of ground forces to nuclear fires and the reduced importance of conventional operations, the Soviets adopted a single echelon strategic force configuration. The first strategic echelon consisted of all active forces, regardless of location. The second strategic echelon and strategic reserve encompassed the remaining mobilization base. The first strategic echelon now numbered three operational echelons, located respectively in the forward groups of forces, the western military districts, and the interior of the Soviet Union.[41]

At the strategic level, strategic rocket forces, long-range aviation and nuclear missile submarines were to strike the economic base, the nuclear delivery means, the armed forces, and the very center of political power of potential enemy nations. Thus, rocket forces, able to achieve principal strategic aims in a relatively short time, broadened the arena of war. Ground forces, equipped with their own operational-tactical and tactical nuclear rockets, performed the lesser role of destroying enemy forces and nuclear weapons and occupying enemy territory within a theater of war. In contrast to earlier wars, however, the ground forces were to exploit the results of strategic rocket strikes and more rapidly and decisively fulfill their missions. *Fronts*, still viewed as strategic-operational formations, conducted strategic offensive operations in cooperation with airborne forces to satisfy strategic missions within the theater of military operations. The rapidity of the operation within the fluid environment of nuclear war dictated direct control of these strategic operations by the General Staff (*Stavka*).

The appearance of nuclear weapons and their proliferation on the battlefield increased the vulnerability of conventional ground forces, required their dispersal on the battlefield, thus negating the old definition of mass, and increased the importance of maneuver by mobile, self-contained operational and tactical units. Concentration of forces to conduct the classic frontal penetration operation, "gnawing through" the defense, became folly; and the Soviets rejected the idea of set-piece battle conducted in carefully patterned arrays.[42] The comparative invulnerability of armor to nuclear strikes, the mobility of armored units, and the growing importance of relatively quick success in initial offensive operations prompted the Soviets to place greater emphasis on the use of

192

tank units in first echelon at every level of command. Thus, the classic function of exploitation forces (mobile groups) blurred a bit. Exploitation could now occur initially in any operation after nuclear strikes by use of reinforced tank units in first or second echelon.

The threat of nuclear attack on the Soviet Union elevated the defense of the homeland to the level of a distinct strategic operation. *PVO Strany* (national air defense) forces performed the mission of defending important economic, political, military, and population centers against enemy attack. To supplement active strategic defense measures, the Soviets instituted a more passive civil defense program as a facet of strategic defense. With the inclusion of missile firing submarines into the Soviet armed forces, the realm of strategic operations broadened to include the sea. Above all other strategic considerations, the Soviets intensified their analysis of the nature of the initial period of war, which loomed more prominently in an age of potential surprise nuclear attack.

While nuclear weapons occupied center stage after 1960 in the strategic realm, they also dominated the field of operational art. Precisely stated, "the main means of destruction in operational large units of all types of armed forces are rocket-nuclear weapons". The outcome of battles and operations:

> depends in large measure on the results of nuclear strikes. The capability of simultaneous and sudden attack with nuclear rocket and conventional means on the entire depth of the enemy's operational formation on land and sea theaters of military operations, regardless of whether they are attacking or defending, and also of destroying objectives in the deep enemy rear has acquired very important meaning. Skillful use of rocket-nuclear weapons secures in a shorter period than in previous wars, the infliction of large enemy losses, the destruction of important objectives and groupings, and the creation of a favorable correlation of forces.[43]

The complexity of conducting rapid operations in the dangerous environment of nuclear warfare "created favorable conditions for perfecting the theory and practice of deep offensive operations".

The scope of *front* operations increased in terms of tempo and depth of operations as a consequence of the requirement to achieve more decisive aims in shorter periods of time. *Fronts*, attacking in sectors of up to 400 kilometers, advanced to depths of up to 300 kilometers to fulfill their missions. Although the requirement to concentrate forces on critical directions still existed, it could only be accomplished by dispersing and fragmenting large units to avoid creating compact formations in restricted spaces vulnerable to nuclear fires and then concentrating forces rapidly, at the last moment, in critical attack sectors. Likewise, it was no longer necessary to establish high operational densities of artillery. Use of nuclear weapons and timely concentration of the most maneuverable forces (tank) on decisive directions provided necessary superiority over a defending enemy.

A *front* offensive began with nuclear attacks on main enemy groups, in particular against enemy nuclear delivery means, and ground forces launched simultaneous attacks along both main and secondary directions. Attacking *front* forces were supported by air armies, by the nuclear strikes of operational-tactical and tactical rocket forces, and by *front* aviation. Their primary initial task was to destroy enemy atomic artillery, rocket units, and tactical aviation to the operational depth of the defense. Because of the enemy nuclear threat, Soviet *front* forces deployed a considerable distance from the front lines and then launched their attack after an extensive approach march from the rear area. While the Soviets maintained that *fronts* could deploy in a variety of formations, the extended two echelon configuration offered better dispersion and lessened the risk of damage from nuclear attack. Tank armies, because of their mobility and strength, attacked from *front* first echelon, particularly if enemy defenses were weak.

Penetration of prepared enemy defenses avoided "gnawing through" the defense in narrow penetration sectors. Instead, nuclear strikes blew holes in the defense through which tank and motorized rifle divisions of first echelon armies passed as rapidly as possible in march formation. Thus, *front* attack sectors were wider than in previous years (up to 400 kilometers). The *front* offensive developed along separate operational directions using maneuver to a maximum extent in order to strike enemy forces in the flanks and rear. Because of the absence of a dense linear front, flexible maneuver of artillery fires and nuclear strikes filled the gaps between units. Airborne units exploited these nuclear fires and assisted in encircling enemy formations.[44] Consequently, the *front* offensive became a complex of fragmented (*ochagovyi*) and separate battles requiring extreme initiative on the part of all combat leaders.

Unlike previous periods, tank forces played a significant role in the *front* penetration operation, as well as in the subsequent exploitation phase.[45] Tank armies (as well as combined-arms armies) deployed in *front* first echelon, and tank divisions deployed in the first echelon of combined-arms armies (and tank armies). They initiated the attack after the initial nuclear strikes and advanced immediately into the operational depth of the enemy defense to achieve the objectives of the *front* operation. They also performed the task of neutralizing enemy nuclear capabilities and of cooperating with airborne forces landed deep in the enemy rear. Combined-arms armies of the *front* second echelon and motorized rifle divisions of first echelon armies followed tank forces and completed the destruction of remaining enemy ground forces. After penetration of the enemy defenses, on such a fluid battlefield, meeting engagements with enemy reserves or counterattacking forces were likely to occur. To deal with these and to ensure high advance tempos, the Soviet forces advanced in march column (pre-combat formation) led by strong forward detachments.* March columns were configured to permit rapid deployment of tank-heavy forces into required operational or combat formations so that they could repel enemy attacks from any direction

Another variant of offensive and exploitation operations involved meeting an enemy force occupying prepared positions on good defensible terrain and supported by nuclear artillery, rockets, air and antitank and antiaircraft missiles. In this instance, enemy infantry and armored divisions would likely be deployed in depth with only covering forces located in forward positions. The Soviets planned to attack these defenses with nuclear rockets, airstrikes, and concentrated conventional artillery fire, while tank units (battalions, regiments and divisions), coordinating with the nuclear strikes and air support, penetrated the defense from the march.

Soviet military theorists believed that *front* offensive operations were most effective if conducted simultaneously along several operational directions to split enemy forces and destroy each part in piecemeal fashion. The Soviets concentrated nuclear strikes and the largest offensive forces by last-minute moves on the most critical attack directions. Continuous high-intensity operations conducted to the depth of the enemy defense were complex and involved the following measures:

- systematic struggle with enemy nuclear delivery means;
- destruction of opposing units by nuclear fires;
- engagement of enemy reserves;
- providing continuous aviation support for advancing forces;
- furnishing continuous engineer and chemical security for advancing forces;
- development of the offensive by day and night.[46]

The necessity for achieving a rapid offensive tempo required ground forces to advance primarily on tanks and in armored personnel carriers, supported by necessary fires. These forces used intervals and gaps in the

---

* Pre-combat (or pre-battle) formation is a march configuration of a unit from which the unit can engage the enemy, regardless of his direction of attack.

enemy operational defense to strike the enemy's flanks and rear, to cut up, surround, and destroy enemy units.

Modern airborne forces had the capability of conducting operational air-landing operations in support of offensive *front* operations. Airborne forces exploited nuclear strikes, neutralized enemy nuclear units, and secured operationally important objectives, such as river crossings, bridgeheads, and mountain passes. Airborne operations were employed only if enemy antiaircraft fire was suppressed and if Soviet forces had a marked superiority over the enemy. Larger operational drops (multi-regimental, divisional) occurred late in an operation in coordination with the advance of large, exploiting tank forces, while smaller drops (battalions or regiments) supported the advance of tactical units.[47]

Depending on how war began, the Soviets believed defensive operations would occur initially, during pauses between offensive operations, or along secondary directions. As in earlier periods, in defensive operations Soviet forces sought to economize forces, win time, defend territory just seized, repulse counterattacks by superior enemy forces, or provide respite when nuclear attack means had been expended. The Soviets, however, considerably altered earlier defensive techniques. They dispersed their defenses in width and depth and concentrated them along the most important directions. Rocket forces, engineer obstacles, and mobile forces covered the gaps between units by both fire and maneuver. Defenses were anti-nuclear and thus involved maximum use of cover, concealment, and defensive measures against enemy employment of chemical and nuclear attack. Air defenses were heaviest over firing positions, command and control centers, airfields, and rear objectives; and the Soviets placed considerable emphasis on antitank defenses, in particular the use of antitank guided missiles. They supported defensive efforts with heavy nuclear and conventional rocket artillery, air counter-preparations, and armor-heavy counterattacks, cooperating with airborne assaults deep in the rear of penetrating enemy units. *Fronts* and armies defended primarily in two-echelon operational formation, with tank units deployed in second echelon, from where they could launch counterattacks.[48]

The 1960 revolution in military affairs drastically altered the nature of air support in both offensive and defensive operations. Until 1959 air operations still involved a struggle for air superiority in the form of the air offensive. The growing importance of nuclear rockets, however, changed the meaning of air superiority and the nature of the air offensive itself. Now the destruction of enemy nuclear rocket and nuclear air forces became the principal mission of air and rocket forces. Consequently, the Soviets armed the *front*, long-range aviation, and fighter aviation forces

POST-SECOND WORLD WAR SOVIET MILITARY STRATEGY

with more capable bombs, rockets, and guns. The longer ranged Soviet aircraft permitted air operations to cover the *front* rear areas and the deep enemy rear. In addition, *front* aviation cooperated more closely with front air defense units. The most important mission of *front* aviation became the destruction of smaller enemy mobile targets, primarily nuclear delivery means. Long-range aviation conducted reconnaissance, transported troops and equipment, and evacuated casualties. *Front* air defense forces in conjunction with *PVO Strany* forces organized air defense in the front sector during the air offensive and subsequent combat operations.[49]

The nature of combat operations in nuclear war placed a high premium on nuclear and chemical defense, on radio-electronic combat, and on the creation of mobile, survivable command and control systems. Nuclear and chemical defense units and subunits were incorporated into every command level, and necessary defensive equipment proliferated throughout the force structure. Training strongly emphasized chemical and nuclear defense, decontamination, and operations across contaminated zones. Radio-electronic combat, emphasized at all command levels, sought to disrupt enemy command and control, in particular command and control of nuclear delivery units and, simultaneously, to protect friendly communications. The increased dynamism and scope of operations dictated creation of new, more flexible command and control systems and required commanders and staffs to prepare, implement, and alter plans more rapidly. This prompted early Soviet attempts to automate command and control procedures.

The nuclear battlefield also placed a premium on timely collection and dissemination of intelligence. Hence, new types of mobile command posts evolved at all levels, often located in armored vehicles, aircraft and helicopters. Dense, redundant communications nets linked headquarters at each level of command, using radios with greater range and accuracy. Computers assisted rapid communications between rocket units, aircraft, ships, and major land command posts. Logistical measures to support the more intense and complicated operations involved increased emphasis on resupply of fuel and ammunition to front line units. The threat of nuclear interdiction required emphasis on building peacetime logistical stocks in the forward area, creating high-bulk delivery of required materials forward (pipelines), and creating a more formidable transport aviation capability.

While the revolution in military affairs did not abruptly end in the late 1960s, Soviet perceptions regarding the relative importance of nuclear *vis à vis* conventional weapons began shifting as early as 1964. Although Soviet belief that development and use of a single family of weapons systems (nuclear) had fundamentally altered the nature of future war eroded by the late 1960s, an indelible legacy endured – in essence, a gnawing concern that warfare would never again be the same. This concern ebbed in the late 1960s, but would rise again in the late 1980s. It is no coincidence that, in this most recent period, Soviet policies, theories, and practices of the 1960s have again become topics of intense discussion.

THE THIRD POSTWAR PERIOD (1971–1985)

General

International conditions during the decades of the 1970s and much of the 1980s stood in stark contrast to each other. The early Brezhnev years promised an enhanced Soviet stature on the global stage. The Soviet Union's principal strategic opponent, the United States, was bogged down in the unpopular Vietnam War, which sapped its strategic vigor and which, in part, prompted United States' adoption of a policy of *détente* to soften the edge of competition between the United States and the Soviet Union. During the 1970s the Soviets also achieved strategic nuclear parity with the West, which ultimately produced a more active international stance by them.

During the 1980s the Soviet Union flexed its international muscles by adopting a more aggressive foreign policy, characterized by reinvigorated support of revolution and insurgency in the Third World and overt Soviet military intervention outside its contiguous borders. The Afghan War, within the broader context of the Brezhnev Doctrine, which had legitimized Soviet foreign intervention in defense of socialism, exacerbated international relations and brought the Soviet Union into a costly arms race with a reinvigorated United States. The ensuing arms race, with its exhausting economic costs, in turn placed prohibitive burdens on the Soviet economy. By the mid-1980s, Soviet popular and official disillusionment with the seemingly paltry gains of its more aggressive international posture coalesced with concern over equally bleak economic prospects to generate strong impetus for changed policies and reform.

Although Khrushchev had fallen from power in 1964, the "single nuclear option" concept for global war continued to dominate Soviet military thought for several years. As early as the mid-1960s, however, subtle changes began to threaten that dominant view.[50] Preoccupation with the strategy of thermonuclear war began to erode, and Soviet theorists began to display renewed interest in questions of operational art and tactics. An early manifestation of this trend was a revival of interest in research and writing on conventional operational themes, past and present. On the basis of this research, Soviet military theorists focused on distinct themes spanning the strategic, operational, and tactical realms, which were relevant to nuclear as well as conventional war. General and specific works on military art investigated precise ground force operational and tactical techniques (albeit in a nuclear context). The sheer detail unearthed by these investigations distinguished them from earlier works written on military affairs during the zenith of the revolution. Included in this new category were Reznichenko's classic work *Tactics* (*Taktika*), Sidorenko's *The Offensive* (*Nastuplenie*), Savkin's *The Basic Principles of Operational Art and Tactics* (*Osnovnye printsipy operativnogo iskusstva i taktiki*), Babadzhanian's *Tank and Tank Forces* (*Tanki i tankovye voiska*), and Bagramian's text for officers, *History of War and Military Art* (*Istoriia voin i voennogo iskusstva*). All paid lip-service to the assumption that general war would be nuclear, but all also dwelt at length on the techniques of ground force operations in far more detail than their predecessors.[51] During this period the Soviets continued their intense investigation of the nature of the initial period of war (*nachal'nyi period voiny*), a focal point of study since 1958.

In these works and in others, caveats began appearing which qualified the Soviet assumption that general war would inevitably be nuclear. In his 1968 revision of *Military Strategy*, Sokolovsky qualified his 1962 statement that "armed combat in ground theaters of military operations...will be achieved mainly by nuclear rocket strikes" by transforming this blunt statement into a question:

> But in essence, the argument is about the basic method of conducting future war: will it be land war with the use of nuclear weapons as a means of supporting the operations of ground troops [the pre-1960 view], or a war that is essentially new, where the main means of solving strategic tasks will be the nuclear rocket weapon: The theory of military art must give an answer to such important questions as: what types of strategic action will be used in nuclear war, and what form military operations must take.[52]

Sokolovsky's tentative answer was that theater operations would occur, but that on the battlefield "the decisive role will be played by nuclear weapons: the other means of armed combat will utilize the results of nuclear strikes for the final defeat of the enemy".[53] Bagramian, in his *Military History* (*Voennaia istoriia*), more succinctly commented, "while working out the means of conducting war in the nuclear situation, Soviet military science has not excluded the possibility of conventional combat".[54] Subsequent Soviet works of the same generation included the same qualification.

Meanwhile, Soviet military analysts intensified their research on operational matters and produced comprehensive studies on virtually every aspect of the Soviet Army's operational and tactical experience – most dealing with the Great Patriotic War (in particular its later stages). As if to highlight these new concerns, in 1965 the Soviets published an anthology of works written by preeminent pre-Second World War Soviet military theorists. The work, entitled *Questions of Strategy and Operational Art in Soviet Military Works 1917–1940* (*Voprosy strategii i operativnogo iskusstva*), with a preface by M. V. Zakharov, Chief of the Soviet General Staff, signaled the rehabilitation of the purged generation of Tukhachevsky and evidenced renewed interest in deep operations (*glubokie operatsii*) and the techniques necessary to achieve them.[55] The following year the Soviets published P. A. Kurochkin's detailed study on army operations, *The Combined-Arms Army in the Offensive* (*Obshchevoiskovaia armiia v nastuplenii*).[56] Writings during the period 1968 to 1972 reflected patient, deliberate, and extensive study of the traditional nature of war and operations as they had developed from the 1930s to 1960.

While Reznichenko, Savkin, Sidorenko, and others enunciated official doctrine, still others published articles and works which focused on the theory and practice of strategy, operational art, and tactics in the Second World War and speculated on the contemporary relevance of those practices. The periodicals *Military Thought* and *Military-Historical Journal* published extensive studies on the Second World War and postwar trends in military art. By the mid-1970s, the number of major studies investigating virtually every aspect of military art, in historical and contemporary contexts, reached flood proportions. A. I. Radzievsky built upon Kurochkin's studies of combined-arms operations. I. E. Krupchenko, P. A. Rotmistrov, A. I. Radzievsky and O. A. Losik surveyed in detail armored warfare and the evolution of Soviet tank forces, while I. I. Lisov, and later D. S. Sukhorukov, resurrected the long-obscured experiences of Soviet airborne forces. Soviet logistics lessons-learned and the future direction of the rear services in supporting theater operations were addressed in S. K. Kurkotkin's 1977 study. In addition, Radzievsky edited a multi-volume study of tactics by combat example at every combat level from platoon through division.[57]

The intense and ongoing concern for operational art and tactics, paralleled by Soviet restructuring of the armed forces to improve their operational capabilities, elevated the importance of these levels of military art from their relative position of neglect in the early 1960s to major areas of concern in the 1970s. Over the ensuing decade and a half, the total subservience of operational art and tactics to the overall strategic considerations of nuclear war lessened to a remarkable degree. Even the seemingly mandatory nuclear context for the discussion of combat at these levels was often absent. Thus, in 1979, Marshal V. G. Kulikov wrote, "Successful operations by formations and units of the armed forces, or branches of the armed forces, and of specialized forces, especially during combat using conventional weapons, retain their importance."[58]

During this revival of concern for more traditional strategy, operational art, and tactics, the Soviets re-investigated all aspects of military art. Certain topics, however, received greater attention than others. During the 1970s the Soviets formulated the concept of *protivoiadernyi manevr* (anti-nuclear maneuver).[59] First expressed in defensive terms in the early 1970s, by the mid-1980s that concept provided a cornerstone for Soviet operational and tactical techniques designed to pre-empt, preclude, or inhibit enemy resort to nuclear warfare. As articulated in 1987 by V. G. Reznichenko, "The continuous conduct of battle at a high tempo creates unfavorable conditions for enemy use of weapons of mass destruction. He cannot determine targets for nuclear strikes exactly and, besides, will often be forced to shift his nuclear delivery means."[60] The Soviets tentatively decided that even greater emphasis on this type of maneuver was also a partial remedy to countering enemy use of high-precision weaponry.[61]

Among the topics attracting greatest attention during the 1970s was the subject of the nature of the initial period of war. This had been an intense focus of Soviet concern prior to 1941 and between 1958 and 1960, and renewed interest was evidenced by the publication in 1974 of S. P. Ivanov's book, *The Initial Period of War* (*Nachal'nyi period voiny*), and numerous articles.[62] Drawing heavily on research done on the theme "the initial period of war" or, specifically, what a nation's army must do to win rapid victory or avoid precipitous defeat, the Soviets concluded that the principal prerequisites for victory were the surprise conduct of rapid operations by forces concentrated well forward. Hence, the Soviets tended to eschew preliminary large-scale mobilization (the primary indicator of impending war) and, instead, argued for employment of single strategic and operational echelons, supplemented by numerous tailored operational and tactical maneuver forces. Tactically, as well, by 1987 Soviet writers argued, "There arises the problem of defining the optimal structure for the first and second echelons at the tactical level. With the enemy using high-precision weapons, the role of the first echelon has to grow. It must be capable of achieving a mission without the second echelon (reserve)."[63]

Operational and tactical combat in the Soviet's view embraced "simultaneously the entire depth of the combat formation of both contending sides".[64] As a result, combat missions were no longer described in linear fashion by the seizure of lines. Instead missions called for the securing, along multiple axes deep in the enemy's defense, of objectives whose seizure "undermines the tactical stability of the enemy defense".[65] At the tactical level, specifically designated and tailored maneuver forces – usually forward detachments – performed this function, while tailored operational maneuver forces did likewise at the operational level.[66]

This offensive posture significantly altered traditional concepts of echelonment, not only by reducing the number of ground echelons, but also by supplementing the ground echelon with a vertical echelon, which added greater depth to battle. According to Reznichenko:

> One can propose that, under the influence of modern weapons and the great saturation of ground forces with aviation means, the combat formation of forces on the offensive is destined to consist of two echelons – a ground echelon, whose mission will be to fulfill the penetration of the enemy defense and develop the success into the depths, and an air echelon created to envelop defending forces from the air and strike blows against his rear area.[67]

In essence, what emerged was a Soviet concept of land-air battle juxtaposed against the U.S. concept of AirLand Battle.

After the revival of the terms "deep battle" and "deep operations" in the mid-1960s, these topics soon became major focuses of study along with all the techniques for deep operations. In 1975 Marshal Zakharov underscored the importance of the latter, stating, "The theory of deep operations has not lost its significance today. It can serve as a basis for the creative work of command cadres when resolving the many-sided and complex problems of today".[68]

As an adjunct to their concentrated study of deep operations, the Soviets also emphasized the value of the offensive, the importance of surprise and deception, the utility of encirclement operations and exploitation, the necessity to deploy efficiently and to regroup forces flexibly for combat, methods for rapidly effecting and developing penetration of defenses, requirements associated with sustaining large theater combined-arms forces, and the nature and conduct of meeting engagements. Soviet authors accorded special attention to operational maneuver performed by mobile groups and tactical maneuver by forward detachments and investigated in detail virtually every aspect of past mobile operations. In more recent works, published in the early and mid-1980s, the Soviets focused on the conduct of defense operations during offensives, probably in reaction to U.S. development of AirLand Battle doctrine. Among the myriad of operations the Soviets selected for intensive study were the Belorussian Operation (June 1944), the Vistula–Oder Operation (January 1945) and the Manchurian Operation (August 1945), all of which they considered relevant to contemporary operations.

MILITARY POLICY AND MILITARY DOCTRINE

All of these indicators strongly suggested that a basic shift had occurred in the Soviet view of the nature of future war. While the Soviets still considered nuclear war to be a strong possibility, they increasingly hoped that war could be kept conventional in its early stages, or perhaps even throughout its duration. They concluded that the existing strategic and tactical nuclear balance made it increasingly unlikely that either side would use nuclear weapons, a situation of mutual deterrence that increased the likelihood that strategic operations would remain conventional and become decisive in their own right. Accordingly, the Soviets prepared to fight either a nuclear war or (unlike the case of the 1960s) a conventional war in what might be termed a "nuclear scared" posture. They believed the latter would be more likely.

This Soviet version of "flexible response" emphasized the necessity for expanding and perfecting new combined-arms concepts. Foremost among those concepts were methods for fighting operationally and tactically (in essence, anti-nuclear maneuver) that could help to prevent nuclear conflict by inhibiting an enemy's ability to respond with nuclear weapons even if he wished to, while enhancing the chances of rapid success on the conventional battlefield in the initial period of war. Hence, the Soviets developed war-fighting approaches designed to preempt enemy nuclear use by the early destruction of enemy nuclear systems and by the rapid intermingling of friendly and enemy forces by extensive maneuver in the initial period of war.

Reflecting this emerging Soviet faith in the dual war-fighting option, most theorists abandoned the obligatory reference to a nuclear context, and instead carefully distinguished between the two types of conflict. Thus:

> In nuclear war, if it is unleashed by aggressive countries, simultaneous nuclear strikes on the enemy and skillful exploitation of the results of those strikes is most important. During combat with only conventional weaponry, skillful concentration of superior forces and weaponry is required to deliver blows on selected directions and also rapid dispersal of those forces after fulfillment of the combat missions.[69]

This assertion from an article on operational art by Marshal V. G. Kulikov and other articles on offensive operations, *front* operations, army operations, and tactics appeared in the authoritative eight-volume *Soviet Military Encyclopedia*, published between 1976 and 1980. It illustrated changing views by clearly delineating between nuclear and conventional operations. In addition, military theorists stressed the increased capabilities of all types of ground units, the growing scope of the offensive, and the increased dynamism of battle. Articles in professional military journals reiterated the distinction even more clearly. A 1982 article by N. Kireev in the *Military-Historical Journal* described the changing view of war and combat. After recounting the characteristics and techniques necessary to operate in nuclear warfare, Kireev wrote:

> Since the beginning of the 1960s, our military theory and practice conceded the conduct of combat using only conventional means though under constant threat of enemy use of nuclear weapons. This circumstance dictated the necessity of determining modes of employment of tank units and subunits in penetrating a well-prepared enemy defense in conformity with the new demands. A large number of demonstrations, tactical and other exercises, as well as military scientific conferences, were conducted. The experience of penetration of a deliberate enemy defense obtained during the years of the Great Patriotic War began to be more extensively utilized.[70]

To underscore the full development of this new Soviet view, M. A. Gareev, in a 1986 critique of Frunze's works, disputed Sokolovsky's earlier concepts and fully articulated the difference between nuclear and conventional war.[71]

While developing military doctrine that seemed to meet the challenge of escaping from the dangerous grasp of nuclear war, the Soviets continued to build up global military capabilities and put into practice a more active policy to realize Soviet aims in the Third World, the periphery of traditional great power lands, a region from which the capitalist nations obtain much of their economic sustenance. Expanding on Khrushchev's declaration of support for wars of national liberation, Soviet attempts to influence the course of events in the Third World came to embrace a spectrum of military, political, and economic measures which, by the end of the 1960s, included ambitious military assistance efforts for selected countries in the Middle East, Africa, and Latin America.

Soviet military presence in underdeveloped regions was reflected in the proliferation of military advisers in many Third World nations and the use of Soviet proxy advisers and combat forces in Ethiopia and Angola.

Coupled with the announcement of the Brezhnev Doctrine (1968), in which the Soviets reserved the right militarily to maintain the socialist system where it already existed, a more active Soviet global stance sought to aid "progressive governments" against imperialism, increase Soviet influence, and deny the West access to resources either through creation of socialist states or by manipulating disorders in critical regions to paralyze normal economic activity and trade. At the same time, the publication in 1976 of Admiral Sergei Gorshkov's *Sea Power of the State* marked an overt acknowledgement of the fact that the Soviets had embarked on a naval construction program to create an oceanic navy capable of better projecting Soviet power overseas in tandem with the already burgeoning Soviet merchant marine. The 1979 edition of the same work made it clear that Soviet naval presence, while a valuable political tool, was not independent of the war plans of the Soviet General Staff, which retained the duty of formulating all operational plans for the Soviet armed forces, whether the branches of those forces acted jointly or independently.[72]

These trends, reinforced by other motives, encouraged direct Soviet military involvement in Afghanistan, an invasion presumably launched in accordance with the Brezhnev Doctrine. Significantly, the invasion marked the first active incursion of Soviet forces beyond their own borders and the Soviet Bloc proper since the end of 1945 (except for the wartime joint Allied occupation of Iran and joint United States–Soviet occupation of Korea in the immediate postwar years). Soviet intervention in Afghanistan was a *coup de main* aimed at changing the character of a Soviet-sponsored regime by intimidation and the use of internal collaborators. But there was also an armed anti-communist resistance in the field at the time. Soviet international activity was made possible in part by United States' overcommitment around the globe and a Soviet sensing that the nuclear deadlock and general fears of global nuclear war left more room for maneuver at the local war level.

Paralleling these trends the Soviet Armed Forces expanded, in particular the ground forces in light of their rebounding prestige. Between 1968 and 1987, armed forces' strength grew from 2 million and 138 divisions to 5.2 million and over 220 divisions. In peacetime the Soviets kept these formations at three levels, ranging from almost full wartime strength to less than 20 per cent strength. It is likely that the Soviets maintained mobilization and embryonic divisions for mobilization during crises or during wartime from existing formations and training bases. In essence, elements of the mobilization base which had existed since the 1920s endured as tried and true mobilization methods.

Initial Soviet pronouncements in 1987 regarding the new "defensive" nature of their military doctrine represented a sophisticated new stage in how the Soviets perceived the course of the revolution in military affairs.[73]

By emphasizing "defensiveness" and "prevention of war" they capitalized on current global political realities to accent the political aspects of a doctrine, which, by definition, has always been inherently defensive. By stressing "prevention of war", the Soviets further developed their view that nuclear war, by virtue of its destructiveness to all parties, was unthinkable and, hence, avoidable. In essence, the "new" definition of Soviet doctrine articulated an intent *to prevent nuclear war*. As such, this definition found its corollary in Soviet proposals for arms reductions, particularly in the nuclear realm, and, in the extreme, the creation of nuclear-free zones and the outright abolition of nuclear weapons.

Soviet postulation of a "defensive" military doctrine also responded in the military-technical realm to a new phase in the technological revolution – a revolution in conventional weaponry, which, in many ways, promised to make new high-precision conventional weapons as lethal as their nuclear counterparts. This new reality prompted intensive Soviet study of future strategy, operational and tactical concepts and techniques.

MILITARY STRATEGY

As Soviet military doctrine changed, so also did the Soviet view of military strategy. During the period 1970 to 1985, the Soviet military addressed two fundamental military problems reflecting the realities of the times. The first of these was the problem of overcoming contemporary defenses, whether those defenses were in the Far East (China) or in Central Europe (NATO). This problem was a long-standing one made more complex by technological changes, in particular the development of modern, more lethal antitank and other precision-guided weapons. Consequently, the Soviets studied their own experience (1941–45), the experiences of the 1973 Arab–Israeli War, other contemporary conflicts, and a series of key experimental exercises.

The second problem was that of nuclear warfare, or, specifically, how to avoid it, preempt it, or conduct it. The Soviets recognized the possibility that a major war could become nuclear, but, at the same time, they sought ways to avoid nuclear conflict (nuclear freeze, renunciation of first use, nuclear-free zones, etc. in the political realm) and developed operational and tactical concepts designed both to inhibit the enemy's ability to employ nuclear weapons and to reduce the effectiveness of those weapons if they were used. Thus, former Chief of the General Staff N. V. Ogarkov wrote regarding the Soviet declaratory policy of no first use:

> Soviet military strategy assumes that a world war may be started and conducted for a certain period of time with conventional weapons alone. The expansion of military operations, however, can result in its escalation into a general nuclear war, with nuclear weapons, primarily strategic, as the main means of conducting it. Soviet military strategy is based on the position that the Soviet Union, proceeding on the basis of the principles of its policy, will not be the first to employ such weapons.[74]

While expressing a Soviet desire to keep hostilities conventional, Ogarkov warned any aggressor of the consequences of resorting to nuclear warfare, stating: "Any possible aggressor should clearly understand, however, that it will be the target of an annihilating answering strike in the event of a nuclear missile attack against the Soviet Union or the other countries of the Socialist community." Such statements were part of the struggle for retention of the initiative during the initial period of war through deterring an opponent and limiting his options by political means.

Subsequent pronouncements by Gorbachev and Defense Minister Iazov regarding the "defensiveness" of Soviet doctrine and Soviet actions regarding arms limitations (particularly nuclear) were further political manifestations of Soviet desires to denuclearize future warfare, as well as to soften the impact on Soviet military preparedness of the technological revolution in conventional weaponry.

In the event that such a policy failed to deter nuclear war, the Soviets prepared themselves for the worst through study of several distinct areas fundamental to the conduct of general war. They intensely examined the nature of nuclear war and spent immense time and resources to train and equip their forces to operate successfully in a nuclear environment.

However, it remained a clear Soviet intention to achieve theater objectives without the use of nuclear weapons by either side, and Soviet efforts to develop concepts and forces capable of meeting this goal were extensive as well. The Soviets studied in considerable detail the operations of their forces in the Great Patriotic War, especially during the initial stages and the third period of the war, focusing on operational and tactical techniques that could assist in preventing enemy recourse to nuclear weapons while better preparing Soviet forces to win should those weapons be used.[75]

Although they have been reticent on this point, it is likely the Soviets, by the mid-1970s, revived the strategic echelonment concept associated with the period before 1960. That is, they returned to a structure whereby the first strategic echelon consisted of forces in the forward area of eastern Europe, a second strategic echelon of forces in the western military districts, and a strategic reserve of forces in the Moscow, Ural, and Volga Military Districts, and the remaining mobilization base.[76]

During the 1970s the Soviets reaffirmed their faith in the preeminence of the offensive in producing victory, although they recognized that conditions surrounding the outbreak or subsequent course of war required integration of a defensive phase or temporary defensive actions in some sectors into the overall strategic offensive plan. They believed that armor, as but one element of a combined-arms team, still played a significant role in successful offensive operations. Their analysis of successful combat in the past "initial periods of war" led them to several conclusions. First, those nations succeeded which quickly brought overwhelming force to bear on the enemy. The effectiveness of that force was magnified if the enemy was denied time necessary to prepare his defenses fully. Maximum force could best be generated and projected forward if applied simultaneously across a broad front by only the first strategic echelon. The application of such a force in this manner could generate rapid penetration into the depths of the defense along numerous directions, create total paralysis in enemy command and control systems, and result in reduced enemy capability or willingness to respond with nuclear weapons.[77]

Second, in initial and subsequent operations in a potentially nuclear war, the Soviets categorically ruled out the conduct of set-piece battle by forces deployed in deeply echeloned and densely patterned arrays, which were highly vulnerable to nuclear and conventional strikes (the then-existing Western stereotype of Soviet echelonment).[78] Thus, the Soviets altered traditional concepts concerning mass and concentration and continued to stress flexible echeloning techniques. Echeloning was designed to meet the requirements of specific combat conditions (the nature of enemy defenses, depth of objectives, terrain, etc.), and mass and concentration were to be achieved by rapid movement of forces from dispersed positions and by shifting of fires rather than by traditional assembly of forces in dense arrays before an operation.

Soviet study of the last period of the Great Patriotic War led them to conclude that many of the techniques developed in that period were applicable in the early 1980s, despite changing technology. On the basis of their study, the Soviets believed that surprise was absolutely essential for victory: strategically regarding timing; and operationally and tactically regarding the form, location, and nature of the offensive.[79] Moreover, they believed that wartime strategy was inexorably related to political conditions existing before and during the initial period of war.

The Soviets also analyzed the nature of modern defense, in particular that of NATO, its coherence, the time it took to form, and, most important, the time ramifications of political decision-making.[80] They understood how formidable the NATO defense was if fully in place. Although they still credited NATO with the ability to conduct a mobile defense, they understood the forward positional nature of the defense, its limited depth, and its lack of mobile operational reserves. Given the real and potential problems associated with timely establishment of NATO defenses, the Soviets realized that, if hard-pressed, and if given the opportunity, NATO might have chosen to go nuclear. Thus, a cardinal tenet of Soviet planning (supported by their research into operational and tactical techniques) was a recognition of the necessity of preempting the defense or disrupting its full deployment or, failing that, preempting the use of or minimizing the effects of nuclear weapons.[81]

Based on these conclusions, in the event of war, the Soviets sought to achieve surprise by using deception to a maximum extent while politically trying to undermine the unity and resolve of the coalition itself. They would have attempted to preempt or disrupt strategic (theater) defenses and preempt the use or limit the effectiveness of enemy nuclear weapons and precision-guided munitions (PGMs) by launching a massive ground offensive, by emphasizing early neutralization of enemy nuclear delivery means, and by attacking, using operational and tactical techniques designed to disrupt enemy command and control and produce paralysis and confusion in enemy ranks. The Soviets would have attempted to force the capitulation of one or more of the weaker members of the enemy coalition.

To accomplish these ambitious aims, the Soviets sought to keep forward-area forces in a high state of readiness, furnished with first-rate equipment. Combat forces were backed up by a logistical capability sufficient to sustain operations for the duration of the initial strategic operations and – because the potential for protracted operations was recognized – until the defense industrial sector was fully mobilized and producing key materiel and equipment (for example, 60–90 days). The Soviets had to achieve parity or superiority in the strategic and tactical nuclear realm, and, because of the necessity to effect speed and surprise, they had to abandon large-scale advanced mobilization and reinforcement of forward area forces prior to war. Forward area forces had to be capable of attacking on short notice with only limited redeployment and regrouping. Maximum use of cover and deception was essential, and forces had to be structured for and capable of conducting high-speed deep

209

operations. The Soviets, it now appears, were ambivalent over whether they had achieved the bulk of these prerequisites.

They asserted that a war which was nuclear from the outset would have begun with strategic operations by nuclear forces. The initial strategic nuclear exchange – theater or global – would have been massive, affecting all levels of war. In this nuclear variant, the strategic nuclear exchange and subsequent exchanges would have been accompanied by theater strategic operations. The theater-strategic operation, in concept, was a framework for understanding how a nation could achieve its strategic military objectives by armed force in continental theaters. Its scope was a direct function of aim. It could have involved coherent use of all types of forces in multiple theaters to win a global war, or it could have taken more limited form to achieve more modest goals. Thus, it provided a context for operations which required thoughtful balance between aims and the forces used to achieve aims.

At one end of the spectrum, the theater-strategic operation in multiple theaters of military operations involved the mobilization of the nation's entire force to achieve global and theater aims by the conduct of successive strategic operation; at the other end of the spectrum in a single remote theater, the theater-strategic operation involved selective application of force to achieve lesser intra-theater objectives. Thus, the concept of the theater-strategic operation was simply a refinement of previous Soviet thought on strategic offensive operations and was by no means a new subject. Its conceptual roots were found in the 1920s theory of successive operations and in the mature campaigns on the Eastern Front in the Second World War.

The Soviets planned to conduct theater-strategic operations with "the forces of several *fronts*, according to a single concept or plan within continental Theaters of Military Operations (TVDs)". High commands of forces in each TVD or a TVD representative assigned from the *Stavka* was to coordinate operations of all land, air, and naval forces within the theater "under the continuous control of the High Command".[82] The most important feature of a theater-strategic offensive operation in a nuclear context was the delivery of massed nuclear fires. Subsequent offensive operations by *fronts* sought to achieve the final destruction of the enemy and secure the most important regions.

Regardless of whether nuclear weapons were used, the theater-strategic operation in a major continental TVD involved simultaneous and successive operations by *fronts*, each of which "can conduct two or more *front* operations in succession, with brief pauses and even without pauses".[83] In addition to initial and subsequent operations by *fronts*, a theater-strategic operation in a continental TVD included, "on coastal directions, initial and subsequent operations by fleets, air defense, airborne landing, naval landing, combined landing, and other operations, as well as nuclear missile and air strikes".[84] Thus, the theater-strategic operation in its fully developed form included:

- nuclear strikes of strategic nuclear forces;
- air operations;
- anti-air operation;
- *front* operations;
- naval fleet operations;
- landing operations.

The initial *front* operations were designed to have:

> decisive importance. They will be distinguished by surprise, by decisive aims and operations from the very beginning by large spatial scope; by high dynamism, by massive use of forces and weapons to destroy the most important objectives, by participation of large quantities of various types of armed forces, by intense radio-electronic combat, and by the complexity of command and control and rear area support.[85]

Forces within the theater of war (TV) sought to achieve rapid victory by conducting successive *front* operations without pause in the theater's TVDs. A first strategic echelon consisted of combat-ready forces (*fronts*) within the TVD (primarily forward), backed up by a second strategic echelon and a strategic reserve consisting of *fronts* (and, in some cases, individual armies) mobilized within the Soviet Union on the basis of the strength and status of each military district.[86] Stronger peacetime military districts provided second strategic echelon forces and weaker districts provided reserves. The theater-strategic offensive relied for success primarily on the use of first strategic echelon forces to preserve strategic surprise by avoiding more than essential pre-hostility mobilization and reinforcement. The Soviets committed second strategic echelon forces and reserves to combat either in the event the first strategic echelon failed to achieve its aims and a protracted conflict occurred or in the event an offensive against well-prepared defenses was necessary.

The deployment of forces by each TVD command was carried out in accordance with the existing situation. In a nuclear context, or in the more likely context of an offensive launched against unprepared or partially prepared defenses, the Soviets tended to array their *fronts* in single echelon with a combined-arms reserve (one or two armies). Echelonment increased in depth in direct proportion to the increased strength of the defense and in consonance with Soviet capabilities to

211

conceal offensive preparations. Throughout the process the Soviets sought to capitalize on both surprise and strength. They recognized that the former was most critical and that its achievement both produced and accentuated a favorable correlation of forces.[87] On the other hand, an offensive against a fully prepared defense required more substantial deployment of second strategic echelon forces (*fronts* or armies) into the forward area prior to commencement of hostilities. Large-scale strategic airborne or amphibious operations supported the conduct of a theater-strategic offensive in the initial stages by strikes against more vulnerable objectives on enemy flanks, where their use detracted from the main enemy defensive efforts, or against targets of major political or economic value. Large-scale airborne or amphibious operations were also to be used in the later stages of a successfully developing offensive to administer the *coup de grâce* against already beleaguered enemy forces. Smaller-scale airborne or amphibious assaults supported the ground offensive throughout its entire duration.

The mature concept of the theater-strategic offensive, together with the critical sub-elements of operational and tactical maneuver, dominated Soviet strategic thought from the early 1970s right up to 1987. It is clear, however, that during the latter stages of that period, those same theoreticians began paying increased attention to defensive questions at both the strategic and operational level, albeit within the context of the theater-strategic operation. The theme of defensiveness first surfaced in the General Staff journal *Military Thought* (*Voennaia mysl'*) in the form of an initial discussion of the relative importance of offense *vis à vis* defense.[88] It then spread to the operational realm when other open journals such as *Military-Historical journal* began investigating the theme of defense during an offensive to deal with counterstrokes or counterattacks.[89]

It is now clear that this Soviet concern for defense was prompted, in part by Soviet recognition of the new Western concepts of Air Land Battle and Follow-On Forces Attack (FOFA), in part by their realization that a new technological revolution had occurred in weaponry, characterized by the appearance of high-precision weapons, and, finally, in part by an increasing Soviet awareness of the ambitiousness of the very concept of the theater-strategic operation. Despite these changes and apparent doubts, through 1987 Soviet faith in the theater-strategic offensive, seemed to remain solid.

Abruptly, in 1987 and 1988, the tenor of Soviet discussions over strategic issues changed. The 1987 declaration of defensive doctrine and the subsequent 7 December 1988 Gorbachev United Nations speech were accompanied by a virtual end to Soviet discussions of the theater-strategic offensive. The collapse of Soviet political dominance of eastern Europe only reinforced this trend. At the same time, Soviet military theorists have since renounced their most advanced operational concepts, such as the utility and feasibility of conducting operational maneuver with operational maneuver groups.

The apparent rejection of the twin concepts of the theater-strategic operation and reliance upon operational maneuver marked a clear break with traditions dating back to the late 1960s and, in fact, to the 1930s. The most important question was to what extent was this break in tradition valid? It was clear that political and economic realities played the most prominent role in these changes by forcing Soviet military theorists to abandon, at least temporarily, these predominantly offensively oriented concepts. It was less clear whether there was a valid military basis for doing so. Thus today it is important that we remember these traditional concepts lest they return in the future if, and after, the Soviets weather their current political and economic crisis.

CHAPTER 7

FUTURE SOVIET MILITARY STRATEGY AND ITS IMPLICATIONS

ON THE THRESHOLD OF THE FUTURE

During the mid-1980s a wide range of new factors emerged to influence significantly Soviet military strategy. First, the Soviet military began a fundamental reassessment of the nature and requirements of future war, especially regarding what they perceived as an ongoing technological revolution in new weaponry (in particular, high-precision weaponry), whose ultimate effects they could not readily predict. Second, a wave of internal uncertainty swept through the ruling and intellectual circles within the Soviet Union regarding the political, economic, and, finally, ideological bases of the Soviet state. Third, throughout a broad spectrum of Soviet society, disenchantment grew over the questionable nature and seemingly negative effects of existing Soviet military policy and strategy, which was characterized by active Soviet military intervention abroad and an intense and seemingly unlimited arms race, which, in turn, had placed immense burdens on the Soviet economy and seemed to offer in return little real gain in the Soviet Union's international stature.

All of these factors contributed to decisions by a new Party Secretary and future President, Mikhail Gorbachev, to implement a series of programs to reform the Soviet state, principally in an internal sense. These internal reform programs inexorably involved the realm of military policy, doctrine, and, ultimately, strategy as well. In 1987, within the context of these changes, the Soviets adopted a new defensive military doctrine, which is now producing revolutionary changes in Soviet military strategy.

THE PARAMETERS OF STRATEGIC DEBATE

Initial Historical Paradigms for Defensiveness

Beginning in 1985, the Soviets designated a new period in military development, soon defined within the context of a recast military

214

doctrine emphasizing "defensiveness" in its political component, but clearly shaped in many of its military-technical aspects by reassessments begun during the previous decade.[1] Subsequently, Soviet theorists articulated several strategic paradigms, couched analogously in historical terms, which they claimed applied to all periods of history. The Soviet academician A. Kokoshin, and former General Staff theorist, Colonel General V. Larionov publicly advanced four enduring strategic paradigms, which were distinguished from one another by their relative degree of offensiveness or defensiveness. Other theorists have since postulated additional models related to these original paradigms as new political realities emerge.[2] The Soviets advanced these paradigms to provide a framework for discussing future strategy within the General Staff and the Soviet body politic as a whole, and to create a basis for broader international discussions of future global strategic relationships. In essense, the paradigms seemed to offer a basis for mastering future change in a more rational and studied fashion. Quite naturally, the paradigms themselves were subject to interpretation.

On a scale of increasing defensiveness, the four original paradigms proposed by Kokoshin and Larionov were as follows:

1. *Offensive Defense*: Opposing states or coalitions possessing strong, offensively-oriented force groupings, which intend to conduct operations on enemy territory.

Mutual offensive intent and suspicion of their opponent's motives characterize the strategic stance of contending parties in this model. This paradigm replicates traditional strategic circumstances in European history and strategic relationships dominant in the twentieth century, including pre-First World War Europe, and, in the Soviet view, the Cold War as well. Soviet theorists argue that this traditional strategic situation, if permitted to exist in the future, given the technological revolution in weaponry, would be suicidal for all contending parties.

In this paradigm opposing states or coalitions possess a mature strategic posture, that is, multiple strategic echelons of armed forces, either existing in the peacetime force structure or rapidly mobilizable from strategic reserves (see Figure 34). Depending on the actual circumstances surrounding the outbreak of war, each side, using covert measures, can achieve a considerable degree of strategic surprise and an initial superiority of three to one over its opponent. That superiority will, however, dissipate as mobilization continues, and ensuing warfare would be prolonged and have catastrophic impact on both sides.

2. *Strategic Counteroffensive Defense*: The Kursk paradigm for premeditated defense, which postulates one state or coalition absorbing a

215

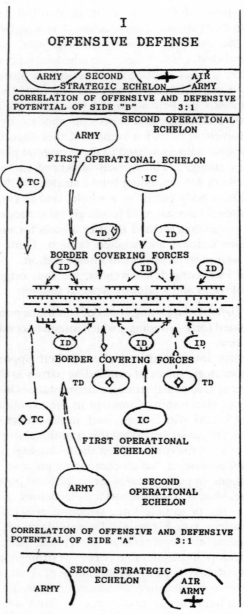

34. Strategic posture: offensive defense (according to V.V. Larionov)

major enemy blow and then delivering a decisive counteroffensive that carries well into enemy territory.[3]

Although labelled by the Soviets as "defensive", characteristics of the historical example used (the Kursk operation) underscore the inherently offensive nature of this paradigm. For this reason, many Soviet theorists have since turned away from the Kursk paradigm as a suitable example of future defensiveness to another which seems more appropriate.

The Kursk paradigm postulates a semi-mature strategic posture on both sides, consisting of a single strategic echelon and a strategic reserve (see Figure 35). In a period of crisis, either state or coalition could achieve operational-strategic advantage over its opponent on the basis of a two-to-two overall correlation of forces. Depending upon the course and outcome of initial operations, the defending side has the capability of launching counteroffensive operations, which can propel its forces into the territory of its opponent.

3. *Operational Counteroffensive Defense*: The Khalkhin-Gol paradigm, which replicates Soviet 1939 operations against the Japanese and United Nations operations in Korea (1951–1953), postulates that each state or coalition possesses the capability of routing an enemy force on its own territory, but is not capable of penetrating enemy territory.[4] Although this paradigm seems more appropriate to today's situation than does that of Kursk, close examination of the circumstance at Khalkhin-Gol reveals other facets of the historical example which make it less relevant and somewhat more suspect. These facets include the secret Soviet force build-up before the 1939 operation, which accorded the Soviets considerable surprise; Soviet numerical advantage; and political circumstances associated with the German threat to the Soviet Union, which restrained the Soviets at Khalkhin-Gol.

The Soviets also cite the period from 10 June 1951 to 21 July 1953 during the Korean War as representative of this paradigm. During that period warring parties tacitly agreed not to cross a certain demarcation line and not to expand the scale of military operations. Here, difficulties in determining the territorial limits of combat, compensation for losses and degree of restraint on both sides cloud the model's utility.

According to this paradigm, a state or coalition can achieve only temporary operational advantage (see Figure 36). Because the postulated peacetime strategic posture of both sides involves only an incomplete and partial strategic echelonment (in the form of a partial single strategic echelon), surprise and resulting advantage are only transitory. The defender has the capability of parrying the initial offensive blow and responding with operational counterstrokes, which clear his territory of enemy forces. Inherent in this paradigm is the assumption that the

217

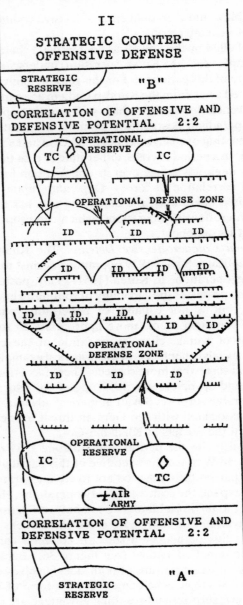

35. Strategic posture: strategic counteroffensive defense (according to V.V. Larionov)

defender will be unable to conduct offensive action on the territory of the initial invader.

4. *Non-Offensive Defense*: Opposing states or coalitions, possessing only limited tactical capabilities, neither of which is able to undertake any operations of strategic consequence.[5]

This paradigm addresses relative capabilities and falters on the amorphous definition of defensive adequacy or, in current parlance, "sufficiency". It implies that neither side considers war imminent, and both sides agree on how to define "limited tactical capabilities". Within the parameters of this paradigm, neither warring state or coalition possesses operational or strategic offensive potential (see Figure 37). Both sides lack strategic echelons and instead possess only tactical or limited operational capabilities. In this circumstance tactical incursions are met by tactical counterattacks. These limited capabilities preclude achievement by either side of operational or strategic advantage.

In postulating these four enduring paradigms, Soviet theorists have created an analytical framework suited for internal strategic debates and, more importantly, for international discussion of critical strategic issues.

President Gorbachev's current program of "defensiveness" postulates Soviet maintenance of a defensive capability sufficient to absorb and repulse any enemy blow. The program leaves several fundamental questions unanswered. First, Is defensiveness genuine? Second, if it is genuine, Is it based upon the Kursk or Khalkhin-Gol paradigms or on yet another model? And, finally, will future developments in the Soviet Union permit a rational model based on military considerations to be implemented, and will the General Staff and Ministry of Defense view of strategic paradigms and models prevail in the face of other realities?

There are additional models set within the context of the Kokoshin and Larionov paradigms which may better suit future Soviet strategic conditions, capabilities and intentions should Soviet defensive doctrine persist. The Soviets surfaced the first of these new models in 1989 when they published a document purporting to be their strategic defensive plan for operations by the Group of Occupation Forces Germany (GOFG) in the late 1940s.[6] This "pre-Cold War" model for defensiveness seemed to provide an excellent guide for a Soviet forward defensive strategic posture in the post-Cold War years. Militarily, it resembled both the Kursk and Khalkhin-Gol paradigms. Political events in eastern Europe throughout 1989 and 1990 rendered the model irrelevant.

The Soviets have since commenced extensive discussion on new

219

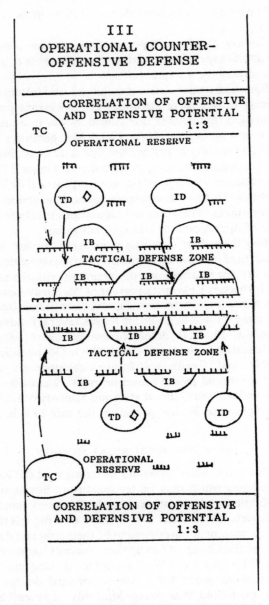

36. Strategic posture: operational counteroffensive defense (according to V. V. Larionov)

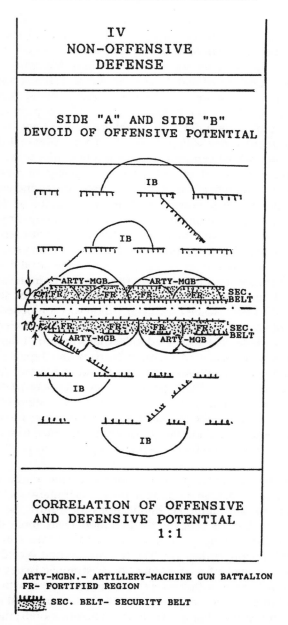

36. Strategic posture: non-offensive defense (according to V. V. Larionov)

models related to the Soviet strategic posture from 1921 to the commencement of war on the Eastern Front in 1941. Recent and prospective changes in the Soviet Union and in the European political and economic structure also, to some extent, recall conditions that existed during that period. Close analysis of that 20-year period reveals a second and third potential model. The more optimistic second model regards Soviet military strategy during the 1920s and up to 1935. It postulates a Soviet Union beset by severe internal problems, attempting to develop a military strategy to cope with post-Treaty of Versailles realities – specifically, a Europe whose central feature was a militarily weak but dissatisfied Germany bordered on the east by a group of newly-emerged independent, but politically unstable, successor states and on the west by war-wearied capitalistic powers bent on maintenance of the post-1919 status quo. The reduced threat to the Soviet Union posed by post-World War European states and the necessity for dealing with serious internal problems dictated Soviet adoption of a defensive military strategy characterized by maintenance of a smaller peacetime armed force and a mechanism permitting a transition to stronger forces in the event of war.

The third and more pessimistic model reflects Soviet strategy from roughly 1935 to 1941, when the Soviet Union was compelled to meet the challenge of sharply changing conditions within the Soviet Union and Europe as a whole. The increased industrial strength of the Soviet state and the emerging threat of German Nazism and Japanese militarism sharply increased the potential external threat and Soviet capabilities of responding to it. The 1930s paradigm was characterized by a more aggressive Soviet military strategy (although still ostensibly defensive) involving the maintenance of a large peacetime military force and a more efficient system for making the transition from peace to war – a system ultimately characterized by the term "creeping up to war" (*vpolzanie v voinu*).

The last two potential models address a wide range of emerging military and political realities and can provide a framework for analysis of likely political and military implications of future Soviet military strategies. The Soviets believed the first model was applicable at a time when the USSR planned to retain the groups of forces in the forward area. That is no longer the case. The two pre-Second World War models provide a framework for analyzing Soviet strategic issues when Soviet forces complete their withdrawal to a national bastion within the Soviet Union. All three models require detailed examination and analysis. The first is of interest for what it reveals about Soviet mobilization plans and defensive/counteroffensive procedures and the latter two for what they may indicate about the shape and form of future strategy.

THE CONTEMPORARY STRATEGIC ENVIRONMENT

A wide variety of internal and external political, economic, and social factors have coalesced to produce striking change in the Soviet Union and its former satellites. Although no one can predict with any degree of certainty what these changes will ultimately produce, they must be considered as the context for future Soviet military policy, doctrine, and strategy.

Within the Soviet Union economic stagnation has reached the crisis point. The decay of the Soviet economy and ineffective attempts to deal with it have reduced the economy's productivity and, more important in a military sense, denied it the prospect of mastering the rapid technological changes sweeping the developed world. Economic crisis has, in turn, fostered political and social turmoil which threatens the fabric of Soviet political life and society. Democratization, unleashed in a conscious attempt to legitimize official programs for economic reform, has concurrently released new political forces, which have altered the rigid political structure of the Soviet state, and nationalism, which has simultaneously generated both centripetal forces within the Russian nation and centrifugal forces on the part of the Soviet Union's national republics. Democratization has also severely undermined the power and authority of its natural targets, the Communist party and the *nomenklatura*.[7]

These economic and political crises have, in turn, underscored vividly the class and ethnic nature of the Soviet state, have exacerbated class, ethnic and religious distinctions, and fostered virtual low-level social warfare among classes and nationalities. This is a particularly vexing problem in view of the impending minority of Great Russians within their Soviet state. For the first time, the Soviet Union leadership must now directly ponder the possible dissolution of the Soviet state. All of these forces, singly or in combination, will affect both the nature of the future Soviet state and the shape and form of its military establishment as the Soviet leadership strives to achieve a consensus regarding its position in relation to Europe and the rest of the world.

While internal factors continue to condition the Soviet Union's reaction to the world, in a political and military sense the principal future variable affecting the Soviet Union is the structure of the international arena itself. There, major changes have occurred and are occurring that the Soviet leadership must take into account as it formulates its policies and strategies. The Soviet perspective now reflects recognition of the following factors:

- The arms race of the 1980s which, while creating enormous economic pressures on both sides, failed to accord military

223

> advantage to the Soviet Union (and, in fact, may have accorded advantage to the West and simultaneously shattered the Soviet economic base);
> – The changing international political balance, characterized, in part, by the increased political and economic power of Europe (EEC) and Japan; the opening of China to limited Western influence; the unleashing of politically potent religious forces in the Middle East and potentially in southern Asia; and the continued pauperization and political weakness of friendly Third World governments;
> – The new technological revolution, principally in cybernetics, and high-precision weapons, which, because of an inability to compete, places the Soviet Union at increasing disadvantage;
> – The world-wide revival of nationalism and its negative effects on the internal and external status quo;
> – The collapse of communism in Eastern Europe and, with it, diminished Soviet influence in Europe (in a Cold War sense);
> – The unification of Germany;
> – The limited success of Soviet-sponsored or supported wars of national liberation, the curtailment or asserted abandonment of many military assistance programs, and the ensuing political and economic enfeeblement of Soviet client states world-wide.

All of these complex internal and external factors have impelled change within the Soviet Union, and these changes have evolved in a dialectical sense with one generating another. Gorbachev's initial economic program of acceleration (*uskorenie*), designed to speed up economic activity, failed and instead underscored the need for openness and debate of vital issues. The policy of *perestroika* followed, a revitalization program of both the economy and the military, which, like a germ developing in a petri dish, had to be accompanied by a program of *glasnost'* to lend it credence and vitality. When it became clear that institutional constraints threatened to throttle *perestroika*, the ensuing program of democratization (*demokratizatsiia*) sought to break the institutional log-jam and legitimize reform, but in so doing destroyed much of the institutional base of the Soviet Union.

Each of these stages has reinforced the dialectical truth that all trends are interrelated, and one cannot have genuine progress in one realm without commensurate progress in other important realms. This truth propelled Gorbachev in the spring of 1990 to embrace reform on all fronts, with inherent risks, while attempting to control the entire process through the new institution of President of the Soviet Union. The military corollary of these fundamental internal and external political, economic and social changes has been a revision of Soviet military policy and declared Soviet intent to implement a defensive military doctrine. That, in turn, requires articulation of a new military strategy.

Future Soviet military strategy will reflect five basic realities: the shape and form of the future Soviet (or Russian) state; Soviet (or Russian) national interests and objectives; the nature of perceived threats; Soviet perception of the nature of future war; and the potential of the national material base (economy, manpower, etc.). As the Soviet political and military leadership study these realities, they are driven by habit and inclination to consider what the past has to offer in the way of solutions. They understand that study of the past offers no panaceas. But it does offer hints as to proper action at a time when conditions existed which may have been similar to those existing today or which will exist in the future.

When and if the Soviets fully comprehend current and future realities and resolve their most acute problems, their military strategy must address the critical issues of peacetime strategic force posture, force generation, strategic deployment, and the nature and conduct of strategic operations within the framework of their understanding of future war. This analysis now turns to the principal issues of strategic force posture and strategic deployment and also addresses the related questions of peacetime force strength, manning, disposition, and readiness; force generation during transition from peace to war (mobilization); and strategic force deployment and concentration, all within the traditional and necessary context of perceived national interests and threats. Most important, this analysis presumes that the *process* of formulating strategy, which has characterized the work of the General Staff and political leadership in the past will continue to be valid in the future.

NATIONAL INTERESTS AND DEFINING THE THREAT

Whereas in the past many in the West have assumed the Soviet Union's national interests and policy objectives envisioned the ultimate destruction of capitalism, current realities argue that Soviet interests today focus more on insuring the security and survival of the Soviet state. Whether or not Soviet national interests during the Cold War (1949–89) were offensive, there is now considerable similarity between Soviet interests today, and probably in the future, and analogous Soviet interests in the 1920s and 1930s. Specifically, there are strong reasons to accept the validity of Soviet claims that their national policy, in general, and their military policy, in particular, is now defensive. In the last analysis, the concrete nature of future strategic Soviet posture will settle this question.

One reality concerning future Soviet military strategy, which is as true today as it was yesterday, is that it will continue to reflect perceived threats. Threat analysis in a time of change is difficult at best, and it inherently involves defining a range of threats and then fashioning a strategy which can cope with a combination of the most likely and most dangerous. One can postulate a range of future international political relationships differentiated from one another by the degree to which each poses a threat to the Soviet Union. Four principal threat variants based on these relationships may evolve, listed here in descending order of favorability. Recent commentary by Soviet strategists and political figures and available evidence concerning the process of past Soviet threat analysis argues that the General Staff has and will continue to accept these variants as a valid base for formulating military policy and strategy. The categorization of specific states within each variant is partial, and obviously tentative.[8]

THREAT VARIANTS

Variant 1 (Best Case)

Characteristics: Economically, and to a lesser degree, politically unified Europe with German, Soviet, and East European states' participation. Abolition of all military alliances and general disarmament of all European states. Stability based on status quo in Asia. This variant has never before existed.

National Attitudes

Group 1: Potentially hostile to the Soviet Union: Japan, China, Iran, Afghanistan (if Mujahadin rules), Pakistan, Romania, South Korea, Turkey, Israel

Group 2: Neutral or ambivalent: Great Britain, France, Germany, Hungary, Finland, U.S.A. (could be friendly depending on events in Asia), Poland, Czechoslovakia, Italy, Spain, Egypt, Austria, Switzerland, Sweden, Iraq

Group 3: Friendly to the Soviet Union: Bulgaria, Serbia (Yugoslavia), Syria, Vietnam, India, North Korea

Variant 2 (Good Case)

Characteristics: NATO as a reduced-scale political alliance without Ger-

226

man participation. Unified, neutralized, and partially demilitarized Germany. Soviet Union with limited bilateral political, economic, or military agreements with selected Eastern European states. Continued United States security role in Asia and Pacific with growing Japanese participation. This somewhat resembles political conditions existing in the 1920s.

National Attitudes

Group 1: Potentially hostile to the Soviet Union: U.S.A., Great Britain, France, Japan, Turkey, Italy, Hungary, Iran, China, Israel, Pakistan, South Korea, Romania, Afghanistan (if Mujahadin rules)

Group 2: Neutral or ambivalent: Austria, Germany, Sweden, Poland, Czechoslovakia, Finland, Greece, Switzerland, Egypt, Iraq

Group 3: Friendly to the Soviet Union: India, Serbia (Yugoslavia), Bulgaria, Vietnam, North Korea, Syria

Variant 3 (Satisfactory Status Quo)

Characteristics: Potentially hostile NATO with military power restricted by CFE arms limitations. Participation in NATO of unified Germany with a reduced military establishment. Token United States military presence in Europe. Soviet bilateral agreements with selected East European states. Continued United States security in Asia and the Pacific shared with Japan. This continues some of the unpleasant uncertainties of Cold War relationships but, in favorable conditions, can evolve into Variant 2.

National Attitudes

Group 1: Potentially hostile to Soviet Union: NATO nations, Japan, Iran, Hungary, China, Pakistan, Romania, South Korea, Israel, Afghanistan (if Mujahadin rules)

Group 2: Neutral or ambivalent: Poland, Finland, Sweden, Austria, Czechoslovakia, Iraq

Group 3: Friendly to Soviet Union: India, Serbia (Yugoslavia), Bulgaria, Vietnam, North Korea, Syria

Variant 4 (Worst Case)

Characteristics: NATO dissolved and replaced by bilateral political and military agreements between U.S., France, and Great Britain. Unified, militarized revisionist Germany. Competition between Soviet Union and Germany for influence in Eastern Europe. Remilitarized, expansionist Japan and diminished U.S. influence in Asia and the Pacific. These international relationships, to some degree, resemble conditions in the 1930s.

National Attitudes

Group 1: Hostile to Soviet Union: Germany, Japan, Hungary, Romania

Group 2*: Potentially hostile to Soviet Union: U.S.A., Iran, China, Great Britain, Pakistan, South Korea, France, Turkey, Israel

Group 3*: Neutral: Poland, Sweden, Czechoslovakia, Netherlands, Finland, Norway, Belgium, Austria, Denmark, Spain, Iraq

Group 4: Friendly to Soviet Union: Vietnam, India, Bulgaria, Syria, Serbia (Yugoslavia), North Korea

---

*This is a particularly volatile relationship, in that, depending on Japanese and German policies, states in groups 2 and 3 (including the United States) could become friendly with the Soviet Union, in a virtual return to the structure of the wartime Grand Alliance.

Juxtaposed against these threat variants based on international relationships and national attitudes are a series of alternatives regarding the Soviet future internal situation, which can have an influence on the former. Although there are numerous possibilities, they can be lumped into three general categories, each with a specific set of probable impacts on the threat variants and vice versa.

Alternative 1: Gorbachev or a successor succeeds in reforming the Soviet state. This would require some positive economic reform and a degree of democratization in the Soviet Union and would involve probable outright loss of Soviet sovereignty over the Baltic States, Moldavia, and possibly other regions. Some form of federal structure would likely govern the relationship between existing republics and the Soviet Union. International variants 1 and 2 would facilitate this process, variant 3 would only marginally affect it, and variant 4 could definitely inhibit the process. On the other hand, successful reform within the Soviet Union would tend to foster the development of variants 1 and 2 internationally. This alternative has no precedents.[9]

Alternative 2: The reforms of Gorbachev or his successor fail and either democratic revolution or authoritarian reaction ensues. Although this might occur in any circumstance for internal reasons, international variant 4 could undoubtedly speed this outcome. A "democratic" revolution would probably fragment the Soviet Union, produce a new federal structure, and contribute to international variants 1 or 2. Return to a more authoritarian regime (rule by party, nationalist movement, police, union, military, or a combination of all four) would resist national fragmentation, probably by force, and promote international variants 3 and possibly 4. In addition, there is no guarantee that victorious authoritarianism would be able to stave off ultimate revolution or reform. The precedents for this alternative are, on the one hand, February 1917 and, on the other, Stalin's authoritarianism or that of his successors.

Alternative 3: Gorbachev or his successors muddle through with enough reform to maintain a shaky status quo. In this instance the Soviet government will have to contend with continuous, long-term economic, political, and ethnic problems. These internal contradictions would be exacerbated by international variants 3 and 4 and would, in turn, certainly hinder achievement of variant 1, and possibly variant 2. This characterizes earlier failed Soviet attempts at reform (1954, 1960, 1970s).

If one were to distill from the four threat variants all conceivable threats to the Soviet Union, they would include the following:

All Conceivable Threats: 1995

1. Continued full NATO threat to the Soviet Union;
2. Emergence of a hostile unified Germany and a remilitarized and aggressive Japan;
3. Strategic nuclear and peripheral threat by the U.S.A.;
4. Residual threat from a truncated NATO;
5. Foreign support of ethnic unrest in the Soviet Union;
6. Unrest in Eastern Europe with Western intervention;
7. Unrest in Eastern Europe with Soviet domestic implications;
8. Domestic ethnic unrest;
9. Nuclear and chemical weapons proliferation in hostile or potentially hostile border states;
10. Transnational threats with military implications (including religious fundamentalism in southern Asia, narcotics, and terrorism).

In terms of likelihood and desirability, these threats break down as follows:

– Threats 1 and 2 least desirable
– Threat 4 desirable and most likely

229

- Threats 3, 5, 6, 9, and 10 possible
- Threats 7 and 8 probable

Since it is awkward, if not impossible, to predict one's own demise, the Soviet General Staff must plan on the basis of some sort of stability being maintained. Likewise, the Soviets cannot anticipate or meet every threat. It is reasonable to assume that threat variants 2 or 3 are most likely to evolve and can provide a reasonable and valid basis on which to formulate future military policy and strategy. It is these two variants that a majority of Soviet policy makers and military strategists are today addressing. They would like to see variant 2 result, but must prudently plan for the circumstances of variant 3. The trick is to encourage the evolution of variant 2 (or even 1) by formulating a strategy (and hence a threat for the West) which does not impel Western powers to continue variant 3, but still satisfies Soviet security needs if variant 3 should persist. In this respect, and in many others, the 1920s model looks increasingly attractive.

There is, however, a sizeable and vocal minority of military strategists who, for emotional or other reasons, raise the specter of threat variant 4 (worst case) as a valid, and even necessary, planning consideration. There are indications that this group may predominate within the current General Staff. These strategists tend to view the 1930s model with much greater concern and, hence, urge political leaders to maintain a more powerful military establishment and seek closer ties with Britain and the United States.

Assuming that more moderate forces predominate, Soviet strategists will distill from threat variants 2 and 3 a finite list of possible threats, which can provide a reasonable, and safe, basis upon which to formulate future military strategy. This pared-down list might be as follows:

Possible Threats: 1995

1. Strategic nuclear and peripheral threat by the U.S.A.;
2. Residual threat from a reduced-strength NATO;
3. Foreign support of ethnic unrest in the Soviet Union;
4. Domestic ethnic unrest;
5. Unrest in Eastern Europe with Western intervention;
6. Unrest in Eastern Europe with Soviet domestic implications;
7. Nuclear and chemical weapons proliferation in hostile or potentially hostile border states;
8. Transnational threats with military implications.

Soviet military strategy will likely be fashioned to cope with these potential threats. Should, however, those strategists who fear the worst case (variant 4) prevail, a markedly different picture of the threat will emerge, characterized by preeminent Soviet concern with threat 2 (emergence of a hostile Germany and Japan) and a corresponding reduction in Soviet fear of the United States and non-German Western states.

MASTERING FUTURE WAR

A second reality Soviet military planners must contend with in formulating a future military strategy is the nature of future war, in general, and the traditional concept of the initial period of war, in particular. The General Staff, the institution customarily entrusted with this task, has always experienced difficulty preparing the Soviet armed forces to conduct war 30 years in the future. The difficulty has not been with developing an accurate image of future war, for, in fact, as the experiences of the 1920s and 1930s have indicated, Soviet theoretical concepts were quite visionary. Rather, the General Staff has found it difficult to translate that vision of warfare into reality. They readily imagined the conceptual, technological, and force structural change required to exploit their vision, but could not impart these changes to the armed forces quickly or thoroughly enough.

Today that long-standing dilemma is even more serious, for, in fact, the General Staff is experiencing difficulty with the very process of foresight and forecasting. Increasingly, they cannot envision the nature of future war with the degree of surety they had in the past. Compounding that dilemma are the increasing problems Soviet industry is experiencing in developing and fielding new technology. It is the technical realm of future war that most confounds and frustrates Soviet military theorists, for they know the state they serve is increasingly unable to respond to their needs. Moreover, they understand that new families of weapons, based on new physical principles, will appear, whose impact on warfare cannot now be understood.

The Soviets are experiencing two problems as they attempt to analyze future war: the first relates to who is doing the analysis and the second to the results of the analyses. The General Staff and its supporting research organizations, the traditional sources of truth regarding future war, have been challenged by political and social scientists and economists of civilian academic institutes, whose *institutchiki* now also study the subject of war on the assumption that matters of war and its consequences are too great to be left to military men alone. General Staff analysis embodies continuity in Soviet military thought, and their views on future war are evolutionary and thoroughly consistent with those that they embraced in the 1970s and early 1980s. They recognize the significant impact of

231

technological changes on warfare, but generally reject the idea that future war is now inconceivable.[10]

The General Staff has argued that, although the risk of global war still tends to deter political-military action in peacetime, war can still occur, and, if it does, fundamentally new types of weaponry are creating completely new forms of combat and increasing the complexity of warfare. The six key elements of Soviet General Staff assessments remain:

(1) The initial period of war
(2) The likely intensity and scale of combat
(3) The means (weaponry) to be employed
(4) The consequences for the USSR economy and population
(5) The duration of war
(6) The influence of U.S. and NATO doctrine on "reasonable sufficiency".[11]

In the General Staff view, Soviet ground forces' "defensive" operations would not be defensive throughout the entire war. Instead, the Soviet armed forces would act "decisively" if the enemy did not cease operations immediately. This seems to be consistent with Kokoshin's and Larionov's second paradigm (Kursk), but the "character of modern war" which they describe suggests a picture of warfare rather different from that postulated by the proponents of defensivism (the *instituchiki*), who tend to argue for an armed force whose strategy is consistent with Kokoshins and Larionov's third (Khalkhin–Gol) paradigm. The General Staff postulates that future war will be characterized by the following:

- Extremely high density, dynamic, and rapidly developing operations
- Broad global extent, including operations in space
- Extremely destructive combat of unprecedented scale
- High expenditure of resources, particularly to seize and maintain the initiative
- Fragmented (*ochagovyi*) combat. Disappearance of the "frontline" or "first echelon," so that traditional terms like Forward Edge of the Battle Area (FEBA), Forward Line of Own Troops (FLOT), or of Enemy Troops (FLET) are no longer meaningful. Rather "zones" of combat", up to 100 kilometers wide and deep would be created.
- No country or region would be safe from enemy action, since no "deep rear" (*glubokiy tyl*) would exist beyond the range of future weapons.

232

- Strategic goals would be achieved through combined arms operations: no particular weapons systems could be singled out as having overwhelming significance
- The destruction of nuclear power generation and chemical production facilities during the course of a war, whether nuclear or conventional, would have disasterous effects on the theater of operations. The lessons of Chernobyl' are clearly dominant here.
- Nuclear war could liquidate the world's population.[12]

On the other hand, the *institutchiki* point out the utter folly of war as Andre Kokoshin argued in November 1988:

> Recently, at a time when the idea is taking root that war can no longer serve as a rational means of politics (at least not in Soviet-American relations, between the WTO and NATO), the need for the highest state and political leadership to know the fundamentals of military strategy, operational plans, the functioning of the military mechanism of carrying out decisions and so on, has by no means been eliminated. On the contrary, it is increasing. This is because decisions made at the boundary between politics and strategy may have fatal and irreversible consequences.[13]

In a major article published in December 1988, General G.I. Salmanov presented a classic view of modern war in the language of the General Staff:

> What, then, is new in the make-up of Soviet military doctrine, and how is it reflected in the nature of modern war?
>
> In the first place – it is the reinforcement, and accentuation of its defensive orientation ...
>
> Defense in the initial period of a war is now regarded, not only as a means of bleeding the enemy with comparatively fewer forces, as a means of stopping him as quickly as possible and creating the necessary conditions for active counter-offensive action, but also as a means, and this is most important, of making the enemy think over and over again (*mnogo raz podumat'*) before he decides to attack in the first place. In individual TVDs, defense can also be used to inflict prolonged delay on the enemy with comparatively small forces on previously prepared sectors.
>
> At the present time, one must take issue with those who assert, that with approximate parity of forces within the TVD, and with the sophistication of modern reconnaissance, the deployment of forces by an aggressor in, for example, Europe, is a chimera. Defending

this opinion, they quite reasonably assert, that an aggressor can decide on an attack only if he will attain important strategic aims (for example, reaching the state frontier of the USSR) as a result of the first strategic operation.

To accomplish such an objective the aggressor would have to have a three- or four-to-one superiority in forces on main axes (and it is impossible not to agree with this). Evidently, to build up such a superiority secretly before the start of a war would hardly seem possible.

All this is true, if you do not consider a completely new qualitative improvement in the enemy's firepower, the sharply increased mobility of his shock grouping and what he recognizes as the main means of unleashing war – the surprise attack.

Even with a roughly equal balance of forces before the start of military action, the enemy, having started the war by surprise, will attempt to shift this balance in his favour on individual axes. Evidently, such a situation can be attained during an air-land operation with the use of powerful fire strikes (*ognevymi udarami*) on corridors through our combat formations and by rapid insertion of strong groupings from mobile enemy infantry units, large scale air assaults (*desanty*), army aviation, specially trained diversionary and reconnaissance detachments (groups), and so on. The activity of these groups, evidently, will unfold with their flanks covered by unbroken fire. The bringing up of our reserves will be impeded by deep fire strikes undertaken by aviation and long-range high-precision weapons.

Many might consider such a variant of the course of events as fantastic. But if we are not prepared for it in every way, this fantasy could become a terrible reality.[14]

Salmanov then underscored the central issue preoccupying the General Staff today, that of technology, stating:

In modern conditions, special timeliness and relevance (*aktual'nost'*) is accorded to those assets able to oppose new enemy weapons, which they plan to introduce into their armed forces during the next 10 to 15 years. It is very important to find answers in time, which will guarantee reduction in the effectiveness of enemy land, air and sea-launched high precision weapons, low-power lasers designed to blind people and put observation instruments and sights out of action radar-absorbent coverings, which can significantly reduce the effectiveness of our air defences in combating tactical aircraft, and so on.

... it is necessary to pay special attention to achieving reliable cover for second echelons, reserves, and also (logistic) targets in the rear against strikes by enemy aviation and high-precision weapons during the course of an air-land operation by them.[15]

Salmanov's arguments concerning the nature of war at the strategic and operational level, particularly the predominance of non-linear warfare, were consistent with earlier General Staff analyses and evolutionary in nature. What was new was the extent to which non-linear war embraced also the tactical level. In the 1970s the Soviets developed the concept of anti-nuclear maneuver (*protivoiadernyi manevr*), which their maneuver specialist, F.D. Sverdlov, defined as "the organized shifting of subunits with the aim of withdrawing them out from under the possible blows of enemy nuclear means, to protect their survival and subsequent freedom of action to strike a blow at the enemy. Therefore, anti-nuclear maneuver is also one of the forms of maneuver."[16] The defensive aspect of this maneuver was complemented by offensive measures "to disperse rapidly subunits or change the direction of their offensive ... and to conduct other measures related to defense against weapons of mass destruction".[17]

The work of Sverdlov and other theorists in the 1970s led the Soviets to conclude that the most effective manner in which to conduct anti-nuclear maneuver was through expanded reliance upon operational and tactical maneuver. These concepts provided the basis for the emerging Soviet preoccupation with conducting operational maneuver (by maneuver groups – the OMG) and tactical maneuver (by forward detachments), which had reached full maturity by 1980.

As recently as 1987 the concept of anti-nuclear maneuver still provided a cornerstone for Soviet operational and tactical techniques designed to preempt, preclude, or inhibit enemy resort to nuclear warfare. As articulated in 1987 by V.G. Reznichenko, "the continuous conduct of battle at a high tempo creates unfavorable conditions for enemy use of weapons of mass destruction. He cannot determine targets for nuclear strikes precisely and, besides, will be forced to shift his nuclear delivery means often."[18] In addition, by the mid-1980s, the Soviets had identified Western development of a wide variety of high-precision weapons as a major new threat. These weapons posed the same threat to attacking forces as tactical nuclear weapons, and in addition, the weapons promised a capability of more flexible engagement of attacking forces before such forces made actual contact with the enemy. The Soviets tentatively decided that even greater emphasis on operational and tacti-cal maneuver was also a partial remedy to countering enemy use of high-precision weaponry.[19] To capitalize fully on the effects of maneuver, the Soviets believed that they had to reduce planning time and execute command and control more precisely. This required increased emphasis on the use of cybernetic tools, including automation of command and expanded reliance on tactical and operational calculations (nomograms, etc.).

The Soviets also realized that advantage accrued to that force which could quickly close with the enemy, thus rendering high-precision weapons less effective. This judgement, in turn, increased the significance of first echelons, operationally and tactically. Thus by 1987, in the tactical realm, Soviet writers were able to argue "there arises the problem of defining the optimal structure for the first and second echelons at the tactical level. With the enemy using high-precision weapons, the role of the first echelon has to grow. It must be capable of achieving a mission without the second echelon (reserve)."[20]

Operational and tactical combat, in the Soviet view, "embraces simultaneously the entire depth of the combat formations of both contending sides".[21] As a result, combat missions are no longer solely described in linear fashion by the seizure of lines. The new approach, according to Reznichenko in the 1987 edition of his book *Taktika*, is "to determine them not by line, as was done before, but rather by important area (objective), the seizure of which will secure the undermining of the tactical stability of the enemy defense".[22]

Reznichenko and others now suggest that tactical missions call for securing objectives along multiple axes throughout the depth of the enemy's defense, whose seizure fragments the defense and renders it untenable. At the tactical level, specifically designated and tailored maneuver forces (usually forward detachments) had earlier performed this function, while tailored operational maneuver forces did likewise at the operational level.[23] Today, and in the future, all tactical units and subunits are likely to operate in this fashion.

This description of operational and tactical combat in future war has significantly altered traditional concepts of echelonment, not only by reducing the number of ground echelons, but also by supplementing the ground echelon with a vertical (air assault) echelon, which adds greater depth to battle. According to Reznichenko:

> One can propose that, under the influence of modern weapons and the great saturation of ground forces with aviation means, the combat formation of forces on the offensive is destined to consist of two echelons – a ground echelon, whose mission will be to complete the penetration of the enemy defense and develop the success into

the depths, and an air echelon created to envelop defending forces from the air and strike blows against his rear area.[24]

A 1988 article rounded out these descriptions by adding:

> Modern combined arms battle is fought throughout the entire depth of the enemy combat formation, both on the side's contact line (FLOT) and in the depth, on the ground and in the air.[25]

Consequently, the fragmented (*ochagovyi*) nature of battle will result in "mutual wedging (overlap) of units and subunits, which will have to operate independently for a long time".[26]

Rounding out this description of future war, the Polish theorist, Colonel S. Koziej, recently identified five basic tendencies in ground force tactics driven also by the technological revolution. These he identified as:

> the transformation of traditional ground combat into air-land combat; broadening the role of mobility in all actions of troops; the development and generalization of training of combat actions within enemy formations, especially raiding actions; the initiation of battle at increasingly greater distances; (and) the growth of the significance of the "information struggle", which has as its objective to steer the enemy in the direction of one's own plans and intentions.[27]

In essence, what has emerged is a Soviet concept of land-air battle juxtaposed against the U.S. concept of air-land battle.

These operational and tactical debates over the nature of combat had severe repercussions in the strategic area. Acceptance of the idea that combat would be non-linear required the creation and equipping of forces capable of engaging in non-linear combat on a fragmented battlefield. This meant that all forces down to battalion size had to function relatively independently. To do so required formation of forces which could sustain their own operations and the training of leaders who could display requisite initiative to lead their units successfully in combat.

By 1987 Soviet theorists were discussing such forces (usually by analogy), and the General Staff was testing them in the field (corps in the Soviet Union and brigades in Afghanistan). These new maneuver forces were closely modeled after their earlier counterparts, the mobile corps and brigades of the Second World War. Unlike the Second World War, however, the Soviets also experimented with such forces at battalion level (combined-arms battalion).

237

In 1988, in the midst of this study and experimentation, economic and political realities intervened and halted the implementation of those changes. The new restructuring program was expensive, and, moreover, it seemed dysfunctional with ongoing arms reduction negotiations and "defensiveness".

Thus, while the military rationale for restructuring to wage non-linear war was valid (and will remain so), political, economic, and international conditions subverted the program. In essence, restructuring was incompatible with newly emerging strategic concepts. Whether or not it will reemerge in the future depends on those very same conditions which halted its progress.

Thus, systematic General Staff study of the nature of future war noted the emergence of new factors and influences which have altered traditional frameworks for planning, conducting, and studying war. Technological changes, such as development of high-precision weapons, electronic warfare systems, new heliborne systems and forces, and even space weapons and weapons, whose nature and effects cannot now be imagined have challenged the traditional linear nature of war, and in so doing have required redefinition of the geographical content of war (theaters, TVDs, and types of axes (directions – *napravlenii*)), and the nature of missions and objectives. In essence, war has become multi-dimensional or, in the General Staff's language, "fragmented" (*ochagovyi*) – a war without front lines.

Given these profound changes and their inability to respond to them conceptually or structurally, General Staff analysts are accepting (albeit, often reluctantly) some of the arguments for defensiveness advanced by political authorities and argued for by the *institutchiki*. They find Kokoshin and Larionov's four paradigms for a defensive strategy useful, but, unlike their civilian counterparts who look favorably on the Khalkhin–Gol variant, they take a more jaundiced view of the threat, being inclined to support the Kursk variant. As defenders of and advocates for military truth (and, to an increasing extent, political and social order as well as Russian tradition), the General Staff cannot permit itself to become transfixed by "defensiveness", which may be driven more by political and economic realities than by objective military factors.

What sort of synthesis can result from these dichotomous views? Certainly any synthesis must recognize international and domestic political, economic and social realities, as well as military ones. Reasonable and prudent military assessments argue that Kokoshin and Larionov's second and third paradigms (those of Kursk and Khalkhin–Gol) are valid and useful. Political realities associated with the collapse of communism in eastern Europe have spelled the demise of the Soviet Union's forward defense strategy as well as the older concept of an offensive theater-strategic operation. These realities have forced the General Staff to consider anew some version of a "bastion strategy" for defense of the Soviet Union, based either upon Soviet experiences in the 1920s, which seem to correspond to the Khalkhin–Gol paradigm, or founded upon Soviet experiences in the late 1930s, which seem to fall within the parameters of the Kursk paradigm. It is this stark fact that compels Soviet analysts to a thorough study of the 1920s and 1930s, times when a bastion strategy was operative. *The only question which then remains is the degree to which domestic conditions will permit traditional General Staff analysis to continue to govern the manner in which the Soviets shape their strategy to the requirements of future war.*

As an adjunct to this critical study of future war, the General Staff has been obliged to continue its study of the nature and impact of initial periods of war. The most recent published judgements are refinements of General S. P. Ivanov's major work on the subject, published in 1974, and subsequent articles written through the mid-1980s.[28] By this time General Staff theorists had identified the following tendencies characterizing contemporary, and likely future, initial periods of war:

TENDENCIES IN THE INITIAL PERIOD OF WAR

- Increased importance of the initial period due to massive use of new means of armed conflict
- Increased influence of the results of the initial period on the subsequent course and outcome of hostilities
- Enlarged scale of military operations
- Increased use and importance of surprise
- Shortened duration because of improved weaponry
- Enhanced role and importance of maneuver

While Soviet theorists earlier stressed the necessity for gaining the strategic initiative, ostensibly through offensive action, since 1987 their emphasis has been on defense during an initial period of war. Salmanov's declaration, cited earlier, emphasized the utility of defense during the initial period as a deterrent to war in the first place, as well as a prelude to counterattacks in the Khalkhin–Gol and Kursk sense.

In Salmanov's view, "The new doctrinal approach to the interrelationship of offensive and defense, and the extraordinary importance of effective preparedness to conduct the first defensive operations of the initial period of war", urgently dictates the following measures be taken to insure success in an initial period of war:[29]

239

THE MILITARY STRATEGY OF THE SOVIET UNION

(1) Special efforts in preparing forces for their organization, .6.10deployment, and successful fulfillment of missions to repel aggression, whether conventional or nuclear, in particular, well-organized intelligence (*razvedka*) to prevent surprise attack.

(2) Maintenance of well-prepared and protected (in advance) defensive grouping capable of increasing its combat preparedness commensurate with an enemy build-up for an attack. Thus:

> Our peacetime grouping and especially the first strategic echelon must be prepared, in the event of enemy attack, to conduct first defensive operations, independently and without reinforcement, and to prevent the enemy from penetrating into the depths of (its) territory, and to create conditions for successful conduct of subsequent operations to destroy him.[30]

(3) Creation in a short time of a system of fire which can deal with an enemy attack, and particularly his second echelon – and immediately achieve fire and air superiority. (This involves anticipation of enemy technological achievements in the next 10 to 15 years.)

(4) Protection of one's own second echelon, reserves, and critical rear area objectives. "In these conditions, defense proves to be not only a means capable of repelling an enemy invasion, but also creating the prerequisites for seizing the initiative and conducting successful subsequent operations to destroy him." Defense must be active and strong because "it is very important ... not to permit losses of a considerable portion of (one's) territory".[31]

Salmanov once again underscored the deterrent value of such a strategy, stating, "The logic of military-political thought is such that an enemy, reflecting on our preparation and constant readiness to repel aggressors rapidly and by the firmness, activeness, and power of our defense, will think more than once over the well-known truth, which says that 'to begin war is simpler than to end it'".[32]

Numerous Soviet theorists have joined with Salmanov in studying the initial period of war, using as a principal vehicle the experiences of June 1941. All have reinforced his conclusions.[33] These recently published Soviet analyses on the initial period of war correspond, in their general description of the nature of combat, with similar studies written through 1985. When addressing the particular theme of offense versus defense, the recent studies accord with Soviet declarations of defensiveness promulgated since 1987. In this sense these descriptions directly relate to Kokoshin and Larianov's Kursk and Khalkhin–Gol paradigms. The main thrust of all this literature, however, directly relates to the single most notable case where a "defensive" strategy failed, that is in June 1941.

Traditionally, the Soviets have analyzed future conflict on an ideological basis and have defined a spectrum of wars among capitalist states or between capitalist and socialist states, which were the inevitable result of dialectical contradictions. This relatively neat framework, which has persisted from the 1920s through the Cold War, ostensibly still exists today. The essentially ideological approach has provided context for identifying types of war, assessed the likelihood of their occurrence, and identified the most probable scenarios for the outbreak of war. Moreover, ideological imperatives have, to a large extent, undergirded the solution of all other strategic questions, such as determining strategic posture, specifying the geographical limits of conflict (TVD), and defining the role of *fronts*, war planning, and force generation.

Today, as the importance of ideology rapidly withers, many ideological assumptions are also being questioned. This has led the civilian *institutchik*, Kokoshin, the military theorist, General V. N. Lobov, and others to state cautiously:

A qualitatively increased level of interdependence has changed the nature of the struggle of capitalist states for a market and sources of raw materials – it has become different than it was, not only between the two world wars, but also during the first postwar decades. Most significant in this respect is the policy of Japan, which does not possess many types of raw materials (beginning with energy resources) and is significantly inferior to other capitalist states in military power.

When assessing the military-political situation in the world, we do not fully take into account the fact that today's bourgeois-democratic regimes in the leading capitalist countries, even if conservative governments are in power, differ sharply from the extreme right-wing regimes of the likes of Hitler or Mussolini. To this day, in assessing the likelihood of war, some of our scientists virtually do not take into consideration either these differences or the fact that the results of World War II had a profound effect on the social consciousness in the majority of developed capitalist states. Of course, this does not rule out the need to be constantly aware of the activities and the scale of influence of various extremist groups and organizations on the masses and the governments. They are capable

241

of changing the political, and through it the military-political, situation.

The nature of the military-political interrelations between the USSR and the United States and between the Warsaw Pact and NATO has changed noticeably, the international situation has become less tense, and the immediate danger of aggression has decreased; however, the threat of war remains. Consequently, vigilance is required; it is necessary to know how the armed forces of the United States, NATO, and a number of other states are developing.[34]

This softening of the ideological content of Soviet policy has contributed to prospects for arms control and lessened the likelihood of either general nuclear war or European-wide conventional war. Ideology is likely to continue to wither, if not altogether disappear. This has, in turn, increased the need for further study of previous strategic "truths".

Kokoshin, Lobov and others suggest that study of the 1920s is an appropriate approach in the search for new answers to questions hitherto harnessed to ideology:

> Now, when these problems of the theory of strategy, the art of war as a whole, and limiting and reducing armed forces and arms are being widely discussed, it is important to consider them in a historical context and turn to the forgotten or half-forgotten works of Soviet politologists and military theorists of the 1920s and early 1930s, a prominent place among whom belongs to A. A. Svechin.[35]

Complicating this new approach to formulating strategy is the fact that the Leninist explanation of colonial war between imperialist powers and oppressed colonial states is also subject to doubt:

> One should bear in mind that the period of the struggle by colonial and dependent countries for national liberation has to a considerable extent ended in the traditional idea. More and more conflicts are taking place among developing countries themselves, who are in the stage of forming their own national and multinational (multi-tribe) statehood. The scale of the use of military force in this zone is not decreasing, and is increasing for a number of parameters. The process of devaluating the role of military force here has not yet begun, so the question of just and unjust wars must be largely resolved anew.[36]

This fact increases the need to study local wars, both for their political content as it has affected socialist and capitalist great powers and for their

242

military content, since wars between great powers have become less frequent, and any new system to foster global order must solve the dilemma of controlling the frequency and effect of local conflicts.

Kokoshin, Lobov and others also cast doubt on the utility of studying the experiences of the last major world conflict (the Second World War), which to date has provided the basis for much Soviet military analysis:

> The experience of the Great Patriotic War, illuminated with considerable distortions, given all its unquestioned value and given all the outstanding achievements of our military art, was often made absolute. This interfered with full-scale consideration of the increasingly new political, economic, scientific and technical, and operational-strategic factors which, following the Second World War, fundamentally changed, using A. A. Svechin's expression, the "strategic landscape". These factors included, above all, nuclear weapons, as well as the evolution of conventional weapons, a different appearance of local battlefields, and the use of military force not only on the battlefields, but also for direct and mediated political influence.[37]

The last major anomaly arising from the erosion of the classic Marxist–Leninist framework for articulating military strategy is the growing tendency for conflict within the socialist camp:

> The armed conflicts of the postwar decades between socialist states – the USSR and the PRC, the PRC and the PRV – have also not been studied. Conclusions and recommendations which could completely preclude such conflicts in the future have not been formulated sufficiently clearly.[38]

The existence of these conflicts demonstrates the extent to which previously held assumptions are becoming invalid. Soviet theorists are considering all of these factors as they attempt to translate threat assumptions into a military strategy for the 1990s and beyond.

All of these developments will also affect future Soviet typology of war, which, although now unclear, may include the following:

(1) Wars among capitalist states;
(2) Wars between capitalist states and socialist states;
(3) Wars among socialist states;
(4) Wars among developing states;
(5) Wars between capitalist states and developing states;
(6) Ethnic or religious struggles within states.

While inevitable struggles between large capitalist and socialist coalitions and between imperialist powers and a unified proletariat of under-developed states (revolutionary wars) have diminished, and with them the specter of inevitable cataclysmic struggle, the prospect for an increased number of "classic" conflicts among competing states and smaller local wars has increased. In short, large wars of limited frequency may now be replaced by smaller wars of much greater frequency but of equal ferocity and destructiveness. This has placed a premium on the necessity to prevent proliferation of weapons of massive destruction (nuclear, chemical, and high-precision). This tendency accords with historical reality which tells us when great "concerts" of states, such as existed during the Cold War, erode, international relations become more complex until a new "concert" is formed. Today, we seem to be entering such a period.

MILITARY STRATEGY

Based on existing and potential threats and their view of the nature of future war, Soviet theorists must develop a military strategy which suits the political-military aims of the state. It is not unreasonable to assume that those aims, given political and economic realities, are essentially defensive. If so, that defensive posture, as Salmonov argues, must be adequate to meet potential threats. We earlier suggested that the threat, a combination of threat variants 2 (good) and 3 (satisfactory status quo), consisted of eight principal elements:

1. Strategic nuclear and peripheral threat by the U.S.;
2. Residual threat from a reduced strength NATO;
3. Foreign support of ethnic unrest in the Soviet Union;
4. Domestic ethnic unrest (internal threat);
5. Unrest in Eastern Europe with Western intervention;
6. Unrest in Eastern Europe with Soviet domestic implications;
7. Nuclear and chemical weapons proliferation in hostile or potentially hostile border states;
8. Transnational threats with military implications.

Since the last five elements are essentially internal or of an indirect nature, Soviet military strategists must deal primarily with the first three. These represent the general threat the General Staff and Soviet political authorities must contend with. The nuclear and conventional threats posed by reduced-strength NATO are familiar ones whose nature is now being altered to some extent by the arms control process. That process, as it develops, provides a rational mechanism for measuring and, if necessary, scaling down the seriousness of the threat. The third element,

244

foreign support for ethnic unrest is a new dimension, which requires further clarification and definition. It also merges with the internal issue of maintaining order within the Soviet Union, which the Soviets anticipate and hope will be a matter for internal security (MVD) forces.

Given the more complex Soviet typology of war, the three most likely threats to the Soviet Union (strategic nuclear and peripheral U.S. threat, residual threat of NATO, and foreign support of ethnic unrest in the Soviet Union) and the two likely threat variations (number two: demilitarization of NATO – neutrality of Germany, and number three: status quo with reduced NATO military threat) Soviet strategists must determine a range of war scenarios in terms of threat, form, and timing. Since threat variant 2 is far less threatening, it is only prudent to plan on the basis of variant number 3. In increasing order of seriousness, this variant could result in the following spectrum of hostile action against the Soviet Union:

Case 1: covert or overt support of ethnic unrest within the Soviet Union by bordering states (China, Afghanistan, Iran, Turkey, Romania, Poland, Finland);

Case 2: covert or overt support of ethnic unrest or indigenous generated unrest within the Soviet Union by bordering states with great power assistance (Japan, U.S., Britain, France, Germany);

Case 3: military intervention within the Soviet Union for any reason by NATO or any combination of great powers;

Case 4: deliberate major conventional or nuclear attack on the Soviet Union by opposing alliances or the U.S. in concert with other powers;

Case 5: attack of unpredictable scope resulting from long-term crisis between major powers and the Soviet Union.

Analysis of the first four cases within the context of current and prospective arms limitations and other political and economic negotiations argues that the likelihood of their occurring is inversely proportional to their seriousness. In short:

(1) Nuclear or conventional attack by NATO or the U.S. is unlikely and will become less so as CFE negotiations progress;

(2) For the same reasons as cited in (1), direct Western military intervention in the Soviet Union is unlikely;

(3) Probable unrest in the Soviet Union is likely to afford increasing opportunity for foreign intervention in virtually all border regions, but, in particular, in eastern Europe, and in southern and eastern Asia;

(4) Planners must keep in mind the possibility of variant 5 (creeping up to war during crisis) and tailor the Soviet strategy posture accordingly.

While the first three judgements support Soviet desires to truncate their armed forces' structure and reduce its readiness posture, uncertainties associated with the fourth possibility will act as a natural brake on this process.

Based on this analysis, the geographical aspect of the threat will change considerably. During the Cold War, the principal threat to the Soviet Union emanated from the west (Europe), and only during the late 1960s did a new threat emerge in the east (China). Thus, Soviet strategists formulated a strategic posture and war plans geared to protecting those two high-priority regions.[39] Given the altered threats, these priorities will probably change. While CFE agreements produce (and in fact mandate) a reduction in Soviet strategic strength oriented westward, the Soviets will have to continue to maintain defenses in the east and, in addition, look carefully at their defensive posture in the south. These new realities argue for increased Soviet attention to building up strategic reserves in areas outside CFE guidelines regions, such as east of the Urals.[40] While satisfying CFE requirements, a build-up east of the Urals will also help the Soviets cope with new strategic threats to border regions in central and eastern Asia. This geographical reapportionment of strategic resources in response to an altered threat will require the Soviets to rethink their geographical framework for planning and conducting war – specifically the current TVD concept.

The Soviets must also judge how future wars will begin, specifically, to what extent traditional views on that issue remain valid today and will do so in the future. As before, the central issue remains the ability to secure the strategic initiative. The traditional view originated during the 1920s, governed Soviet strategic thought prior to the Second World War and, although somewhat modified, remained valid during that war and the Cold War. The variants were:

(1) Mobilization and concentration of forces by all contending parties prior to war;
(2) Partial mobilization and concentration prior to war, but completed during war;
(3) One state attacks to achieve operational-tactical advantage, while its opponent mobilizes and concentrates;
(4) One state attacks by surprise to achieve strategic advantage before its opponent can mobilize and concentrate. The most dangerous new facet of this variant is the nuclear "first strike".

During the 1920s the Soviets planned on the basis of variants 1 and 2 and during the 1930s on the basis of variants 2 and 3. On the eve of the Second World War, variant 4 matured in the form of German blitzkrieg, and the Soviets were only partially prepared to deal with it. Since the end of the Second World War, and particularly since the appearance of nuclear weapons, variants 3 and 4 have become the preeminent Soviet concerns in an alliance sense, for they have forced Soviet strategists to address such concepts as "first-strikes", which vastly increases the importance of the strategic initiative.

Soviet strategy in the early 1960s focused on denying any opposing state or alliance a first-strike capability, and in the 1970s and 1980s the Soviet concept of the theater-strategic offensive was designed to counter variants 3 and 4 in both a nuclear and a conventional sense.

Today, as the force reduction process unfolds, Soviet military strategists must study a wider array of variations. They must remain concerned about dealing with a nuclear first-strike in the sense of variant 4, and they must also deal with the potential for full or partial mobilization and concentration of enemy forces during periods of crisis (a modern variation of creeping up to war). In addition, they must be prepared to deal with new variations, that is, ethnic unrest and foreign support of domestic unrest with no overt mobilization or with only partial mobilization by a foreign power (in particular, in the case of a neighbor possessing a large peacetime standing army). In essence, they face the threat of revolutionary or guerrilla war on their own territory, with or without covert foreign support. This prospect blurs the traditional threat indicator of mobilization.

These judgements are based on the assumption that Soviet strategists will confine their judgements within the framework of threat variations 2 and 3 (good and satisfactory cases). Certainly contemporary domestic (particularly economic) conditions will encourage them to do so. As noted before, however, there are a significant minority of theorists who consider it prudent to base their strategic judgements on threat variant 4 (the worst case). Growing chaos in the Soviet Union would strengthen this view as would a resurgence of authoritarianism or "Great Russian" nationalism.

Predominance of this worst case view would have significant impact on the, more or less, rational process of strategy formulation outlined above. At the least, it would complicate not only the Soviet Union's (or Russian) strategic position, but also require fundamental strategic reassessments by all major world powers. Setting aside this more complex question, Soviet study of these issues will proceed within the context of the likely threats outlined above and the national and geographical sources and foci of those threats. The ensuing analytical process is determining and will continue to determine Soviet judgements regarding armed forces strength, strategic posture, strategic deployment, and force generation.

STRATEGIC POSTURE

Strategic Requirements

The Soviet view of future war, potential threats, and possible threat scenarios generates a series of strategic requirements which must be satisfied by future Soviet military policy and doctrine. Among these are:

(1) maintenance of a peacetime force adequate to deal with prospective threats in an initial period of war;

(2) preparation of a force generation infrastructure capable of generating and sustaining main forces sufficient to satisfy Soviet defense needs throughout the duration of any foreseeable conflict;

(3) development of detailed mobilization, concentration, and operational-strategic deployment plans to meet any wartime contingency;

(4) creation of requisite command and control entities for peacetime and wartime forces;

(5) realignment of deployment patterns (strategic echelons) to cope with all reasonable threats and permit orderly transition from peace to war;

(6) Engineer preparation of all prospective TVDs;

(7) deployment of sufficient air defense and ABM capability to protect the nation's industry and mobilization base (*PVO Strany*);

(8) Development of force generation schemes, which can deal with threats short of general war (partial mobilization).[41]

These requirements must be tailored to meet the minimum threat posed by threat variant 2 (demilitarized NATO), but be flexible enough to defend against any aspect of threat variant 3 (reduced strength NATO). It must also address all five possible cases of how hostilities might begin. Moreover, while providing for a balanced response to all possible threats, the overall Soviet strategic posture must respond to internal pressures for assisting internal economic reform by decreasing the military burden on the economy. In this respect, analogies with the 1920s situation are useful, since that period replicated many of the internal and external conditions the Soviet Union faces today and will face in the immediate future.

MILITARY STRENGTH

The first basic question concerns requisite levels of peacetime and wartime military strength, which should directly reflect corresponding global and regional correlation of forces. It is reasonable to postulate Soviet acceptance of peacetime and wartime military strength levels commensurate with those of its most likely wartime opponents in a general confrontation or war. In the 1920s the Soviets adhered to this policy by maintaining a peacetime force of 560,000 (or about 75 divisions), roughly equal to the strength of her two most likely opponents (Poland and Rumania). This peacetime manning level was expandable in several stages during crisis and war to 103 and 131 divisions (or 1 to 1.5 million men) respectively, enough to deal with the two most challenging and likely threat variants.[42]

Replication of this process in the 1990s would require the Soviets to maintain peacetime forces at least on a parity basis with opposing forces existing in threat variant 3, a reduced-scale NATO, plus other peripheral threats the Soviets may face in Asia. Wartime strength would have to correspond to the mobilized version of that threat. (Application of the late 1930s paradigm would require postulation of a threat far beyond that which exists today and maintenance of a vastly larger armed force, which would contravene and rule out future arms control discussions and unnecessarily burden, if not ruin, the Soviet economy.) Actual Soviet force levels will be dictated by levels negotiated within the CFE framework and additional requirements outside the Western theater as assessed by the General Staff.

By presuming Soviet efforts to capitalize on the economies of defense in northwest or south Asia, it is reasonable to assume Soviet strength in these regions could be cut by up to 25 per cent, reducing the approximately 89-division existing force to about 66.[43] Force reductions in Europe under CFE could eventually be as extensive as 50 per cent, reducing the 105 divisions (forward groups of forces, Leningrad, Baltic, Belorussian, Carpathian, Odessa, and Kiev Military Districts) of the current first and second strategic echelons to about 52. Part or all of the remaining divisions of the current strategic reserve of 20 divisions, strengthened by transfers from the west to about 30 divisions, could then constitute either a new second strategic echelon east of the Urals or part

THE MILITARY STRATEGY OF THE SOVIET UNION

of a new strategic reserve. Forces transferred from active status into the mobilization base would constitute the nucleus of a new strategic reserve. This overall force of between 140–150 divisions would have an overall peacetime strength of about 1.5 million.[44] By accepting a higher degree of risk in the belief that threat variant 2 may evolve, even more of the active strength could be subsumed into the mobilization base or into units with lower personnel manning levels (like fortified regions), for a peacetime strength of 1.0 million, manning a ground force of roughly 100–110 divisions.[45] These strength estimates accord with Soviet declarations and actions since December 1988.

The Soviets will calculate necessary wartime strength based on the assessed strength of potential foes. As a rule of thumb, however, in virtually all peacetime periods, the Soviets have assumed the necessity for expanding their force structure during wartime three- to four-fold and have created the mechanism for doing so. This would mandate a future wartime mobilized strength of about 4.5 million (as opposed to 1.5 to 2 million men in the 1920s, 5.4 million today, and 9.0 million in 1941) and creation of a mobilization mechanism capable of carrying out that expansion.

ARMED FORCES DEPLOYMENT: PEACETIME DISPOSITIONS

Force strength is but one dimension of strategic posture. Equally important is the interrelated concept of armed forces deployment (*razvertyvanie vooruzhennykh sil'*), which, in turn, depends directly on the nature, principally geographic, of the threat. Armed forces deployment involves creation of force groupings to conduct war (operations). At the highest level, strategic deployment includes:

- transition of the armed forces from a peacetime to a wartime footing
- concentration of forces on selected strategic directions within theaters of military operations
- operational deployment of forces to requisite wartime locations;
- deployment of rear services.[46]

The point of departure for strategic deployment is the peacetime disposition of active and mobilizable forces in time of crisis and war. Currently, Soviet forces are disposed to meet threats in three strategic theaters: Western, Southern, and Far Eastern. The vast territorial expanse of these theaters precludes effective strategic command and control of all forces operating within them by a single strategic headquarters. To facilitate command and control, as in the past, the Soviets have designated specific theaters of military operations (TVDs), in which strategic forces operate.

The size, number, and even the existence of TVDs has varied in the past. In the 1920s the Western Theater (from the Arctic to the Black Sea) consisted of six TVDs, in which groups of armies operated under loose *front* control. By the late 1930s the Western Theater had shrunk to include five TVDs, each of which was the responsibility of a single *front*. This system proved inadequate during the initial stages of the Second World War, and the Soviets replaced the TVDs with three strategic direction (*napravlenie*) headquarters (Northwestern, Western, Southwestern), each consisting of several fronts responsible to a small direction (*napravlenie*) headquarters. When this arrangement also proved unsatisfactory, they shifted to groups of fronts temporarily formed to conduct strategic operations under *Stavka* control (through its designated personal representative).[47]

In the late 1970s the Soviets again formed ground and oceanic TVDs, ultimately five ground TVDs contiguous to the Soviet Union (three in the Western theater and one each in the Southern and Far Eastern theaters). These suited the strategic circumstance of having groups of Soviet forces disposed deep in central Europe. Now that these forward groups are returning to the Soviet Union, the General Staff must reassess the nature and utility of TVDs, both as defined geographical areas and as specific strategic headquarters. Although the ultimate outcome of that redefinition is not yet clear, it is likely the Soviets will retain at least Western and Far Eastern TVDs and perhaps a skeletal organization for a Southern TVD.[48] Other former TVDs will become strategic directions.

Even more vexing for the General Staff is the matter of establishing strategic depth for its force deployments, which it has classically achieved through echelonment. Strategic echelons, traditionally and by definition, are distinct parts of the Soviet Union's armed forces designated to accomplish strategic missions in wartime. The first strategic echelon consists of forces designated to conduct initial operations, while the second echelon includes Soviet main forces located or forming in the depth of the nation. Strategic reserves under High Command control consist of additional mobilizable forces and materiel.

In the recent past (and currently) in the Western theater, the forward groups of forces with their massive command and control and support infrastructures made up the first strategic echelon (see Figure 38). This 30-division force was backed up directly or indirectly by the 75 divisions of the border military districts (plus the Kiev Military District), which comprised the second strategic echelon, and by a strategic reserve of about 20 active divisions and an indeterminate number of mobilization divisions.[49] Similar echelonment applied to the Far East and Southern theaters.

With the withdrawal of the forward groups of forces from eastern and central Europe, the Soviet General Staff will have lost its first strategic echelonment in the most critical theater and must now reassess strategic echelonment in general. The most appropriate model for echelonment within the contiguous borders of the Soviet Union is that of the 1920s and 1930s, the last occasion when the Soviets were forced to address that question. At that time the first strategic echelon consisted of forces in the

38. Soviet strategic echelonment: 1989

border military districts, and the second strategic echelon of forces in internal military districts. There are two major problems with Soviet adoption of a similar system. First, because of the likely pace of operations and range of weapons systems, the border districts may lack requisite depth to conduct successful strategic initial operations, particu-

252

larly if some western republics separate from the Soviet Union (the Baltic republics for example). Second, and more unsettling, the strategic echelonment system of the 1920s and 1930s failed in 1941, and the Germans overcame first strategic echelon forces within only three weeks.

One solution to this dilemma would be to seek bilateral military and political agreements with eastern European states (such as Poland), which are uneasy with the newly evolving international political structure, in particular, the unification of Germany. Such an agreement could permit the token stationing of Soviet forces on Polish soil so long as NATO retains its own military force, and United States forces on European soil. An even stronger, although unlikely, version of this solution could involve continued stationing of Soviet forces in eastern Germany, even after German unification. Although this could be justified while United States troops are still stationed in western Germany, if and when they left Germany, such an arrangement would become increasingly awkward and destabilizing. There are indicators that some Soviet strategists favor a continued, although reduced, United States force presence in Europe, either to justify reciprocal Soviet presence in eastern Europe or, in the case of those who fear the worst case threat variant, to act as a check on potential increases in German political and military power. Stationing of Soviet forces somewhere in eastern Europe would, in any case, provide additional arguments for Soviet adoption of the pre-1941 mode of strategic echelonment.

There are then principally two methods for the Soviets to echelon forces strategically in peacetime. Both will be shaped by the provisions of CFE agreements. The first would involve formation of a relatively shallow first strategic echelon (with possible but unlikely limited forward basing of forces in western Poland and perhaps even a token force in eastern Germany) (see Figure 39). The first strategic echelon would extend eastward to the Sozh and Dnepr River lines and include the Leningrad, Baltic, Belorussian, Carpathian, Odessa, Kiev, and Trans-Caucasus Military Districts. The second strategic echelon would then include portions of the Ural–Volga, Moscow, and North Caucasus Military Districts, while a strategic reserve could consist of forces in part of the Ural–Volga and the Siberian Military Districts and in the mobilization base elsewhere in the nation. Analogous echelonment would exist for the Southern and Far Eastern theaters, although strategic echelons would not be as clearly delineated along military district lines. Soviet loss of sovereignty over the Baltic republics or Moldavia would preclude adoption of this option.

A second echelonment variation would include a first strategic echelon extending eastward to the Urals, backed up by strategic reserves east of the Urals (see Figure 40). The strategic reserve in this circumstance would also encompass the mobilization base throughout the entire nation and would have no specific geographical limits.

The relative strength and force composition of strategic echelons will depend directly on overall Soviet armed forces strength and on constraints imposed by arms control negotiations. In general, the closer that reality is to threat variant 3 (the satisfactory case), the stronger will be overall Soviet strength and the strength and readiness of the first strategic echelon. In this instance, Soviet dispositionscould strongly resemble those of June 1941, although on a markedly lighter scale. Close examination of the 1941 defense can provide hints as to what the future structure of such defense might involve.

In June 1941 Soviet strategic plans called for defense by rifle, fortification, and mechanized forces echeloned in considerable depth (see figure 41). The first operational echelon of rifle and fortification forces, arrayed in the immediate border regions, consisted of several tactical echelons backed up by the most combat-ready mechanized corps. To their rear, a

39. Soviet strategic echelonment: 1995 (variant 1)

second operational echelon of rifle forces and mechanized corps defended at a depth of up to 150 kilometers. A third operational echelon of reserve armies and mechanized corps deployed before or shortly after the outbreak of hostilities along the line of the Dnepr River from Vitebsk in the north to west of Kiev in the south. The first defending operational echelon had the task of slowing and wearing down enemy forces, the

40. Soviet strategic echelonment: 1995 (variant 2)

second with halting the enemy drive, and the third with counterattacking to expel the invader. The 1941 plan weighted defenses along the south-western (Kiev) direction (axis) where Soviet strategists (Stalin) thought the main enemy blow would fall.

Closer examination of the best-developed defensive sector (south-western) more clearly shows force mix, configuration, and disposition (see Figure 42). The basic building blocks of the Soviet defense were fortified regions, rifle divisions and corps, and mechanized corps. The fortified regions (*ukreplennyhi raion*) of about 5,000 men each consisted of machine gun and artillery battalions. Light in manpower and heavy in firepower, these units occupied prepared or semi-prepared defenses immediately adjacent to the border astride major projected axes of

255

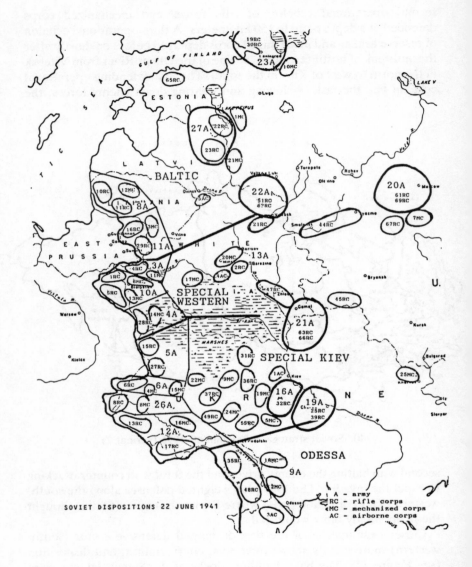

41. Soviet strategic defense, Western Theater, June 1941

enemy advance and other prepared defense lines deeper in the rear area. Their function was to block the enemy advance in specific sectors, tie down and cause attrition in enemy forces, and generally disrupt the coherence of the enemy advance. These formations correspond in structure and function to modern machine gun-artillery divisions, which the Soviets have recently announced are now being created and deployed.

Rifle forces, being larger and more maneuverable than the fortified regions, defended from field fortifications along the front or at intermediate positions to the rear. Mechanized forces, depending on their initial locations, launched counterattacks in support of the forward defense, counterstrokes from the depths, or, in combination, conducted counteroffensives. Mechanized corps disposed at shallow depths were positioned to strike the flanks of the enemy advance. Successive commitment of mechanized corps, in support of successive defense lines, provided depth to the defense and theoretically would wear enemy forces down to a point where reserve armies and mechanized corps could launch a concerted and decisive counteroffensive.

The general post-1945 straightening of the Soviet border will facilitate future Soviet strategic defense of her western borders. The new border

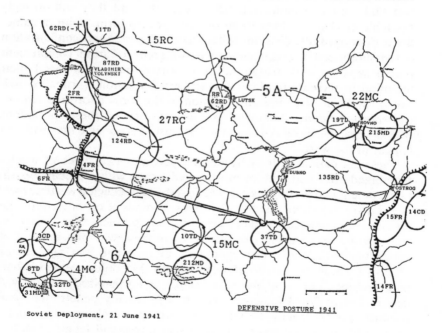

Soviet Deployment, 21 June 1941

DEFENSIVE POSTURE 1941

42. Soviet strategic defense, Southwestern Front, June 1941

257

configuration has eliminated the infamous Bialystok and L'vov salients and provided a far more linear front, which offers better lateral communications west of the Pripiat Marshes. This configuration will remain favorable if the Soviets retain control over the Baltic states, Belorussia, the western Ukraine, and Bessarabia. Their loss, however, would seriously jeopardize Soviet western strategic defenses.

The Soviets have already sketched out the likely structure of their new reformed "defensive" force.[50] Its combat backbone will be new tank and motorized rifle divisions (or corps), restructured to deemphasize reliance on armor and, instead, emphasize better-balanced combined-arms entities at every level of command, which can operate more efficiently in non-linear future war. Weaponry and materiel hitherto employed at division level will devolve to regiment, battalion, or army level, depending on where it will be of the greatest use. To enhance the defensive look of forces at division and below, air assault and assault bridging assets will be removed from some divisions and armies and be concentrated at *front* level. (This, of course, does not preclude reassignment and employment of these forces at lower levels in wartime.)

At least some tank divisions will convert to a square configuration of two tank and two motorized rifle regiments, and they will strongly resemble mechanized formations of yesteryear in form, if not in name. Some motorized rifle divisions will similarly adopt a square configuration of four motorized rifle regiments, each with a reduced armor complement plus a separate tank battalion.[51] The Soviets have announced their intention to recreate machine gun-artillery formations (probably divisions) similar in structure and function to the former fortified regions (*ukreplennyi raion*). Although they have associated these formations with defense in central Asia and the Far East, it is possible they will also appear in the west.

These formations will likely be grouped into two types of armies (combined-arms and tank or mechanized), each with a specific operational function to perform as part of a first strategic echelon wartime *front* (see Figure 43). Combined-arms armies, composed of motorized rifle divisions, machine-gun-artillery divisions, and perhaps a tank division, will operate as covering (or defensive) armies, with the mission of conducting initial defensive operations to slow and halt any enemy offensive. These armies will defend to a depth of 150 kilometers with their tank divisions poised to the rear. Tank (or mechanized) armies will deploy 150 to 300 kilometers deep to halt enemy penetrations and conduct counterstrokes. Other deeper-deployed tank armies, supplemented by mobilized reserve (secondary) forces will launch counteroffensives, if required. Thus, this structure could include both peacetime forces maintained at or near combat strength and a large mobilizable force, maintained at cadre strength in peacetime.

This force will be disposed in depth and integrated into an extensive engineer defense, consisting of prepared or semi-prepared defensive belts or zones. Engineer preparation will be most-developed in the forward area to a depth of 150 kilometers. A more detailed look at one sector reveals how defenses might look at tactical and operational depths (see Figure 44). In this instance, one first strategic echelon *front* defends along the western (Minsk) direction north of the Pripiat Marshes and one defends on the southwestern or Kiev direction. Each *front* consists of two combined-arms and two tank or mechanized armies. The combined-arms armies defend forward to a depth of 150 kilometers with motorized rifle

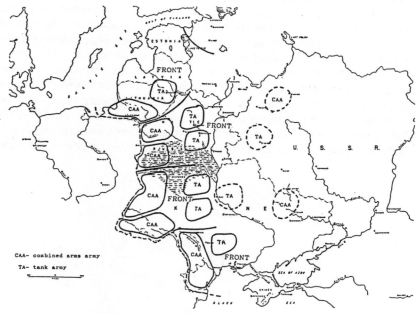

43. Soviet strategic defensive posture, 1995 (variant)

and machine gun-artillery divisions located to their front, deployed to depths of up to 70 kilometers. Machine-gun-artillery divisions (shown as fortified regions – FRs) cover more difficult terrain or built-up areas, while motorized rifle divisions deploy covering forces forward along the border (up to one regiment) on main avenues of approach and occupy more extensive defenses up to 50 kilometers to the rear (depending on terrain).

Second-echelon or reserve motorized rifle divisions of combined-arms armies occupy prepared defenses up to 100 kilometers in the army rear and coordinate closely with combined-arms army tank divisions, also located on main axes, which are designated to deliver counterattacks. Further to the rear (150–300 kilometers) *front* tank armies, covered by a second belt of fortified regions, prepare to conduct counterstrokes in support of first-echelon combined-arms armies. The tank divisions of combined-arms armies and the *front* tank armies are reinforced with requisite antitank, self-propelled artillery, and air defense artillery units (regiments and brigades).

The strength, number and disposition of these peacetime forces will have to be reconciled with force reduction provisions negotiated under CFE. If the force balance decreases proportionately and approaches conditions of threat variant 2 (the good case), Soviet posture will also decrease in terms of overall strength and combat readiness. The bulk of reductions will probably be absorbed by the force generation system, which serves as a mobilization vehicle in the event of war.

The readiness state of peacetime forces of first strategic echelon wartime *fronts* will correspond to the perceived threat. Should a large NATO or German force exist in peacetime, all forward forces will be maintained at nearly full wartime strength. Should a residual NATO force exist in Central Europe, readiness requirements would correspondingly decrease. In this instance, elements of forward combined-arms

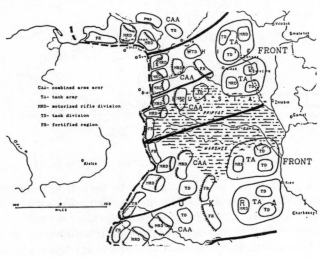

44. Soviet defensive posture, 1995 (variant)

armies in peacetime are likely to remain near full strength, while the remainder of these armies and tank armies would be kept at cadre strength (perhaps one full-strength regiment in peacetime).

In this model Soviet forces decrease considerably from current levels. Presently, Soviet forces in the forward groups and western military districts (Baltic, Belorussian, Carpathian) number about 70 divisions, half at or near full strength. In this strategic model, there are 44 divisions in the western military districts, nine of which are machine-gun-artillery, while 15 of the tank divisions and nine of the motorized rifle divisions can be maintained at cadre strength. Without mobilization this force possesses very limited offensive capability, but sufficient force for defensive purposes. Moreover, this force configuration, given a proper correlation of forces and suitable political context, negates the more serious flaws of 1941. The Soviets will also adjust this force to accord with the requirements of CFE negotiations. In this configuration the Soviets are likely to retain a formal TVD structure for the Western TVD.

The Soviets, if confronted with the less menacing threat variant 2, could adopt a deeper echelonment modeled somewhat after that of the 1920s and involving fewer forces. In fact, as CFE negotiations further reduce force strengths permitted in the CFE guidelines area, the Soviets may be forced to adopt this deployment scheme, which involves maintaining an ever larger proportion of the force either east of the Urals or in the mobilization base.

In this instance, the first strategic echelon would comprise all military districts west of the Urals. Half of these forces would be located west of the Sozh and Dnepr Rivers in the border military districts and would represent the most combat-ready Soviet forces. In wartime these forces would constitute the first two operational echelons of covering armies. East of the two rivers the other half of the forces, dispersed in the Moscow, Ural–Volga, and Kiev military districts, would constitute the first strategic echelon's reserves. The strategic reserve, east of the Urals, would contain the bulk of Soviet main forces and the large segment of the mobilization base.

FORCE GENERATION

The second, and perhaps most critical aspect of strategic armed forces deployment is that of generating forces adequate to satisfying wartime strategic needs. Simply stated, that encompasses both manning the force in peacetime and providing sufficient manpower to effect the transition from peace to war. Although it is a major subject of study in its own right, it warrants brief comment here.[52]

Force generation includes three critical elements: First, establishment and maintenance of a peacetime force and, second, creation of a mechanism for expanding that force to meet wartime needs in terms of manpower, combat force structure, and materiel. Last, it is desirable, in so far as possible, to conceal full wartime strength. In the past the Soviets have employed a variety of systems to perform this critical function.[53] In simplified terms, these systems have produced the following results as regards both mobilization and demobilization:[54]

	Dec 1920	May 1925	1935	1 Jan 1938	Dec 1940
Manpower	5.3m	560,000	1.3m	1.52m	4.2m
Divisions	78	88	102*	142**	206

	21 June 1941	Dec 1941	Dec 1943	April 1945
Manpower	5.0m	4.19m	5.9m	6.2m
Divisions	303	300	480	570

	Jan 1948	1965	1975	1989	1990
Manpower	2.8m	2.0m	1.8m	1.9m	1.59m
Divisions	170	147	166	211	217

*includes 2 mechanized corps
**includes 4 tank corps

Over time the Soviets have employed two basic systems for force maintenance and force mobilization during transition from peacetime to wartime. From 1924 to 1938, they relied on a mixed territorial/militia and regular/cadre system, which permitted maintenance of low peacetime strength levels, but created a large pool of trained manpower to expand the structure in the event of war.[55] From 1938 to 1941, and after the Second World War, they relied on a regular/cadre system based on universal military service.[56] This is the system they still employ. In the regular/cadre system, the Soviets maintained these forces at distinct levels of cadre manning or truncated them in peacetime on the basis of one full-strength cadre regiment or brigade per division. This cadre force provided the nucleus around which the full unit could mobilize and provided additional cadre for the completely mobilized force. In addition, the Soviets have maintained in their mobilization base formations difficult to detect, such as embryonic or "mobilization" divisions, which can be quickly spun off their parent unit containing their cadre leadership.

Today the Soviets are studying these two traditional force generation schemes as well as two others, the pure territorial/militia and volunteer systems, both of which are partly derived from the experiences of other nations.[57] Each system has its own strengths and weaknesses, which, when reduced to chart form, appear as follows:

FUTURE SOVIET MILITARY STRATEGY

FEATURES OF CADRE SYSTEM

Manpower

Universal military service
Two- or three-year service obligation
Long-term reserve obligation
Large, well-trained manpower base

Formations

Varying cadre strength
Level of personnel and equipment readiness dependent on force location
Extra-territorial manning

Examples

Cold War category system
Pre-World War II (1938–41)

FEATURES OF MIXED CADRE/TERRITORIAL SYSTEM

Universal military service
Varied active duty service
Long-term reserve obligation
Large manpower base, with varied training

Formations

Complex manning levels
Variations in training and mobilization exercises
Mixed extra-territorial and territorial manning

Example

1924–38

FEATURES OF TERRITORIAL MILITIA SYSTEM

Manpower

Universal military service
Short-term active duty
Long-term reserve obligation
Large, less well-trained manpower base

Formations

Low personnel strength, full equipment set
Short, frequent training cycle
Periodic mobilization exercises
Territorial (local) manning (reliability question)

Example

1924–38 (never purely territorial)

FEATURES OF VOLUNTEER SYSTEM

Manpower

No universal military service
Contracted active service obligation
Short-term reserve obligation
Small, trained reserve base

263

Formations

Most units full strength (manpower and equipment)
Smaller force
Uniform national training cycle
Extra-territorial manning

Examples

Tsarist times
Current U.S. Army

Today there are fairly clear criteria the Soviets must satisfy in whatever force generation system they adopt. Some of these criteria are basic, others transitory, but none can be violated without incurring certain risks. The five most critical criteria are: "sufficient" force available to meet peacetime need; "sufficient" rapidly mobilizable reserve force to satisfy wartime contingencies; budgetary savings *vis-à-vis* current force expenditures; optimal (efficient) use of scarce manpower resources, *vis-à-vis* the state economy; and an army which is reliable. Expressed in matrix form, the extent to which each force generation system satisfies the criteria becomes clear:

Criteria		*System*	
	Cadre	*Mixed Cadre/Territorial*	*Territorial/Militia*
Sufficient peacetime force	Yes	Yes	No
Sufficient reserves (universal military service)	Yes	Yes	Yes
Budgetary savings	No	Yes	Yes
Optimal use of manpower	No	Yes	Yes
Reliable army?	Yes	Primarily (Distasteful to Soviets)	Questionable (Condemned by Soviets)

	Volunteer
Sufficient peacetime force	Yes
Sufficient reserves (universal military service)	No
Budgetary savings	No
Optimal use of manpower	Yes
Reliable army	Yes

Judged against these criteria, the present regular/cadre system is best suited to satisfying purely military needs, but fails to meet the short-term economic and manpower requirements of the state. In addition, as the threat environment moderates, the necessity for a large, expensive regular/cadre system decreases. The mixed regular/cadre and territorial/ militia system better satisfies current and future Soviet economic and military needs, but raises the question of reliability in ethnic territorial units. A purely territorial/militia system is unsatisfactory because it produces neither a large enough peacetime force nor requisite reliability. The volunteer force, which would guarantee reliability, is unsuited because of its questionable expense and the resultant lack of mobilizable reserves.

It is likely the ultimate solution the Soviets adopt will incorporate elements from all systems, plus some imaginative new measures derived from past practices. First, the Soviets would like to retain universal military service, but to do so they must solve serious problems (draft evasion, desertion, etc.) and consider an alternative service. Failure to solve these problems could result in greater reliance on purely contract (volunteer) service. Force manning will probably be based on a mixed cadre/territorial structure with a heavier regular/cadre component than existed in the 1920s and more extensive reliance on volunteers in critical segments of the military establishment (airborne, strategic rocket forces, submarine, NCOs). Whereas, in the 1920s the ratio of regular/cadre to territorial divisions was roughly 3:4, in the future that ratio will be at least

265

2:1. In a prospective force of 150 divisions, this would result in about 100 regular/cadre and 50 territorial divisions or divisional equivalents. Territorial formations would have some leavening of all-union command cadre and be restricted to only nationalities considered reliable. Politically, the creation of territorial formations could have considerable appeal and bargaining value if Soviet political reforms result in some form of federal system (a pleasanter alternative than outright secession or forced retention in the Soviet Union).

The burden of maintaining a large regular/cadre force could be mitigated by maintaining distinctly different cadre manning levels in peacetime (similar to today's categories and the "line" system of the 1920s and 1930s) or by maintaining cadre nuclei (regiments or battalions) of large units and formations in peacetime. Some regular/cadre formations could be maintained in peacetime as fortified regions, which in wartime could convert to fully fledged divisions.[58]

This regular/cadre force could be expanded in time of crisis or during wartime by pre-assignment of personnel within active cadre formations to newly formed formations, which would then be filled out with reservists, or augmentees, and stored equipment (similar to embryonic formations of the 1920s and 1930s). Another means of creating new formations during mobilization would be to maintain mobilization sites and training centers in peacetime with sufficient cadre and mobilization equipment sets to form the nucleus of up to two new mobilization formations, which could then be filled out with reservists and conscripts.[59] Past practice indicates that a force of 100 cadre and 50 territorial formations, augmented by one training center and one mobilization center per military district (for a total of 30) could produce between 360 and 400 division-size wartime formations, an adequate force to deal with any foreseeable threat. Whereas in the past the Soviets believed it was necessary to triple their peacetime structure in wartime, in a nuclear and high technology age a more than two-fold increase should be adequate to meet strategic requirements.

The debate over armed forces reform continues and is reflected in numerous articles in the Soviet press. This debate is likely to continue for some time until all issues are resolved. To date, virtually all proposals fall within the parameters of the judgements made above, that is, the Soviet Union will field a reformed ground force structure of between 1 and 1.5 million men organized into between 100 and 150 active divisions. Appendix 3 encapsulates in outline form the gist of the debate as reflected in three articles published in late 1990.

CHAPTER 8

CONCLUSIONS

If Soviet military strategy continues to evolve in accordance with defensive Soviet military policy and doctrine, a Soviet strategic posture will emerge that is altogether different from that of the 1970s and early 1980s. The new posture is likely to accord with paradigms or models, which the Soviets have either already openly discussed or implied. Whichever paradigm and model emerges, it is clear that it will be based on thorough analysis of past Soviet strategic experiences juxtaposed against changes in the contemporary and future political and military environment. Analysis of past Soviet strategic defensive experiences permits further speculation regarding other prospective models within the proposed range of paradigms. It remains for us to judge which model is most likely to emerge and then to assess its ramifications.

The original range of paradigms proposed by Kokoshin, Larionov and others are a good starting point for analysis, for they offer a thorough range of options and two which seem to meet modern demands. The first useful paradigm the Soviets suggested, the third, based on premeditated defense at Kursk, appeared defensive only in a superficial historical light. Closer examination revealed features which contradicted its purported defensive nature. Specifically, defensive fighting took place within the framework of a Soviet strategic offensive plan, and large Soviet strategic reserves earmarked to conduct the offensive tilted the correlation of forces decisively in the Soviets' favor. Future Soviet maintenance of similarly large combat-ready forces and reserves in peacetime would contradict the principal of "defensive sufficiency" and render the strategy clearly offensive.

The Khalkhin–Gol and Korean-based paradigms (number two), which Soviet theorists emphasized after the flaws of the Kursk paradigm became apparent, better matches articulated Soviet intent. It too, however, has weaknesses which cast doubt on its applicability. Soviet strategy regarding the Japanese in 1939 was but a part of a larger strategy toward the more menacing foe, Germany. While overall Soviet strategy had, as yet, not become totally defensive in Europe, clearly the Soviets were adopting a defensive posture in the Far East. Restraint against the Japanese at Khalkhin–Gol served the larger purpose of greater readiness

267

against the Germans. Moreover, Soviet secret reinforcement of its forces in Mongolia and her achievement of surprise make the case of Khalkhin–Gol less convincing.

Subsequently, the Soviets suggested a new model based on a pre-Cold War strategy, which seemed to correspond with Kotoshin's and Larionov's second (Kursk) or third (Khalkhin–Gol) paradigms. By providing details of the 1946 GOFG operational plan, the Soviets argued that their pre-Cold War strategic posture was defensive and provided strong hints as to the nature of their desired post-Cold War strategy in a circumstance of forward defense. When it was advanced in early 1989, this "pre-Cold War" forward defense model clearly postulated the basis for a new post-Cold War defensive strategy, provided the Soviets retained their forward groups of forces in central and eastern Europe (see Figure 45). Although it now seems clear the Soviets will continue to withdraw their forward groups of forces, under this model the Soviets probably planned to organize WGF forces into covering (defensive) armies, backed up by armies designated to conduct the counteroffensive. The Soviets would have called the counterattacking armies mechanized or combined-arms in accordance with current and future force structuring. It is likely the Soviets planned to employ two combined-arms armies to conduct initial forward defensive operations and two heavier armies to engage in early counterstrokes. If they resorted to some degree of "cadreing" as they did from 1946 to 1949, they had the capability of reinforcing these forces with up to two more mechanized armies within the seven-day time frame indicated in the 1946 plan. After full reinforcement, the four heavy armies had the capability of launching a full counteroffensive or even an offensive in their own right.

The offensive capabilities of a Western Group of Forces organized in such a fashion depended entirely on the relative correlation of forces in sector, the efficiency of Soviet mobilization and long-distance movement schemes, and the degree to which they could have concealed required mobilization. What is fairly certain is that, until recently, within seven days they could have fielded a WGF force of from 19 to 20 divisions to employ for whatever purpose they envisioned. It is now clear that, as this force is further reduced in the future, its offensive capabilities will continue to erode if, throughout the process, NATO retains sufficient forces to ensure the correlation of forces remains appropriate for successful defense.

Soviet plans for the employment of forward groups of forces after the mid-1950s also encompassed non-Soviet Warsaw Pact forces, which became a key ingredient in the ensuing concept of the theater-strategic offensive. Soviet resurfacing in 1989 of the 1946 model signaled Soviet

CONCLUSIONS

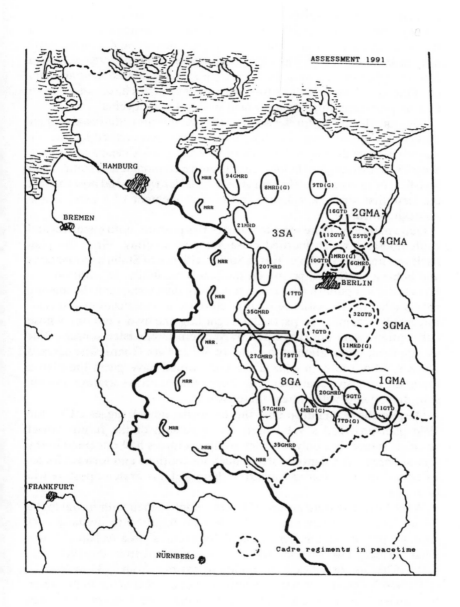

45. Assessment of probable Western Group of Forces dispositions in 1991

269

realization that non-Soviet Warsaw Pact armies, other than perhaps the East Germans, were less relevant to Soviet strategic planning. Changes in the political climate since February 1989 bear this out and, additionally, have made it unlikely that any forward-based Soviet forces will remain in eastern and central Europe. In short, events have rendered this paradigm obsolete as the status of these forward groups of forces has changed from that of a military threat to a hostage to developing events.

Far more disturbing for the Soviets, the precipitous withdrawal of their forward groups of forces into the Soviet Union has created for them a major strategic dilemma. The loss of forward groups means loss of the Soviet's first strategic echelon, with its entire command and control and logistical infrastructure. They must now consider where and how to erect the new first strategic echelon as the vital element of a new, viable strategic posture.

Quite naturally, there were features of this posture, both historical and contemporary, which merited close Western scrutiny. First, the plan itself was not fully credible. Harsh Soviet criticism of Stalin's motivations and behavior reflected poorly on the plan's reliability. In addition, the Soviets did not publish the plan in full. More disturbing than the missing paragraphs was the absence of any reference to mobilization and rein-forcement schemes, in particular regarding the two divisions whose designations were not confirmed by Western intelligence sources. Nor was there an explanation of the roles of 3rd and 4th Guards Mechanized Armies, whose fully mobilized presence would have given the plan a markedly offensive character. One hopes that in future strategic discussion, the Soviets will address these issues.

Despite these qualifications, the defensive model suggested by the 1946 plan provided a valid basis for discussion of the future Soviet strategic stance, but only if Soviet groups of forces had remained in the forward area. As balanced force reductions continue and forward forces withdraw, the justification for and credibility of this strategic posture will disappear.

When Soviet forward groups of forces complete their withdrawal to the Soviet Union, entirely new models will be required to define Soviet strategic posture and its degree of "defensiveness" in a reshaped European balance. Two such models exist, one derived from the 1920s and early 1930s and one based on conditions existing from 1935 to 1941.

The model which warrants the most attention is that of the 1920s, when the Soviet Union assessed the threat potential of Eastern European successor states, alone or in concert with Western powers. This model is advanced most fervently by those who adhere to the Khalkhin–Gol paradigm.

There are compelling reasons to reflect on Soviet military strategy in the 1920s as a potential indicator of future Soviet strategy. First and foremost, the Soviets are faced with an array of internal and external conditions today, which, to a degree, replicate those of the 1920s. Internally, the Soviet Union faces severe political, economic, and social problems resembling those of the 1920s, including:

(1) political instability associated in the 1920s with a struggle for power and a debate over democracy, albeit within the party; as opposed to a similar struggle for more general democracy today;

(2) economic crisis in the 1920s associated with Civil War dislocation of the economy and the adoption and subsequent rejection of the economic reforms of the New Economic Policy (NEP); juxtaposed against contemporary economic stagnation and attempted acceleration of the economy (*uskorenie*), restructuring of the economy (*perestroika*) and now more radical reforms (such as private ownership of property);

(3) Ethnic unrest, associated in the 1920s with Civil War and incorporation into the Soviet Union of nationalities, which, for a time during the Civil War, had regained their independence; as opposed to agitation for independence by numerous nationalities today;

(4) military discontent in the 1920s associated with tension between "Red" officers and Tsarist "experts" and enlisted alienation connected with the collectivization and industrialization program of the late 1920s; corresponding to ferment within the contemporary Soviet Army over ethnic issues, the role of the army as guardian of order and tradition, and demoralization produced by democratization, the Afghan War, and demobilization;

(5) Uncertainty concerning the emerging threat to the USSR, the need to plan for several variants, the uncertain impact of technology on military affairs, the apparent need to incorporate projected changes, and, of course, relationships with Germany in the midst of change.

Compounding these internal difficulties, the Soviets are now watching a Europe and world emerge experiencing changes as drastic as those which occurred after the First World War (although one hopes it is a world which will not be burdened with a modern equivalent of the Treaty of Versailles, which exacerbated international relations). Specifically, old alliances and blocs, which have kept a tense peace for over 40 years, are crumbling with no apparent replacements, a unified Germany is emerging (without "historic" borders); independent successor states are emerging in eastern Europe, subject to political instability, economic weakness and ethnic tensions of their own; the global military and economic balance is shifting; and the world is experiencing a revolution in conventional military weaponry.

Each of these stark realities can have unpredictable consequences, and all resemble dilemmas of the past. It is only reasonable that the Soviets will intensely review that past in their search for hints as to how to deal successfully with those same dilemmas in the future. In particular, the Soviets will critically examine basic concepts and systems developed in the 1920s and early 1930s concerning their methodology for studying the question of future war, the initial period of war, threat definition, and strategic posture. They may also find much of use from the 1920s in assessing future schemes for force generation and transition from peace to war.

The 1920s paradigm best represents future geopolitical, strategic, economic, and military relationships within a post-CFE Europe and addresses the key issue of Soviet attitudes toward Eastern European successor states and to new European threats. As such it offers the most valuable insights into probable Soviet military strategy of the 1990s. The 1920s paradigm suggests that the Soviets will maintain lower peacetime levels of military preparedness, supplemented by a complex mobilization system capable of rapidly transforming the Soviet Army to a wartime footing.

If Soviet military strategy and resultant force posture during the 1920s provides an analogy for an optimistic version of what Soviet military strategy may look like in the future, the late 1930s period also provides a far more pessimistic model for the West. In that decade international conditions turned ugly and threatening for all actors on the international stage. Economic dislocation, growth of totalitarianism, and rampant social discord raised international tensions, increased the likelihood of future war, and altered the very nature of war. In the Soviet Union, it resulted in a major rearmament program and an intense focus on war plans and strategic defense. In the end, despite all Soviet exertions, the strategic defense essentially failed.

It is at least conceivable that unenlightened world leadership in the future, if it fails to comprehend the intricacies of the 1930s, may contribute to a repetition of many of those unpleasant phenomena. Just as the Soviet Union was a major player shaping events in the 1930s, it will continue to figure significantly in the future European and world structure. Likewise, just as other states played or refused to play a role in the developments of the 1930s, they will continue to play critical roles in the future. In short, those same states which provided context for international events in general, and for developments within the Soviet Union in particular, during the 1930s, will similarly contribute to the context of the future.

In the period before 22 June 1941, a strong and hostile Germany in the west and Japan in the east had borders contiguous to the Soviet Union. Now that the Soviets have admitted that their failed 1941 prewar strategy was defensive, the Soviet strategic posture of that period can provide a basis for thoroughly analyzing future strategies for defense of the Soviet Union. While this emerging model will provide an excellent basis for evaluating military "defensive sufficiency," it will also inherently require detailed discussion of the political and military context – namely the European political and military balance as a whole.

The model of June 1941, which is advanced primarily by those who support the Kursk paradigm, poses three problems for the Soviets. First, Soviet theorists have recently accorded the adoption of a 1941 model a very low degree of probability because nuclear deterrents have largely neutralized all analogous threats.[1] Second, Soviet military theorists have only recently admitted their military strategy on the eve of war was defensive. Third, and most important, the defensive strategy of 1941 failed. Despite these problems the 1941 model warrants attention. Soviet implementation of a similar strategy in a post-cold war period will have to deal more effectively with potential threats similar to that of 1941, particularly if nuclear deterrence erodes as a valid defensive concept. Adoption of a new 1941-type strategy will provide the Soviets with the potential collateral benefit of being able to insist on external political and military concessions to reduce the threat and, hence, validate the strategy.

It is clear that today, under pressure of revolutionary changes in the European and world geopolitical balance, accelerated de-Stalinization and possible democratization in the Soviet Union, and the Soviet need for a "strategy for defense of the homeland", both the 1920s model and the 1941 model – with its positive and negative lessons – will become more critical models or, at least, subjects of intensive study as the Soviets shape their new strategy. In fact, that study has already begun.

Should the Soviets rid themselves of the ghosts of 1941, the late 1930s defensive strategic model or that of the 1920s has the potential for offering considerable leverage to the Soviets in their political and military negotiations with the West. If, in fact, defensiveness failed in 1941 because the Soviets seemingly underestimated the external threat, then Soviet adoption of a similar strategy in the future will require the negation of any possibility of such a threat.

Two such potential threats immediately come to mind. The first, in the form of NATO, exists today in Soviet perceptions. The second, in the form of a unified and militarily powerful Germany, within or outside of NATO, looms as a potential future threat. Each threat, in its own right, must be dealt with for a Soviet 1920s- or 1941-type strategy to be viable in the future. It is indeed possible that such a Soviet strategy could become a vehicle for resolving both problems. This strategy would be viable if the USSR (and Europeans themselves) can be convinced that NATO's military power has been reduced to clearly defensive proportions, and if a weaker NATO emerged in lieu of the creation of a larger German military establishment. This would offer better chances for future political stability in Europe through continued (although reduced) U.S. presence, thus avoiding the major problem following the First World War, when a power vacuum existed in Europe, which was ultimately filled by warring nations.

Throughout any discussions concerning whatever model the Soviets propose and implement, another model requires tangential study – that of Manchuria.[2] The Manchurian model stands as a classic case when a clearly defensive posture was secretly transformed into an offensive one. Admittedly, Manchuria was an extreme case, carried out within a particular political and military context. Yet it was representative of a host of lesser examples when a defensive or less threatening posture was secretly and effectively transformed into a major offensive threat. Although many would argue that such a transformation would be unlikely to occur in contemporary or future circumstances, prudence dictates caution. In short, verification must ensure that at all times and in all circumstances, in the case of whatever model emerges, Soviet forces are not "more than they seem".

The 1990s promise revolutionary changes in existing political and military relationships in Europe and, in fact, throughout the world. In large part, this revolution has occurred because of important political, economic, and social pressure within the Soviet Union and Eastern Europe, which are, in addition, affecting Soviet military policy, doctrine, and strategy. The most apparent effects to date have been the Soviet Union's proclamation of "defensiveness" in its military doctrine and its ensuing search for new strategic solutions. Whatever future strategic posture the Soviet Union adopts, it will be a key element in this revolution. It will dictate the nature of future political and military relationships in Europe and the world and the degree of stability of any new political and military structures.

The future Soviet strategic posture will, in the last analysis, reveal the true nature of Soviet military doctrine and dictate the form and mission of the Soviet Army. There are issues within the realm of strategy that the Soviets must work out anew or refine. Among these issues are the nature of the threat; concept of future war; scope of theaters of war and military operations; peacetime military strength, dispositions, and force readiness; and strategic deployment and force generation (mobilization) schemes. All of these issues must be resolved without violating Soviet security interests, and each must facilitate smooth transition from peace to war.

Resolution of these strategic issues will have major implications at lower levels of military science, for operational and tactical concepts will be constrained and governed by strategy and the realities of contemporary and future war. Hence, operational art and tactics will emphasize concepts for non-linear warfare, maneuver, long-range fires and evidence greater defensiveness than before. Force structure at all levels will likewise conform to strategic, political, and budgetary constraints to become smaller, leaner, more flexible, defensively oriented, and, if Soviet desires are realized, of a higher quality. Most important, the force structure will be more expandable to meet wartime requirements.

All of these critical issues have their roots in the past. A clearer understanding of the past will better enable us to comprehend and manage the transition to the future.

NOTES

CHAPTER 1

1. N. V. Ogarkov, "Strategiia voennaia" [Military strategy], *Sovetskaia voennaia entsiklopediia* [Soviet military encyclopedia], 8 vols. (Moscow: Voenizdat, 1976–80), 7:555–6. Hereafter cited as *SVE* with appropriate volume.
2. A. M. Plekhov, "Politika voennaia" [Military policy], *SVE*, 6:413.
3. Ibid.
4. Ogarkov, 556.
5. Ibid.
6. I. N. Khaustov, "Razvertyvanie vooruzhennykh sil" [Deployment of the armed forces], *SVE*, 7:38.
7. Ibid.
8. A. K. Zaporozhchenko, "Strategicheskii echelon" [Strategic echelon], *SVE*, 7:554; V. I. Beliakov and N. I. Reum, "Strategicheskie reservy" [Strategic reserves], *SVE*, 7:553
9. S. P. Ivanov, M. M. Kir'ian, "Nachal'nyi period voiny" [The initial period of war], *SVE*, 5:554–5.

CHAPTER 2

1. V. I. Lenin, *Imperialism: The Highest Stage of Capitalism* (New York, NY: International Publishers, 1939).
2. "Lenin," *Voennyi entsiklopedicheskii slovar'* [Military encyclopedic dictionary] (Moscow: Voenizdat, 1983), 397, hereafter cited as *VES*; N. N. Azovtsev and E. I. Rybkin, "Lenin" *SVE*, 1977, 4:599–611.
3. Ibid.
4. V. D. Sokolovsky, ed., *Voennaia strategiia* [Military strategy] (Moscow: Voenizdat, 1962), 129.
5. Lenin, *VES*, 397.
6. Sokolovsky, 129–30.
7. Lenin, *VES*, 398.
8. Sokolovsky, 130.
9. Ibid., 132–3.
10. Soviet views of Allied intervention detailed in G. V. Kuz'min, *Razgrom interventov i belogvardeitsev v 1917–22 gg.* [Destruction of the interventionists and White Guards in 1917–22] (Moscow: Voenizdat, 1977); M. I. Svetachev, *Imperialisticheskaia interventsiia v sibiri i na dal'nem vostoke (1918–22 gg.)* [Imperialist intervention in Siberia and the Far East (1918–22)] (Novosibirsk: "Nauka", Siberian Department, 1983).
11. Most thorough investigation of Civil War campaigns in N. N. Azovtsev *et al.* (eds.), *Grazhdanskaia voina v SSSR 2T.* [The Civil War in the Soviet Union, 2 vols.] (Moscow: Voenizdat, 1980–86); archival materials in *Direktivy komandovaniia frontov Krasnoi Armii, 4T. (1917–22)* [Directives of Red Army Front commands, 4 vols. (1917–22)] (Moscow: Voenizdat, 1978).
12. Among many sources, see A. I. Denikin, *Pokhod na moskvu* [Advance on Moscow] (Moscow: Voenizdat, 1989). Contains selections from memoirs of former White Guard

276

NOTES: CHAPTER TWO

commander.
13. Kuz'min, 316–73. Among the many declassified U.S. Army G-2 documents relating to the Russian-Polish war is "Polish-Bolshevik Operations in 1920", *Report No. 1311, American Legation, Office of the Military Attache, Warsaw, Poland* (Washington, DC: Office of the Chief of Staff, War Department, 17 March 1921), declassified from secret.
14. A good account of Wrangel's operations in M. Akulov and V. Petrov, *16 Noiabria 1920* [16 November 1920] (Moscow: "Molodaia gvardiia, 1989); "Final Military Operations in the Crimea", *Monograph Report, Combat. No. 540 from Constantinople (Russia)* (Washington, DC: Office of the Chief of Staff, War Department, 1 December 1920).
15. Sokolovsky, 133.
16. Ibid.
17. Ibid.
18. N. V. Ogarkov, "Strategiia voennaia", 7:560.
19. Sokolovsky, 134.
20. V. I. Lenin, *Voennaia perepiska (1917–22 gg.)* [Military notes (1917–22)] (Moscow: Voenizdat, 1966), 84.
21. Sokolovsky, 134–5.
22. Ibid., 135.
23. Ibid., 137.
24. N. Kh. Bagramian (ed.), *Istoriia voin i voennogo isskusstva* [A history of wars and military art] (Moscow: Voenizdat, 1970), 83; A. A. Strokov (ed.), *Istoriia voennogo iskusstva* [A history of military art] (Moscow: Voenizdat, 1966); and N. M. Kozlov, "Frontovaia nastupatel'naia operatsiia" [The *front* offensive operation], *SVE* 1980, 8:336–9, cite differing figures. Bagramian's figures include the prolonged Eastern Front offensive in 1919–20.

	Strokov	Kozlov
offensive sector	300–500 km	40–600 km
offensive depth	200–300 km	200–300 km
duration of offensive	30–50 days	25–30 days
tempo of advance	6–10 km/day	6–10 km/day
		– rifle forces
		15–20 km/day
		– cavalry forces

For a thorough survey of Civil War military theory and practice and force organization, see G. V. Kuz'min, *Grazhdanskaia voina i voennaia interventsiia v SSSR* [The Civil War and military intervention in the USSR] (Moscow: Voenizdat, 1958); *Direktivy komandovaniia frontov, 4.*
25. Sokolovsky, 136.
26. Ibid.; see also I. Krasnov, "Kharakternye cherty nastupatel'nykh operatsii Krasnoi Armii v grazhdanskoi voine" [The characteristic features of offensive operations of the Red Army in the Civil War], *Voenno-istoricheskii zhurnal*, No. 3 (March 1976), 96–192. Hereafter cited as *VIZh.*
27. Sokolovsky, 140.
28. Ibid.
29. Ibid., 141.
30. Ibid.
31. Ibid., 142.
32. Ibid. Vivid descriptions of partisan warfare found in M. Sholokov's novels *Quiet Flows the Don* and *The Don Flows Home to the Sea.*
33. Ibid.
34. Ibid., 143.
35. Ibid.
36. Ibid.
37. Ibid., 144.
38. Ibid.

39. Ibid.
40. Ibid., 148.

CHAPTER 3

1. Among the many works which describe the NEP and the "New Socialist Offensive", see Geog von Rauch, *A History of Soviet Russia* (New York, NY: Praeger, 1957).
2. S. V. Lipitsky, "Voennaia reforma 1924–25 godov" [The military reforms of 1924–25], *Kommunist* [Communist], No. 4 (March 1990), 102.
3. The Civil War involved widespread ethnic, social, and class conflict in addition to the struggle between "Whites" and "Reds" and the Bolshevik regime and intervening Western forces. Ethnic conflict continued into the early 1920s, in particular in the Caucasus and central Asia. For example, the fight against the Moslem Basmachy in central Asia endured to 1923.
4. R. A. Savushkin, *Razvitie sovetskikh vooruzhennykh sil i voennogo iskusstva v mezhvoennyi period 1921–1941 gg.*) [The development of the Soviet armed forces and military art in the interwar period] (Moscow: Lenin Military-Political Academy, 1989), 6.
5. Ibid., 7.
6. Ibid., 8.
7. Ibid., 9–10. This is confirmed by numerous reports from U.S. Army attachés in Riga and Warsaw during the 1920s.
8. Ibid., 10.
9. In this assessment the Soviets bore in mind their experiences of the Civil War and Polish War of 1920, when two of the principal threats were intervention by Western powers along their sea coasts (White Sea, Baltic Sea, Black Sea, and Sea of Okhatsk) and Turkish, Afghan, Chinese, and Polish support of nationalities struggling against Bolshevik authority.
10. Savushkin, *Razvitie*, 10. This threat judgment and the ensuing "war scare" in 1927–28 led inexorably to Soviet (Stalin's) 1928 decisions to collectivize the peasantry and undertake rapid industrialization of the Soviet Union. The "war scare" was associated in part with negotiations in 1926 of the Locarno Pact, which served to end German isolation, the Zinov'ev Letter crisis with England, and political changes in Poland and China, which produced new governments less friendly to the Soviet Union.
11. "Edinaia voennaia doktrina i Krasnaia Armiia" [Unified military doctrine and the Red Army], *SVE*, 1977, 3:300. See also R. H. Baker, "The Origins of Soviet Military Doctrine", *Journal of the Royal United Services Institute for Defense Studies*, No. 3 (March 1976), 38–42.
12. Baker, 39.
13. M. V. Frunze, "Front i tyl v voine budushchege" [The front and rear in future war], *Voprosy strategii i operativnogo iskusstva v sovetskikh voennykh trudakh 1917–40 gg.* [Questions of strategy and operational art in Soviet military works – 1917–40], (Moscow: Voenizdat, 1965), 64–5, hereafter cited as *Voprosy strategii*.
14. Savushkin, *Razvitie*, 47–8.
15. Ibid., 57, is virtually identical with definition found in Ivanov, Kir'ian, 553.
16. Ibid.
17. Ibid., 57–8. The covering army was part of the armed forces in peacetime, deployed along the state borders to prevent an enemy surprise attack and protect mobilization, concentration, and deployment of main forces after the declaration of war and beginning of military operations.
18. Ibid., 58–9.
19. V. K. Triandafillov, *Kharakter operatsii sovremennykh armii* [The nature of operations of modern armies] (Moscow: Voenizdat, 1929), 96–7, adds up to five Polish cavalry divisions to the threat.

20. The key position which Poland and Rumania occupied in Soviet war planning during the 1920s is also attested to by numerous U.S. attaché reports. See attache assessments of Soviet war plans as interpreted by the Estonian and Latvian General Staffs, "Mobilization-General: War Plans," *Russia (Combat), G-2 Report No. 5868–6600* (Washington, D.C.: Military Intelligence Division, War Department, 2 June 1927); "Mobilization of Personnel: Strength of Russian Army on Mobilization", *Russia (Combat), G-2 Report No. 6038–6610* (Washington, D.C.: Military Intelligence Division, War Department, 27 September 1927).

21. Savushkin, *Razvitie*, 51.

22. S. K. Timoshenko, *Zakliuchitel'naia rech' na voennom soveshanii 31 dekabria 1940 g* [Concluding speech at a military conference of 31 Dec. 1940] (Moscow: Voenizdat, 1941), 24.

23. When assessing the work of Soviet military theorists of the 1930s, a recent Soviet critique noted the lack of attention to the subject of *front* operations:

    This [Triandafillov's] and other works had several problems. For example, the questions of preparing and conducting operations only regarded the force of a shock army, that is a reinforced combined-arms army operating on the main direction in the *front* offensive sector. In addition, these works devoted their main attention to the preparation and organization of operations and weakly illuminated questions of their conduct, the operational penetration, the action of mobile groups in the operational depths, operational pursuit, etc. Nothing was said concerning the nature and context of *front* operations. Special work on *front* operations appeared only in the beginning of the 1940s.

    See V. Semenov, "Operativnoe iskusstvo v trudakh sovetskikh avtorov" [Operational art in the work of Soviet authors], *Voennaia mysl'* [Military thought], No. 5 (May 1967), 85. Hereafter cited as *VM*.

24. V. N. Lobov, "Aktual'nye voprosy razvitiia teorii sovetskoi voennoi strategii 20-kh – serediny 30-kh godov" [Timely questions on the development of the theory of Soviet military strategy in the 1920s and the 1930s], *VIZh*, No. 2 (Feb. 1989), 43.

25. Ibid., 42.

26. Ibid., 43.

27. Ibid.

28. Ibid., 43–4.

29. Ibid., 44.

30. A. A. Kokoshin, V. N. Lobov, "Predvidenie" [Foresight], *Znamia* [Banner], No. 2 (Feb. 1990), 174–5.

31. Lobov, 44.

32. Ibid.

33. Ibid.

34. Ibid.

35. Ibid., 50.

36. Ibid.

37. S. S. Kamenev, "Ocherednye voennye zadachi" [Successive military objectives], *Voprosy strategii*, 149–52.

38. M. Zakharov, "Preduslovie" [Preface], *Voprosy strategii*, 12.

39. V. K. Triandafillov, "Kharakter operatsii sovremennykh armii" [The character of operations of modern armies], *Voprosy strategii*, 291–345.

40. Bagramian, 103. For details on the nature of successive operations, see R. Savushkin, "K voprosu o zarozhdenii teorii posledovatel'nykh nastupatel'nykh operatsii – 1921–29 gg." [Concerning the creation of the theory of successive offensive operations – 1921–29], *VIZh*, No. 5 (May 1983), 77–83.

41. V. Matsulenko, "Razvitie operativnogo iskusstva v nastupatel'nykh operatsiiakh" [The development of operational art in offensive operations], *VIZh*, No. 10 (October 1967), 39–40.

42. A. A. Svechin, "Strategiia" [Strategy], *Voprosy istorii*, 238.

43. Bagramian, 103.
44. V. Matsulenko, "Razvitie taktiki nastupatel'nogo boia" [The development of the tactics of offensive battle], *VIZh*, No. 2 (February 1968), 28–9; M. Zakharov, "O teorii glubokoi operatsii" [Concerning the theory of deep operations], *VIZh*, No. 10 (October 1970), 10–13.
45. A. Svechin, *Strategiia* [Strategy] (Moscow: Voenizdat, 1926). Soviet exercises and war games in the 1920s, as reflected by articles in the journal, *Voina i revolutsiia* [Revolution and war], and in attaché reports, postulated defense of the Soviet Union against Rumanian incursions via Odessa and Polish operations through the "Moscow Gate" (Smolensk area). See also A. A. Kokoshin and V. N. Lobov, "Predvidenie (General Svechin ob evoliutsii voennogo iskusstva)" [Foresight (General Svechin concerning the evolution of military art)], *Znamia* [Banner], No. 2 (Feb. 1990), 170–82, which thoroughly reviews the strategic emphasis in Svechin's works. They noted:

A. A. Svechin wrote in "The Evolution of the Art of War": "Defense in strategy has the opportunity of using the boundaries and depth of the theater, which forces the attacking side to waste forces in order to strengthen the spaces and to waste time crossing it, and any gain in time is another plus for the defense. The defending side reaps where it sows ..., since an offensive is often stopped by false reconnaissance data, false fears, and inertness." He directed attention to the statements by Clausewitz, who considered the defense to be the strongest form of waging war for the materially weaker side. Noting that even the most ardent admirers of Clausewitz failed to take his ideas into account, he recalled the tragic consequences to which this led, particularly in World War I. With respect to modern military-political conditions, A. A. Svechin did not consider it a mistake to recognize the defense as the strongest form of waging war: "at least in the conditions of Europe, not enveloped by the revolutionary movement. The national economic fences of Europe have a tremendous historical standing ..."

Svechin believed that a revisionist Germany was the most likely European power to provoke a general European war, and that war would probably begin with a German attack on Poland, a prescient observation. Consequently, Svechin argued for a defensive strategy involving an initial defensive phase of operations designed to wear down enemy forces prior to launching a counteroffensive to destroy the enemy [resembling Kokoshin and Larionov's Kursk and Khalkhin Gol paradigms], see V. N. Lobov, "Aktual'nye voprosy razvitiia teorii sovetskoi voennoi strategii 20-kh – serediny 30-kh godov" [Real questions concerning the development of Soviet military strategy in the 1920s and mid-1930s], *VIZh*, No. 2 (February 1989), 44.

Relating Svechin's analysis to contemporary circumstances, Kokoshin and Lobov connected Svechin's concepts to current "reasonable defensive sufficiency:"

Today, when the thesis that war cannot serve as a rational instrument of policy [at least in relations between the United States and the USSR and between the Warsaw Pact and NATO] is receiving recognition, it is all the more important that the top state and political leadership know the theory and practice of military strategy and the implementation by the military mechanism of decisions made by policy. After all, such decisions on the boundary of politics and military affairs can lead to the most fatal, irreversible consequences. They should especially know, it seems, the real capabilities of command and control systems and equipment – theirs and the enemy's – communications and reconnaissance systems, and missile warning systems. The general public should also understand the basic military-strategic issues, so *glasnost* is necessary here, too. Otherwise policy will not be able to exercise real, but only declarative control over military strategy, and there will be no correspondence between the political and military-technical components of a state's military doctrine ... One of the chief principles of organizational development of the Soviet Armed Forces today is the principle of reasonable defensive sufficiency. For all practical purposes, this means giving them a non-offensive structure; limiting to the maximum extent their number of strike systems; changing deployment on the expectation of carrying out strictly defensive missions; lowering the parameters of mobilizational deployment of the armed forces and also the volume of military production.

46. For an excellent cross-section of Soviet military thought in the 1920s and 1930s, see *Voprosy strategii*.

47. "Mobilization-General: War Plans", *Russia (Combat), G-2 Report No. 5868–6000*.

48. Ibid., 1.

49. For example, see "Distribution of Troops. Red Army", *Russia (Combat), G-2 Report No. 7687–6180* (Washington, D.C.: Military Intelligence Division, War Department, 14 February 1929).

50. "Mobilization-General. War Plans for S.W. Front", *Russia (Combat), G-2 Report No. 5509–6600* (Washington, D.C.: Military Intelligence Division, War Department, 13 October 1926).

51. Lipitsky, 105.

52. Ibid.

53. Ibid., 106.

54. Ibid., 69. A U.S. attaché report written in 1927 noted that before the revolution the Tsarist government was careful with recruiting minorities into the army:

> Certain areas and peoples were entirely and other areas partially exempt from conscription: for example, in the Caucasus only the Cossacks were called to service, the Armenians, Georgians, and such, being exempt; the tribes of Turkestan and the Kirghiz were exempt, as were the Lapps in the tundra regions of the north; conscription in Finland was started partially only late in the war.

"Mobilization-General. War Plans", *Russia Combat, G-2 Report No. 5868–6600* (Washington, D.C.: Military Intelligence Division, War Department, 2 June 1927), 1–2.

55. Lipitsky, 106–7.

56. See I. Berkhin, "O territorial'no-militsionnom stroitel'stve v Sovetskoi Armii" [Concerning the territorial-militia construction in the Soviet Army], *VIZh*, No. 12 (December 1960), 15–16; I. B. Berkhin, *Voennaia reforma v SSSR (1924–25)* [Military reform in the USSR (1924–25)] (Moscow: Voenizdat, 1958), 97–101; John Erickson, The Soviet High Command (London: St. Martins Press, 1962), 181–2. These accounts conflict regarding peacetime strength, but the system rather than the precise numbers is what is important.

57. Ibid.

58. Among numerous attaché reports on the system, see "Territorial Divisions", *Soviet Russia (Combat), G-2 Report No. 8216–6140* (Washington, D.C.: Military Intelligence Division, War Department, 14 February 1933). These reports refer to "spin-off" mobilization divisions as "reserve" divisions.

59. This chart is composed from several sources including: Lipitsky; Berkhin; John Erickson, *The Soviet High Command* (London: St. Martins Press, 1962); W. F. de B. Whittaker, "The Red Army Today II", *The Army, Navy and Air Force Gazette*, 12 July 1928, 593; N. N. Golovine, "The Red Army", *The Infantry Journal*, No. 4 (July–August 1936), 303; P. Malevsky-Malevitch, *Russia U.S.S.R.* (New York: William Farquhar Payson, 1933), 262–3. These all track closely with orders of battle maintained by the Military Intelligence Divisions, U.S. Army War Department, throughout the 1920s and 1930s. For a review of experiments with national formations, see V. I. Varennikov, "Iz istorii sozdaniia i podgotovki natsional'nykh voinskikh formirovanii" [From the history of the creation and training of ethnic military formations], *VM*, No. 2 (February 1990), 3–13.

CHAPTER 4

1. Savushkin, *Razvitie*, 11–12.

2. Ibid., 12.
3. Ibid., 13–14.
4. Ibid., 14. Advanced preparations, according to Svechin, included diplomatic action. "The diplomatic plan is obliged to study international relations on a global scale, and not concentrate its attentions [only] on probable enemies." A. A. Svechin, *Strategiia*, 108.
5. Savushkin, *Razvitie*, 21–22.
6. Ibid., 22.
7. Ibid., 23; V. A. Melikov, "Problemy strategicheskogo razvertivaniia" [Problems of strategic deployment], *Voprosy strategii*, 521.
8. Savushkin, *Razvitie*, 23.
9. Graphic prewar Soviet writings about battles of encirclement (*boi v okruzhenii*) attest to Soviet realization of the perils that the forward defending echelons faced. See, for example, B. K. Kolchigin, "Vykhod iz boia" [Withdrawal from battle], *VM*, No. 7 (July 1940); P. I. D'iacheko, "Razvedka v okruzhenii" [Reconnaissance in an encirclement], *VM*, No. 9 (September 1940); A. I. Starunin, "Boi v okruzhenii" [Battle in encirclement], *VM*, No. 10 (October 1940); A. I. Shtromberg, "Operativnoe ispol'zovanie tankov v oborone" [Operational use of tanks in the defense], *VM*, No. 11–12 (November–December 1940); P. I. Vedenichev, "Protivovozdushnaia oborona v sovremenoi voine" [Antiaircraft defense in contemporary war], *VM*, No. 11–12 (November–December 1940). Among the works demonstrating Soviet appreciation of German capabilities, see A. I. Starunin, "Operativnaia vnezapnost'" [Operational surprise], *VM*, No. 3 (March 1941), 27–35; A. Kononenko, "Boi v flandrii (Mai 1940 gg)" [The battle in Flanders (May 1940)], *VIZh*, No. 3 (March 1941), 3–20. Starunin's superb analysis of German use of surprise in Poland and France ended with the enjoinder, "One requires high vigilance and constant combat readiness so that the enemy cannot take forces by surprise." Three months later, Starunin's warning went unheeded, and his lessons were not learned.
10. Savushkin, *Razvitie*, 24; V. N. Lobov, "Strategiia pobedy" [Strategy of victory], *VIZh*, No. 5 (May 1988), 6, has written:

   The distortion of military doctrine caused serious mistakes in working out a series of theoretical strategic positions and in conducting measures to prepare the armed forces for war. As a result, the problems of strategic defense, the escape of the mass of forces from under enemy blows, and going over to the counteroffensive were weakly worked out. General recognition of the importance of the initial period of war in circumstances of surprise were not in full measure confirmed by practical measures to increase the capabilities of forces to repel aggression. In particular, arising from the positions of military doctrine, it was outlined that the first onslaught would be repelled by limited numbers of covering forces, while the main forces of the Soviet Army deployed for conducting a decisive offensive to carry combat actions to enemy territory. The variant of prolonged strategic defense was not contemplated, and, in this connection, the creation of defensive groupings of the armed forces was not planned. This was based on mistaken assumptions that the enemy would begin combat operations with only part of his forces, with subsequent strengthening of them during the course of war.

11. Savushkin, *Razvitie*, 24.
12. Ibid.
13. Ibid., 59, citing *Voprosy strategii*, 377–83.
14. Ibid., 60.
15. Berkhin; Lipitsky; D. M. Glantz, *The Motor-Mechanization Program of the Red Army During the Interwar Years* (Ft. Leavenworth, KS: Soviet Army Studies Office, 1990); D. M. Glantz, *Observing the Soviets: Army Attachés in Eastern Europe During the 1930s* (Ft. Leavenworth, KS: Soviet Army Studies Office, 1990).
16. Savushkin, 61, citing Sokolovsky, 169.
17. M. Zakharov, "O teorii glubokoi operatsii" [Concerning the theory of deep opera-

tions], *VIZh*, No. 10 [October 1970], 18.
18. G. Zhukov, *Reminiscences and Reflections*, Vol. 1 (Moscow: Progress Publishers, 1985), 255.
19. Savushkin, *Razvitie*, 62.
20. Ibid., 63.
21. Ibid., 64.
22. Zhukov, 264. The Russian language version, p. 250, published in 1974, uses the proper term for "special threatening military period". The English language version obfuscates the terminology, stating, "In the last few prewar months, the leadership did not call for any steps that should have been taken when *the threat of war was particularly great.*" (My italics)
23. Savushkin, *Razvitie*, 63.
24. Ibid., 50.
25. Timoshenko, 30.
26. Savushkin, *Razvitie*, 52.
27. Timoshenko, 24.
28. Ibid., 36.
29. Savushkin, *Razvitie*, 54.
30. N. V. Ogarkov, "Glubokaia operatsiia" [The deep operation], *SVE*, 1976, 2:574; V. Daines, "Razvitie taktiki obshchevoiskovogo nastupatel'nogo boia v 1929–1941 gg" [The development of the tactics of combined-arms offensive battle – 1929–41], *VIZh*, No. 10 (October 1978), 96.
31. I. Korotkov, "Voprosy obshchei taktiki v sovetskoi voennoi istoriografii – 1918–41 gg" [Questions of general tactics in Soviet military historiography – 1918–41], *VIZh*, No. 12 (December 1977), 89.
32. Daines, 96.
33. Kozlov, "Frontovaia ...," 337.
34. Bagramian, 106.
35. Ogarkov, "Glubokaia operatsiia", 576; Matsulenko, "Razvitie operativenogo iskusstva ...," 40, states that shock armies contained three to four rifle corps.
36. Strokov, 316.
37. Sokolovsky, 169; M. M. Kozlov, "Frontovaia oboronitel'naia operatsiia" [The *front* defensive operation], *SVE*, 8:340.
38. Savushkin, *Razvitie*, 54.
39. Ibid., 55.
40. Ibid., 55–6.
41. Ibid., 56.
42. Ibid., 57; see also *Voprosy strategii*, 346–60.
43. Zakharov, "O teorii", 18; D. M. Glantz, *The Soviet Airborne Experience*, Research Survey No. 4 (Ft. Leavenworth, KS: Combat Studies Institute, 1984), 11–12.
44. M. V. Zakharov, *General'nyi shtab v predvoennye gody* [The General Staff in the prewar years] (Moscow: Voenizdat, 1989), 111–16.
45. Ibid., 125.
46. Ibid., 126–7.
47. An excellent German study of this question, translated into Russian, is A. Filippi, *Pripiatskaia problema* [The Pripiat problem] (Moscow: Izdatel'stvo Inostrannoi literatury, 1959).
48. Zakharov, *General'nyi shtab*, 129–30. Shaposhnikov assessed Japanese forces to consist of 27–33 infantry divisions, 4 security and 5 cavalry brigades, 2,827 guns, 1,400 tanks, and 1,000 aircraft. The General Staff estimated Japanese main forces would concentrate within 22–25 days on the Kirin, Muleng, Chiamussu, Liunchen, Tsitsihar, and Mukden sectors, where rail and road nets would support strategic deployment. The Japanese main force, based in eastern Manchuria, covered by an extensive fortified zone, would attack to seize the Far Eastern coastal regions, Iman and Blagoveshchensk, while Japanese forces in northwestern Manchuria would conduct an active defense along the Great Khinghan Mountains. A smaller Japanese force, consisting of

one–two infantry divisions and mobile units located around Dolonnor and Kalgan, would attack into eastern Mongolia. The General Staff assessed the Japanese could also attack Soviet Kamchatka and northern Sakhalin Island. Until, however, Japanese deployment was complete, the existing first echelon of 12 divisions in northern Manchuria and Korea was too weak to initiate combat.

49. Ibid., 130–31.
50. Ibid, 163–71, 174. Zakharov concentrates on diplomatic aspects of the Polish crisis and provides little concrete information on military preparations. He does mention the correlation of forces between the Soviet proposed coalition (Great Britain, France, Poland, and the Soviet Union) and the Nazi bloc (Germany and Italy), which, in the Soviet view, was as follows:

	Allies	Nazi Bloc
Divisions	311	168
Tanks	15,400	8,400
Heavy Guns	9,600	4,350
Aircraft	11,700	7,700

A more detailed view of Soviet deployments during the crisis appears in A. V. Antosiak, "Osvobozhdenie Zapadnoi Ukrainy i Zapadnoi Belorussii" [The liberation of Western Ukraine and Western Belorussia], *VIZh*, No. 9 (September 1989), 51–60; and formerly classified U.S. attache reports, including "Military Operations-General-Soviet Invasion of Poland", *USSR (Combat-Army), C-2 Report No. 1589–6900*, (Washington, D.C.: Military Intelligence Division, War Department, 25 October 1939).

51. Zakharov, *General'nyi shtab*, 175; A. G. Khor'kov, "Ukreplennye-raiony na zapad-nykh granitsakh SSSR" [Fortified regions on the western borders of the USSR], *VIZh*, No. 12 (December 1987), 47–54; V. F. Abramovich, "Nuzhny li nam bastionnye, kreposti, forty i doty" [Do we need bastions, fortresses, forts, or pillboxes?], *VIZh*, No. 6 (June 1989), 68–71. For a survey of similar units in the Far East, based on Japanese intelligence records, see "Study of Strategical and Tactical Peculiarities of Far Eastern Russia and Soviet Far East Forces", *Japanese Special Studies on Manchuria, Volume XIII* (Headquarters, Army Forces Far East Historical Section, 1955), 95–109.
52. Zakharov, *General'nyi shtab*, 213–14.
53. Ibid., 215.
54. Ibid., 217–19.
55. Ibid., 219.
56. Ibid., 239–50. Zakharov also provides considerable detail on the December 1940 conference in Moscow, which preceded the war game (see Ibid., 195–211), hitherto discussed more briefly in the memoirs of I. A. Eremenko, K. A. Meretsov, and Zhukov. In a lengthy explanation, Zakharov asserts that the association of Zhukov, N. F. Vatutin (Chief of the General Staff's Operational Directorate), and others with the Kiev Special Military District, along with Stalin's fixation on the southwestern direction, influenced Soviet war planners' penchant for emphasizing the importance of that region.
57. Ibid., 240.
58. Not coincidentally, the objective line of the "Westerners" was chosen to match the rail system, specifically where the rail gauge changed – which, in wartime, would have become a natural final objective or pause point.
59. During the first stage of the Soviet-Finnish War (November–December 1939), the Soviets experienced massive difficulties in penetrating Finnish defenses prepared in depth throughout the Karelian Isthmus.
60. Zakharov, *General'nyi shtab*, 247.
61. Ibid., 248–50.
62. Alan Clark, *Barbarossa: The Russian-German Conflict 1941–1945* (New York: Signet, 1965), 49–96.

63. For details on Soviet intelligence collection, see V. I. Beliaev, "Usilenie okhrany zapadnoi granitsy SSSR nakanune Velikoi Otechestvennoi voiny" [Strengthening the security of USSR's western borders on the eve of the Great Patriotic War], *VIZh*, No. 5 (May 1988), 50–5; A. G. Khor'kov, "Nakanune groznykh sobytii" [On the eve of threatening events], *VIZh*, No. 5 (May 1988), 42–9; L. M. Sandalov, "Stoiali nasmert" [Stand to the death], *VIZh*, No. 11 (November 1988), 3–10; "Nakanune voiny (1940–1941 gg.): O podgotovke germanii k napadeniiu na SSSR" [On the eve of war (1940–1941): Concerning the preparations of Germany for the attack on the USSR], *Izvestiia Tsk KPSS*, No. 4 (April 1990), 198–222. The latter contains intelligence documents from the KGB archives relating to German offensive preparations.
64. Zakharov, General'nyi shtav, 251–64.
65. V. Karpov, "Zhukov," *Kommunist vooruzhennykh sil*, No. 5 (May 1990), 67.
66. Ibid., 68.
67. "Nakanune voiny", 219–20.
68. Zakharov, *General'nyi shtav*, 259–61.
69. Karpov, 68, comments:

And now just imagine what might have happened if that plan of Zhukov's had been accepted and carried out. On one May or June dawn, thousands of our aircraft and ten of thousands of our guns could have struck concentrating (crowded) forces, the dispositions of which were well-known with an accuracy down to battalion. There would never have been such a surprise – very likely, more probable than the German attack on us. No one in Germany, from the private soldier to Hitler, could ever conceive of such actions by our army. Thousands of our aircraft, destroyed on the ground, and hundreds of thousands of shells, abandoned in the retreat – all of these would have rained down on the sleeping, assembling invasion forces of the aggressors. Following this, thousands of tanks and 152 divisions in a powerful blow would dash upon the pulverized enemy. It seems to me that what occurred during the first days on our land, after the blows of the Hitlerites, would have developed on German territory by the exact same scenario. The Hitlerites absolutely did not have experience of operating in such extreme situations. Panic or shock undoubtedly would have enveloped their commands and armies. But even if, after a week or ten days, the Hitlerites had succeeded in regaining consciousness, during the first months, they would have undertaken defensive efforts, and our armies, being in the immediate rear services area with all types of ammunition, fuel and equipment, could perhaps have developed success.

It is absolutely certain: after a preventative strike, Fascist Germany would have lost the capability for large-scale offensive operations and could not speak of or conduct "lightning war". Most likely, the Nazis would have postponed war for several years, and if they had continued combat operations after our preventative strikes, they could have advanced from the border and reestablished their position, and even greater, and almost unbelievable – reach the Dnepr River line. In this case the strategic initiative would have been in our hands, because our army would have been mobilized, would not have lost many millions of casualties, which happened in June 1941; would not have experienced the shock of surprise attack; and further industry and agriculture, not having had their productive rhythm disrupted, would remain in place (without evacuation); would firmly have supplied the front with all that was necessary.

70. I. B. Pavlovsky, *Sukhoputnye voiska SSSR* [The ground forces of the USSR] (Moscow: Voenizdat, 1985), 65–8.
71. Ibid., 65.
72. Ibid., 66.
73. The chart is a composite compiled in part from I. Kh. Bagramian (ed.), *Istoriia voin i voennogo iskusstva* [History of war and military art] (Moscow: Voenizdat, 1970); V. A. Anfilov, *Proval blitskriga* [The failure of blitzkrieg] (Moscow: "Nauka", 1974); A. Ryzhakov, "K voprosu o stroitel'stve bronetankovykh voisk krasnoi armii v 30-e gody"

[Concerning the question of the formation of armored forces of the Red Army in the 1930s], *VIZh*, No. 8 (August 1968).

74. S. A. Tiushkevich, ed., *Sovetskie vooruzhennye sily* [The Soviet armed forces] (Moscow: Voenizdat, 1978)), 236.

75. A. G. Khor'kov, "Nekotorye voprosy strategicheskogo razvertyvaniia Sovetskikh Vooruzhennykh Sil v nachale Velikoi Otechestvennoi voiny" [Some questions concerning the strategic deployment of the Soviet armed forces in the beginning of the Great Patriotic War], *VIZh*, No. 1 (January 1986), 11.

76. Ibid.; Zakharov provides the exact date. See Zakharov, *General'nyi shtab*, 259.

77. Khor'kov, "Nekotorye voprosy", 11.

78. A. A. Grechko, et. al., ed., *Istorii vtoroi mirovoi voiny 1939–45, T-3* [History of the Second World War, Vol. 3] (Moscow: Voenizdat, 1974), 441.

79. Savushkin, *Razvitie*, 19.

80. *OSOAVIAKHIM*

[Obshchestvo Sodeistviia Oborone, Aviatsionnomu i Khimicheskomu Stroitel'stvu] [Society for Assistance to Defense, Aviation and Chemical Construction], mass voluntary public military-patriotic organization which existed in the USSR from 1927 to 1948. Principal tasks: assistance in development of the aviation industry, dissemination of military knowledge among the general public, and conduct of mass-defense work among the workers for the purpose of strengthening this country's defense capability. Awarded the Order of the Red Banner (1947). On 16 February 1948 DOSARM, DOSAV, and DOSFLOT were formed to replace Osoaviakhim, which in turn were consolidated into USSR DOSAAF on 29 August 1951.

See "OSOAVIAKHIM," *SVE*, 6:141.

81. Among the many articles describing the failed process, see G. P. Pastukhovsky, "Razvetyvanie operativnogo tyla v nachal'nyi period voiny" [Deployment of the rear in the initial period of war], *VIZh*, No. 6 (June 1988), 18–27; Iu. G. Perechnev, "O nekotorykh problemakh podgotovki strany i Vooruzhennykh Sil k otrazheniia fashistskoi agressii" [About some problems in preparing the nation and armed forces to repel fascist aggression], *VIZh*, No. 4 (April 1988), 42–50; M. M. Kir'ian, "Nachal'nyi period Velikoi Otechestvennoi voiny" [The initial period of the Great Patriotic War], *VIZh*, No. 6 (June 1988), 11–17; V. D. Danilov, "Sovetskoe glavnoe komandovanie v preddverii Velikoi Otechestvennoi voiny" [The Soviet high command on the threshold of the Great Patriotic War], *Novaia i noveishaia istorii*, No. 6 (June 1988), 3–20.

82. A. D. Borshchov, "Otrazhenie fashistskoi agressii: uroki i vyvody" [Repelling Fascist aggression: lessons and conclusions], *VM*, No. 3 (March 1990), 15.

83. Ibid., 20–2. Borshchov provides distinct lessons with the implication that they are relevant today as well. He writes:

An analysis of the content of prewar theoretical views on the initial period of war and of experience in carrying out a set of practical measures for realizing them in western border military districts provides grounds to note a number of what we view as *instructive lessons*.

First. The failures of 1941 above all are the result of distortions in defense policy on the part of the country's supreme military-political leadership, I. V. Stalin's subjectivism and monopoly in choosing the means and methods of achieving objectives, and the ignoring of that scientific store which had been accumulated in the 1930s. Therefore, fulfillment of all defense programs under present-day conditions, and especially measures for preparing to repulse a possible external attack *must be based on a scientifically grounded theoretical concept and be conducted on a purposeful, planned basis without any conditionalities or manifestations of subjectivism and dogmatism*. This conclusion also wholly conforms to 19th All-Union CPSU Conference lines on strengthening the ties of science and practice.

Second. Experience teaches that in the stage of planning to cover the state border and the first defensive operations *it is important to consider comprehensively the full set of economic, sociopolitical and strictly military conditions of the situation.* USSR Minister of Defense Army General D. T. Yazov notes: "The Soviet Union is forced to prepare for whatever war an aggressor prepares." In this connection the intensifying danger of a surprise attack by a probable enemy who is taking steps to outfit his armed forces with fundamentally new models of weapons and military equipment merits special attention today.

It is also important to emphasize that operational plans of border military districts and groups of forces for conducting the first defensive operations must provide for several options of troop operations depending on possible conditions of the aggressor's initiation of war.

Third. Its essence is that *combat documents* being drawn up under peacetime conditions *must be sufficiently specific and simultaneously flexible* and permit necessary corrections to be made in the course of a war which has begun, and the command authority and personnel of the covering forces should be oriented, not toward the automatic triggering of documents, but toward actions in conformity with the existing operational-strategic situation. The consequences resulting from fascist Germany's attack on the Soviet Union, a surprise for border military district forces, insistently demand that the USSR Armed Forces be kept in such a condition as to ensure their organized entry into a war even in a more complicated situation than the one which took shape on the morning of 22 June 1941. The efforts of command personnel, political entities and staffs at all levels must be directed toward this above all back in peacetime. In our view, those forces earmarked for disrupting an aggressor's invasion, conducting the first defensive operations and delivering retaliatory attacks and surprise retaliatory counterstrikes against him should be kept in the highest state of readiness. Given past experience, *troops of border military districts and groups of forces must be capable of executing their assigned combat missions without additional redeployments and reorganizations, i.e., essentially at any moment.*

Fourth. Advance preparation of theaters of military operations is an important direction for increasing the readiness of covering forces for repelling a possible invasion by a ground enemy. The extent and nature of engineer preparation of installations and the terrain must conform fully to combat missions assigned to those forces stationed in border areas. Past experience teaches that in support of the covering forces' first commitment, it is important to take a substantiated approach to determining the correlation of the distance from the border of defensive lines and positions, lines of operational and other obstacles, deployment lines of counterthrust force groupings, and so on, on one hand, and the distance of the disposition areas and the locations of corresponding units on the other hand.

Fifth. Operational and combat training as well as political upbringing and agitation-propaganda work in the covering formations and units must aim personnel above all at ensuring execution of the primary mission – *maintaining troops and command and control entities at the level of the threat of the onset of war and reacting promptly to all changes in the probable enemy's plans and intentions.* Experience also indicates that with an aggressor's surprise initiation of war, demands increase sharply for autonomy of operations by formations, units and subunits. This obviously can be achieved without great outlays *by stationing them in the same locations and areas* with planned means of reinforcement and support and by active joint drills, practices and exercises.

Sixth. It is common knowledge that in preparing for war, the fascist German command concentrated its invasion forces in advance and under other various pretexts at the Soviet border. That operating method from the probable enemy's arsenals cannot be ruled out even now. A series of exercises held in NATO Armed Forces simultaneously in a vast territory from the Barents Sea to the Mediterranean during August–September 1989 is clear proof of this. Such exercises are dangerous in that they are not always subject to unequivocal qualification and are difficult to distinguish from an actual deployment of forces for war. And in order not to repeat past mistakes, the question of the possibility and advisability of granting commanders of formations stationed on territories of border military districts and groups of forces and having missions of covering the state border *the right of independently taking adequate steps when the enemy conduct measures for increasing his forces' combat readiness* requires very careful study under present-day conditions. First of all, this will permit reducing the probability of an aggressor's surprise attack; secondly, it will facilitate keeping forces in an appropriate state of readiness to repel possible invasion.

And finally the seventh lesson from past experience. It is that everything previously accumulated must not be taken unequivocally and transferred to modern conditions in its initial form. As a matter of fact, attempts in 1941 to canonize the experience of the initial period of World War I revealed its total groundlessness, as Marshal of the Soviet Union G. K. Zhukov admitted. Consequently, in our view even today the reminder that *any past experience requires continuous creative study and practical application only with consideration of the entire set of changes which have occurred since the war and which are occurring now* will not be superfluous even today. In other words, at the present time we should take an identically weighted approach both to conclusions drawn based on the experience of preparing border military district forces to repel fascist aggression on the eve of the Great Patriotic War as well as to assessments of the modern military-political situation with consideration of changes in the means and methods of warfare.

84. According to official Soviet views:

Prior to the beginning of World War II, Soviet military strategy validly presumed that the class nature of a war in defense of the socialist homeland would make the armed struggle uncompromising and decisive, that the war might be prolonged and highly maneuverable, and would be conducted against a coalition of imperialist states. The strategic offensive in the form of successive *front* operations carried out with close interaction among all the services of the armed forces was recognized as the decisive type of strategic operations ... Soviet military strategy considered the defense to be a valid form of military operations, but it did not devote adequate attention to the development of the theory of defensive operations on a strategic scale. It was also considered that a surprise attack by an aggressor was possible, but questions of repelling an unexpected attack by previously fully-mobilized enemy forces as well as the overall problem of the initial period of a war [*nachal'nyi period voiny*] under changing conditions were not properly worked out. Not all of the correct theoretical principles worked out by Soviet military science with respect to military strategy were promptly taken into account in practical work or included in regulations. Ogarkov, 561.

85. Savushkin, *Razvitie*, 170.
86. Ibid., 175.

CHAPTER 5

1. R. A. Savushkin (ed.), *Razvitie sovetskikh vooruzhennykh sil i voennogo iskusstva v Velikoi Otechestvennoi voine 1941–1945 gg.* [The development of the Soviet Armed Forces and military art in the Great Patriotic War 1941–45] (Moscow: VPA, 1988), 48–9, hereafter cited as *Razvitie ...1941–45 gg.* For a survey of wartime strategy as it related to Soviet intelligence, see David M. Glantz, *The Role of Intelligence in Soviet Military Strategy in World War II* (Novato, CA: Presidio Press, 1990).
2. N. V. Ogarkov, "Strategiia voennaia", 562.
3. Savushkin, *Razvitie ... 1941–45 gg.*, 50.

NOTES: CHAPTER FIVE

4. Ibid., 95.
5. "Boevoi opyt ukreplennikh raionov (UR)" [Combat experience of fortified regions], *Sbornik materialov po izucheniia opyta voiny No. 3 noiabr'–dekabr' 1942 g.* [Collection of materials for the study of war experience No. 3 November–December 1942] (Moscow: Voenizdat, 1942), 122–32, (formerly classified secret), hereafter cited as *SMPIOV* with appropriate volume and article; "Oborona" (Defense), *Sbornik boevykh dokumentov velikoi otechestvennoi voiny No. 1* [Collection of combat documents of the Great Patriotic War No. 1] (Moscow: Voenizdat, 1947), 54–61 (formerly classified secret), hereafter cited as *SBD* with appropriate volume and section.
6. Savushkin, *Razvitie ... 1941–45 gg.*, 99.
7. Ibid., 101–6; V. A. Anfilov, *Krusheni pokhoda Gitlera na Moskvu 1941* [The Ruin of Hitler's March on Moscow 1941] (Moscow: "Nauka", 1989), 196–270.
8. Savushkin, *Razvitie ... 1941–1945 gg.*, 102.
9. Ibid., 104–6; V. Zemskov, "Nekotorye voprosy sozdaniia i ispol'zovaniia strategicheskikh reservov" [Some questions concerning the creation and use of strategic reserves], *VIZh*, No. 10 (October 1971), 14; A. G. Khor'kov, "Nekotorye voprosy strategicheskogo razvertyvaniia Sovetskikh vooruzhennykh sil v nachale Velikoi Otechestvennoi voiny" [Some questions concerning the strategic deployment of the Soviet Armed Forces at the beginning of the Great Patriotic War], *VIZh*, No. 1 (January 1986), 13.
10. Savushkin, *Razvitie ... 1941–45 gg.*, 105.
11. Ibid.; "Dokumenty stavki verkhovnogo komandovaniia i general'nogo shtaba Krasnoi armii" [Documents of the *Stavka* of the High Command and General Staff of the Red Army], *SBD*, No. 37 (Moscow: Voenizdat, 1947), 11–13. Includes the orders forming 29th and 30th Armies.
12. Savushkin, *Razvitie ... 1941–45 gg.*, 107.
13. Ibid.
14. Ibid., 110.
15. Ibid.
16. Ibid.
17. Ibid., 111.
18. Ibid., 112.
19. N. A. Sbytov, "Stavka verkhovnogo glavnokomandovaniia" [The *Stavka* of the High Command], *SVE*, 1979, 7:511–12.
20. Savushkin, *Razvitie ... 1941–45 gg.*, 51.
21. G. K. Zhukov, *Vospominaniia i razmyshleniia, T.1* [Reminiscences and Reflections, Vol. 1] (Moscow: Voenizdat, 1978), 1:283.
22. Savushkin, *Razvitie ... 1941–45 gg.*, 52.
23. Ibid., 53.
24. Ibid. As evidence of General Staff work, see the recently declassified 26 volumes of war experiences assembled and published between 1942 and 1948 by the Department for the Study of War Experience of the Red Army General Staff.
25. Ibid., 54.
26. Ibid.
27. Ibid., 56.
28. Ibid.
29. Ibid., 57.
30. Ibid. For details of "strategic direction headquarters", see Volumes 34 to 43 of *SBD*, which contains reports and orders for the period 22 June to 5 November 1941.
31. Ibid.
32. Ibid., 59.
33. Ibid.
34. Ibid., 60. Key *Stavka* directives contained in appropriate sections of volumes 34 to 43 of *SBD* as well as in operational studies published in the series *Sbornik Materialov* [Collection of Materials], Issues 1–18, prepared by the Military-historical Directorate of the General Staff between 1949 and 1968 (formerly classified secret), hereafter cited as *SM*, with appropriate issue and study.

35. Savushkin, *Razvitie ... 1941–45 gg.*, 64.
36. Ibid.
37. Ibid., 65.
38. Ibid., 68.
39. David M. Glantz, *Soviet Military Deception in the Second World War* (London: Frank Cass & Co., Ltd, 1989), 42–56.
40. A. Radzievsky, "Proryv oborony v pervom periode voiny" [Penetration of a defense in the first period of war], *VIZh*, No. 3 (March 1972), 17–18.
41. Strokov, 391; Bagramian, 189–90. More details found in S. Lototsky, "Iz opyta vedeniia armeiskikh nastupatel'nykh operatsii v gody Velikoi Otechestvennoi voiny" [From the experience of conducting army offensive operations in the years of the Great Patriotic War], *VIZh*, No. 12 (December 1965), 3–14.
42. "Prikaz NKO No. 325 ot 16 Oktiabria 1942 g" [Order of the People's Commissariat of Defense No. 325 of 16 October 1942], *VIZh*, No. 10 (October 1974), 68–73.
43. Savushkin, *Razvitie ... 1941–45 gg.*, 104.
44. Ibid., 85–6.
45. N. Pavlenko, "Na pervom etape voiny" [During the first phase of war], *Kommunist* (Communist), No. 9 (June 1988), 92.
46. For example, see "Archives Document Torture of Marshal Meretskov", *JPRS-UMA-88-019*, 19 August 1988, 21. Quoting from an article in *Literaturnaia Gazeta*, 20 April 1989, 13.
47. Ogarkov, "Strategiia voennaia", 562.
48. Savushkin, *Razvitie ... 1941–45 gg.*, 65.
49. Bagramian, 243; Lototsky.
50. G. A. Kavraisky, "Artilleriiskoe nastuplenie" [The artillery offensive], *SVE* 1976, 1:270–1; K. Kazakov, "Sovershenstvovanie artilleriiskogo nastupleniia" [Perfection of the artillery offensive], *VIZh*, No. 10 (October 1970), 33–9.
51. Glantz, *Soviet Military Deception*, 105–292.
52. Savushkin, *Razvitie ... 1941–45 gg.*, 78.
53. "Deistviia aviatsii v kurskom srazhenii" [The actions of aviation in the battle of Kursk], *SMPIOV*, Vol. 11, March–April 1944, 160–87 (formerly classified secret).
54. Savushkin, *Razvitie ... 1941–45 gg.*, 82.
55. David M. Glantz, *From the Don to the Dnepr* (London: Frank Cass & Co., Ltd, 1991).
56. Bagramian, 245–6.
57. Ibid.
58. Savushkin, *Razvitie ... 1941–45 gg.*, 96; *SMPIOV*, Vol. 11, March–April 1944, 3–5 (formerly classified secret).
59. David M. Glantz, "Soviet Defensive Tactics at Kursk", *CSI Report No. 11*, (Ft. Leavenworth, KS: Combat Studies Institute, 1986); "Podgotvoka k oborona kurskogo platsdarma" [Preparations to defend the Kursk bridgehead], *SMPIOV*, Vol. 11, March–April 1944, 24–37 (formerly classified secret). In retrospect, one must recall that, until July 1943, no Soviet defense had been able to contain a major German offensive, either tactically or operationally.
60. David M. Glantz, "Soviet Operational Intelligence in the Kursk Operation, July 1943", *Intelligence and National Security*, Vol. 5, No. 1 (January 1990), 5–49.
61. Savushkin, *Razvitie ... 1941–45 gg.*, 111.
62. Ibid., 112.
63. Ogarkov, "Strategiia voennaia", 562.
64. Zhukov, 1:293.
65. Savushkin, *Razvitie ... 1941–45 gg.*, 70.
66. Ibid., 70. Operational superiorities were much greater. For example, in selected operations, according to formerly classified Soviet documents, superiorities were as follows:

Belorussian Operation (June 1944)

Front	Manpower	Artillery	Tanks/SP Guns
lst Baltic			
(overall – 160 km)	1.7:1	3:1	4.5:1
(penetration			
sector – 25 km)	3.2:1	5.3:1	6:1
3rd Belorussian			
(overall – 130 km)	2.5:1	4:1	4:1
(penetration			
sector-27 km)	3.5:1	6:1	5.5:1
1st Belorussian			
(overall – 240 km)	2:1	3:1	8:1
(penetration			
sector – 28 km)	5:1	17:1	11:1

Source: "Razgrom nemtsev v Belorussii, letum 1944 goda" [Destruction of Germans in Belorussia, summer 1944], *SMPIOV*, Vol. 18, May–June 1944 (Moscow: Voenizdat, 1945), formerly classified secret.

Iassy-Kishinev Operation (August 1944)

Front	Manpower	Artillery	Tanks/SP Guns
2d Ukrainian			
(overall)	1.8:1	2.8:1	4.8:1
(penetration)	3.9:1	10.8:1	3.8:1
3d Ukrainian			
(overall)	1.6:1	1.6:1	2.3:1
(penetration)	8:1	6.7:1	6.6:1

Source: "Iassko-kishinevskaia operatsiia (avgust 1944 g.)" [Iassy-Kishinev operation (August 1944)], *SMPIOV*, Vol. 19, July–August 1945 (Moscow: Voenizdat, 1945) formerly classified secret.

L'vov-Sandemierz Operation (July 1944)

Front	Manpower	Artillery	Tanks/SP Guns
lst Ukrainian			
(overall)	2:1	2:1	2:1
(penetration			
after regrouping)	5:1	6.5:1	3.5:1

Source: "L'vov-peremyshl'skaia operatsiia 1-go ukrainskogo fronta (iiul'–avgust 1944 g.)" [L'vov-Peremysl' operation of the lst Ukrainian Front (July–August 1944)], *SMPIOV*, Vol. 22, January–February 1946 (Moscow: Voenizdat, 1946), formerly classified secret.

German intelligence records for 1 June 1944 show the following estimated correlation of forces for the Nevel–Chernovtsy sector:

	Army Group North Ukraine	Enemy	Ratio
men	633,000	669,000	1:1.16
tanks	811	2,300	1:2.8
	Army Group Center	Enemy	Ratio
men	880,000	1,230,000	1:1.4
tanks	996	1,100	1:1.1

	Total German	Total Enemy	Ratio
men	1,513,000	1,899,000	1:1.25
tanks	1,807	3,400	1:1.88

See "Kraftegegenuberstellung", *Fremde Heere Ost* (IIC), Pruf. Nr. 1058 1.6.44.

67. Bagramian, 417; Strokov, 568.
68. Bagramian, 418; Lototsky, 7–8.
69. Bagramian, 420–22; Matsulenko, "Razvitie operativnogo ... ," 48–50. For a good discussion of forward detachments, see I. Vorob'ev "Forward Detachments in Offensive Operations and Battles", *VM*, April 1965, translated in FDD 957, 6 April 1966. For details on the use of forward detachments in Manchuria, see D. Glantz, *August Storm: Soviet Operational and Tactical Combat in Manchuria, August 1945*, Leavenworth Paper No. 8 (Ft. Leavenworth, KS: Combat Studies Institute, 1983).
70. Bagramian, 426–38; A. Radzievsky, *Tankovyi udar*; Losik. Among the many articles focusing on distinct aspects of tank operations are: P. Kurochkin, "Operations of Tank Armies in the Operational Depth", *VM* (November 1965), 97–166, translated by FDD; A. Maryshev, "Deistviia tankovykh voisk pri proryve oborony protivnika" [Operations of tank forces in penetrating an enemy defense], *VIZh*, No. 6 (June 1982); N. Kobrin, "Iz opyta vydvizheniia tankovykh armii iz raionov sosredotocheniia dlia vvoda v srazhenie" [From the experience of the movement of tank armies from assembly areas for introduction into battle], *VIZh*, No. 9 (September 1976); A. Radzievsky, "Vvod tankovykh armii v proryv" [Introduction of a tank army into a penetration], *VIZh*, No. 2 (February 1976); I. Garkusha, "Osobennosti boevykh deistvii bronetankovykh i mekhanizirovannykh voisk" [The peculiarities of combat operations of armored and mechanized forces], *VIZh*, No. 9 (September 1975); I. Taran and V. Kolesnik, "Organizatsiia sviazi v bronetankovykh i mekhanizirovannykh voiskakh destvuiushchikh na razobshchennykh napravleniiakh" [The organization of communications of armored and mechanized forces operating on separate directions], *VIZh*, No. 5 (May 1982); A. Tsynkalov, "Iz opyta povysheniia zhivuchesti tankov v nastupatel'nykh operatsiiakh" [From the experience of increasing the survivability of tanks in offensive operations], *VIZh*, No. 3 (March 1983).
71. Glantz, *Soviet Military Deception*, 292–557; for complete documentary evidence of deception, see *SBD*, Vol. 27 (Moscow: Voenizdat, 1956), formerly classified secret, which contains more than 200 pages of deception documents and after-action reports.
72. Glantz, *Soviet Military Deception*, 348–60; for example, see "Operativnaia peregruppirovka (po opytu 1-go Pribaltiiskogo Fronta)" [Operational regrouping (based on the experience of the 1st Baltic Front)], *SMPIOV*, Vol. 17, March–April 1945, 3–30 (formerly classified secret).
73. Allied forces included two Polish armies (1st, 2nd) of 3 corps and 15 divisions, two Rumanian armies (1st, 4th) of 4 corps and 15 divisions, one Bulgarian army (1st) of 6 divisions, a Czechoslovakian corps (1st) of 5 brigades, 3 Hungarian divisions, 2 Norwegian infantry battalions, two Yugoslav brigades, and 1 French aviation division ("Normandy").
74. Savushkin, *Razvitie ... 1941–45 gg.*, 79.
75. Ibid., 83.
76. *Stavka* orders to the 1st Ukrainian and 1st Belorussian Fronts, issued in late January, envisioned operations against Berlin. See "Nizhne-Silezskaia nastupatel'naia operatsiia voisk 1-go Ukrainskogo fronta [The Lower-Silesian offensive operation of forces of the 1st Ukrainian Front], *SM*, Issue 10–11 (Moscow: Voenizdat, 1953), 134–8, (formerly classified secret).
77. Savushkin, *Razvitie ... 1941–45 gg.*, 85. In each national formation, there were representatives of Soviet military commands, the Soviet General Staff, operational groups, instructors, advisers; and representatives of national formations, in turn, were assigned to Soviet *front* and army staffs. For thorough coverage on how these allied forces were formed and integrated into Soviet commands, see *SM*, Issue 19 (Moscow: Voenizdat, 1968) formerly classified "for service use".

292

78. Ibid., 84.
79. Ibid. Mutual suspicion is evident in the memoirs of Shtemenko, Vasilevsky, and Zhukov.
80. Among the many documents, see *SMPIOV*, Vol. 18, May–June 1945, which surveyed the entire Belorussian operation; "Deistviia tankovykh i mekhanizirovannykh voisk v operatsii po okruzheniiu i unichtozheniiu bobruiskoi gruppirovki protivnika (iun' 1944g.)" [The action of tank and mechanized forces in operations to encircle and destroy the Bobruisk enemy group (June 1944)], *SMPIOV*, Vol. 17, March–April 1945, 64–84, (formerly classified secret).
81. For operations by armored and mechanized forces, among many new works, see I. M. Anan'ev, *Tankovye armii v nastuplenii* [Tank armies in the offensive] (Moscow: Voenizdat, 1988); also extensive documents in *SBD*, Issue 15 (Moscow: Voenizdat, 1952), which contains over 100 pages of formerly top secret (*sovenshenno sekretnyi*) material on tank and mechanized force operations.
82. See *SMPIOV*, Vol. 25, 1–188, (formerly classified secret), which details the Vistula–Oder operations; "Operativnaia maskirovka voisk 1-go Ukrainskogo fronta v podgotovitel'nyi period Sandomirsko-Silezskoi nastupatel'noi operatsii" [Operational deception of 1st Ukrainian Front forces in the preparation period of the Sandomiercz-Silesian offensive operation], *SBD*, Issue 27, 153–86 (formerly classified secret).
83. David M. Glantz, *August Storm: The Soviet 1945 Strategic Offensive in Manchuria*, Leavenworth Papers No. 7 (Ft. Leavenworth, KS: Combat Studies Institute, 1983); David M. Glantz, *August Storm: Tactical and Operational Combat in Manchuria 1945*, Leavenworth Papers No. 8 (Ft. Leavenworth, KS: Combat Studies Institute, 1983).
84. Savushkin, *Razvitie ... 1941–45 gg.*, 91.
85. Bagramian, 435.
86. *Krasno-znamennyi dal'ne-vostochnyi* [Red Banner Far Eastern] (Moscow: Voenizdat, 1985), 133–200.
87. Ibid., 191.
88. David M. Glantz (ed.), *From the Dnepr to the Vistula: Soviet Offensive Operations – October 1944–March 1945*, 1986 Art of War Symposium (Carlisle, PA: U.S. Army War College, Center for Land Warfare, 1986), 663–788; "Oboronitel'nye boi 64-go strelkovogo korpusa iuzhnee ozera balaton v marte 1945 g." [The defensive battle of 64th Rifle Corps south of Lake Balaton in March 1945], *SM*, Issue 9 (Moscow: Voenizdat, 1953), 121–86 (formerly classified secret); "Oboronitel'naia operatsiia 4-i gvardeiskoi armii zapadnee goroda Budapesht" [The defensive operation of 4th Guards Army west of Budapest], *SM*, issue 5 (Moscow: Voenizdat, 1951), 91–163, (formerly classified secret).
89. As evidence of this Soviet mistrust of Allied intentions, see G. K. Zhukov, *Reminiscences and Reflections*, 2 Vols. (Moscow: Progress Publishers, 1985), 11:338–9. Translation of *Vospominaniia i razmyshleniia* (Moscow: Izdatel'stvo Agentsva Pechati Novosti, 1974); S. M. Shtemenko, *The Soviet General Staff at War, 1941–45*, Book 1 (Moscow: Progress Publishers, 1985), 399–401. Translation of *Sovetskii general'nyi shtab v gody voiny* (Moscow: Voenizdat, 1981).

CHAPTER 6

1. Ogarkov, *Strategiia voennaia*, 563.
2. Ibid.
3. Ibid., 565.
4. Sokolovsky, *Voennaia strategiia*. Two additional editions of the work appeared in 1966 and 1968.
5. Lecture Materials from the Voroshilov General Staff Academy, supplement to the lecture "Principles and Content of Military Strategy". The basic strategy lecture, along with the 1975 supplementary material, may be found in *The Voroshilov Lectures: From the Soviet General Staff Academy–Issues of Military Strategy* (Washington, D.C.: National Defense University Press, 1989). The basic lecture itself, without the

supplement, has been published in *The Journal of Soviet Military Studies*, Vol. 1 (April 1988), 29–53. Theater-strategic operations relied on high-speed combined-arms offensives designed to seize the initiative and achieve strategic objectives quickly and without employment of nuclear weapons.

The concept of the theater-strategic operation provided a broad framework for understanding the full scope and complexity of strategic military endeavors, althought the Soviets never implied that such a complex and risky concept would be fully implemented in future war. The theoretical structure of the full theater-strategic operation provided insights as to what strategic objectives smaller-scale operations over shorter durations could achieve. More importantly, the larger model of the full theater-strategic operation vividly underscored the possible consequences should the smaller-scale operations fail.

The Soviets reassessed the nature of strategic operations in a five-article series appearing in *Voenno-istoricheskii zhurnal* [Military-historical journal, hereafter cited as *VIZh*] from October 1985 to July 1986. The articles in this Soviet-designated "*Diskussiia*" [Discussion or Debate] included V. V. Gurkin and M. I. Golovnin, "K voprosu o strategicheskikh operatsiiakh Velikoi Otechestvennoi voiny, 1941–1945" [On the question of strategic operations in the Great Patriotic war, 1941–45], *VIZh* (October 1985), 11; N. K. Glazunov and B. I. Pavlov, "K voprosu o strategicheskikh operatsiiakh Velikoi Otechestvennoi voiny", *VIZh* (April 1986), 48–50; A. I. Mikhalev and V. I. Kudriashov, "K voprosu o strategicheskikh operatsiiakh Velikoi Otechestvennoi voiny, 1941–45," *VIZh* (May 1986), 48–50; and Kh M. Dzhelaukhov and B. N. Petrov, "K voprosu o strategicheskikh operatsiiakh Velikoi Otechestvennoi voiny, 1941–1945," *VIZh* (July 1986), 46–8. Also appearing at this same time, though not formally a part of the "*Diskussiia*", was the related article, A. P. Maryshev, "Nekotorye voprosy strategicheskoi oborony v Velikoi Otechestvennoi voiny" [Several questions on strategic defense in the Great Patriotic War], *VIZh* (June 1986), 9–16. In the fall of 1987, an unsigned article, "Itogi diskussii o strategicheskikh operatsiiakh Velikoi Otechestvennoi voiny, 1941–45" [Results of the discussions on strategic operations of the Great Patriotic War, 1941–45], *VIZh* (October 1987), 8–24, capped the series. Among the conclusions reached in these assessments was an approach to classifying operations as "strategic". The Soviets have formulated and generally accepted three "fundamental criteria" for describing an operation as strategic. Specifically, a strategic operation: 1, resolves important strategic missions and attains important military-political aims; 2, in most cases consists of combat operations of great spatial scope and includes the participation of a considerable quantity of forces and means; and 3, is planned by the *Stavka* of the Supreme High Command (*VGK*), with the coordination of actions by *fronts*, fleets, and other Services of the Armed Forces carried out by *VGK* representatives. Thus, as these criteria and associated Soviet discussions make clear, a strategic operation is centrally controlled at the highest level of command, is usually large and of combined arms composition, and, most importantly, accomplishes critically important military-political goals regardless of its size and scope, or the length and intensity of operations.

6. The most extensive English language works on these operations are David M. Glantz (ed.), *From the Vistula to the Oder: Soviet Offensive Operations – October 1944 – March 1945, 1986 Art of War Symposium, A Transcript of Proceedings* (Carlisle, PA: Center for Land Warfare, U.S. Army War College, 1986); D. M. Glantz, *August Storm: The Soviet 1945 Strategic Offensive in Manchuria*, Leavenworth Papers No. 7 (Ft. Leavenworth, KS: Combat Studies Institute, 1983); D. M. Glantz, *August Storm; Soviet Tactical and Operational Combat in Manchuria, 1945*, Leavenworth Papers No. 8 (Ft. Leavenworth, KS: Combat Studies Institute, 1983). Soviet formerly classified studies include: *SMPIOV*, Vol. 18, May–June 1944, (Moscow: Voenizdat, 1945); *SMPIOV*, Vol. 19, July–August 1945, (Moscow: Voenizdat, 1945); *SMPIOV*, Vol. 25, (Moscow: Voenizdat, 1947).

7. Among the many works describing the "permanently operating factors," see I. V. Maryganov, *Peredovoi kharakter sovetskoi voennoi nauki* [The advanced nature of

Soviet military science] (Moscow: Voenizdat, 1953).
8. I. Korotkov, "O razvitii sovetskoi voennoi teorii v poslevoennye gody" [Concerning the development of Soviet military theory in the postwar years], *VIZh*, No. 4 (April 1964), 40.
9. M. Cherednichenko, "Razvitie teorii strategicheskoi nastupatel'noi operatsii v 1945–53 gg." [The development of the theory of the strategic offensive operation, 1945–53], *VIZh*, No. 8 (August 1976), 39.
10. *50 let vooruzhennykh sil SSSR* [50 years of the Soviet Armed Forces] (Moscow: Voenizdat, 1968), 459, 474–9. There were 6 million in the "operating armies" in January 1945 and a total of 11,365,000 in the Soviet Army and Navy. Demobilization reduced this total to a strength of 2,874,000 in 1948.
11. V. A. Semenov, *Kratkii ocherk razvitiia sovetskogo operativnogo iskusstva* [A short sketch of the development of Soviet military art] (Moscow: Voenizdat, 1960), 289.
12. M. Burshtunovich, "Bases of Offensive Battle of a Rifle Regiment and Battalion", *VV* (January 1947), as quoted from R. Gartoff, *Soviet Military Doctrine* (Glencoe, IL: The Free Press, 1953), 69.
13. Cherednichenko, 41.
14. Ibid.
15. F. F. Gaivoronsky (ed.), *Evoliutsiia voennogo iskusstva: etapy, tendentsii, printsipy* [Evolution of military art: stages, tendencies, principles] (Moscow: Voenizdat, 1987), 162.
16. Ibid., 42. See also M. M. Kir'ian (ed.), *Voenno-tekhnicheskii progress i vooruzhennye sily SSSR* [Military-technical progress and the armed forces] (Moscow: Voenizdat, 1982), 239–42.
17. Cherednichenko, 42–3; Bagramian, 477; V. Miagkov, "Razvitie teorii boevogo primeneniia aviatsii v 1946–53 gg." [The development of the theory of the combat use of aviation, 1946–53], *VIZh*, No. 2 (February 1976).
18. Z. Zlobin, "Sovremannaia frontovaia operatsiia" [Contemporary *front* operations], *VM*, (April–May 1945), translated by the Directorate of Military Intelligence, Army Headquarters, Ottawa, Canada, 3.
19. Bagramian, 476; Cherednichenko, 42, 44.
20. M. A. Garelov, "Otkuda ugroza" [Whence the threat], *VIZh*, No. 3 (February 1989), 24. This article went to press in November 1988.
21. Ibid.
22. Ibid., 25.
23. "Operativnyi plan", 27.
24. Ibid., 28.
25. Ibid., 29–30.

1st Guards Mechanized Army	2nd Guards Mechanized Army
9th Tank Division	1st Tank Division
11th Guards Tank Division	12th Guards Tank Division
8th Guards Mechanized Division	1st Mechanized Division
18th Guards Mechanized Division	9th Guards Tank Division*

*9th Guards Tank Division was shown on the operational map, but not listed in the order. Presumably it served as GOFG reserve.

26. The order seems to have deleted paragraphs on reinforcement and employment of strategic reserves, as well as the requisite number of annexes and appendices.
27. U.S. Department of the Army, Intelligence Division, GSUSA, *Military Summary: Foreign Ground Forces*, No. 1 (May 1949), Secret (declassified), 39–45.
28. Ibid.
29. Ibid.; see also USAREUR G-2 OBR, *Soviet Order of Battle Handbook GSFG and Installations List Soviet Zone, Germany* (1 January 1957), Secret (declassified). The two armies were organized as follows:

3rd Guards Mechanized Army	4th Guards Mechanized Army
6th Guards Tank Division	10th Guards Tank Division
7th Guards Tank Division	25th Tank Division
9th Mechanized Division	6th Guards Mechanized Division
14th Guards Motorized Rifle Division	7th Guards Mechanized Division

30. Ibid.; see also declassified sources which include the designated volumes of U.S. Department of the Army, *Intelligence Review*, No. 89 (July 1949), Secret (declassified); and No. 58 (July 1949), Secret (declassified); Department of the Army, Intelligence Division, GSUSA, *Military Summary: Foreign Ground Forces*, No. 2 (July 1949); No. 3 (September 1949); No. 4 (November 1949); No. 5 (January 1950); No. 6 (March 1950); and No. 7 (July 1950), Secret (declassified).

Descendant Formations of 3rd and 4th Guards Motorized Armies

3rd Guards Mechanized Army

1950	*1957–58*	*1964*	*1984*	*1990*
6GTD	6GTD (1GTA)	6GTD (1GTA)	6GTD (withdrawn)	
7GTD	7GTD (18GA)	7GTD (1GTA)	7GTD (3SA)	7GTD (withdrawn)
9MD	9MRD (withdrawn)			
14GMD	14GRD (18GA)	14GMRD (20GA)	32GTD (20GA)	32GTD (withdrawn)

4th Guards Mechanized Army

1950	*1957–58*	*1964*	*1984*	*1990*
25TD	25TD (2GTA)	25TD (3SA)	25TD (20GA)	25TD (withdrawn)
10GTD	10GTD (20GA)	10GTD (3SA)	10TD (3SA)	32TD (withdrawn)
6GMD	6GMRD (20GA)	6GMRD (20GA)	6GMRD (20GA)	6GMRD (90GTD) (2GTA)
7GMD	11GMD (withdrawn)			

It is also of more than passing interest that the four divisions presently withdrawing from Western Group of Forces (WGF) (25th Tank, 32d Tank, 12th Guards Tank, and 7th Guards Tank) were the descendants of those earlier cadre divisions of 3d and 4th Guards Mechanized Armies. If portions of these divisions had remained in Western Group of Forces (WGF), they could have performed the same cadre function as their predecessors and played an important part in Soviet mobilization schemes.

31. Based in part on Headquarters, U.S. Forces, European Theater, *The Reserves of the Red Army* (Europe, 18 March 1946), declassified Top Secret study, as cited in Albert Z.

Conner and Robert G. Poirier, Soviet Ground Force Mobilization Potential: Lessons of the Past and Implications for the Future", *Journal of Soviet Military Studies*, Vol. 2, No. 2 (June 1988), p. 227, plus an author's estimate.
32. U.S War Department, *Handbook on USSR. Military Forces*, Washington, D.C.: War Department, 1945), p. II–23.
33. Ibid., pp. II–22 to II–23.
34. For the nature of the "revolution in military affairs", see the collection of articles published in *Problemy revolutsii v voennom dele* [The problems of the revolution in military affairs] (Moscow: Voenizdat, 1965).
35. V. D. Sokolovsky, *Voennaia strategiia* [Military strategy] (Moscow: Voenizdat, 1968), translated by Foreign Technology Division (FTD), 192–3.
36. Ibid., 209.
37. Ibid.
38. Strokov, 612.
39. For the text of this law (amended in various ways over the next two decades), see *Izvestiia*, 13 October 1967, pp. 3–4 of the supplementary edition. The law went into effect in January 1968.
40. Sokolovsky, 209.
41. G. H. Turbiville, G. D. Wardak (eds.), *The Voroshilov Lectures: Materials from the Soviet General Staff Academy*, Vol. 1 (Washington, D.C.: National Defense University Press, 1989), 205–31.
42. Strokov, 616.
43. Bagramian, 501.
44. Ibid., 502; V. Margelov, "Razvitie teorii primeneniia vozdushno-desantnykh voisk v poslevoennyi period" [The development of the theory of the use of airborne forces in the postwar period], *VIZh*, No. 1 (January 1977), 54.
45. Bagramian, 503; N. Kireev, "Primenenie tankovykh podrazdelenii i chastei pri proryve oborony protivnika" [The use of tank subunits and units in penetrating an enemy defense], *VIZh*, No. 2 (February 1982), 37–8.
46. Bagramian, 504.
47. Ibid; V. G. Reznichenko, *Taktika* [Tactics] (Moscow: Voenizdat, 1966), K. Andrukhov, V. Bulatnikov, "The Growing Role of Airborne Troops in Modern Military Operations," *VM*, No. 2 (July 1966). English translation, FPIE 9475/67, 17 May 1967, 175.
48. Bagramian, 505–8.
49. Ibid, 506–7.
50. Evidenced, for example, by publication of General P. A. Kurochkin's "Operations of Tank Armies in the Operational Depth", *VM*, No. 11 (November 1965), 97–126 (translation).
51. A. A. Sidorenko, *Nastuplenie* [The offensive] (Moscow: Voenizdat, 1970); V. E. Savkin, *Osnovnye printsipy operativnogo iskusstva i taktiki* [The basic principles of operational art and tactics] (Moscow: Voenizdat, 1972); A. Kh. Babadzhanian (ed.), *Tanki i tankovye voiska* [Tanks and tank forces] (Moscow: Voenizdat, 1968); I. Kh. Bagramian (ed.), *Istoriia voin i voennogo iskusstva* [History of war and military art] (Moscow: Voenizdat, 1970).
52. Sokolovsky, 289.
53. Ibid., 300.
54. I. Kh. Bagramian (ed.), *Voennaia istoriia* [Military history] (Moscow: Voenizdat, 1971), 345.
55. *Voprosy strategii*. Five years later Zakharov introduced a companion book, *Voprosy taktiki v sovetskikh voennykh trudakh (1917–40 gg.)* [Questions of tactics in Soviet military works (1917–40)] (Moscow: Voenizdat, 1970). Zakharov had served in the General Staff during the late 1930s.
56. P. A. Kurochkin (ed.), *Obshchevoiskovaia armiia v nastuplenii* [The combined-arms army in the offensive] (Moscow: Voenizdat, 1966).
57. A. I. Radzievsky (ed.), *Armeiskie operatsii* [Army operations] (Moscow: Voenizdat,

1977); I. E. Krupchenko (ed.), *Sovetskie tankovye voiska 1941–1945* [Soviet tank forces 1941–45] (Moscow: Voenizdat, 1973); P. A. Rotmistrov, *Vremia i tanki* [Time and tanks] (Moscow: Voenizdat, 1972); O. A. Losik (ed.), *Stroitel'stvo i boevoe primenenie sovetskikh tankovykh voisk v gody Velikoi Otechestvennoi voiny* [The organization and combat use of Soviet tank forces in the Great Patriotic War] (Moscow: Voenizdat, 1979); I. I. Lisov, *Desantniki-vozdushnyi desanty* [Airlanding troops – airlandings] (Moscow: Voenizdat, 1968); D. S. Sukhorukov, *Sovetskie vozdushno-desantnye* [Soviet airlanding forces] (Moscow: Voenizdat, 1980); S. K. Kurkotkin (ed.), *Tyl sovetskikh vooruzhennykh sil v Velikoi Otechestvenoi voine* [The rear of the Soviet armed forces in the Great Patriotic War] (Moscow: Voenizdat, 1977); A. I. Radzievsky (ed.), *Taktika v boevykh primerakh: vzvod, rota, polk, diviziia* [Tactics by combat example: platoon, company, regiment, division] (Moscow: Voenizdat, 1974–76).

58. V. G. Kulikov, "Operativnoe iskusstvo" [Operational art], *SVE*, 6:53. Kulikov uses the terms *soedinenie* and *chast'*, which mean formation and unit and which are equivalent respectively to division and regiment in English parlance. The Russian term *ob'edinenie* means large formation and corresponds to a Soviet *front* (army group) and army.

59. Among the many articles, see F. Sverdlov, "K voprosy o manevr v boiu" [Concerning the question of maneuver in combat], *VV*, No. 8 (August 1972), 31; V. Savkin, "Manevr v boiu" [Maneuver in battle], *VV*, No. 4 (April 1972), 23.

60. V. G. Reznichenko, *Taktika* [Tactics] (Moscow: Voenizdat, 1987), 72.

61. For example, see I. Vorob'ev, "Novoe orushie i printsipy taktiki" [New weapons and tactical principles], *Sovetskoe voennoe obozpenie* [Soviet military review], No. 2 (February 1987), 18.

62. Extensive Soviet analysis of this theme of the initial period of war has produced many studies, including S. P. Ivanov, *Nachal'nyi period voiny* [The initial period of war] (Moscow: Voenizdat, 1974); M. Cherednichenko, "O nachal'nom periode Velikoi Otechestvennoi voiny" [Concerning the initial period of the Great Patriotic War], *VIZh*, No. 4 (April 1961), 28–35; P. Korkodinov, "Facti i mysli o nachal'nom periode Velikoi Otechestvennoi voiny" [Facts and ideas about the initial period of the Great Patriotic war], *VIZh*, No. 10 (October, 1965), 26–34; V. Baskakov, "Ob osobennostiakh nachal'nogo periode voiny" [Concerning the peculiarities of the initial period of war], *VIZh*, No. 2 (February 1966), 29–34; A. Grechko, "25 let tomu nazad" [25 years ago], *VIZh*, No. 6 (June 1966), 3–15; I. Bagramian, "Kharakter i osobennosti nachal'nogo perioda voiny" [The nature and peculiarities of the initial period of war], *VIZh*, No. 10 (October 1981), 20–27; V. Matsulenko, "Nekotorye vyvody iz opyta nachal'nogo perioda Velikoi Otechestvennoi voiny" [Some conclusions from the experience of the initial period of the Great Patriotic War], *VIZh*, No. 3 (March 1984), 35–42; A. I. Evseev, "O nekotorykh tendentsiiakh v izmenenii soderzhaniia i kharaktera nachal'nogo perioda voiny" [Concerning some tendencies in the changing form and nature of the initial period of war], *VIZh*, No. 11 (November 1985), 11–20.

63. Iu. Molostov, A. Novikov, "High-precision weapons against tanks," *Soviet Military Review*, No. 1 (January 1988), 13.

64. Reznichenko, 200.

65. Ibid.

66. David M. Glantz, *Soviet Conduct of Tactical Maneuver: The Role of the Forward Detachment* (Ft. Leavenworth, KS: Soviet Army Studies Office, 1988).

67. Reznichenko, 206.

68. M. Zakharov, "O teorii glubokoi operatsii", 20.

69. Kulikov, 57.

70. N. Kireev, "Primenenie tankovykh podrazdelenii i chastei pri proryve oborony protivnika" [The use of tank subunits and units in penetrating an enemy defense], *VIZh*, No. 2 (February 1982), 38–40.

71. M. A. Gareev, *M. V. Frunze – Voennyi teoretik* [M. V. Frunze – Military theoretician] (Moscow: Voenizdat, 1984), 236–46.

72. S. G. Gorshkov, *Morskaia moshch' gosudarstva* [Seapower of the state] (Moscow: Voenizdat, 1976); S. G. Gorshkov, *Morskaia moshch' gosudarstva* [Seapower of the

NOTES: CHAPTER SIX

state] (Moscow: Voenizdat, 1979).
73. Among the many references to the new military doctrine, see S. Akhromeev, "The Doctrine of Averting War and Defending Peace and Socialism", *World Marxist Review*, XXX No. 12 (December 1987), 40–41; D. T. Iazov, *Na strazhe sotsializma i mira* [On guard for Socialism and Peace] (Moscow: Voenizdat, 1987), 23; D. T. Iazov, "Perestroika v rabote voennykh kadrov" [Perestroika in the work of military cadres], *VIZh*, No. 7 (July 1987), 4.
74. Ogarkov, "Strategiia voennaia", 564.
75. The observation is based on the informed judgments of the author and a reading of extensive Soviet works on experience with deep, mobile operations. Publication of these works has increased geometrically since the late 1960s. For the sake of analysis, the Soviets subdivide their Great Patriotic War (1941–45) into three distinct periods, each characterized by basic unifying conditions: the first period from June 1941 to November 1942; the second from November 1942 through December 1943; and the third from January 1944 through May 1945.
76. This is consistent with Soviet echelonment practices since the 1930s and accords with recent Soviet laments that the loss of forward groups of forces is destroying the first strategic echelon, which now must be reconstructed within the borders of the Soviet Union.
77. The Soviets were also prepared to conduct a protracted war, but only reluctantly, for they understood what that involved. They also understood the difficulties and risks associated with an attack after only limited preparations. In this circumstance, the chances of achieving surprise through *maskirovka* were greater and could outweigh the risks.
   Writings on the initial period of war reached the following conclusions:
   – the tendency for the massive use of new means of armed struggle to have increasing importance in the initial period of war;
   – the tendency for the results of the initial period to have increasing influence over the subsequent course of hostilities;
   – the tendency for the scale of military operations to increase;
   – the tendency of both sides to use surprise as the most important factor;
   – the tendency for the initial period to shorten as a result of improved weaponry;
   – the tendency of the role of maneuver to increase in importance.
78. The Soviets repeatedly renounced the intention of "gnawing through" [*progryzanie*] deeply arrayed defenses. For example, see A. A. Strokov, *Voennaia istoriia*, 616. In some offensive situations, for example, against a prepared defense organized in depth, the Soviets accepted the necessity for deeper echelonment. The echelonment, however, would not be so deep as to deprive the Soviets of the ability to commit forces in sufficient quantities to penetrate enemy defenses and sustain the offensive into the operational depths. In general, deeper, more resilient enemy defenses increased Soviet force requirements, compelled the Soviets to echelon their forces more deeply, increased necessary preparation time, reduced the possibility of achieving surprise, and provided more lucrative potential nuclear targets. Consequently, the enemy had more time to make political-military decisions, which might have included use of nuclear weapons. For all of these reasons and the likelihood that a more protracted military operation could result, the Soviets tended to dismiss this option.
   In their study of past operational experiences, the Soviets concentrated on those operations in which massive Soviet initial blows produced significant strategic gains (for example, Belorussia – June 1944, Iassy-Kishinev – August 1944, Vistula-Oder – January 1945, and Manchuria – August 1945). In all of these operations, multiple Soviet *fronts* attacked in a single echelon and each *front* concentrated the bulk of its forces in first echelon. The results seemed to justify the practice.
79. M. M. Kir'ian (ed.), *Vnezapnost' v nastupatel'nykh operatsiiakh Velikoi Otechestven-noi voiny* [Surprise in offensive operations of the Great Patriotic War] (Moscow: "Nauka". 1986).

THE MILITARY STRATEGY OF THE SOVIET UNION

80. For example, see Soviet analysis of the operational and tactical techniques of U.S. and NATO armies in N. K. Glazunov and N. S. Nikitin, *Operatsiia i boi* [The operation and battle] (Moscow: Voenizdat, 1983); S. V. Grishin and N. N. Tsapenko, *Soedineniia i chasti v boiu* [Formations and units in battle] (Moscow: Voenizdat, 1985).

81. This is the author's judgement based on extensive inferences made in Soviet sources.

82. Cherednichenko, "Strategicheskaia operatsiia", 552. In Russian, *Teatr voennykh deistvii (TVD)* means "theater of military operations". This is synonymous with the current DOD acronym – TSMA – (Theater of Strategic Military Action). TVDa or TSMAs exist within a theater of war (*Teatr voiny – TV*).

83. N. V. Ogarkov, *Vsegda v gotovnosti k zashchite otechestva* [Always in readiness to defend the homeland] (Moscow: Voenizdat, 1982), 35.

84. Ogarkov, "Strategiia voennaia," 564.

85. Kulikov, 56.

86. A. K. Zaporozhchenko, "Strategicheskii eshelon" [Strategic echelon], *SVE*, 7:554; V. I. Beliakov, N. I. Reum, "Strategicheskie reservy" [Strategic reserves], *SVE*, 7:553.

87. The Soviets have experimented with TVD commands in the past. During 1941 and 1942, the *Stavka* controlled operations in key strategic sectors using strategic directions [*strategicheskie napravleniia*], such as the Northeastern, Western, and Southwestern Directions, with a commander and headquarters for each. Only the Western Direction echeloned its *fronts* in depth, while the other directions employed their *fronts* in a single echelon. This command structure proved unwieldy, and, after mid-1942, the *Stavka* controlled strategic operations by groups of *fronts* by using a *Stavka* representative. From 1942 on, the Soviets employed virtually all fronts in a single echelon, except during the Kursk defense, when one front (Steppe) was held in the rear, in *Stavka* reserve, to conduct the counteroffensive.

In late July 1945, the *Stavka* formed a TVD headquarters to control air, ground, and naval operations in the Far East. This headquarters, its staff, and functions became a model for recent Soviet development of a TVD structure.

88. Articles on the relationship of offensive and defense include I. N. Vorob'ev, "Soot-noshenie i vzaimosviaz' nastupleniia i oborona" [The correlation and interconnectivity of offensive and defense], *VM*, No. 4 (April 1980); V. V. Turchenko, "O strategiches-koi oborone" [Concerning the strategic defense], *VM*, No. 7 (July 1982), 16–27; I. G. Zav'ialov, "O roli boevogo potentsiala Vooruzhennykh Sil v nastuplenii i oborone" [Concerning the role of combat potential of the Armed Forces in the offensive and defense], *VM*, No. 3 (March 1983), 4–14; A. T. Levchenko, "Nekotorye voprosy oborony obshchevoiskovykh soedinenii" [Some questions concerning the defense of combined-arms formations], *VM*, No. 4 (April 1984), 32–40.

89. See, for example, A. Maryshev and V. Iminov, "Iz opyta podgotovki i provedeniia kontrudarov v oborone" [From the experience of preparing and conducting coun-terstrokes in the defense], *VIZh*, No. 1 (January 1981), 17–24; M. Kozlov, "Osoben-nosti strategicheskoi oborony i kontranastupleniia i ikh znachenie dlia razvitiia sovets-kogo voennogo iskusstva" [The peculiarities of the strategic defense and counteroffen-sive and their importance for the development of Soviet military art], *VIZh*, No. 10 (October 1981), 28–35.

CHAPTER 7

1. This assessment, for example, appeared in connection with a review of A. Babakov, *Vooruzhennye Sily SSSR posle voiny (1945–86)* [The Armed Forces of the USSR after the war (1945–86)] (Moscow: Voenizdat, 1987) in V. G. Reznichenko, "Sovetskie vooruzhennye sily v poslevoennyi period" [Soviet armed forces in the postwar period], *Kommunist vooruzhennykh sil* [Communist in the armed forces] (January 1988), 86–8.

2. A. Kokoshin and V. Larionov, "Protivostoianiia sil obshchego naznacheniia v kon-tekste obespecheniia strategicheskoi stabil'nosti" [The counterposition of general

300

purpose forces in the context of strategic stability], *Mirovaia ekonomika i mezhdunarodnye otnosheniia* [World economics and international relations, hereafter cited as *MEMO*] (June 1988), 23–31. These have been widely discussed by Western analysts to include a number of forums with Western, Soviet, and East European participation.

3. Considerable Western interest in the "Kursk model" was generated by the article by A. Kokoshin and V. Larionov entitled "Kurskaia bitva v svete sovremennoi oboronitel'noi doktriny" [The Kursk battle in light of contemporary defensive doctrine], which appeared in the August 1987 issue of *MEMO*. Numerous other Soviet analyses of Kursk have appeared before and after this article.

4. Kokoshin and Larionov, 27.

5. "Soviets' Shifting Military Strategy", *The Kansas City Times*, 11 March 1989, which quotes testimony of A. A. Kokoshin in March 1989 before the U.S. Congress' House Armed Services Committee.

6. "Operativnyi plan deistvii Gruppy sovetskikh okkupatsionnykh voisk v Germanii" [Operational plan for actions of the Group of Soviet Occupation Forces in Germany], *VIZh*, No. 2 (February 1989), 26–31 (with map).

7. The *nomenklatura* is the finite group of party members in rank order who occupy key party, governmental, economic, and other positions within virtually all Soviet institutions. In essence it represents an upper class of communist "nobility".

8. The listed grouping of nations are representative and by no means include all nations. Assignment to a category is subject to a variety of finite political and economic conditions.

9. One could argue that the Soviet Union faced similar conditions after it signed the Treaty of Brest-Litovsk (1918). By virtue of that treaty and other postwar conditions (Civil War and allied intervention), for varying lengths of time, the Soviet Union lost possession of the Baltic states, the Ukraine, Georgia, Armenia, Azerbazhan, the Far East, and Tanu Tuva. As soon as the Soviets regained their strength, most of these regions were re-incorporated into the Soviet Union.

10. For a superb study of how the Soviets approach future war in an historical and contemporary sense, see Christopher Bellamy, *Soviet Future War*, 2 vols. (Ft. Leavenworth, KS: Soviet Army Studies Office, 1990).

11. Ibid., 51. The source is referred to as a "confidential discussion". It does, however, match the traditional Soviet approach followed in earlier periods when the General Staff analyzed future war.

12. Ibid. This reflects the contents of G. I. Salmanov, "Sovetskaia voennaia doktrina i nekotorye vzgliady na kharakter voiny i zashchitu sotsializma" [Soviet military doctrine and some views on the nature of war in the defense of socialism], VM, No. 12 (December 1988), 7–20; see almost identical concerns expressed in A. Kokoshin, A. Konovalov, V. Larionov and V. Mazing, *Problems of Ensuring Stability with Radical Cuts in Armed Forces and Conventional Armaments in Europe* (Moscow: Institute of USA and Canada Studies, USSR Academy of Sciences, 1989).

13. A. Kokoshin, "Alexander Svechin on War and Politics," *International Affairs*, No. 11 (November 1988), 121.

14. Salmanov, 9–10.

15. Ibid., 10–11.

16. Among the many articles, see F. Sverdlov, "K voprosu o manevre v boiu" [Concerning the question of maneuver in combat], *Voennyi Vestnik*, No. 8 (August 1972), 31; V. Savkin, "Manevr v boiu" [Maneuver in battle], *Voennyi Vestnik*, No. 4 (April 1972), 23. Hereafter cited as VV.

17. Sverdlov, "K voprosu", 31.

18. V. G. Reznichenko, *Taktika* [Tactics], (Moscow: Voenizdat, 1987), 72.

19. For example, see I. Vorob'ev, "Novoe oruzhie i printsipy taktiki" [New weapons and tactical principles], *Sovetskoe voennoe obozrenie* [Soviet military review], No. 2 (February 1987), 18.

20. Iu. Molostov, A. Novikov, "High precision weapons against tanks", *Soviet Military Review*, No. 1 (January 1988), 13.

301

21. Reznichenko, 200.
22. Ibid.
23. David M. Glantz, *The Soviet Conduct of Tactical Maneuver* (Ft. Leavenworth, KS: Soviet Army Studies Office, 1989).
24. Reznichenko, 206.
25. Molostov, Novikov, 13.
26. Ibid.
27. Stanislaw Koziej, "Anticipated Directions for Change in Tactics of Ground Forces," *Przegled Wojsk Ladowych* [Ground Forces Review], No. 9 (September 1986), 9. Translated by Harold Orenstein in *Selected Translations from the Polish Military Press*, Vol. 1 (Ft. Leavenworth, KS: Soviet Army Studies Office, 1988), 7.
28. See note 62, Chapter 6.
29. Salmanov, 10.
30. Ibid.
31. Ibid., 11.
32. Ibid.
33. See note 83, Chapter 4.
34. A. A. Kokoshin and V. N. Lobov, "Predvidenie [Foresight]," *Znamia* [Banner], No. 2 (February 1990), 182.
35. Ibid.
36. Ibid.
37. Ibid., 181. This questioning of the validity of World War II experience echoes similar questioning by Soviet military theorists in the late 1950s and early 1960s, when they argued that the nuclear revolution (the revolution in military affairs) had negated the value of older forms of war. By 1962, however, theorists began having second thoughts, and they ultimately rejected the "single nuclear option" in favor of studying and preparing for both nuclear and conventional operations. See G. H. Turbiville, Jr. and G. D. Wardak (eds.), *The Voroshikov Lectures: Materials from the Soviet General Staff Academy, Vol. 1* (Washington, D.C.: National Defense University, 1989), 26–7.
38. Ibid., 182.
39. In August 1969 the Soviet Union added a 16th military district by separating the Central Asian Military District from the Turkestan Military District, ostensibly to respond to an increased threat from China.
40. In 1989 the Soviets again combined the Central Asian and Turkestan Military Districts. The recent combination of the Ural and Volga Military Districts into a single Ural-Volga Military District reduced the overall number of military districts to 14. This marks a diminution in the perceived threat from China, and perhaps increased Soviet concern for its southern flank.
41. Compare with Borshchev's critique of 1941 strategic deficiencies (Note 83, Chapter 4) and Savushkin's descriptions of missions of June 1941, which were not fulfilled (Savushkin, *Razvetie ... 1941–45 gg.*, 48).
42. In a longer duration mobilization scenario, the Red Army could have expanded well beyond these figures to approximately Civil War strength of over 5 million.
43. The Soviet Union has traditionally employed fortified regions along its southern and eastern borders to fulfill defensive roles, conserve manpower, and provide a base around which mobilization could occur. During wartime the fortified regions served as economy of force formations, permitting main forces to better concentrate. During mobilization fortified regions were sometimes converted into full-fledged divisions, and the reverse occurred during demobilization.

The quantities of divisions are according to IISS *The Military Balance 1989–90*. As such they incorporate none of the announced Soviet troop reductions, which to date include four tank divisions from Western Group of Forces and one each from the Central and Southern Groups.

In addition, the Soviets have announced withdrawal of three of four divisions from Mongolia, 12 from Asia (facing China), and conversion of other divisions to artillery-machine gun divisions, the modern equivalent of the older fortified region.

44. It is likely that 140–150 divisions would be maintained at varying manning levels, depending on the international political climate, missions, and their geographical orientation.
45. As the threat decreases, manning levels could decrease and the Soviets could rely to a greater extent on artillery/machine gun divisions (fortified regions), mobilization divisions, and a variety of mobilization bases (existing divisions, training or mobilization centers, etc.).
46. Khaustov, 38.
47. In late July 1945 the Soviets created a Theater of Military Operations (TVD) headquarters under Marshal A. M. Vasilevsky to control all air, sea, and land operations against Japanese forces in Manchuria. This was necessitated by the huge size of the region of conflict, the complexity of envisioned operations, the requirement for offensive speed, and the distance of the theater from the western Soviet Union.
48. This is based on the assumption that the most serious threat faced by the Soviets, besides those in the West, will be threat of foreign intervention on behalf of rebellious nationalities in Central Asia.
49. The approximate breakdown of divisions by military district and group of forces is:

Group or Military District	Tank	Divisions Mot Rifle	Abn	Total
Western Group	11	8	0	19**
Northern Group	1	1	0	2**
Central Group	2	3	0	5**
Southern Group	2	2	0	4**
	16	14	0	30
Leningrad	0	11	1	12
Baltic	3	7	2	12
Belorussian	10	2	0	12*
Carpathian	4	9	0	13
Odessa	0	9	1	10
Kiev	8	7	0	15
	25	45	4	74
Moscow	2	7	1	10
Ural–Volga	1	9	0	10
	3	16	1	20
North Caucasus	1	8	0	9
Trans-Caucasus	0	12	1	13
Turkestan	1	16	0	17
	2	36	1	39
Siberian	0	8	0	8
Trans-Baikal	2	11	0	13*
Far Eastern	3	21	0	24***
Mongolia	2	2	0	4**
	7	42	0	50

*does not include experimental "unified army" corps, each consisting of about two divisions, which have only recently been disbanded
**troop withdrawals underway
***includes one coastal defense division
According to *The Military Balance 1989–90* (London: International Institute for Strategic Studies, 1989), 28–42.

50. For example, see D. T. Iazov, "V interesakh obshchei bezopasnosti mira" [In the interest of general security and peace], *Izvestiia* [News] (February 27, 1989), 3.
   In January 1990 at the Vienna Doctrinal meetings, the Soviet delegation stated that

THE MILITARY STRATEGY OF THE SOVIET UNION

new motorized rifle divisions would have between 85 and 155 tanks and would be organized with two to three motorized regiments equipped with BMPs and one to two with BTRs. See Graham Turbiville, Jr., *Trip Report–Seminar on Military Doctrine* (Ft. Leavenworth, KS: Soviet Army Studies Office, 9 February 1990).

51. Based on the declared tank strength of 155, new Soviet motorized rifle divisions will probably contain five tank battalions with 31 tanks each. One battalion will be assigned to each of the four motorized rifle regiments, to employ as a single subunit or to subdivide on the basis of one tank company for each regimental motorized rifle battalion (to form a combined-arms battalion). The fifth battalion will serve as a separate tank battalion under division control (similar to the former separate tank battalion of motorized rifle divisions of forward groups of forces).

52. See Appendix 3 for the parameters of the ongoing debate.

53. Glantz, *Soviet Military Deception*. The aforementioned case of the 1946 GOFG operational plan is also an example of concealing wartime force structure in peacetime.

54. Chart based on the following sources: *Direktivy komandovaniia frontov Krasnoi Armii 1917–22 gg* [Directives of the Red Army's front commands 1917–22], (Moscow: Voenizdat, 1978); Berkhin, *Voennaia reforma*; V. A. Anfilov, *Proval blitskriga* [The failure of blitzkrieg] (Moscow: "Nauka", 1974), *50 let Sovetskikh vooruzhennykh sil* [50 years of the Soviet armed forces]; I. Kh. Bagramian (ed.), *Istoriia voin i voennogo iskusstva* [History of war and military art] (Moscow: Voenizdat, 1970); *The Military Balance* (London: International Institute for Strategic Studies, 1965, 1975, 1989). See also Erickson.

55. Berkhin, "O territorial'no"; Berkhin, *Voennaia reforma*; Erickson.

56. Pavlovsky, 65; Bagramian, *Istoriia voin*; Anfilov; Tiushkevich, 238.

57. In particular, the U.S. and British volunteer systems. The Soviet navy has begun experimenting with volunteers in selected areas of service. See "Officers, Deputies Discuss Professional Military", *Moscow World Service 1030 GMT 8 March 90* states "General Nikitin of the General Staff reported that the navy has already prepared an experiment in which some of the sailors will serve by contract."

58. The Soviets employed nuclei cadre regiments in GOFG between 1946 and 1949 and converted fortified regions into rifle divisions and *vice versa* in Manchuria between 1939 and 1946.

59. Future Czech Army mobilization plans are based on maintaining a peacetime force of ten divisions, five ready divisions at 50 to 70 per cent strength and five reduced strength (cadre) divisions at ten to 22 per cent strength. The former will be mobilizable in two to three days. The latter will form as equipment storage sites (3) or training centers (2) and can mobilize in 17 days. During mobilization five additional divisions will form as spin-offs from existing divisions, using "second equipment sets". Thus, a peacetime force of 10 divisions can evolve after mobilization into a wartime force of 15 divisions. See Graham Turbiville, Jr., *Trip Report–Seminar on Military Doctrine* (Ft. Leavenworth, KS: Soviet Army Studies Office, 9 February 1990). This report contains comments made by the Czech delegation at Vienna Doctrinal discussions 22–26 January 1990. In all likelihood, the Czech system is based on similar Soviet practices.

CHAPTER 8

1. V. V. Zhurkin, S. A. Karaganov, and A. A. Kortunov, "Vyzovy bezopostnosti–starye i novye" [Challenges to security–old and new], *Kommunist*, No. 1 (January 1988), 43.

2. A more disturbing model, which the Soviets have understandably not advanced, is the Manchurian model. In this case, a defensive force structure and posture is rapidly converted into an effective offensive one through a combination of *khitrost'* [strategem], *maskirovka* (deception), and a massive covert strategic and operational regrouping of forces with the use of fortified regions to cover the mobilization. This extreme example

replicates numerous documented cases of similar transformations during operations on the Eastern Front in the Second World War. In a future context, this model embraces the circumstances of creeping up to war over an extended period. Inherent in it are issues such as transition to war and mobilization of the front and rear. Soviet military theorists and planners continue to assess this three-*front* strategic operation in detail. L. N. Vnotchenko, *Pobeda na dal'nem vostoka* [Victory in the Far East] (Moscow: Voenizdat, 1966), is one of the best book-length Soviet assessments of the Manchurian operation, while David M. Glantz, *August Storm: The Soviet 1945 Strategic Offensive in Manchuria*, Leavenworth Papers, Vol. 7 and 8 (Ft. Leavenworth, KS: Combat Studies Institute, 1983), is the most substantial Western treatment.

APPENDIX 1

SOVIET MOBILIZATION IN THE SECOND WORLD WAR

In the last analysis, effective and extensive Soviet mobilization plans on the eve of Operation Barbarossa proved to be the decisive factor in the Soviet Union's ultimate victory over Germany. At each critical strategic turning-point, particularly at Moscow in December 1941 and Stalingrad in November 1942, newly mobilized Soviet forces, which appeared on the battlefield just as the Germans had expended their offensive strength and reserves, turned the tide in the Soviets' favor, halted the German offensive, and provided forces for Soviet counteroffensives. Compounding this factor was the congenital German tendency to underestimate Soviet mobilization potential and the subsequent failure of German intelligence to detect critical newly-formed and concentrating Soviet strategic reserves.

What then was the scale of that German intelligence failure? During the planning period for Operation Barbarossa, German intelligence underassessed the active strength of the Red Army and maintained a flawed picture of its composition, in particular *vis à vis* the Soviets' armored force. Curiously enough, this had not been the case when German planning commenced in summer 1940, but it became increasingly true as the Germans apparently failed to detect Soviet General Staff mobilization measures implemented throughout the ensuing year (or, as the Soviets referred to it, the "creeping up to war").

In August 1940 the Germans estimated Soviet military strength at 151 infantry divisions, 32 cavalry divisions, and 38 mechanized brigades, at a time when actual Soviet ground force strength was 152 rifle divisions, 26 cavalry divisions, and nine newly forming mechanized corps (each composed of two tank divisions and one motorized rifle division).[1] Although German estimates of Soviet regular infantry and cavalry forces were close to accurate, the Germans began a long-lasting process of underestimating Soviet armored strength. Against this force the Germans postulated their own attack force of 147 divisions (24 panzer, one cavalry, 12 motorized infantry, and 110 infantry), a force which would remain stable throughout subsequent planning.[2]

APPENDIX 1

The final German assessment of Soviet strength, dated 11 June 1941, estimated a force of 175 infantry divisions (15 motorized), 33½ cavalry divisions, seven tank divisions, 43 motorized and armored brigades (equivalent to 15 divisions), and seven parachute brigades. At this time the Red Army active strength was 196 rifle divisions, 13 cavalry divisions, 61 tank divisions (58 with mechanized corps and three separate), and 31 motorized rifle divisions (29 with mechanized corps and two separate). Of this total the Germans assessed Soviet strength in the border military districts at 125 infantry divisions, 22½ cavalry divisions, seven tank divisions, and 34 mobile brigades (a total of about 150 divisions) whereas actual Soviet strength was 171 divisions of all types. In the remainder of European Russia, German intelligence estimated about 32 Soviet divisions, when, in fact, about 100 existed. The Germans credited the Red Army with the ability to raise a maximum of 209 new divisions.[3]

These figures underscore two major faults in German assessments of existing Soviet military strength. First, the Germans did not adequately keep track of the scale of Soviet readiness efforts. While this was true of military districts along the border, it was even more pronounced in the internal military districts where mobilization could be better concealed. Second, the Germans had an inadequate appreciation of Soviet force restructuring, in particular restructuring associated with the Soviet mechanization program. As late as 22 June, German intelligence continued to count older Soviet tank brigades and cavalry divisions without realizing that most of these had reformed into tank and mechanized divisions and mechanized corps. By 22 June the Germans had identified one mechanized corps each in the Baltic, Special Western, and Special Kiev Military Districts out of the 16 actually there (in various stages of formation). Nor did the Germans detect the large antitank brigades formed in the border districts designated to cooperate with the new mechanized corps.[4] It is true, however, that German operational and tactical proficiency largely compensated for this intelligence failure. Nevertheless, the failure established a pattern which would persist in the future with inevitable negative effects.

Far more serious than this problem was the German failure to appreciate the size and efficiency of the Soviet mobilization system. German estimates tended to look only at active Soviet forces, that is, those maintained in peacetime at various levels of combat readiness. They did not, however, detect or closely examine Soviet mobilization or spin-off divisions, which had seemingly insignificant cadre and equipment complements in peacetime. This was perhaps understandable in light of German estimates that the Barbarossa operation would be over in about four months, before the Soviets could generate significant new

307

combat-ready forces. The German High Command reasoned that any new Soviet units could be dealt with in successive stages of the operation.

To appreciate the scale of this German failure, it is only necessary to review the actual Soviet mobilization record. Soviet armed forces strength on 22 June 1941 was 20 armies (14 along the western border and six in the Far East), 303 divisions (81 in the process of forming), and about 5.0 million men.[5] By 1 July 1941 the Soviets had called 5.3 million men into military service. Between 22 June and 1 December 1941, increased personnel call-ups permitted the Soviets to field 291 new divisions and 94 brigades. Of this total 70 were brought to strength and transferred westward from internal military districts and 27 were dispatched westward from the Far East, Central Asia, and Trans-Baikal Military Districts. The remaining 194 divisions and 94 brigades were formed anew from cadre in the mobilization base. Subsequently, in 1942 the Soviets formed 50 new divisions and reformed 67 divisions.[6]

By November 1942, the Soviet mobilization system had created a total of 367 rifle divisions, 193 rifle brigades, and 118 tank or mechanized brigades. This was followed by the creation of 42 divisions and 44 brigades between November 1942 and December 1943. While prewar German estimates had postulated an opposing force of up to 300 divisions, in fact, by December 1941 the Soviets had been able to mobilize and deploy a force of over 600 divisions. This permitted the Soviets to lose well over 100 divisions during the initial period of war and still survive.[7]

The Soviets mobilized and deployed these forces in waves of reserve armies throughout the first year of war. The wave effect put at the disposal of the *Stavka* (High Command) sizeable fresh strategic reserves after each operational disaster and provided staying power for the Red Army.

The first wave of Soviet reserve armies mobilized before the outbreak of war. Between 13 May and 22 June, to bolster existing forces in the border military districts, the Soviets deployed forward five armies from interior military districts (16th, 19th, 20th, 21st, 22nd), two of which closed into the forward area in June and the remainder in early July. After the German offensive swallowed up these armies, along with covering armies along the border, in July 1941 a new wave of eight Soviet reserve armies took up positions east of Smolensk, where they were joined in August by a ninth reserve army (43rd) (plus three more on the northern and southern flanks).[8] The presence of these armies in July and August prompted the stiff Soviet resistance around Smolensk that slowed German progress and contributed to the German decision to strike at Kiev in order to clear their southern flank.

In early October 1941, after the Soviets had fielded three more armies, the Germans broke through Soviet positions near Viaz'ma and Briansk and, by mid-November, approached Moscow, certain that one final successful lunge would secure the Soviet capital. As Soviet resistance on the approaches to Moscow stiffened, Stalin again marshaled his strategic reserves, amassing in the Moscow region six reserve armies, which he ultimately employed to spearhead the Soviet December counteroffensive. Simultaneously, on the flanks the Soviet threw into combat four more reserve armies to stiffen defenses in the Leningrad and Rostov regions (see Figure 46).[9]

This mobilization and deployment process continued even after the German 1941 strategic drive had been blunted. In spring 1942, anticipating a new German strategic thrust, the Soviet High Command formed ten new reserve armies (numbered 1–10) and an experimental 3rd Tank Army (see Figure 47). It deployed the mostly conscript reserve armies on a broad front from Vologda in the north to Saratov and the Volga River in the south. While German Operation "Blau" unfolded, propelling German forces across southern Russia into the Don River bend and on to Stalingrad and the Caucasus, the *Stavka* renumbered these armies and threw them into combat, primarily in the Voronezh and Stalingrad regions. At the same time, the *Stavka* formed three additional tank armies (1st, 4th and 5th), which participated in the summer and fall operations in southern Russia.

All the while, additional Soviet armies formed on the base of armies defeated or depleted in earlier operations (for example, in April 1942 53rd Army was created from 34th Army, in October 1942 65th Army formed from badly damaged 4th Tank Army). The force generation process also drew NKVD forces into the regular force structure when, in October 1942, 70th Army formed in the Ural Military District on the base of NKVD troops from the Far Eastern, Trans-Baikal, and Central Asian Military Districts.[10]

After November 1942 the process of forming new reserves slowed, in part because of the already existing Soviet numerical superiority. From November 1942 to December 1943, the Soviets created two new combined-arms armies and three new tank armies and a total of 42 divisions and 44 brigades. From that time forth, most new conscripts were used to fill existing formations.[11]

The net result of this comprehensive mobilization program was Soviet creation between 13 May 1941 and December 1943 of over 40 armies of various types and composition. The formation and almost constant maintenance of a sizeable strategic reserve enabled the Soviet High Command to survive crisis after crisis in the first 18 months of war by fielding fresh troops after each operation had run its natural course, and

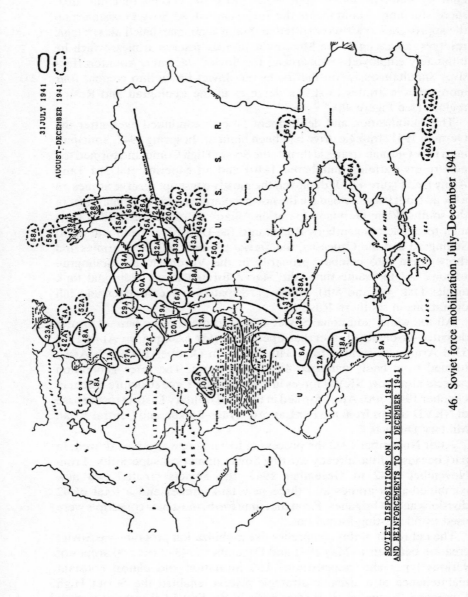

46. Soviet force mobilization, July–December 1941

47. Soviet force mobilization, 1942

311

at a time when German forces were most vulnerable. This, in large part, explained the extraordinary staying power of the Red Army.

NOTES

1. For German estimates of Soviet strength, see "The German Campaign in Russia, Planning and Operations (1940–41)," *DA Pamphlet No. 20–261a*, (Washington, D.C.: Department of the Army, March 1955), 7; Soviet figures in V. A. Anfilov, *Proval blitskriga* [The failure of blitzkrieg] (Moscow: "Nauka", 1974), 117–24, and numerous other sources.
2. Ibid., 7.
3. Ibid., 42. Soviet strength figures from V. Danilov, "Sovetskoe glavnoe komandovanie v predverii otechestvennoi voiny" [The Soviet high command on the threshold of the patriotic war], *Novaia i noveishaia istoriia* [New and newest history], No. 6 (November–December 1988), 4. German estimates from captured German documents contained in SM, Issue 18 (Moscow: Voenizdat, 1960), 86–8, 134–7 (formerly classified top secret).
4. See *Lage der Roten Armee im europaischen Russland abgeschlossen am 20.VI.41*. Abteilung Fremde Herre Ost, H3/1346, NAM T–78, 677, which shows all assessed Soviet unit locations in the border military districts.
5. Danilov, 4.
6. V. Zemskov, "Nekotorye voprosy sozdaniia i ispol'zovaniia stratigicheskikh reservov" [Some questions of the creation and use of strategic reserves], *VIZh* (Military-historical journal), No. 10 (October 1971), 14; A. G. Khor'kov, "Nekotorye voprosy strategicheskogo razvertyvaniia Sovetskikh Vooruzhennykh Sil v nachale Velikoi Otechestvennoi voiny" [Some questions of the strategic deployment of the Soviet armed forces at the beginning of the Great Patriotic War], *VIZh*, No. 1 (January 1986), 13.
7. V. Golubovich, "Sozdanie strategicheskikh reservov" [The creation of strategic reserves], *VIZh*, No. 4 (April 1977), 12–19. Soviet losses during 1941 are difficult to determine because many divisions listed by the Germans as destroyed were, in fact, reformed around surviving remnants of the former divisions. It is clear that the Soviets lost more than 100 division equivalents.
8. Zakharov, *General'nyi shtab*, 258–62, provides details of the April–July mobilization process. Subsequent mobilization described by Khor'kov, 11–13; and A. I. Evseev, "Manevr strategicheskimi rezervami v pervom periode Velikoi Otechestvennoi voiny" [The maneuver of strategic reserves in the first period of the Great Patriotic War], *VIZh*, No. 3 (March 1986), 11–13.
9. Evseev, 12–14. See also Robert G. Poirier and Albert Z. Conner, *Red Army Order of Battle in the Great Patriotic War*, draft manuscript.
10. Poirier and Connor; *SVE*.
11. Evseev, 13–14. By 31 December 1943, the Soviets had created 11 guards armies from existing armies, as well as five tank armies and a fifth shock army.

SOVIET STRATEGIC OPERATIONS IN THE SECOND WORLD WAR

No.	Name of Operation and Dates	Field Forces Involved in Operation	Opposing Enemy Forces	Scope of Operation		Results of Operation
				Along Front, km	In Depth, km	
1	2	3	4	5	6	7
	First Period of War (22 June 1941-18 November 1942)					
1	Defensive operation in Baltic (22 Jun-9 Jul 41)	NW Front, Baltic Fleet	Army Group North, part of 3d Panzer Group & 9th Army of Army Group Center, 1st Air Fleet, German and Finnish Navies on Baltic Sea	350-450	400-450	Enemy plan thwarted to destroy troops of front in border area. By counterstrikes of III and XII Mechanized Corps and by defense on intermediate lines, great damage caused to advancing enemy grouping, its strike force weakened and rate of advance declined. This allowed our troops to prepare defensive lines in depth and bring up fresh reserves.
2	Defensive operation in Belorussia (22 Jun-9 Jul 41)	Western Front, Pinsk Naval Flotilla	Army Group Center, 2d Air Fleet	450-800	450-600	By resistance on frontier and intermediate lines, by counterstrikes of mechanized corps and rifle formations great damage caused to main Wehrmacht grouping, its rate of advance slowed down. This provided opportunity to deploy troops of second strategic echelon on line of Western Dvina and Dnieper from Kraslava to Loyev.

3	Defensive operation in Western Ukraine (22 Jun-6 Jul 41)	SW and Southern Fronts, part of Black Sea Fleet	Army Group South, VIII Hungarian Corps, 4th Air Fleet	600-700	300-350	By resistance on frontier and intermediate defensive lines, by counterstrikes of mechanized corps in areas of Dubno, Lutsk and Rovno, great damage caused to enemy, the offensive of its main grouping checked and this made it possible to withdraw troops for taking up fortified areas on old frontier on line of Korosten, Novograd-Volynskiy, Shepetovka, Starokonstantinov, Proskurov.
4	Defensive operation in Arctic and Karelia (29 Jun-10 Oct 41)	Part of Northern Front from 23 Aug 41, Karelian Front), Northern Fleet, White Sea Naval Flotilla	German Army Norway, III Finnish Army Corps, Finnish Army Karelia, part of 5th Air Fleet and Finnish Air Forces, operations group of German Navy	800	50-150	In stubborn defensive battles Soviet troops halted enemy offensive, defeated it and thwarted plan to capture Murmansk and Murmansk Railroad.
5	Kiev Defensive Operation (7 Jul-26 Sep 41)	SW Front, part of Bryansk and Southern Fronts, Dnieper detachment of Pinsk Naval Flotilla	Army Group South, part of Army Group Center, 4th Air Fleet	300	600	During more than 2 months of defensive battles great damage caused to enemy and forced German Command to achieve its aims on this axis to use a portion of Army Group Center (2d Army and 2d Panzer Group) thereby checking enemy advance on main (Moscow) axis.

315

1	2	3	4	5	6	7
6	Leningrad Defensive Operation (10 Jul-30 Sep 41)	Northern (from 23 Aug 41 Leningrad), NW Fronts, Baltic Fleet, Ladoga Naval Flotilla	Army Group North, SE Army of Finns, part of Finnish Air Force and Navy	450	70-300	In stubborn fighting enemy was defeated, its advance halted, and plan to capture Leningrad without a halt checked.
7	Smolensk Engagement (Smolensk Defensive Operation) (10 Jul-10 Sep 41)	Western, Central, Bryansk and Reserve Fronts	Army Group Center, part of 16th Army of Army Group North, 2d Air Fleet	600-650	200-250	Major defeat to enemy, its advance checked on main axis for 2 months and this played important role in thwarting the plan for a "blitzkrieg" against USSR.
8	Donbass-Rostov Defensive Operation (29 Sep-16 Nov 41)	Southern Front and portion of SW Front, Azov Naval Flotilla	Army Group South, 4th Air Fleet	400-670	150-300	Enemy plan thwarted to surround and destroy Southern Front and continue offensive to Caucasus. Enemy suffered heavy losses and its offensive halted.
9	Moscow Defensive Operation (30 Sep-5 Dec 41)	Western, Kalinin, Reserve and Bryansk Fronts	Army Group Center, part of 16th Army of Army Group North, 2d Air Fleet	700-1100	300-350	Major defeat dealt to main enemy grouping and its offensive halted. Conditions created for going over to counteroffensive and defeating enemy at Moscow.
10	Tikhvin Offensive Operation (10 Nov-30 Dec 41)	5th Army of Leningrad Front, 4th and 52d Separate Armies (from 17 Dec 41)	16th Army, part of 18th Army of Army Group North, part of 1st Air Fleet	300-350	100-120	Major damage done to 10 enemy divisions, significant territory liberated, and enemy plan thwarted to completely isolate Leningrad from nation and

	combined into Volkhov Front), Novgorod Army Group of NW Front				starve it out. Operation helped establish conditions for going over by Soviet troops to counteroffensive at Moscow.
11	Rostov Offensive Operation (17 Nov-2 Dec 41)	Southern Front, 56th Separate Army (from 23 Nov 41 part of Southern Front)	170	80	Major defeat to enemy 1st Panzer Army, its troops pushed back 80 km from Rostov and enemy breakthrough to Caucasus prevented. Operation helped establish conditions for going over of our troops to counteroffensive at Moscow.
12	Moscow Offensive Operation (5 Dec 41-7 Jan 42)	Western and Kalinin Fronts, part of SW Front, Air Forces Ost Bryansk Front (from 21 Dec 41)	1000	100-250	Soviet troops defeated enemy assault groupings, routed 38 enemy divisions, including 15 panzer and motorized, advanced 100-250 km to west, liberated over 11,000 population points, including cities of Volokolamsk, Kalinin, Kaluga, Klin and so forth. Direct threat to Moscow eliminated.
13	Kerch-Feodosiya Landing Operation (25 Dec 41- 2 Jan 42)	Transcaucasus (from 30 Dec 41, Caucasian) Front, and part of 4th Air Black Sea Fleet, Fleet Azov Naval Flotilla	250	100-110	Amphibious force landed on Kerch Peninsula, consisting of 2 combined arms armies which advanced 100-110 km and captured important bridgehead, where Crimean Front was deployed. This forced enemy to break off offensive against Sevastopol and shift part of forces to fight Crimean Front.

1	2	3	4	5	6	7
14	Rzhev-Vyazma Offensive Operation (8 Jan-20 Apr 42)	Kalinin and Western Fronts	Army Group Center, Air Force Operations Group Ost	650	80-250	Soviet troops dealt major defeat to enemy, completely liberated Moscow and Tula Oblasts, many rayons of Kalinin and Smolensk Oblasts. In course of operation, enemy lost 330,000 men. Flanks of Army Group Center were deeply enveloped by our troops.
15	Voronezh-Voroshilovgrad Defensive Operation (28 Jun-24 Jul 42)	Bryansk, Voronezh (from 7 Jul 42), SW and Southern Fronts	Army Group South, from 9 Jul 42, Army Groups A and B, 4th Air Fleet	900	150-400	In course of stubborn fighting, enemy plans thwarted to defeat main forces of Soviet troops on southwestern sector. Its assault grouping suffered heavy losses.
16	Stalingrad Defensive Operation (17 Jul-18 Nov 42)	Stalingrad (Don), SE (Stalingrad) Fronts. Volga Naval Flotilla	Army Group B, part of 4th Air Fleet	250-500	150	Enemy defeated, its offensive stopped and conditions created for going over of our troops to counteroffensive.
17	Northern Caucasus Defensive Operation (25 Jul-31 Dec 42)	Southern (until 28 Jul 42), Northern Caucasus and Transcaucasian Fronts, Black Sea Fleet, Azov Naval Flotilla	Army Group A, part of 4th Air Fleet, German and Romanian Navies on Black Sea	320-1000	400-800	As a result of operation, enemy offensive halted, enemy suffered great losses, and its plans to capture oil fields of Caucasus and bring Turkey into war against USSR were thwarted.

Second Period of War (19 November 1942-31 December 1943)

#	Operation	Forces/Fronts			Description
18	Stalingrad Offensive Operation (19 Nov 42- 2 Feb 43)	SW, Don and Stalingrad Fronts, 22 Nov 42, Army Group Don), 4th Air Fleet	850	150-200	Main forces of German 6th and 4th Panzer Armies surrounded and destroyed, 3d and 4th Romanian Armies and 8th Italian Army defeated. Enemy losses were over 800,000 men, up to 2,000 tanks and assault guns, over 10,000 guns and mortars, around 3,000 aircraft. Soviet Army firmly took strategic initiative.
19	Northern Caucasus Offensive Operation (1 Jan- 4 Feb 43)	Transcaucasian, Northern Caucasus Fronts, part of Southern Front, Black Sea Fleet	840	300-600	Army Group A defeated, its troops pushed 300-600 km to west, and threat to Caucasus oil fields lifted.
20	Operation to break Leningrad blockade (12 Jan-30 Jan 43)	Part of Leningrad, Volkhov Fronts and Baltic Fleet	45	60	In course of offensive, enemy blockade broken and overland communications of Leningrad with rest of country restored. Enemy plan thwarted to starve out millions of people in city.
21	Voronezh-Kharkov Offensive Operation (13 Jan- 3 Mar 43)	Voronezh Front, part of Bryansk and SW Fronts	250-400	360-520	Soviet troops dealt major defeat to Army Group B. The 2d Hungarian Army and 8th Italian Army which were part of it were almost completely destroyed. Significant territory and a number of major industrial and administrative centers such as Voronezh, Kursk, Belgorod and Kharkov were liberated from occupiers.

1	2	3	4	5	6	7
22	Kharkov Defensive Operation (19 Feb-25 Mar 43)	SW and Voronezh Fronts	Army Group South, part of Army Group Center, 4th Air Fleet	300-350	100-150	Enemy suffered heavy losses, its counteroffensive stopped and enemy plan to surround our troops in Kursk area thwarted.
23	Kursk Defensive Operation (5 Jul-23 Jul 43)	Central, Voronezh and Steppe Fronts	2d and 9th Armies of Army Group Center, 4th Panzer Army and Operations Group Kampf, Army Group South, 4th and 6th Air Fleets	550	10-35	In course of defensive engagements, enemy assault groups were ground down, bled white and halted. Conditions created for going over to counteroffensive by our troops.
24	Orel Offensive Operation (12 Jul-18 Aug 43)	Bryansk, Central Fronts and part of Western Front	2d Panzer and 9th Armies of Army Group Center, 6th Air Fleet	400	150	15 enemy divisions defeated. Soviet troops advance 115 km and liberate significant territory from occupiers. Strongly fortified enemy bridgehead eliminated from which it advanced in Kursk Battle.
25	Belgorod-Kharkov Offensive Operation (3 Aug-23 Aug 43)	Voronezh and Steppe Fronts	4th Panzer Army and Operations Group Kampf of Army Group Center, part of 4th Air Fleet	300-400	140	15 enemy divisions defeated. Our troops advanced 140 km in depth, having widened breach to 400 km, and liberated Kharkov Industrial Area.
26	Smolensk Offensive Operation (7 Aug-2 Oct 43)	Kalinin and Western Fronts	3d Panzer, 4th and 9th Armies of Army Group Center, 6th Air Fleet	400	200-250	Smolensk and part of Kalinin Oblasts liberated, start made to liberation of Belorussia. 17 enemy divisions were defeated and 14 divisions suffered heavy losses.

No.	Operation	Fronts	German Forces			Results
27	Donbass Offensive Operation (13 Aug-22 Sep 43)	SW and Southern Fronts	1st Panzer and 6th Armies, part of 8th Army of Army Group South and 4th Air Fleet	450	250-300	Soviet troops defeated 13 enemy divisions, liberated Donbass, reached approaches to Dnieper. Major economic area returned to nation.
28	Chernigov-Poltava Offensive Operation (26 Aug-30 Sep 43)	Central, Voronezh and Steppe Fronts	2d Army of Army Group Center, 4th Panzer and 8th Armies of Army Group South, part of 4th and 6th Air Fleets	600	250-300	Troops of 3 fronts reached Dnieper and captured bridgehead on right bank. In course of operation 17 enemy divisions defeated.
29	Novorossivsk-Taman Offensive Operation (10 Sep-9 Oct 43)	Northern Caucasus Front, Black Sea Fleet, Azov Naval Flotilla	17th Army of Army Group A, portion of 4th Air Fleet	80	150	Liberation of Caucasus completed, important enemy bridgehead eliminated which gave it good conditions for defense of Crimea. Liberation of Novorossivsk and Taman Peninsula significantly improved basing of Black Sea Fleet and created good conditions for attacking the Crimean enemy grouping from the sea and across the Kerch Strait.
30	Lower Dnieper Offensive Operation (26 Sep-20 Dec 43)	Steppe (Second Ukrainian), SW (Third Ukrainian), Southern (Fourth Ukrainian) Fronts	1st Panzer and 8th Armies of Army Group South, 6th Army of Army Group A, 4th Air Fleet	750-800	100-300	Troops of 3 fronts complete liberation of Left-Bank Ukraine in lower courses of Dnieper, blockade from land the Crimean enemy troop grouping and capture bridgehead on western bank of Dnieper up to 400 km along front and 100 km in depth.

1	2	3	4	5	6	7
31	Kiev Offensive Operation (3 Nov-13 Nov 43)	First Ukrainian Front	2d Army of Army Group Center, 4th Panzer Army, part of 8th Army of Army Group South and 4th Air Fleet	320-500	150	Troops of front liberated capital of Ukraine, Kiev, and formed strategic bridgehead on right bank of Dnieper more than 300 km along front and 150 km in depth playing important role in carrying out operations to liberate Right-Bank Ukraine. In course of operation 15 enemy divisions defeated.

Third Period of War (January 1944–May 1945)

1	2	3	4	5	6	7
32	Offensive Operation to liberate Right-Bank Ukraine (24 Dec 43-17 Apr 44)	First, Second, Third and Fourth Ukrainian and Second Belorussian Fronts	Army Groups South and A, 4th Air Fleet, Romanian Air Force	1300-1400	250-450	Soviet troops liberated Right-Bank Ukraine, reach Carpathian foothills and state frontier with Romania, split southern wing of strategic enemy front. In course of operation 10 divisions and 1 brigade were destroyed and over 59 divisions suffered losses from one-half to three-quarters of personnel.
33	Leningrad-Novgorod Offensive Operation (14 Jan-1 Mar 44)	Leningrad, Volkhov and Second Baltic Fronts. Baltic Fleet	Army Group North, 1st Air Fleet, Naval Operations Group on Baltic	600	220-280	Major defeat dealt to Army Group North. 26 divisions routed, including 3 destroyed. Leningrad completely freed from enemy blockade.

APPENDIX 2

No.	Operation	Soviet Forces	Enemy Forces			Results
34	Crimean Offensive Operation (5 Apr-12 May 44)	Fourth Ukrainian Front, Separate Maritime Army, Black Sea Fleet, Azov Naval Flotilla	17th Army of Army Group Southern Ukraine, part of 4th Air Fleet, Romanian Air Force, German and Romanian Navies on Black Sea	160	200-260	Enemy 17th Army (to 12 divisions) completely routed, Crimea liberated, better conditions for basing and combat of Black Sea Fleet.
35	Vyborg-Petrozovodsk Offensive Operation (10 Jun-9 Aug 44)	Part of Leningrad and Karelian Fronts, Baltic Fleet, Ladoga and Onega Naval Flotillas	Troops of Finnish Operations Groups Mosel, Karelian Isthmus and Olonets, Finnish Air Force	280	110-250	Major defeat to enemy troops defending Karelian Isthmus and Southern Karelia and this created conditions for liberation of Arctic and withdrawal of Finland from war.
36	Belorussian Offensive Operation (23 Jun-29 Aug 44)	First Baltic, Third, Second and First Belorussian Fronts, Dnieper Naval Flotilla, 1st Polish Army	Army Group Center, portion of 16th Army of Army Group North and 4th Panzer Army of Army Group Northern Ukraine, 6th Air Fleet	1100	550-600	Defeat dealt to Army Group Center with 17 divisions and 3 brigades destroyed and 50 divisions losing over one-half of personnel. Belorussia and part of Lithuania liberated, good conditions created for attacking enemy groupings in Baltic, East Prussia and Poland.
37	Lwow-Sandomierz Offensive Operation (13 Jul-29 Aug 44)	First Ukrainian Front	Army Group Northern Ukraine, part of 4th Air Fleet	440	350	Defeat of Army Group Northern Ukraine, western oblasts of Ukraine and southeastern regions of Poland liberated from occupiers. Major bridgehead captured on west bank of Vistula and of great importance for subsequent offensive on Silesian axis.

1	2	3	4	5	6	7
38	Iasi-Kishinev Offensive Operation (20 Aug-29 Aug 44)	Second and Third Ukrainian Fronts, Black Sea Fleet and Danube Naval Flotilla	Army Group Southern Ukraine, part of 4th Air Fleet, Romanian Air Force	500	300-320	Army Group Southern Ukraine completely destroyed: 22 German divisions destroyed and virtually all Romanian divisions on the front routed. Moldavia liberated and Romania withdraws from Nazi bloc, declaring war on Germany.
39	Eastern Carpathian Offensive Operation (8 Sep-28 Oct 44)	Fourth Ukrainian Front, portion of First Ukrainian Front, I Czechoslovak Army Corps	Army Group Heinrici (German 1st Panzer Army and 1st Hungarian Army), portion of 4th Air Fleet	400	50-110	Defeat of Army Group Heinrici. Ciscarpathian Ukraine liberated. Soviet troops, having crossed Main Carpathian Range enter Czechoslovak territory.
40	Baltic Offensive Operation (14 Sep-24 Nov 44)	First, Second and Third Baltic Fronts, part of Leningrad and Third Belorussian Fronts, Baltic Fleet	Army Group North, part of 3d Panzer Army of Army Group Center, 1st Air Fleet and portion of 6th Air Fleet	1000	300	Liberation of Baltic (except Kurland) completed. Of 79 enemy formations existing at start of operation in Baltic, 29 were defeated and rest sealed off in Kurland.
41	Belgrad Offensive Operation (28 Sep-20 Oct 44)	Third Ukrainian Front, portion of Second Ukrainian Front, troops of Yugoslav PLA, 1st, 2d and 4th Bulgarian Armies, Danube Naval Flotilla	Army Group Serbia of Army Group F, part of Army Group E, Air Force Operations Group Southeast	400-620	200	Army Group Serbia of Army Group F defeated, defeat of Army Group E, eastern regions of Yugoslavia and its capital Belgrad liberated. Enemy forced to hurriedly pull troops out of Greece over Yugoslav mountain roads.

324

42	Petsamo-Kirkenes Offensive Operation (7 Oct-29 Oct 44)	Karelian Front and Northern Fleet	20th German Mountain Army, 5th Air Fleet, German Navy in Berents Sea	80	150	Soviet troops under harsh Arctic conditions defeat enemy, reach frontier with Norway and liberate a portion of its territory, including city of Kirkenes, from occupiers. In course of operation around 30,000 men destroyed and 156 enemy ships and vessels sunk.
43	Budapest Offensive Operation (29 Oct 44-13 Feb 45)	Second and Third Ukrainian Fronts, Danube Naval Flotilla, 1st and 4th Romanian Armies	Troops of Army Group South, portion of 4th Air Fleet, Hungarian Air Force	420	250-400	Enemy troop liberated central regions of Hungary and its capital Budapest. A 188,000-strong enemy grouping surrounded and destroyed. Hungary out of war, good conditions created for offensive in Czechoslovakia and Austria.
44	Vistula-Oder Offensive Operation (12 Jan-3 Feb 45)	First Belorussian and First Ukrainian Fronts, 1st Polish Army	Troops of Army Group A (from 26 Jan 45, Army Group Center), 6th Air Fleet	500	500	Soviet troops liberated larger portion of Polish territory, entered German territory and reached Oder, having captured number of bridgeheads on its western bank. In course of operation 35 enemy divisions were destroyed and 25 routed.
45	Western Carpathian Offensive Operation (12 Jan-18 Feb 45)	Fourth and Second Ukrainian Fronts, 4th Romanian Armies	1st Panzer Army, part of 17th Army, 1st Hungarian Army of Army Group A (from 26 Jan 45, Army Group Center), 6th and 8th Armies of Army Group South, portion of 4th Air Fleet	440	170-230	In course of operation, Soviet troops defeat enemy, liberate southern regions of Poland, a portion of Czechoslovak territory and cross Western Carpathians.

1	2	3	4	5	6	7
46	East Prussian Offensive Operation (13 Jan-25 Apr 45)	Second and Third Belorussian Fronts, portion of First Baltic Front and Baltic Fleet	Army Group Center (from 26 Jan 45, Army Group North), portion of 6th Air Fleet, German Navy on Baltic Sea	550	120-200	Soviet troops capture East Prussia. In course of operation 25 enemy divisions destroyed, 12 divisions suffer heavy losses. German Navy deprived of number of major naval bases sharply impeding supply of Kurland enemy grouping.
47	East Pomeranian Operation (10 Feb-4 Apr 45)	First and Second Belorussian Fronts, part of Baltic Fleet	Army Group Vistula, part of 6th Air Fleet, German Navy on Baltic Sea	460	130-150	21 enemy divisions and 8 brigades defeated, threat eliminated of its counterstrike in flank and rear of First Belorussian Front, East Pomerania cleared of Nazi troops. Soviet troops reach Baltic Seacoast and secure flank of main strategic grouping of our troops fighting on Berlin axis.
48	Vienna Offensive Operation (16 Mar-15 Apr 45)	Third Ukrainian Front, part of Second Ukrainian Front, Danube Naval Flotilla, 1st Bulgarian Army	Troops of Army Group South, part of Army Group E, 4th Air Fleet	230	150-250	Liberation of Hungary completed, enemy cleared out of southern regions of Czechoslovakia and Eastern Austria with its capital Vienna. In course of operation Soviet troops defeated 32 enemy divisions.

49	Berlin Offensive Operation (16 Apr–8 May 45)	Troops of First and Second Belorussian Fronts and First Ukrainian Front, part of Baltic Fleet, Dnieper Naval Flotilla, 1st and 2d Polish Armies	300	100-120	Army Group Vistula, 4th Panzer and 17th Armies of Army Group Center, 6th Air Fleet, Air Fleet Reich	In course of operation Soviet troops defeat 70 infantry divisions, 23 panzer and motorized divisions, capture 480,000 men and take capital of Germany, Berlin, linking up with Anglo-American troops on Elbe and forcing Nazi Germany to unconditionally surrender.
50	Prague Offensive Operation (6 May–11 May 45)	First, Second and Fourth Ukrainian Fronts, 2d Polish Army	1200	160-200	Army Group Center, 8th Army, portion of 6th Panzer Army SS of Army Group Austria. 4th Air Fleet	In course of operation, 860,000-strong German troop groupings surrounded and taken prisoner. Czechoslovakia and its capital Prague liberated from Nazi occupation.
	Campaign in Far East (August 1945)					
51	Manchurian Offensive Operation (9 Aug–2 Sep 45)	Transbaykal, First and Second Far Eastern Fronts, Pacific Fleet, Amur Naval Flotilla, formations of Mongolian Army	2700	200-800	Kwantung Army (1st, 3d, 17th Fronts, 4th Army, 2d and 5th Air Armies), Manchukuo Army, Army of Prince Dewan and Suiyuan Army Group of Inner Mongolia, Sungari Naval Flotilla	Kwantung Army and puppet armies of Japan in Manchuria and North China defeated. Soviet troops advance 200-800 km, liberate Manchuria, Northeast China, and northern part of Korea. Defeat of Kwantung Army and loss of military-economic base in China and Korea deprive Japan of real forces to continue war.

Soviet Troop Strategic and Front Operations
Carried Out in Battles of the Great Patriotic War

Strategic Operations and Front Operations Carried Out Within Strategic Ones	Front Operations Conducted Outside Strategic Ones
1	2

I. Battle of Moscow (30 Sep 41 - 20 Apr 42)

1. **Moscow Strategic Defensive Operation (30 Sep - 5 Dec 41)**

   Involving troops of Western, Kalinin, Reserve, Bryansk and portion of forces of the Southwestern Fronts.

   Within the operation, the following front operations were carried out:

   - Orel-Bryansk Defensive Operation of the Bryansk Front (30 Sep - 23 Oct 41);
   - Vyazma Defensive Operation of Western and Reserve Fronts (2-13 Oct 42);
   - Kalinin Defensive Operation by right wing of Western Front, from 17 Oct the Kalinin Front (10 Oct - 4 Dec 41);
   - Mozhaysk-Maloyaroslavets Defensive Operation of Western Front (13-30 Oct 41);
   - Tula Defensive Operation of Bryansk Front, from 11 Nov the left wing of the Western Front (24 Oct - 5 Dec 41);
   - Klin-Solnechnogorsk Defensive Operation by right wing of Western Front (15 Nov - 5 Dec 41);
   - Naro-Fominsk Defensive Operation of Western Front (16 Nov - 5 Dec 41).

2. **Moscow Strategic Offensive (Moscow Counteroffensive) Operation (5 Dec 41 - 7 Jan 42)**

   Involving Western, Kalinin, Bryansk (from 24 Dec 41), the right wing of the Southwestern (to 20 Dec 41) Front.

   Within the operation, the following front operations were carried out:

   - Kalinin Offensive Operation by Kalinin Front (5 Dec 41 - 7 Jan 42);
   - Klin-Solnechnogorsk Offensive Operation by right wing of Western Front (6-25 Dec 41);
   - Tula Offensive Operation by left wing of Western Front (6-16 Dec 41);
   - Yelets Offensive Operation by right wing of Southwestern Front (6-16 Dec 41);

1	2
- Naro-Fominsk--Borovaya Offensive Operation of Western Front (13-25 Dec 41); - Kaluga Offensive Operation by left wing of Western Front (17 Dec 41 - 5 Jan 42). From 24 Dec 41, the operation involved the Bryansk Front.	
3. Rzhev-Vyazma Strategic Offensive Operation **(8 Jan - 20 Apr 42)** Involving Western and Kalinin Fronts. Within the operation, the following front operations were carried out: - Sychev-Vyazma Offensive Operation by the Kalinin Front (8 Jan - 20 Apr 42); - Vyazma Offensive Operation of Western Front (10 Jan - 20 Apr 42).	Bolkhov Offensive Operation by Bryansk Front (8 Jan - 20 Apr 42)

II. Battle of Leningrad (10 Jul 41 - 9 Aug 44)

1	2
1. Leningrad Strategic Defensive Operation **(10 Jul - 30 Sep 41)** Involving troops of Northern, Leningrad (from 23 Aug 41), Northwestern Fronts, Baltic Fleet and Ladoga Naval Flotilla. Within the operation, the following front operations were carried out: - Pskov-Novgorod Defensive Operation of Northwestern Front (10 Jul - 23 Aug 41); - Luga-Narva Defensive Operation by left wing of Northern Front (from 23 Aug, the Leningrad) (10 Aug - 8 Sep 41); - The defensive operation of the Leningrad Front on the near approaches to Leningrad (8-30 Sep 41).	1. Vyborg-Keksgolm Defensive Operation by portion of forces of Northern (from 23 Aug 41, the Leningrad) Front (10 Jul - 23 Sep 41) 2. Tikhvin Defensive Operation of 4th and 52d Separate Armies and portion of forces of Leningrad Front (16 Oct - 10 Nov 41) 3. Lyuban Offensive Operation of Volkhov and partially the Leningrad Fronts (7 Jan - 30 Apr 42)
2. Tikhvin Strategic Offensive Operation **(10 Nov - 30 Dec 41)** Involving 54th Army of Leningrad Front, 4th and 2d Separate Armies combined from 17 Dec 41 into the Volkhov Front, the Novgorod Army Group of the Northwestern Front.	4. Sinyavino Offensive Operation of Volkhov and Leningrad Fronts (19 Aug - 10 Oct 42) 5. Mga Offensive Operation of Leningrad Front (22 Jul - 22 Aug 43)

1	2
3. **Strategic offensive operation to breach Leningrad blockade (12 Jan - 30 Jan 43)** Involving troops of Leningrad and Volkhov Fronts, portion of forces of the Baltic Fleet.	6. Narva Offensive Operation of Leningrad Front (24-30 Jul 44)
4. **Leningrad-Novgorod Strategic Offensive Operation (14 Jan - 1 Mar 44)** Involving troops of Leningrad, Volkhov and Second Baltic Fronts, part of forces of Baltic Fleet. Within the operation, the following front operations were carried out: - Krasnoye-Selo--Gdov Offensive Operation of Leningrad Front and forces of the Baltic Fleet (14 Jan - 1 Mar 44); - Novgorod-Luga Offensive Operation of Volkhov Front (14 Jan - 13 Feb 44); - Staraya Russa-Novorzhev Offensive Operation of Second Baltic Front (18 Feb - 1 Mar 44).	
5. **Vyborg-Petrozavodsk Strategic Offensive Operation (10 Jun - 9 Aug 44)** Involving troops of Leningrad and Karelian Fronts, Baltic Fleet, Ladoga and Onegin Naval Flotillas. Within the operation, the following front operations were carried out: - Vyborg Offensive Operation of Leningrad Front with support of Baltic Fleet (10-20 Jun 44); - Svir-Petrozavodsk Offensive Operation of Karelian Front (21 Jun - 9 Aug 44).	

III. Battle of Stalingrad (17 Jul 42 - 2 Feb 43)

1. **Stalingrad Strategic Defensive Operation (17 Jul - 18 Nov 42)**

   Involving troops of Stalingrad (Don), Southeastern (Stalingrad) Fronts, Volga Naval Flotilla.

   Within the operation, the following front operations were carried out:

   - Defensive Operation of Stalingrad and Southeastern Fronts on distant approaches to Stalingrad (17 Jul - 17 Aug 42);
   - Defensive Operation of Stalingrad and Southeastern Fronts on near approaches to Stalingrad (18 Aug - 18 Nov 42);
   - Counterstrikes by Don Front against enemy assault group advancing against Stalingrad (30 Sep - 18 Nov 42).

1	2
2. **Stalingrad Strategic Offensive Operation** (19 Nov 42 – 2 Feb 43) Involving troops of Southwestern, Stalingrad and Don Fronts. In the course of the operation, the following front operations were carried out: - Offensive Operation by Southwestern Front to encircle enemy troop grouping in Stalingrad area (19-30 Nov 42); - Offensive Operation by Stalingrad Front to encircle enemy troop grouping in Stalingrad area (20-30 Nov 42); - Offensive Operation by Don Front to encircle enemy grouping in Stalingrad area (19-30 Nov 42); - The Kotelnikovo Operation by the left wing of the Stalingrad Front to repel enemy counterstrike and defeat its grouping endeavoring to break through to Stalingrad (12-30 Dec 42); - Middle Don Offensive Operation of Southwestern Front (16-30 Dec 42); - Offensive Operation of Don Front to eliminate encircled enemy troops in Stalingrad (10 Jan – 2 Feb 43).	

IV. Battle of the Caucasus (25 Jul 42 – 9 Oct 43)

1	2
1. **Northern Caucasus Strategic Defensive Operation** (25 Jul – 31 Dec 42) Involving troops of Southern (to 28 Jul 42), Northern Caucasus Fronts, Northern and Black Sea Groups of Transcaucasus Front, Black Sea Fleet and Azov Naval Flotilla. Within the operation, the following front operations were carried out: - Defensive Operation of Southern (to 28·Jul 42) and Northern Caucasus Fronts on the Stavropol and Krasnodar axes (25 Jul – 5 Aug 42); - Armavir-Maykop Defensive Operation of Northern Caucasus Front (6-17 Aug 42); - Novorossiysk Defensive Operation of Northern Caucasus Front, from 1 Sep 42, the Black Sea Troop Group of the Transcaucasian Front (19 Aug – 26 Sep 42); - The Mozdok-Malgobek Defensive Operation of the Northern Troop Group of the Transcaucasus Front (1-28 Sep 42);	

331

1	2
- Tuapsi Defensive Operation of Black Sea Troop Group of Transcaucasus Front (25 Sep - 20 Dec 42); - Nalchik-Ordzhonikidze Defensive Operation of Northern Troop Group of Transcaucasus Front (25 Oct - 12 Nov 42).	
2. **Northern Caucasus Strategic Offensive Operation** (1 Jan - 4 Feb 43) Involving troops of Transcaucasus, Northern Caucasus Fronts, a portion of forces of the Southern Front*, the Black Sea Fleet. Within the operation, the following front operations were carried out: - Mozdok-Stavropol Offensive Operation of Northern Troop Group of Transcaucasus Front (1-24 Jan 43); - Novorossiysk-Mykop Offensive Operation of Black Sea Troop Group of Transcaucasus Front (11 Jan - 4 Feb 43); - Tikhoretsk Offensive Operation of Northern Caucasus Front (24 Jan - 4 Feb 43).	Krasnodar Offensive Operation of Northern Caucasus Front (5 Feb - 24 May 43)
3. **Novorossiysk-Taman Strategic Offensive Operation** (10 Sep - 9 Oct 43) Involving troops of Northern Caucasus Front, forces of the Black Sea Fleet and Azov Naval Flotilla.	

V. Kursk Battle (5 Jul - 23 Aug 43)

1. **Kursk Strategic Defensive Operation** (5-23 Jul 43)

Involving troops of Central, Voronezh and Steppe Fronts.

Within the operation, the following front operations were carried out:

- Defensive Operation of Central Front on Orel-Kursk Axis (5-11 Jul 43);
- Defensive Operation of Voronezh Front and portion of forces of the Steppe Front on the Belgorod-Kursk Axis (5-23 Jul 43).

2. **Orel Strategic Offensive Operation** (12 Jul - 18 Aug 43)

Involving troops of Bryansk, Central and portion of forces of the Western Front.

Within the operation, the following front operations were carried out:

- Volkhov-Orel Offensive Operation of Bryansk Front (17 Jul - 18 Aug 43);

1	2
- Kromy-Orel Offensive Operation of Central Front (12 Jul - 18 Aug 43).	
3. Belgorod-Kharkov Strategic Offensive Operation (3-23 Aug 43)	
Involving troops of Voronezh and Steppe Fronts.	
Within the operation, the following front operations were carried out:	
- Offensive Operation of Voronezh Front on Belgorod-Bogodukhov Axis (3-23 Aug 43);	
- Offensive Operation of Steppe Front on Belgorod-Kharkov Axis (3-23 Aug 43).	
VI. The Battle for the Dnieper (Aug - Dec 43)	
1. Chernigov-Poltava Strategic Offensive Operation (26 Aug - 30 Sep 43)	Gomel-Rechitsa Offensive Operation of Belorussian Front (10-30 Nov 43)
Involving troops of Central, Voronezh and Steppe Fronts.	
Within the operation, the following front operations were carried out:	
- Chernigov-Pripyat Offensive Operation of Central Front (26 Aug - 30 Sep 43);	
- Sumi-Priluki Offensive Operation of Voronezh Front (24 Aug - 30 Sep 43);	
- Poltava Offensive Operation of Steppe Front (24 Aug - 30 Sep 43).	
2. Donbass Strategic Offensive Operation (13 Aug - 22 Sep 43)	
Involving troops of Southwestern and Southern Fronts.	
Within the operation, the following front operations were carried out:	
- Barvenkovo-Pavlograd Offensive Operation of Southwestern Front (13 Aug - 22 Sep 43);	
- Mius-Mariupol Offensive Operation of Southern Front (18 Aug - 22 Sep 43).	
3. Lower Dnieper Strategic Offensive Operation (26 Sep - 20 Dec 43)	
Involving troops of Steppe (from 20 Oct 43, Second Ukrainian), Southwestern (from 20 Oct 43, Third Ukrainian) and Southern (from 20 Oct 43, Fourth Ukrainian) Fronts.	
Within the operation, the following front operations were carried out:	

1	2

- Kremenchug-Pyatikhatki Offensive Operation of Second Ukrainian (to 20 Oct 43, Steppe) Front (15 Oct - 20 Dec 43);
  - Zaporozhye Offensive Operation of Southwestern Front (10-14 Oct 43);
  - Dnepropetrovsk Offensive Operation of Third Ukrainian Front (23 Oct - 20 Dec 43);
  - Melitopol Offensive Operation of Southern (from 20 Oct 43, Fourth Ukrainian) Front (26 Sep - 5 Nov 43).	

4. Kiev Strategic Offensive Operation (3-13 Nov 43) Involving troops of First Ukrainian Front.	Kiev Defensive Operation of First Ukrainian Front (13 Nov - 22 Dec 43)

* The main forces of the Southern Front at this time were carrying out the Rostov Offensive Operation.

Source: "Itoggi diskussii o strategicheskikh operatsiiakh Velikoi Otechestvennoi voiny 1941–45 gg." [Results of the discussion about strategic operations of the Great Patriotic War 1941–45], *VIZh*, No. 10 (October 1987), 8–24; V. V. Gurkin, M. I. Golovnin, "Operatsii i bitvakh (K voprosu o strategicheskikh i frontovykh operatsiiakh provedennykh v khode bitv Velikoi Otechestvennoi voiny)" [Operations and battles (To the question of strategic and *front* operations conducted during the Great Patriotic War)], *VIZh*, No. 9 (September 1988), 318. Chart translated by JPRS. Note differing transliteration of Russian place-names.

APPENDIX 3

RECENT SOVIET VIEWS ON MILITARY REFORM

PROGRAM PROPOSED BY MAJOR GENERAL V. IVANOV IN AN
ARTICLE ENTITLED "FUNDAMENTAL RENOVATION AND NOT
COSMETIC REPAIR"[1]

Armed Forces Composition

- First Contingent: Combat-ready forces, weapons, and equipment
- Second Contingent: Reserve forces, weapons, equipment; and materiel-technical reserves for the formation of units and formations in the event of war
- Third Contingent: Training and alternative service

First Contingent (Combat-Ready)

- Nuclear and space weapons
- PVO forces (main)
- Military aviation
- Naval forces
- Highly mobile ground forces

(Composition and quantity depend on military-political international conditions and the economic situation – should be sufficient for defense in an individual region and to support deployment of the second contingent in case of war.)

Second Contingent (Reserve)

- Most massive
- Reserve units
- Cadre base
- Equals one-third of first contingent

(Composition and quantity depend upon strategic plans.)

Third Contingent (Training and Alternative Service)

- Fulfills conscript service based on universal military service law

335

- 600,000–700,000 men
- Period of service: Up to 6 months in training units
- Full period in first or second contingent unit or longer period in alternative service in republican formations
- Basic source of fill for first and second contingent on a volunteer (contract) basis or otherwise

Forms of Armed Forces Control

- Administrative control
- Strategic control
- Operational control

Administrative Control

- Council (*Sovet*) form of control to replace high commands of types of forces
- Councils consist of representatives of the Ministry of Defense, military industry, scholarly institutions, and training organs
- Councils consist of 100–150 personnel
- Councils determine military-technical and organizational-TO&E (establishment) policies; military production requirements and quality levels; and supply of forces
- Councils work under the Minister of Defense and in close cooperation with the General Staff and strategic commands

Strategic Control

- Strategic commands plan the combat use of the armed forces, or a portion thereof, in limited conflict or general war
- Commands organic to the General Staff:
  - Strategic Forces Command
  - Constant Readiness Forces Command
  - Conventional Forces Command
  - Training Forces Command
  - Republican Units and Civil Defense Forces Command
  - Command of Organs of Local Military Control
- Command Administrative Apparatus: 50–200 Personnel

Strategic Forces Command

- Consists of nuclear forces and space forces including:
  - Strategic Rocket Forces
  - Military Aviation units and formations
  - Naval Forces
  - PVO and Space Defense Forces

336

- Space Forces ("units and forces capable of striking enemy objectives from space")
- Support units
- Use planned by General Staff and approved by the President
- Initially 400,000 personnel, but will be reduced depending on international military and political conditions
- Will conduct independent operations in cooperation with other forces
- Supreme High Command in charge of combat employment
- Maintained by state budget
- Used only in time of war

Constant Readiness Forces Command

- Forces maintained in peacetime at established TO&E (establishment) norms
- Used in peacetime and wartime to repel aggression or resolve limited, regional conflicts, in independent operations under TVD High Command
- President decides on deployment and use
- Employed within *fronts* in wartime
- Maintained by state budget
- Size depends on military-political situation
    Can be 1,000,000–1,300,000 total
    700,000 – Ground Forces
    170,000 – Military Aviation
    250,000 – Air and Space Defense
    150,000 – Navy

Conventional Forces

- Basic and most numerous component
- Reserve units, formations, and large formations of ground forces, military aviation, air and space defense forces, and navy
- Equipment and materiel reserves kept at bases, arsenals, and storage depots maintained by contract servicemen
- Personnel assigned by military commissariats
- Peacetime strength 630,000
    400,000 – Ground Forces
    80,000 – Military Aviation
    80,000 – Navy
    70,000 – Air and space defense forces
- Brought up to wartime strength by contract and conscript servicemen
- Maintained by state budget
- Deployment determined by General Staff and sanctioned by Supreme High Command

337

Training Forces

- With republican units, embodies entire draft contingent under Law of Universal Military Service
- Thereafter personnel conclude contract service in some element of the force or perform alternative service in republican units
- Strength 300,000–500,000 for 5–6 months of training
- Prepares 25,000 for Strategic Forces
    200,000 for Ground Forces
    30,000 for Military Aviation
    15,000 for Air and Space Defense Forces
    40,000 for Navy
- Maintained by state budget
- Subordinate in peacetime to military districts
- Deployed by Minister of Defense
- Form reserve units and prepare replacements in wartime
- Training bases can form line units in wartime
- Call-ups twice a year

Republican Units and Civil Defense

- Consist of companies and battalions limited to .5 per cent of republic's population
- Used for harvesting, agricultural and industrial work, protective measures, maintaining order, and disaster control
- Provides alternative service
- Republics control in peacetime
- Military Districts (*fronts*) control in wartime for use within the republic

Organs of Local Military Control

- Includes military departments and military commissariats
- Military departments, within local Councils of People's Deputies, conduct pre-induction training; draft men into training forces, republican and civil defense units; conduct military-patriotic work; and assist military organs in organizing mobilization
- Military commissariats, under military departments, amass contract volunteers, handle pensions, and assist in mobilization

Operational Control

- Independent authority under the Supreme Command (Minister of Defense and General Staff)
- In peacetime and in wartime, TVD high commands, military districts, and armies plan and prepare TVD, *front*, and army operations (and independent operations by fleets, flotillas, and squadrons)

- In peacetime, constant readiness forces, conventional forces, and training forces are subordinate to military districts, who work in close coordination with local councils and republican commands, and who are subordinate to the TVD high command
- All peacetime military districts (except the northern fleet and the Moscow, North Caucasus, Volga–Ural, and Siberian Military Districts, which are subordinate to the General Staff) are subordinate to the TVD high commands

Additional Proposals

- In peacetime, TVD high commands, military districts, and fleets maintained at numerical strength necessary to prepare for combat employment of subordinate forces
- Remaining functions (support, training, etc.) carried out by force commands
- Administrative or construction functions carried out by civilian organizations
- Restrict military rank to military functions
- Create system for training military cadres (NCOs)
- Tie foreign language training to actual service requirements
- Enforce Law on Universal Military Service

Summary of Armed Forces Strength

Command	Total	Ground
Strategic Nuclear Command	400,000	–
Constant Readiness Force Command	1,100,000–1,300,000	700,000
Conventional Forces	630,000	400,000
Training Forces	300,000–500,000	200,000
Total Strength	2,430,000–2,830,000	1,300,000

REFORM PROPOSALS OF REFORMIST DEPUTIES "ON THE PREPARATION AND CONDUCT OF MILITARY REFORM IN THE USSR"[2]

The Need for Military Reform

- Contemporary conditions necessitate reform
- Armed forces do not conform to modern demands
- Cost of the armed forces is excessive
- Tension exists within the armed forces

- Armed forces do not reflect political, republican, constitutional, or societal transformations
- Armed forces prestige is falling
- Individuals in the armed forces are suppressed

Basic Principles of Military Reform

1. Guaranteed assurance of national security based primarily on qualitative factors
2. Optimization of structures formulating military policy and ensuring rights and obligations of each
3. Military accountability to state and society on basis of *glasnost'*
4. Conformity of armed forces organization, equipping, and financing with real threats and principle of "defensive sufficiency"
5. Phased professionalization of the army and strengthening of every citizen's personal incentive for quality accomplishment of national defense missions
6. Democratization of the army and commitment to rule-of-law and international law
7. Consideration of national-historic traditions and progressive domestic and world experience

Contents of Military Reform

- Formulation of military policy
- Armed forces reorganization
- Reserve training

Formulation of Military Policy

1. Military policy formulation and execution is in concert with the threat as determined by the USSR Congress of Deputies, the USSR president, and the USSR Supreme Soviet
2. Military policy is optimized by dividing leadership and command and control levels into inter-related and mutually responsible political, administrative, and military levels
   A. The USSR president heads the system by lawfully serving as supreme commander
   B. The president serves this function constitutionally
   C. Legislative bodies have the right to:
      - Approve armed forces organization and concepts of military policy and doctrine
      - Determine armed forces size, terms of service, weaponry, and the budget
      - Organize studies and hearings on military-political and military-economic problems

340

- Appoint a civilian Minister of Defense

Necessary conditions to implement the above include:
- Legal transition from party to state leadership
- Passage of law on parties to govern political activity in the armed forces
- Creation and definition of defense and state security committee to limit executive power
- Creation of legal consultative national security body under the president
- Creation of USSR Supreme Soviet research and information service
- Assuring of political and public involvement in formulation of military policy on the basis of *glasnost'*

D. Administratively, the Ministry of Defense draws up military policy for consideration by legislative bodies, including such questions as:
- Assessing the threat
- Planning details of the budget

Necessary conditions to implement the above include:
- Division of functions of the Ministry and General Staff
- Transformation of the Ministry into an administrative control organ under a civilian
- Concentration of the budget under ministry
- Reorganization of the armed forces rear and military-industrial complex (eliminate redundancy)
- Restructuring of military-scientific research under the Ministry

E. The General Staff implements military-political and military-technical decisions by strategic and operational planning and through the armed forces

Necessary conditions to implement this include:
- Elimination of main commissariats of directions
- Reorganization of armed forces branches and military districts to accord with General Staff functions

3. New Union treaty should govern all questions of organizing defense, the armed forces, and national security, on a joint USSR-republican basis. This assumes:

A. Republics delegate powers to the center
B. Republics contribute to national defense
C. USSR armed forces include national-territorial elements and professional (territorial) reserves in each republic administratively subordinate to the center and the republics and operationally and strategically subordinate to the center

D. Territorial forces available for use in disasters and to stop disorders

Necessary conditions to implement this include:

- Incorporation of republican rights and obligations *vis-à-vis* defense in USSR constitution and Union treaty
- Cooperation between Ministry of Defense and republican military departments

4. A new system of special services based on legal and political entities must ensure rights and freedoms of servicemen as they fulfill their service obligations. Services include:

A. Basic training and professional orientation by a reorganized DOSAAF

B. Institution of new professional training system at civilian higher education institutions and military institutions (in reduced numbers)

C. Creation of new in-depth training system at a network of comprehensive training centers

D. Formation of military academies for each armed forces branch

Necessary conditions to implement this include:

- Reorganization of cadre entities and competitive officer selection
- Guaranteeing the rights of servicemen to a civilian speciality
- Organization of military cadre training to reflect country's multi-ethnic makeup
- Adequately equipping and computerizing training systems

Reserve Training

1. Military reform presumes formation of a system of territorial reserves, including:

A. Professional first-order reserve organized on a voluntary contract basis

B. Second-order reserve formed from former regulars and first-order reservists

C. Third-order reserve composed of retired servicemen

D. Increased reserve quality through reduction in numbers and increase in professional reserves and permanent party

Necessary conditions to implement this measure includes:

- Reorganization of DOOSAF to train high-quality technical specialists
- Transformation of the system for training first- and second-order reserves
- Establishment of territorial training centers and territorial national forces

- Formation of union of armed forces veterans to unite former servicemen and assist third-order reserves
- Reorganization of military commissariats to select and orient future servicemen

Financing

Seek budget appropriations for military reform measures by the following:

A. Consolidate the military budget in the Ministry of Defense and structure it to support army personnel
B. Reduce significantly armed forces' strength to benefit the national economy
C. Reduce the armed forces equipment inventory, centralize production and procurement under the Ministry of Defense, and decrease equipment loss
D. Establish an optimal cadre training system, reduce numbers of academies, and reorient them to train junior command personnel and specialists
E. Reduce the size of command and control entities, eliminate intermediate levels, and automate command and control
F. Expand the use of civilian specialists in place of servicemen
G. Unify civilian and military production, exploit advanced technology, and reduce classification and secrecy
H. Eliminate the shadow military economy and privileges for high-level personnel

Phases in the Preparation and Conduct of Military Reform

1. *Phase 1*:

A. Discuss reform in USSR Supreme Soviet committees and commissions and with the public in the mass media
B. Discuss and adopt military reform by a decree of Supreme Soviet
C. Establish a USSR Supreme Soviet commission for preparing and conducting military reform within the framework of the formation of a general USSR security system
D. Discuss the reform program with the nation's scientific personnel, armed forces specialists, and the public
E. Organize large-scale research in the army and society
F. Prepare and implement programs to reduce the armed forces and convert military production

2. *Phase 2*:

A. Experiment comprehensively with a program for transition to a new

343

armed force as outlined above

B. Develop and adopt legal documents to implement military reform (law on USSR defense, new regulations, service laws, etc.)

3. *Phase 3*:

Fulfill the tasks and provisions of military reform to the fullest extent

"MILITARY REFORM: REALITY AND PROSPECTS" INTERVIEW WITH ARMY GENERAL M. A. MOISEEV, CHIEF OF THE USSR ARMED FORCES GENERAL STAFF AND USSR FIRST DEPUTY DEFENSE MINISTER

20 November 1990

1. Military reform is being elaborated by a representative and competent commission headed by the Minister of Defense, with participation by the USSR Supreme Soviet, USSR Council of Ministers, military-industrial enterprises, military scientists, and staff and troop workers.
2. Purpose of reform is to create a mechanism for safeguarding national security, ensuring effective military organizational development, and bringing the armed forces in line with the real threat and new political, economic, and social conditions.
3. Reform encompasses all spheres of defense organization and presupposes radical restructuring throughout the entire country, including military-political, military-economic, military-legal, military-technical, military-scientific, and purely military spheres.
4. Reform so far has encompassed:
- Emphasis on non-offensive means of achieving national security
- Demilitarization of international affairs
- Mutual cuts in accordance with defensive sufficiency
- Conversion of 400 military and 100 civilian plants
- Defensive budget cut by 8.2 per cent
- New defensive doctrine
- Troops withdrawn from Afghanistan
- Forces cut by 500,000 men
- Two classes of missiles abolished
- New defensive force grouping established within the USSR
- Railroad and internal troops removed from the armed forces
- Army and navy being democratized

5. Subsequent reforms depend on progress at Geneva talks.

The Reform Program

1. *Purpose*: To reorganize and qualitatively renew all components and the main aspects of armed forces activity, while simultaneously reducing strength and lending a profoundly defensive thrust to staffing, structure, technical procurement, and training in accordance with the principle of reasonable and reliable sufficiency.

2. *First Stage (Up to 1994)*:

- In accordance with CFE agreements, cut nuclear and conventional arms and withdraw forces from Czechoslovakia, Hungary (1991), Mongolia (1992), and Germany (1994)
- Remove civil defense and construction forces from the armed forces and disband other ministry construction organs
- Rework all operational and mobilization plans
- Draw up new acts for organizational development
- Redeploy and resettle troops from forward groups
- Prepare mobilization resources for social welfare for discharged troops

3. *Second Stage (1994–1995)*:

- Complete cuts in armed forces
- Form strategic armed forces grouping on Soviet territory
- Reorganize central armed forces apparatus
- Clarify structure of military districts
- Optimize military educational structure
- Adopt new specialist training program

4. *Third Stage (1996–2000)*:

- Complete 50 per cent cut in strategic offensive arms
- Technically reequip the army and navy
- Continue to improve quality in all forces
- Reorganize and amalgamate branches of armed forces, troop categories, and administrative organs
- Implement social welfare programs
- Optimize all organizations
- Elaborate a long-term military-political and technical procurement policy
- Restructure cadre and democratize military relations
- Change staffing and training systems
- Transform political organs in military
- Strengthen the legislative foundations of draft service

Optimization and Improvement of the Army and Navy Structure

1. *Purpose*: To create a more economic, efficient, and capable armed force.

2. *Contents*:
- By 2000, cut strategic forces by more than 30 per cent
- Cut ground forces by 10–12 per cent
- Retain rapid deployment capability
- Reduce the number of armies, corps, and divisions
- Reorganize all forces
- Cut air defensive troops by 18–20 per cent, but retain in constant readiness
- Cut the air force by 6–8 per cent to a level of reasonable defensive sufficiency, improve quality of flight training, and enhance aviation basing
- Maintain the navy at sufficient level and renew qualitatively
- Keep rear services at level of less than 2.6 per cent of armed forces
- Cut non-branch elements of the armed forces by 30 per cent (administration, institutions)
- Cut armed forces to 3–3.2 million, eliminate duplicate organs, and cut central, district, and army directorates by 15–20 per cent

Restructuring of Military-Technical Policy

1. *Purpose*:

To ensure the country's defense capabilities under conditions of a sharp reduction in arms and armed forces by reliance on qualitative parameters

2. *Contents*:
- Make use of competition
- Emphasize "cost effectiveness"
- Transfer R&D appropriations to Defense Ministry

Transformation of the Armed Forces Cadre Training and Staffing System

1. *Purpose*:

To raise the role of the human factor and enhance professionalism of army and navy personnel

2. *Contents*:
- Reduce generals by 1,300, officers by 220,000, and warrant officers by 250,000
- Cut 15–20,000 officer posts (at institutions) by civilianization
- Cut 50 per cent of officers in civilian ministries
- Reform military-educational institutions to make them more flexible and able to meet contemporary requirements
- Beginning with command and engineering officers, shift to five year courses

- Continue to staff armed forces with combination of volunteers and draftees as the most acceptable system for political, economic, social, and purely military reasons
- Expand the volunteer system for army and navy to increase professionalism
- During 1991, conduct an experiment with "contract service" in the Navy. If successful, expand the program during the third stage of reform
- Implement contract service for warrant officers and ensigns, partially in 1993 and wholly in 1996
- Include provisions for alternative service of from 1.5 to 3 years on national economic projects in new law on universal military obligations.

Changes in the Sphere of Political Work and Education

1. *Purpose*:

To improve the forms and methods of educating army and navy personnel and reshape political organs into military-political organs of state policy.

2. *Contents*:

- Improve financial backing for armed forces development and the social protection of servicemen
- Base the social and legal guarantees for servicmen on the principles of socialist rule-of-law and the norms of international law
- Permit career officers to request discharge into the reserves after 10 years' service and, in the future, even less
- Define by law improved rights of servicemen in a wide range of areas including social welfare for discharged servicemen; increased pay for all officers, warrant officers, ensigns, extended-service personnel, and draftees; compensation for injured servicemen; annual leave; indexed pay; better housing; and other benefits.

NOTES

1. V. Ivanov, "Korennoe obnovlenie a ne 'kosmeticheskii remont'" [Fundamental renovation and not cosmetic repair], *Kommunist vooruzhennykh sil* [Communist of the Armed Forces], No. 15 (August 1990), 15–20.
2. "O podgotovke i provedenii voennoi reformy v SSSR (proekt)" [Concerning the preparation and conduct of military reform in the USSR (Project)], *Mirovaia ekonomika i mezhdunarodnye otnosheniia* [World economics and international relations], No. 9 (September 1990), 117–24.
3. D. Yazov, "USSR Ministry of Defense Draft: Military Reform Concept," *Pravitel'-stvenny vestnik* [Governmental herald], No. 48 (November 1990), 5–10, cited in FBIS-Sov-90-239, 12 December 1990, 62–75.

POSTSCRIPT

The August 1991 revolution in the Soviet Union, which was prompted by the ill-planned and abortive coup attempt, opened a new chapter in Soviet (Russian) military affairs. As has been the case in any revolution, accurate prediction of ultimate outcome is futile in the face of the immensely dynamic forces which revolutions inevitably unleash. It is safe to say, however, that, as in the past, months, and perhaps years, will pass before those forces stabilize. In the meantime, some rudimentary judgements can be made regarding basic forces and general tendencies.

First, individuals tend to shrivel in importance and become transitory in the face of contending forces, leaving history and fate to accord fame to those now unknown persons who will emerge to prominence in the future. Second, issues of national security, whether of the Soviet Union, of Russia, or of the likely numerous successor states, will continue to be a major concern to the nations themselves, to neighbouring countries, and to remaining world powers. The enduring strategic paradigms, which were articulated by Kokoshin and Larionov after 1986 and were born as a synthesis of reform and tradition, will retain their validity for whatever states emerge and in whatever circumstances they are applied.

Successor states to the Soviet Union must address perceived threats and challenges, singly or in combination. They will respond with security policies and strategies, only in part reminiscent of those of the past. Where reformist views prevail, strategists will tend to reject "traditional" threats and instead focus on the internal economic, social, and political challenges, which they perceive as the most important obstacles to future development. New military reform programs will reduce the size and stature of military establishments to levels analogous to those of the 1920s. This means for the Soviet (Russian) state the maintenance of a force at near or well below the 100 division level. Nuclear deterrence, supplemented by a smaller and leaner conventional military establishment formed around a nucleus of combat-ready, rapid-reaction forces, will likely emerge as the military component backing up strategic concepts. Military doctrine and military art will focus on the fundamentals of defense, internal security, low intensity conflict and local war. In time, and as reform mellows, traditional aspects of strategy will tend to reemerge.

348

In the newly independent republics a mixture of reform and traditional strategies will predominate, depending on the conditions surrounding the achievement of independence and individual political and economic circumstances which each confronts. Because of these varied conditions, the ultimate strategic stance of successor states is difficult to predict. At a minimum, their strategies will react to the stance of the Soviet (Russian) central state and the policies of their immediate neighbours. In this regard, the RSFSR may advance the concept of a political commonwealth as a substitute for the former Union and a Soviet military "NATO", that is, a consensual alliance of those sovereign republics which wish to participate, as the best option for all. The thorniest question will remain: to what extent will the only institution spanning the breadth of the former Union, the military, abide by these fundamentall political and military changes? The answer to this question will determine, along with the severity of the ongoing economic crisis, whether future transformations proceed peacefully or produce civil disorder and civil war.

The overwhelming predominance of reform and republican sentiments will, for a time, largely negate traditional Soviet General Staff concepts of military strategy and future war. In the mid- and long-term, however, many of those traditional concepts will reemerge both in the Soviet (Russian) state and in some of the successor states as well. Economic, political, and strategic realities will cease operating as centrifugal forces drawing these states apart and will instead act as centripetal forces impelling greater cooperation and perhaps even unity.

In the mid- and long-term, fundamental national, economic, and geographical factors will likely reassert themselves as new, more mature political systems evolve, as they must, in the lands of the former Soviet Empire. The great Soviet strategic debates of the 1980s and 1990s, influenced by reformer and traditionalist alike, which preceded the August Revolution will leave a lasting imprint on the future. Ultimately the debates and their legacy will affect the successor states of the Soviet Empire and those other nations of the world, which now rest easy in the bright light and euphoria of a new global order.

INDEX

Transliteration note: In general, this volume employs the Library of Congress transliteration system. In some maps, charts, and quotes, other systems will occasionally be encountered. Index entries of ia, iu, or e may be written ya, yu, or ye, or in German style.

350

INDEX